The
Social Bases
of Politics

Other Titles of Related Interest in Sociology

Research Methods and Statistics

Earl Babbie, *The Practice of Social Research*, 4th
Earl Babbie, *Observing Ourselves: Essays in Social Research*
Earl Babbie, *Survey Research Methods*
Margaret Jendrek, *Through the Maze: Statistics with Computer Applications*
John Lofland / Lyn Lofland, *Analyzing Social Settings: A Guide to Qualitative Observation and Analysis*, 2d
Joseph Healey, *Statistics: A Tool for the Social Sciences*
June True, *Finding Out: Conducting and Evaluating Social Research*
John Hedderson, *SPSS-X Made Simple* (forthcoming)

Introductory Texts

Rodney Stark, *Sociology*, 2d (forthcoming)
Sheldon Goldenberg, *Thinking Sociologically* (forthcoming)
Paul J. Baker / Louis Anderson / Sharon Baker, *Social Problems: A Critical Thinking Approach* (forthcoming)
Richard Peterson / Charlotte Vaughan, *Structure and Process: Readings in Introductory Sociology*
Judson R. Landis, *Sociology: Concepts and Characteristics*, 6th
William Levin, *Sociological Ideas: Experiencing Concepts*
Leonard Cargan / Jeanne Ballantine, *Sociological Footprints: Introductory Readings in Sociology*, 3d

Specialized Texts

James Spates / John Macionis, *Sociology of Cities*, 2d (forthcoming)
Martin Marger, *Elites and Masses*, 2d (forthcoming)
Martin Marger, *Race and Ethnic Relations: American and Global Perspectives*
Robert Atchley, *Social Forces in Aging*, 4th
Robert Atchley, *Aging: Continuity and Change*, 2d (forthcoming)
Donald Cowgill, *Aging Around the World*
Judith Perrolle, *Computers and Social Change: Information, Property, and Power* (forthcoming)
John Weeks, *Population*, 3d
David Miller, *Introduction to Collective Behavior*
James Wood / Maurice Jackson, *Social Movements: Development, Participation, and Dynamics*

Computer Software for the Social Sciences

William Bainbridge, *Experiments in Sociology* (in the *Study Guide to Accompany Sociology* by Rodney Stark)
William Bainbridge, *Sociology Laboratory: Computer Simulations for Principles of Sociology*
Cognitive Development Company, *Showcase: Demonstrating Sociology Live in the Classroom*, with demonstration scripts by Rodney Stark

The
Social Bases
of Politics

Arnold K. Sherman

Aliza Kolker
George Mason University

Wadsworth Publishing Company
Belmont, California
A Division of Wadsworth, Inc.

Sociology Editor: Sheryl Fullerton
Editorial Assistant: Cynthia Haus
Production Editor: Sandra Craig
Print Buyer: Ruth Cole
Text and Cover Designer: Lisa S. Mirski
Copy Editor: Mary Roybal
Compositor: Graphic Typesetting Service

Printed in the United States of America   19

1 2 3 4 5 6 7 8 9 10——91 90 89 88 87

ISBN 0-534-06864-2

Library of Congress Cataloging-in-Publication Data

Sherman, Arnold K., 1939–
    The social bases of politics.

    Bibliography: p.
    Includes index.
    1. Political sociology. 2. Political science—
History. I. Kolker, Aliza. II. Title.
JA76.S46   1987   306'.2   86-13281
ISBN 0-534-06864-2

Acknowledgments

Pages 46–47: Excerpt from Max Weber, *Economy and Society*. Reprinted by permission of University of California Press.

Box 5.1: "How Britain Managed the News" by Leonard Downie, Jr. © Washington Post. Used by permission.

Pages 146–150: Excerpts from Gaetano Mosca, *The Ruling Class*. Reprinted by permission of McGraw-Hill, Inc.

Pages 193, 194: Table 10.3, Figure 10.2 from Raymond E. Wolfinger and Steven J. Rosenstone, *Who Votes?* Reprinted by permission of Yale University Press.

Page 240: Excerpts from Herbert Blumer in *Review of Sociology: Analysis of a Decade*. Reprinted by permission of Dr. Joseph B. Gittler.

Pages 255–259: Excerpts from Eric R. Wolf, *Peasant Wars of the Twentieth Century*. Copyright © 1969 by Eric R. Wolf. Reprinted by permission of Harper & Row, Publishers, Inc.

Pages 267–269: Excerpts from Donald L. Barnett and Karari Njama, *Mau Mau from Within*. Copyright © 1966 by Donald L. Barnett. Reprinted by permission of Monthly Review Foundation.

*To Jeanette Marian Ullman Sherman,
who challenged me to think, allowed me
to be independent, provided opportunities
to take responsibility, questioned my
decisions, and taught me the Vermont
way of trying to leave things a little
better than you found them.*

AKS

*To my husband, Kenneth Leon Heitner,
and my children, Ariel Ron and Ethan
Sam Heitner, who have taught me what
the real priorities are.*

AK

Contents

Part 2 / The Social Bases of Politics 51

Part 3 / Power 119

Part 4 / Political Participation 181

Preface

When we first took political sociology as graduate students in the 1960s, it was one of the most popular courses in the sociology department, with brimming enrollments and overflowing classrooms. Now that we teach political sociology—we have taught it for a combined total of more than twenty years—we still find it exciting and relevant. Possibly more than any other course in sociology, political sociology fulfills C. Wright Mills's vision of the sociological imagination: It enables us to understand the broad historical scene in terms of its meaning for our lives, to translate private "troubles" into public "issues," and to comprehend the connection between history and biography.

Like many textbooks, this book grew out of our frustration with the existing textbooks in the field. We could not find a textbook that suited the way we teach this course, so we decided to write one. Little did we realize that this project would take seven years to complete. In the course of these seven years the political world moved on, as it inevitably does, so each chapter had to be rewritten many times just to keep abreast of political events.

This book is innovative both intellectually and stylistically. Intellectually, the book attempts to link the past with the present, the individual with the collectivity, the socioeconomic with the political. Stylistically, it aims at making abstract concepts and theories come alive.

Unique Features

- This book provides up-to-date information on rapidly changing political phenomena, such as voting trends, campaign financing, and the ideological underpinnings of political behavior.

- It incorporates a feminist perspective on a number of issues, including power, stratification, and voting patterns.

- It stresses both a historical and comparative approach to social thought, providing both an overview of historical events and the intellectual background of specific issues within political sociology.

- It provides a balanced appraisal of different theoretical models, including the social construction of reality, the consensus, and the conflict models.

- It stresses the reciprocities among social structure, ideas, and political institutions. The chapters on stratification, socialization, and ideology link those concepts to the political system.

- It distinguishes between substantive and functional rationality and between utopian and diagnostic thinking and uses these concepts to understand problems in contemporary society.

- It links the political process and the PEWS (political economy of the world system) models to provide a solution to the problem of levels of analysis with respect to understanding social change and social movements.

- It provides a theoretical and empirical critique of the oversocialized view of the political person, replacing this view with a concept of the political actor as potentially changeable.

Organization and Style

Stylistically, we belive this book will appeal to professors and students of political sociology for a number of reasons:

- It is written clearly and succinctly with student readers in mind.

- Each chapter is clearly organized with a preview that introduces the topic and links it to material previously covered, a main substantive section, and a summary.

- There are numerous examples from current and historical events that help to clarify theoretical concepts and bring them to life. These examples illustrate the relevance of political sociology to students' lives and encourage them to apply the concepts toward a better understanding of the world around them.

- In addition to the examples in the text, several self-contained boxes provide more detailed illustrations of specific issues, such as politics in the Sunbelt, the press coverage of the Falklands War, and big-city political machines.

- Difficult theories and concepts are illustrated by tables and charts, as are comparisons among different theories.

We hope that this book will do justice to students' needs and professors' expectations and convey the excitement we have felt in teaching political sociology and in writing about it.

Acknowledgments

During the seven years it took to plan, write, and produce this book, many individuals helped us make it a better book. First, we wish to thank our editors at Wadsworth, Sheryl Fullerton, Liz Clayton, and Sandra Craig. We would also like to thank the following reviewers, who read various drafts of the manuscript and made helpful suggestions for improvement: Ford Cleere, University of Northern Colorado; Charles Green, University of Wisconsin; Philip Kasnitz, New York University; Pat Lengerman, George Washington University; Anthony Orum, University of Texas; and Allan Silver, Columbia University.

We thank the following colleagues who have read and commented on parts of the manuscript: Kevin Avruch, Peter Black, Eleanor Gerber, Lois Horton, Shepard Krech III, Ann Palkovich, Karen Rosenblum, Joseph A. Scimecca, and Thomas Rhys Williams.

We would like to thank Mary Blackwell, May Thompson, and Sandra Slater for their patient typing of endless drafts and for finally making it possible for us to do our own revisions on our personal computers. We especially thank Gerald Holmes and Tina Brundage of the George Mason University Library for their generous and competent help with facts and references.

We would like to thank the Sherman, Kolker, and Heitner families, who put up with outrageous encroachments on what should have been their time.

We would also like to thank the directors

and teachers at the Iliff School, who lovingly looked after Ariel and Ethan so that we could work. Finally, we would also like to thank the following people, who helped in various ways: Loren Anderson, Kathy and Earl Hall, David Allen and Cathy Hemenway, Chalmers Hood, Dawn Hultslander, Richard Joas, Hal and Jill Pepinsky, George and Colleen Sabo, Diane Southall, Bryant Wedge, and Tom and Charlene Willess. Special thanks to Jonathan Frederick Sherman for helping to make it possible to complete this project. Thanks also to my brother Richard Bruce Sherman.

This book is the result of a truly joint effort. The order in which the coauthors are listed does not reflect any priority of authorship.

It goes without saying that we take all the responsibility for any errors.

AKS and *AK*

The
Social Bases
of Politics

1

Issues, Perspectives, and Political Variations

CHAPTER ONE

Political Sociology: Developments, Issues, and Perspectives

Preview

We live in a time of contradiction and change. We are moving into a new postindustrial age, an age as distinct from nineteenth- and early twentieth-century industrialism as industrialism itself was different from the feudal, aristocratic-agricultural period that preceded it. We enter this new age without ideological, utopian, or diagnostic views to provide direction or coherence.

As the United States moves into the new era, 80 percent of the world's population still live in agricultural societies. More than 80 percent of the world's population make less than $1,300 per year, and 30 percent, or 1.3 billion people, have an average per capita yearly income of only $260 (The World Bank 1985). The people of the eighteen industrialized countries have a daily caloric intake that is 131 percent of the daily requirement, while the people of the thirty-eight underdeveloped countries have a daily caloric intake that is only 91 percent of the daily requirement. This figure does not take into account periodic famines.

Beyond the contrasts of affluence and poverty are additional contradictions. The number of nation-states has grown dramatically as previously colonial states achieve independence, but the drive for autonomy operates at the regional as well as the national level. Conflict exists both within and between nation-states on the basis of ethnic identity and the desire for regional self-determination. Political and bureaucratic centralization and the increasing dominance of powerful multinational corporations are accompanied by a resurgence of regional ethnicity. Thus, the trend toward centralization is counterbalanced by the trend toward fragmentation and decentralization (see Ronen 1979).

Other recent phenomena include the rise in political and religious fundamentalism and political violence; increasing unemployment and a growing awareness of the limits of economic growth; improved technology in transportation, communications, and weaponry; and the replacement of the Protestant ethic, a philosophy of hard work and little pleasure, with consumerism, a practice that ceases to make sense in light of the limits on economic growth.

We live at a time when the old conceptions of reality no longer apply. The field of political sociology, too, is wracked by controversy. We start our discussion with the basic question of knowledge: How can we know anything?

What Is Political Sociology?

The Problem of Knowledge

The problem of knowledge stems from the fact that there is a separation between the things about which we want to know, our perceptions or observations of those things, and the symbols that stand for them. Since a separation exists between things, concepts, and symbols, each is a possible starting point for political analysis. In the political world it is possible to start with the written record, that is, the symbols that represent knowledge in the realm of political sociology. It is also possible to start with concepts such as revolution, political participation, and conflict and with theories about their causes and consequences. Finally, it is possible to start with specific revolutions, elections, civil wars, and other historical events. The last approach avoids the pitfalls of imposing preconceived notions on reality. Political sociologist Theda Skocpol (1979) argues that she was fortunate in having read the histories of the French, Russian, and Chinese revolutions before she read the theories about the causes of these revolutions, since she was not tempted to accept theories that seemed plausible if they did not fit the facts as she knew them. The fact that most people start with observations, concepts, and symbols has far-reaching implications for both perceptions of reality and political actions.

Analysts with different perspectives give different versions of what has happened in a given situation. People see the world differently depending on the symbols and concepts that organize their perception and knowledge. Republicans and Democrats, for example, have different assumptions about the proper roles of government and business, atheists and Christians have different assumptions about the validity of religion, Americans and Russians have different assumptions about the importance of freedom and dissent, husbands and wives have different assumptions about the division of labor in the household, and parents and children have different assumptions about the benefits or harm of television.

Sociologists Karl Mannheim (1936), Alvin Gouldner (1970), and others have come to the conclusion that people operate on the basis of **domain assumptions**, unexamined and powerful assumptions that stem from life experiences. Those with different experiences have different domain assumptions. In political sociology domain assumptions are important. Karl Marx, for example, assumed that the most important thing to know about the world is its mode of production and that the mode of production influences the way people think and act as well as the shape of government and other institutions. Philosopher Thomas Hobbes believed that the key to political theory lies in understanding human nature and that assumptions about the individual lead deductively, through a process of abstract reasoning, to a theory of government. Social scientist Max Weber argued not only that knowledge about individuals is necessary (for example, whether they are rationally or emotionally oriented) but also that human action is influenced by both the material and the symbolic world. Thus, different approaches produce very different theories. Approaches to political sociology include the scientific, or positivist, perspective and the comparative, or historical, perspective.

The Scientific Approach to Political Sociology

On the basis of the philosophy of science developed by philosopher Karl Popper, many contemporary political sociologists start with the assumption that there is a real world that can be known in an objective manner. The political world may be assumed to be real and external to our senses. That world may be described and analyzed objectively; it actually works the way we say it does. Thus, we can construct theories about the world, derive specific hypotheses from these theories, and test these hypotheses. If the hypotheses are not disconfirmed, the theory becomes more credible. For example, we may theorize that people's socioeconomic status affects their political ideology. Socioeconomic status may be defined operationally in terms of income category, and political ideology may be defined operationally in terms of opinions on public issues ranging from military defense spending to prayer in the schools.[1] Next, we hypothesize that the higher the person's income level, the more conservative he or she is likely to be. We test this hypothesis by administering a survey to a representative sample of respondents. We then have data that either support the theory, leading us to test it further, or disconfirm it, leading us to search for another one.

The Comparative-Historical Approach to Political Sociology

Some political sociologists argue that the scientific approach, by focusing on that which is measurable, neglects the really important questions: What impact does the individual nonelite participant, whatever her income level

---

1. Operational definitions are pragmatic, concrete definitions that necessarily leave out much of the complex meaning of a concept.

or political opinions, really have on societal decisions? Who wields real power, and how did they come to possess it? How is power legitimated (that is, justified) by those subordinate to it? How do individuals come to define their place in society, and when do they decide to revolt? Questions like these are better answered by studies that place societies within a historical and comparative context. In the tradition of Karl Marx and Max Weber, many political sociologists focus on macrosociological concepts such as authority and domination or revolution and social protest by utilizing a comparative and historical approach (see, for example, Bendix 1978; Lenski 1966; Ronen 1979; Schumpeter 1950; and Skocpol 1979). Regardless of the approach chosen, the first step is to delineate the subject matter. This requires proper definitions.

The Importance of Definition

Since the time of Aristotle, the hallmark of intellectual endeavor has been proper definition. To define a field of study, we must decide to what category of things it belongs. Then we must discover the specific thing (*differentia specifica*) that makes what we are studying separate from the general class. If we are studying politics, we first have to define *politics*. Then we must find the specific thing that distinguishes politics from other social sciences, such as economics.

Without clear definitions about the subject matter, we cannot develop logical propositions or obtain verified knowledge. Such a body of knowledge is the defining criterion of a scientific discipline.

What Is Politics?

The *differentia specifica* of political sociology is obviously politics. **Politics**, in its most general terms, is the process by which two or more people maneuver for relative advantage. The advantage may be personal or collective. Per-

sonal advantage is served, for example, when an individual uses her influence with the highway commission to have a new highway run through her property, thus making a profit. An example of collective advantage is elderly citizens organizing to defeat cuts in social security benefits. Whether fought over personal or collective advantage, politics is, in one sense, everywhere. But in another sense, the term *political struggle for advantage* may be limited to cases involving agencies of the government.

Politics and Symbolic Meanings. Politics is not just a contest over things. Agreements over meanings are negotiated and renegotiated constantly and become binding for a period of time. When meanings cease to be controversial, they may be taken for granted, thus becoming self-fulfilling prophecies; that is, a thing is defined as real and therefore becomes real in its consequences (see Thomas and Thomas 1928).

The binding reality and political consequences of symbolic meanings are illustrated in a tongue-in-cheek manner by humorist Art Buchwald (1981). Buchwald invents a fictional character, Professor Applebaum of the Institute for Political Spectrums, who, for a fee, determines which foreign leaders are moderates and which fanatics, which foreign movements involve freedom fighters and which militants. He bases his conclusions on demonstrated anti-Soviet or anti-American tendencies. Thus, Moammar Khadafy of Libya, previously considered a moderate because of his country's oil fields, has been reclassified a fanatic. The reason is that although he has been exporting revolution all along, only recently have his activities been aimed against American interests. Thus, the same person, regime, or political movement may be defined as foe or friend, desirable or dangerous, depending on the ideological tilt of those doing the defining and on their ability to enforce their definitions. Obviously, such definitions matter, since they determine whether we send aid to the countries or movements in question, ignore them, or send troops against them.

Anthropologist Peggy Reeves Sanday (1981) explores the way externally imposed meanings constrain individual identity by examining how cultural patterns interact with patterns of power and dominance in societies. Looking through the historical and anthropological record, she finds that females are not subordinate in all societies, that male dominance is not a universal phenomenon, and that women must share equally in positions of power and influence if women and men are to create a future world of equality.

Culture plays a role in our taken-for-granted view of the world. Sanday's finding that patterns of male dominance are not universal refutes the belief that male dominance and female submission are part of the natural order of things. The determination of what it means to be a man or a woman is an example of what we mean by the negotiation over meaning. The results of such negotiation make things real, and such defined realities do have consequences.

Politics as a process of goal attainment, then, may be oriented either toward material things or toward systems of definitions, meanings, agreements, and ideologies. It is not just a question of fact but a question of whether or not the facts are believed, or, indeed, if what is believed has a basis in reality.

Politics, Participation, and Power. The original meaning of the term *politics* comes from the Greek term for city, *polis;* those with the right to participate in deliberations were *politicians.* Politics, then, is about the right to participate in decisions governing one's life. Political decisions involve choosing goals and the means appropriate to obtain those goals. Such decisions may bring us into alliance with some and conflict with others.

The right to participate, however, does not mean that all participate equally. Without equal resources such as time and information to vote or money to run for office, equal participation is not possible. Since those with greater resources may get their way more often than others, many political sociologists believe that the most important defining criterion of political sociology, the *differentia specifica,* is power. Power is the ability of persons or groups to have their will prevail. The ability to use power depends on control of resources.

In ancient Greek city-states, the ability to take part in decision making (to participate in politics) was based on one's residence in the city. Yet, in city-states such as Athens, only about 20 percent of the population were allowed to participate in making governmental decisions. The remaining 80 percent of the population, including slaves, the foreign-born, and women, were excluded.

A definition of political sociology as the study of participation in making decisions about one's life is both too broad and too narrow. Like Greek city-states (which are often considered the prototype of democracy), repressive regimes today block large numbers of people from political participation, yet we would not define such political systems as being outside the realm of political sociology.

Political and Nonpolitical Decisions. Some say that politics, as suggested by the origin of the term, is about decisions affecting the life of a political entity. Others use a broader definition and argue that politics exists wherever there are competing claims. From this broad perspective, politics is everywhere. Since both views involve decision making, one of our first tasks in defining politics is to distinguish political from nonpolitical decisions.

The broad definition of politics includes all decision-making processes. Thus, the resolution of conflicts between fathers and sons, husbands and wives, teachers and students, business partners, and so on can be considered political in nature. In common parlance, we speak of "office politics," the process by which deals, licit or illicit, are struck in order that two or more parties can come to an agreement or that one party can advance at the expense of others. Office politics also involves how decisions are made concerning such things as who gets what resources (for example, bigger offices closer to the boss) and how promotions are made. Similarly, the decision of a family whether to spend Sunday going on a picnic or to stay home and clean the house or mow the lawn may be called by some a political decision. In fact, deciding who mows the lawn and who cleans the house is often referred to as "sexual politics." In the broad sense, as long as people have defended what is theirs from others, squabbled among themselves as to how resources should be divided, and argued over whether or not the antelope should be pursued, they have been making political decisions.

Perhaps the first political act, in this sense, occurs when a child grasps a toy and says "that's mine," and the adult responds "you should share." In the long run, politics is about who gets what and about when and where they get it; therefore, politics concerns the ability to make and control these decisions. Thus, politics is about power, and power, as we have seen, depends on resources.

Some argue that not all decisions, and not all uses of power, are political. They would argue that the statement "that's mine" within the context of the family is not of interest to political sociology. In this view, the question of "what's mine" is of interest to political sociologists only within the context of the public or the collective domain. Thus, the child's claim that the toy is "mine" is not political except in the broad sense that learning what is "mine" and what is "ours" is part of political socialization. The parents' claim that the land their house sits on is "ours" is political when raised against a claim of the state to seize the property under the right of eminent domain. Similarly, the decision of a bank to give an individual a loan is an economic or business decision, not a political one. Yet, to reject a prospective borrower on the basis of nonbusiness criteria such as age, sex, or race may bring the process back within the political sphere if such discrimination violates specific laws or statutes. Certainly the decision of government to regulate the bank, including the imposition of rules that may influence loan

decisions, is part of the political process. The lobbying attempts of the bank to influence the regulation process are also political, as is protest against the bank for making loans to South Africa. Robbing a bank to provide resources for terrorist activity is not directly political, but the laws against bank robbery and the functions of the police, courts, and correction facilities are political, as are those activities of terrorist groups motivated by political goals.

The difficulty of separating politics from everyday life is illustrated by the following case. In Sicily, a student who needs a favor from a professor she does not know approaches a local politician. The politician arranges the meeting through an intermediary, and the student promises to campaign for the politician in the next election (see Eisenstadt and Roniger 1984, pp. 43–47). Similarly, in the United States, political bosses have gained loyalty and votes from officials and legislators by obtaining jobs for them and for their clients (see chapter 11).

How, then, can political processes be distinguished from nonpolitical ones? The answer lies in a conception of the social system. Societies as types of social systems can be divided analytically into three subsystems related to each other and to the physical environment: social structure, culture, and personality. **Social structure** refers to the positions people occupy (for example, fathers, students, or cashiers) and the ways in which these positions are interrelated. **Culture** includes the norms, values, and beliefs that guide behavior (such as the norm of monogamy) and the ways in which these norms and values are crystallized in institutions. **Personality** includes the array of needs people have (such as the need for sex); their thoughts, feelings, and actions; and their internalized predispositions to comply with or deviate from the requirements of structure and culture in order to satisfy these needs.

Institutions are defined as particular ways in which societies articulate and fulfill persistent social and personal needs. The basic social institutions are education, the family, the economy, religion, and politics. Sociologists define the **institution of politics** as that component of society that deals with articulating societal goals and solving problems of internal and external order. The former function refers to making such decisions as balancing expenditures on guns and butter. The latter function includes the role of the military, police, and courts as well as law creation and administration. In industrial societies, the structural component of the institution of politics is to be found within the government.

Thus, the family decisions discussed above are not political decisions, nor are business decisions about loans political decisions if they occur outside the realm of the institution of politics. Family and business decisions have political dimensions only to the extent that they affect the government or are affected by it. When there are governmental aspects to business decisions, we may say that such business decisions are politically related or that they form a part of the political economy of society.

The Unit of Analysis in Political Sociology. The distinction between political and nonpolitical decisions and institutions raises another question: Are nation-states the only viable unit of analysis for political sociology? In the modern industrial world we think in terms of nation-states and thus tend to define political sociology as the study of the nation-state. Yet such formal political systems have not always existed, nor do they exist in all societies today. In the past, there were many kin-based, acephalous (headless) societies; and societies of this type still exist. In 1945, when the United Nations was founded, only 51 nation-states were members. Today, the United Nations numbers approximately 160 nation-states among its members.[2] Where did the more than a hundred new states come from? How many nation-states will there be twenty years from now? Is the

nation-state the final form of political association? And, more important, are non–nation-states devoid of political processes?

Our position is that no society is devoid of political processes. Even in prehistoric hunting and gathering societies, political decisions were made about whether or not to hunt the antelope, whether to move east or west, whether to invite a neighboring tribe for a feast of unity, or whether, instead, to go steal a few of their goats.

One may consider political activity among the early hunting and gathering and pastoral societies as going back to at least 40,000 B.C., though the state did not emerge until the coming of the first permanent settlements around 10,000 B.C. (see chapter 2). The prototype of the modern state emerged with the Greek city-states in the middle of the first millennium B.C., and the modern state as we know it arose around the 15th century A.D. Both the Greek city-states and the modern state differ from bands, clans, tribes, feudal kingdoms, and empires. The modern state, then, is a latecomer on the historical scene; clearly, politics existed before its arrival.

Furthermore, looking at the world today in terms of the 160 nation-states misses the more than two thousand societies contained both within and outside the boundaries of these nation-states. These ethnic groups or tribal societies may exist entirely within a political society, as, for example, the various Indian groups of the United States or the Ainu of Japan, or they may exist across national boundaries, as do the Ibo in western Africa. A large number of societies have become extinct. These groups, together with the nation-states, make up the universe of political systems and are the subject matter of political sociology.

Many examples of politics outside the context of the nation-state exist. One example is blood-feuding among leaderless people such as the Nuer. When conflicts occur among relatives over property or personal injury, the Nuer do not use courts as agencies of government to adjudicate such disputes. Since Nuer society

2. Thirteen additional states are not members of the United Nations. These are Andora, the Republic of China (Taiwan), Kiribati, North and South Korea, Liechtenstein, Monaco, Nauru, San Marino, Switzerland, Tonga, Tuvalu, and Vatican City.

is based on kinship rather than on residence, the function of settling disputes is handled by kin equally distant from the disputants (see Sahlins and Service 1960). Another example is the precarious peace maintained in Africa by the Organization of African States, which has stipulated that the nation-states will not cross national boundaries in an attempt to reunite tribal groups. But while the demand for re-unification persists in Africa, as it does be-tween East and West Germany, in other parts of the world a demand for secession or regional autonomy persists, as, for example, in Quebec, Northern Ireland, and the Basque country in Spain.

Where nation-states do exist, disputes arise concerning sovereignty over certain areas. In northern New York State, a group of whites was cutting down trees on a Mohawk Indian reservation. The Native Americans found the whites on the reservation, appropriated their tools, and removed them from the reservation. The New York State police moved in and arrested the Native Americans. Did the state police have jurisdiction on the reservation? The Mohawk Indians are split between those who see themselves as the remnants of an indepen-dent Mohawk nation and those who take a more assimilationist position. The former argue that they have sovereignty on land defined by inter-national treaty as theirs and that they can be dealt with only by the Secretary of State, cer-tainly not by the state police.

The relevance of the concept of the nation-state is also challenged by proponents of the paradigm (theoretical model) of a world polit-ical economy (see, for example, Wallerstein 1974, 1979, 1984; Chirot 1977). From this perspective, the dominant force in the modern political world is a group of capitalist core societies that have been in place since roughly A.D. 1450. While the members of the core change, they play an important part in world affairs by helping impose statehood on peripheral societies (such as former colonies in Asia and Africa) as a means of controlling them politically while extracting mineral resources or cheap labor. Here the basic unit is not the nation-state, but the world polit-ical economy (see chapter 13).

To the extent that social systems need to reg-ulate economic interaction or trade, maintain the peace, defend their boundaries, and pro-tect any surplus they may generate, they have political functions to perform. To the extent that the performance of these functions entails costs, some mechanisms for raising funds to pay for military, police, and public administration are necessary. Funds may be raised through taxa-tion, as in contemporary American society, through tithes, as in the Mormon Church, through forced labor, as in ancient Egypt, or through appropriating a portion of the crop, as in feudalism. The processes of politics or gov-ernment, then, include the formation of laws, redistribution of wealth, education, and wel-fare as well as the accumulation of resources through mechanisms such as taxation to pay for these functions.

We have said that politics includes the notion of power. **Power** involves the use of economic resources, force, violence, persuasion, or whatever means an individual or group com-mands to obtain what it wants and to exert domination over a subordinate (minority) group. But there is another important factor in addi-tion to power. People both inside and outside the governmental structure expect the occu-pants of powerful positions to act in ways that benefit society as a whole. When these expec-tations appear to be met (in reality they may not be), the government is said to have **legitimacy**.

In short, while we exclude from the notion of politics that which does not fall within the sphere of political institutions, we include processes that occur outside the context of the nation-state. We take a historical, develop-mental, and comparative point of view. Each age in human history should be included in the universe of units available for the study of political sociology, and within each age, all existing units should be legitimate objects of study. Thus, we strive for a conception of political sociology that is broader than the view that the study of politics should be limited to the nation-state and narrower than the view that politics is everywhere that power is used in making decisions.

Theoretical Perspectives in Political Sociology

Theoretical perspectives are broad frameworks that determine the issues selected for analysis and the methods used to examine them. Political sociologists often distinguish between two major theoretical perspectives: the consensus perspective and the conflict perspective. To these we shall add a third, which encompasses aspects of both yet adds distinctive insights: the social construction of reality perspective.

Consensus theorists, including the structural-functional and the pluralist schools, hold that people in Western democracies, whatever their quarrels over specifics, subscribe to a broad agreement (consensus) over principles. This consensus includes the belief in widespread opportunity for political participation based on the principle of one person, one vote and on the use of constitutional guarantees such as the right of free speech and the right of assembly. The consensus also includes the belief that economic equity (although not equality) exists through equal opportunity to move up or down the ladder of social mobility and the belief that disputes and grievances should be adjudicated by the courts under the guidelines set by the Constitution and not settled by violence or other unconventional tactics. Consensus theorists believe that this is how democratic governments actually operate.

Consensus theorists tend to take a relatively narrow view of political sociology. Their basic unit of analysis is the nation-state, in particular, democratic nation-states. When these theorists address the problem of social and political change, their underlying question tends to

be how democracy is to be spread in the world. They tend to see Western societies as run by several competing elites, all contending for the favor of the voter (the pluralist view), rather than by a single, all-powerful elite (the power elite view of conflict theory). Since one of their key variables is a consensus of fundamental norms and values, they tend to see the socialization process (learning and internalization of the norms, values, and beliefs of a culture) as playing a critical role in the emergence and maintenance of democratic political systems. Education thus is an important concern in this perspective, as are free mass media, since both education and the media are agents of political socialization. Since the major expression of political freedom is the electoral process, these theorists also tend to pay keen attention to voting and elections.

From the 1920s to the 1960s, political sociology came into its own in the United States as an empirical body of knowledge concerned primarily with the study of attitudes and behaviors in democratic countries. This work, dominated by the consensus perspective, was epitomized by political sociologist Seymour Martin Lipset's book *Political Man* (1981). Beginning in the 1960s, in the wake of intensive social change and political upheavals, political sociologists increasingly questioned and finally rejected the earlier model. Taken together, these later works present a new paradigm called conflict sociology (see Anderson 1974, Tilly 1978, Gamson 1975, Szymanski 1978, and Wallerstein 1974, 1979, 1984).

The debate between proponents of the different perspectives actually began before the 1960s. The conflict perspective was pioneered by Karl Marx in the nineteenth century and was continued by the radical sociologist C. Wright Mills in the 1950s. Yet it is convenient to maintain that the consensus perspective held sway until the late 1960s or early 1970s and to consider the period from 1968 to 1973 as a transition period during which conflict sociology began to win ever-widening acceptance.

Conflict theorists, who encompass the Marxist, radical, and power elite schools, tend to believe that whatever consensus exists is illusory, masking significant differences in power, in influence, and in the objective interests of different groups. They further tend to believe that these differences, rather than any manipulated consensus, set the tone of the political system.

Conflict theory tends to see the mechanisms that ensure stability as less important than the potential of the system for change. It sees the electoral process as a manipulative device to maintain the legitimacy of the ruling elite, it sees social structure (in particular, class division) as being more important than cultural norms and values in determining the behavior of individuals and societies, and it tends to see society as run by a more or less cohesive power elite rather than by several competing elites.

The third major perspective discussed in this book is that of the social construction of reality (see Berger and Luckmann 1967), which includes the theory of symbolic interactionism and the sociology of knowledge. **Social construction theorists** emphasize that the meanings of different aspects of the political system are construed and negotiated rather than being given and that these meanings reinforce or, alternatively, undermine the stability of the system. The social construction position accepts both the existence of conflict and the consensus over basic values and needs, but it does not take the position that universal knowledge that will solve societal problems can be obtained or that particular classes of society are the carriers of the truth or of a better future. According to the social construction perspective, the struggle for social order and social change takes place, among other struggles, over the ability to define meaning. Social order and social change may be explained by social constructions or interpretations of reality.

In the next section, we introduce several key concepts and controversies that cut across specific topics within political sociology. These concepts will be analyzed more fully in later chapters.

Key Concepts and Issues

The Role of the State in Society

Political sociology arose out of the economic and political crises that shook Europe and North America in the seventeenth and eighteenth centuries. These crises included the Protestant Reformation, the industrial revolution, and the French and American revolutions. In the wake of these shock waves, people increasingly questioned the authority of the government, an authority they had previously accepted—or at least acquiesced to—as sanctioned by God. Political philosophers such as Hobbes, Locke, and Rousseau attempted to spell out the rights of citizens and the limits on the authority of the state. Revolutionary masses overthrew oppressive regimes and occasionally executed the reigning monarchs. Political leaders such as James Madison in the United States and Maximilien Robespierre in France issued declarations of human rights and designed constitutions that severely restricted the powers of government. As Lipset notes, "the distinction between man and citizen and between society and state became clear" (1959, p. 82; see chapter 2).

In the nineteenth century, as conflicts between classes and nationalities intensified and revolutions spread around Europe, the debate on the role of government in society intensified. Three major views on the role of the state were propounded by Hegel (1770–1831), Marx (1818–1883), and Tocqueville (1805–1859) (see chapter 3).

German philosopher Georg Hegel asserted that the state, in particular the absolutist Prussian state, was everything. It embodied the resolution of all social conflicts, the highest form of progress, and the ultimate moral authority. Karl Marx, who in his youth was a disciple of

Hegel, later argued that the state was merely an instrument used by the propertied class to oppress the propertyless masses. Thus, to Marx the state was simply one party in the confrontation between the classes and not, as Hegel had contended, an entity above the class struggle. In fact, as Marx wrote in his *Preface to a Contribution to the Critique of Political Economy* (1859), neither governmental machinery ("legal relations") nor political ideas could be understood apart from the economic institutions of society:

> I was led by my studies to the conclusion that legal relations as well as forms of state could neither be understood by themselves, nor explained by the so-called general progress of the human mind, but that they are rooted in the material conditions of life, which are summed up . . . under the name *civil society*, and that the anatomy of civil society is to be sought in political economy. (1956, p. 51)

Alexis de Tocqueville emphasized the autonomous role of political institutions in transforming social and economic life. In particular, Tocqueville believed that the democratic form of government would bring about greater social and economic equality, since the newly enfranchised groups would press for such benefits as minimum wage laws and old age pensions.

The relationship between the state and society, although no longer phrased the same way, continues to form a key issue in political sociology. Some political sociologists, especially those with a pluralist or a functionalist orientation (such as Lipset [1959, 1981]), are concerned with how governmental stability, and in particular the stability of democratic governments, can be preserved in the face of societal forces of instability including class divisions, ethnic tensions, and social movements that demand change.

Democracy is more likely to survive, according to these theorists, when a modicum of economic development has been reached and when

an agreement (often implicit) on fundamental values prevails over disagreements on specific programs (see Bollen and Jackman 1985 for a contrasting view). For example, in the United States, although labor and business groups disagree on the amount of governmental intervention needed in the economy, all sides allegedly agree that capitalism is the best economic system. Hence, truly fundamental change—the overthrow of capitalism in favor of socialism, for example—is unlikely. Political sociologists with a conflict orientation, on the other hand, contend that the consensus, if it exists at all, is illusory and contrived, a product of false consciousness. Conflict sociologists argue that capitalism is neither in the best interests of the lower classes nor the only viable economic system. Yet the dominant economic class, composed of the owners and managers of large corporations, exerts just enough pressure on public policy to assure that its own interests are protected and that the lower classes acquiesce. Thus, the economy, society, and government interlock. Following Marx, sociologists sometimes refer to this interlocking of the major societal institutions as the political economy (see Domhoff 1983; Miliband 1969). Regardless of their orientation, then, political sociologists are concerned with the relationship between the state and society (see chapter 9).

Political Power

What is power? Is it held by a narrow elite or spread pluralistically among a number of interest groups? Is the amount of power in a social system finite (zero-sum), or is it expandable (non-zero-sum), like money? In conflicts where power is viewed as expandable, are there alternatives to winning and losing? In some conflicts, is it possible for both sides to win? How is power tied to intention (that is, does power still exist if we lack the will to use the resources available to us)? Is it enough for people to think they have the resources and the intention to use them? (See chapter 7.)

Sociologist Joseph C. Young (personal communication) says that when you don't know what something is, call it a phenomenon; when you don't know how it works, call it a force. Power is a difficult concept. Although we are tempted to simply call power a phenomenon and a force and let it go at that, we must try to define power and distinguish it from other phenomena.

Political sociology deals with the "nature and distribution of power in society" (Orum 1978, p. 3). Sociologist Lewis Coser (1956, p. 1) defines political sociology as "that branch of sociology which is concerned with the social causes and consequences of given power distributions within or between societies and with the social and political conflicts that lead to changes in the allocation of power."

Sociologist Robert Bierstedt (1974, p. 229) defines what power is and what it is not. Not all power is political; political power is but one kind of social power. Power is different from prestige, dominance, and influence. For example, influence persuades; power coerces. Power is located in groups; dominance is a psychological property of individuals. Power also differs from rights; one may have a legal right without the power to exercise it. Power is not strength, since strength is an attribute of the individual, not of the group. "Power is not a force and power is not authority. Power is latent force, force is manifest power, and authority is institutionalized power" (see chapter 7).

According to political scientist Nancy C. M. Hartsock (1983), the distribution of power is related to the nature of the community and the degree of equality of participation. The power distribution in society is evidenced by the kinds of activities that people from various classes, ethnic groups, age groups, and genders are encouraged to pursue or discouraged from pursuing. This focus moves the key concept in the analysis of power from exchange to production. Exchange theories are based on the concept of a rational individual operating on the basis of self-interest. For Hartsock, this view is too simple because it ignores the way in which activities are organized by community relations, including the prevalent patterns of male domination and female subordination. To move to a more adequate theory as well as to a more liberating concept of community, Hartsock argues that it is time to derive theories inductively from the life experiences of women rather than from the life experiences of men.

The perception of power as a zero-sum or non-zero-sum game is a critical issue in the growing field of conflict management. The modern notion of conflict management is based on the possibility that what appear to be zero-sum situations may be converted into mixed-sum or win-win situations. If participants believe that it is possible for all sides to win (or at least not to lose), they may be motivated to resort to mediation rather than confrontation (see Burton 1979; see also chapter 13).

Ideology and Utopia

One of the key issues in political sociology is the relative importance of ideas, beliefs, and values versus economic and social forces in the shaping of political events. Consensus theorists such as Talcott Parsons (1951) argue that cultural beliefs and values are more critical than economic factors. In this view, the American belief in equality is translated both into the economic practice of free competition for financial rewards (presumably based on the initial equality of competitors) and into the political practice of one person, one vote. Conflict theorists such as Michael Parenti (1978) and Albert Szymanski (1978) argue that the consensus view is a biased position that does not explain how the political system in the United States really works. Marx, they recall, claimed that the crucial force in history was the economic mode of production. Thus, they claim, politics in America is more influenced by the capitalist-industrial mode of production than by the American belief system (see chapters 3 and 9).

In fact, ideas like equality are seen by some conflict theorists as reflecting socioeconomic forces in that the ideological superstructure reflects the economic base. The idea of equality of opportunity, they claim, was developed by the rising entrepreneurial class in seventeenth- and eighteenth-century Europe and America to justify its own struggle against aristocratic privilege. Conflict theorists further claim that ideas are shaped not only by the type of economic system prevalent in a given age but by one's position within that socioeconomic structure.

Max Weber, while agreeing with Marx that socioeconomic forces play a crucial role in social change, argued that ideas, too, are causally important. He asserted that without the ideas of the Protestant Reformation, the economic system of capitalism would not have developed (see chapter 3).

Following sociologist Karl Mannheim (1936), we would like to suggest that all ideas are a part of knowledge. Specifically, ideas about politics are part of political knowledge. Knowledge about the political or social situation that rests on evidence and facts may be called **diagnosis**, **description**, or **analysis**. Ideas about the social or political situation that see the world only from the perspective of the actor may be called ideology.

The term *ideology* may be used in two senses. First, *ideology* may be used as a generic term for a particular political point of view. In this sense, communism, liberalism, and conservatism are all ideologies (see chapter 6). Mannheim argued, however, that these points of view were not ideologies; his generic term was *world view* or *Weltanschauung*. The most inclusive term is *knowledge*. Within this world view, the three relevant forms of knowledge are **ideology**, ideas not realistically wedded to the present but rooted in past situations; diagnosis, ideas based on present evidence; and **utopia**, ideas that are oriented to the future but not realistically based on the present. This second meaning of *ideology* is used in contrast to utopia and diagnosis.

Political analysts examine political thought and sort out how it influences, and is influenced by, social structure. According to Mannheim, this analysis involves the sociology of knowledge. In addition, the question of how people from one political perspective perceive and deal with those from another political perspective must be considered. Take, for example, conflicts between those who are for or against nuclear power. When analysts ask how the participating people or groups are influenced by their social background and by their stakes in the issue (for example, whether their jobs are in the nuclear industry), they are using a sociology of knowledge approach. When political participants ask this question only about their opponents but not about themselves, in the hope of discrediting their adversaries' position without having to seriously address the issues, they are using an ideological approach.

Irrational beliefs may take other forms. Most Americans, for example, believe that Columbus discovered America, ignoring the Scandinavian explorer Leif Erikson and the Mongolians who thousands of years before Columbus had come across the land mass that used to connect Alaska with Siberia. Columbus is believed to have discovered unoccupied land, that is, land occupied only by savage barbarians. The Europeans called the Indians "savage barbarians," conveniently forgetting that it was the whites who taught them such savage ways as taking scalps to prove the number of enemy they claimed to have killed. Even today, we ignore the fact that the Indians, or at least some tribes or nations, belonged to fairly sophisticated civilizations. By the same token, blacks, who were imported from Africa, were defined as uncivilized and irrational, although they came from ancient and civilized cultures. If a group is defined as barbarian, inhuman, savage, incompetent, or irrational, it then becomes possible to acquire that group's land, treat its members as slaves, and in general exclude it from equal participation in the political process (see chapter 13).

Two kinds of rationality may be described: functional and substantive (see Weber 1978; Mannheim 1940). **Functional rationality** refers to organization. When action is organized in ways that are calculable and efficient, organizations are said to be functionally rational. Weber describes free-market capitalist economies as the most functionally rational economic systems yet produced because their efficiency can be measured by profit and loss. Yet while each organization operates efficiently, as a whole, capitalism may produce undesired and unanticipated consequences; for instance, inequality, injustice, and ideological distortion. The alternative is a system based on a substantively rational principle such as equality or distributive justice, for example, socialism. Some socialist systems, however, lack ways of calculating efficiency; that is, they have no way of measuring efficiency in terms of profit and loss and hence are functionally irrational.

Substantive rationality consists of "acts of thought which reveal intelligent insight into the interrelations of events" (Mannheim 1940, p. 53). Substantive rationality, then, is close to the sociology of knowledge or social diagnosis. Substantively irrational thought is ideological or utopian thinking, that is, "whatever is false or not an act of thought at all" (Mannheim 1940, p. 53).

As functional rationality increases, substantive rationality may decline. A limited number of social positions allow for the comprehensive view necessary for true understanding. The result is a growing gap between the knowledge elite, which is in a position to have an overall view, and the masses, who are not. This is a paradoxical development in an age characterized by both increasing democratization and an explosion of information.

Political Socialization

Socialization refers to the process by which an individual is taught and learns the culture of a society. **Internalization** is the process by which the individual makes a part of that culture an important element in his or her concept of self. The traditional view of socialization has been that values, beliefs, and patterns of behavior learned at an early age set the basic character

of the individual. This basic character persists throughout life, guiding the individual in various directions. Political socialization is presumed to take place primarily in the home and in the formal educational system. The study of political socialization deals with the learning of democratic or nondemocratic beliefs, of a particular ideology such as socialism, or of support for a given political party.

From the consensus perspective, socialization is seen as the way to form people with democratic personalities who will be the bulwark of democracy. From the conflict perspective, socialization is often seen as reflecting the interests of the power elite that controls education and the media. Such manipulation complements other mechanisms of domination or external constraints (see chapters 5 and 9).

Seen from the consensus perspective of political socialization, the son or daughter of an upper-class American family would, regardless of allegiance to a specific political ideology, be expected to believe in the consensus ethic as previously described. Such a family would find it incomprehensible that its child could become involved in violent political protest or join a religious cult. Yet such transformations have taken place in these young men and women, and traditional political socialization theory fails to account for these transformations. An alternative view casts doubt on the importance and persistence of early socialization. In this view, people are not governed solely by internal beliefs but respond to external forces (cultural or structural) of their situation.

The social construction of reality perspective views things in a different light from both the consensus and the conflict perspectives. From this perspective, candidates for political office are seen as arguing in the media not over the social diagnosis of a situation or over real issues, but over defining themselves as competent and the opponent as incompetent (irrational). Social construction theorists recognize that socialization, both past and present, has some effect, but the effect is to promote the image rather than the substance of democracy. Public debate is seen from this perspective as part of the elaborate machinery that, in conjunction with the socialization process, maintains the position of the elite through creating false consciousness among the masses.

Between the extreme views that see human behavior as influenced either by socialization and internalization or by external forces, there is another view, humanism, which rests on the social construction of reality perspective. **Humanism** holds that individuals have the capacity for intelligence, creativity, analysis, and imagination and are able to understand the pressures that surround them and redefine situations and alter them in important ways (see Scimecca 1981).

In sum, human beings are powerfully affected by both socialization processes and external constraints. There is no doubt, however, that they have the capacity, within limits, to choose between alternatives and even to alter their circumstances.

Political Participation

Much empirical work in political sociology has focused on the nature of political participation in democratic nation-states. Participation in democratic politics is often defined as including voting, campaigning, and lobbying but excluding such phenomena as social movements, riots, rebellion, revolution, and terrorism (see Milbrath 1965). Consensus and pluralist traditions argue that any attempt to influence the political process from outside, using what may be considered illegitimate means, is beyond the scope of the study of democratic political participation (see chapters 10 and 12).

Voting studies, which often utilize the consensus and pluralist perspectives, focus on the vote as a mechanism for the allocation of power. The popular vote is believed to decide which competing elite, or which political program, will prevail. Voting is seen as having the additional function of maintaining equilibrium in democratic societies. The principle of one person, one vote is believed to offset inequalities of power and stratification based on income, resources, sex, race, and religion.

The conflict tradition, however, asserts that voting is ineffectual in influencing key societal decisions and that its real, latent function is to promote the illusion of popular participation. From this perspective, voting serves to maintain the legitimacy of the ruling elite. Individuals are seen as having unequal access to political influence, while some groups are systematically excluded from it. These groups may, under some conditions, participate through channels that lie outside conventional politics, such as protest movements and revolutions (see chapters 12 and 13).

One such noninstitutionalized channel of political participation is social movements. The consensus perspective holds that social movements are powered by people who have banded together on the basis of a common irrational frustration rather than on the basis of a rational understanding of their interests and needs. Because people acting from frustration use "irrational" means of social protest such as riots rather than "rational" means such as petitioning the government, consensus theorists consider them to be outside the legitimate political process. From the conflict perspective, on the other hand, for the underdog not to act violently is seen as irrational.

Recent works by sociologists Charles Tilly (1978), William Gamson (1975), Douglas McAdam (1982), Mayer Zald and John McCarthy (1979), and others argue that social movements may be treated within political sociology's continuum of political participation. American labor's right to unionize and to bargain collectively was won through violent means. The civil rights movement of the 1950s and 1960s resulted in the civil rights legislation of the 1960s. The "Mau Mau" movement in Kenya from 1952 to 1960 helped pave the road to independence. The suffragette movement, though often violent, won women the right to vote. The activities of the Irgun, the violent anti-British underground, helped achieve the state of Israel. As Gamson (1975) has shown, violence is at times an effective political means on the part of the subordinate group.

Summary

The first part of this chapter introduced some of the foundational material in political sociology. It addressed the following questions: What is the problem of knowledge created by the split between symbols, things, and concepts? How is the problem of knowledge addressed by the scientific and comparative methods? What is a body of knowledge? What is politics? What is political sociology? What are the domain assumptions that underlie theory and research in the field? Political sociology was defined as the study of political processes, that is, processes by which people come to know what they want and maneuver for relative advantage, whether material or symbolic. Political processes include participation in decisions about collective goals and the use of power to obtain these goals.

The second part of the chapter introduced the basic theoretical perspectives in political sociology—the consensus, conflict, and social construction of reality perspectives. An overview was presented of key concepts and issues that will be explored in later chapters. These concepts include the reciprocities between the state and society; the nature and distribution of power; the role of ideological, utopian, and diagnostic thought; the functions of political socialization; and the functions and forms of political participation.

Two major conceptions guide this book. The first is that the universe of politics includes all societies existing in the present and those that have existed in the past. Political sociology is not simply concerned with structures of government within the nation-state. Rather, it includes processes of collective self-regulation within nonsovereign societies in the past and in the present.

The second underlying conception is that social structure, political thought, and political institutions interact. Social and economic forces such as the nature of the productive system and the division among classes give rise to ideas about how society is organized and what its goals should be. Political ideas, in turn, give rise to political action by elites and masses. Conversely, elites also shape ideas and create the conditions that influence the lives of all individuals in society.

The organization of the book follows these underlying conceptions. In chapters 2 and 3, we see how the prehistoric and historic circumstances of humankind gave rise to political thought. In chapters 4, 5, and 6, we examine how fundamental divisions in the social structure shape the political thought of individuals in modern society. Chapters 7, 8, and 9 explore the nature and distribution of power. Finally, chapters 10, 11, 12, and 13 analyze modes of participation that link the social structure and the world of thought to the political structure.

The purpose of this book is not to impart knowledge carved in stone but rather to show a method for asking questions and obtaining answers. We hope the reader will improve his or her own substantive rationality and become his or her own diagnostician, since issues and realities change rapidly, and knowledge gained from the past is not adequate for understanding the problems of the present and the course of action for the future.

CHAPTER TWO

—

Historical Background
of the Major Issues

Preview

Scientists tell us that the world began with a cosmic explosion; a poet tells us that it will end with a whimper. In the meantime, we are faced with the problem of creating meaning in a world that many view as devoid of any meaning other than the simple joys and beauty of sharing and being. Some argue that our earliest ancestors—the hunters, fishers, and gatherers—solved problems of meaning and order better than we have. They claim that in preindustrial society life was full of sharing and meaning and that conflict and power struggles came only later. Others argue that conflict is inherent in human relations and at best can be only moderated. We believe that the nature of meaning changes from one society to another. Meaning is created, sustained, or changed through the political process.

The conditions that produce aggression and hostility are created within a society, as are the conditions under which conflict and war exist between societies. Understanding the conditions that create war or peace, cooperation or competition, a sense of meaning or a sense of helplessness and despair allows us to control our destiny. Some people believe, however, that while understanding may be possible, control is not. Since these issues are debatable, individuals should attempt to develop their own answers by examining the various types of societies and political systems that have emerged, and changed, throughout history. The orientations to the field of political sociology are varied, and the stakes are high.

The social and political worlds have changed dramatically since the first hominid (human-like) creatures appeared on earth over five million years ago. To understand the changing nature of social life and political life and our ideas about them, we need to trace the emergence of the human species and some of the major political, economic, social, and ideological changes that have occurred over the course of history.

This chapter illustrates two basic assumptions of political sociology. First, societies have a political system; second, different types of political systems exist in different types of societies. The examination of various societies and their political systems provides a foundation for defining political sociology and analyzing its basic issues.

The kaleidoscopic view of the emergence of increasingly complex structural arrangements is endlessly fascinating. From small bands of hunters and gatherers ranging over a twenty-five-square-mile area, increasingly complex units such as the clan, tribe, kingdom, empire, and nation-state have emerged. Notice that we refer to size (small), type of social organization (band), economic mode of production (hunters and gatherers), density (small number of people per square mile), and complexity of social organization. Each of the types of societies mentioned has a particular mode of production. Early hunters and gatherers are followed by simple horticultural (small-garden) societies. Next come agrarian (large-field) societies, followed by modern industrial societies. What emerges from a comparison of the types of societies, governments, and economic systems is a basis for the exploration of the invention of political philosophy by the ancient Greeks and for tracing the modern theories of politics that have developed since the seventeenth century.

The Origins of Humanity and the Development of Political Systems

The Big Bang, the cosmic explosion that is believed to have created the universe, occurred some 18 billion years ago; the whimpering comes later. What we know about ancient peoples is derived from archeological analysis of the material artifacts that remain as evidence of their passing and from extrapolation from our anthropological knowledge of bands and tribes existing today or in the recent past. Examining the earliest known societies enables us to see how political systems developed. Examination of early people's struggle for control of their environment offers insights into the processes that occur in more complex societies.

Nomadic Hunters and Gatherers (2 Million B.C.–7500 B.C.)[1]

Early humankind was well established by two million years ago. The archeological record shows that bipedality had developed and that our ancestors were living in well-organized family groups. Daily tasks included food sharing, tool making, and cooperative hunting. By 650,000 years ago, Homo erectus used simple stone and wooden tools. What was distinctively different about human groups was their selective use of the environment. While animals would hunt whatever was in their area, humans chose what they would hunt. Another difference was that, unlike other primates, humans could not survive outside of the group.

About one hundred thousand years ago, Neanderthal humans emerged. At this stage of evolution, important developments included burial of the dead, the adoption of clothing, and the discovery of handles for tools. Social organization, bipedality, cooperative hunting, and selective use of the environment emerged. Over time, tool making became increasingly sophisticated. By 50,000 B.C., art was introduced, as were a sense of ethnicity and territorial boundaries. By then, our ancestors were able to cope with all environments because a

great cultural capacity to buffer environmental restrictions existed. The average size of these early bands was probably between six and thirty. Density in these hunting and gathering societies averaged one-half to one person per square mile, since it took that much land to produce enough food to support a single life.

About thirty-five thousand years ago, modern people emerged. Early Homo sapiens still lived in hunting and gathering societies but had developed a higher level of technology with regard to both tools and weapons. Examples of tools from this age include lamps, bows and arrows, needles with eyes, and stone saws. Cave paintings and other artifacts give evidence of religious beliefs. These religious beliefs included sympathetic magic, that is, the belief that something done to the image of an individual or animal would have an effect on the actual individual.

The last ice age peaked about twenty thousand years ago and ended around 10,000–9000 B.C. This change in climate affected the rainfall and the growth of plants and, therefore, the abundance of wildlife. The changes depended in part on the shape of ocean basins that generally slope out gradually from the shoreline. Twenty thousand years ago, mile-high ice masses were produced from ocean water, lowering sea levels by 250 to 500 feet and exposing most of the continental shelf. The melting of the glaciers resulted in the following changes:

> Ocean levels rose and waters crept back across the plains of the exposed continental shelf, covering them with a wide sunlit and sun-warmed shallow sea, a natural marine farmland where many forms of life flourished.
>
> Life changed in the interior as well as along the coasts. Salmon and other fish that migrate upstream to spawn could not negotiate high coastal cascades; but when the cascades disappeared, they began using the rivers increasingly as waterways. (Pfeiffer 1969, p. 217)

The result of these changes was a larger and more reliable supply of food over a large por-

---

1. To be technically correct and nonethnocentric, we should follow the current practice in anthropology of using the designation B.P. (before the present). For example, in 1986 one would say 2000 B.P. rather than 14 B.C. For reasons of communication, we have chosen to use the conventional designation B.C.

tion of the year. The decrease in the need to pack up and move on was a major factor in the development of permanent settlements.[2]

Technology continued to improve slowly. The domestication of the dog aided in the hunt, and the invention of spades increased efficiency in felling trees and working with wood. Fishing nets, as well as boats and paddles, were invented. From 10,000 B.C. to 8000 B.C., systematic gathering and planting were introduced, certain herd animals (such as the gazelle) were harvested, and the first beasts of burden were domesticated. These animals provided meat, basic pulling power, and transportation and were, apart from fire, the first nonhuman energy system. As more sophisticated technology changed the relation of humans to the environment, the number of bands, their average size, and the level of complexity of their social and political systems increased.

Evidence exists of some variation in the political systems of hunting and gathering societies. In some, the headman had power and respect; in others, there was no headman, and decisions resulted from informal discussion. A headman's power depended more on personal qualities than on any authority attached to his position. There was no obligation to obey the headman, and no sanctions were imposed for failure to comply with his wishes. The headman's privileges were few, although he may have enjoyed "a bit more power and privilege" than others (Lenski and Lenski 1974, pp. 144–46).

A recent example of a headman's role in a hunting and gathering society is provided by the Bushmen of the Kalahari desert in Africa (see Marshall 1965). Anthropologist Elizabeth Marshall Thomas tells about a Bushman leader by the name of Toma:

> Toma was not, by birth, first in line to be the rightful headman. Tu's brother was the right-

ful headman of Gautscha, but he had abdicated to live with his wife's people in the north. Her elder sister's husband, a man named Gao Big Feet, also had a right to the leadership in that his wife, Dikai, was older than Tu. But neither ever contested Toma's position as leader, for it was not a position which Toma held by force or pressure but simply by his wisdom and ability, and people prospered under him. No Bushman wants prominence, but Toma went further than most in avoiding prominence; he had no possessions and gave away everything that came into his hands. He was diplomatic, for in exchange for his self-imposed poverty he won the respect and following of all the people there. He enjoyed his position, and, being strangely free from the normal strains and jealousies of Bushmen, he saw justice clearly and hence he led his people well. (Thomas 1959, p. 183)

The political structure of many hunting and gathering bands is one "without a permanent office of leadership" (Vivelo 1978). Because warfare is rare, military leaders do not arise.

> The absence of large-scale political organization, coercive authority, formal leadership, and social stratification is related to the lack of control over productive resources. Foraging for naturally occurring foods and the nomadism this entails make the monopolization of resources difficult. Theoretically, all members of the group have equal access to resources. Hence, the idea of private ownership of important resources is absent. If productive and socially valued resources cannot be monopolized and controlled, or if the means . . . for tapping these resources cannot be controlled, then there is little basis for the exercise of power. An individual who is not able to control a valued commodity, so as to create dependence in others, and cannot threaten to withhold that commodity, is in no position to give orders and to be obeyed. The growth of increasingly complex and pervasive forms of political organization and coercive authority systems is tied in with greater investments in land and labor and with reliance on resources and extractive techniques

---

2. Similarly, economist Kenneth Boulding (1981a) argues that the move from feudalism to industrialism was made possible in part by the introduction of the turnip. Using the turnip as a winter crop made it possible to keep more cattle alive during the winter, which in turn made population growth possible at a time when a larger labor supply was necessary.

that can be controlled by some members of the society. (Vivelo 1978, pp. 135–37)

For the most part, nomadic hunting and gathering tribes cannot accumulate more wealth than they can carry. Therefore, material differences within a group are not great, and a substantial amount of cooperation and sharing generally develops. Unlike the hunters and gatherers of prehistoric times, who often lived in lush surroundings, hunters and gatherers today have apparently been pushed into marginal areas by the advance of agricultural and pastoral people. Exceptions, however, exist. Rich ecological systems enable hunters and gatherers to create permanent settlements. When this occurs, surpluses accumulate and problems of redistribution result. Under these conditions, nonhorticultural and nonagricultural societies can develop rather complicated systems of stratification. The creation of differences in wealth primarily depends not on the development of horticulture but on stable sources of food that, under benevolent conditions, can result in a dependable surplus. Such surpluses occur frequently in coastal regions. A recent example of such societies is the Kwakiutl of the Northwest coast, who engaged in harvesting the salmon runs. The Kwakiutl developed the complicated ritual of the *potlatch* to dispose of surplus and generate social status (Drucker 1965). Anthropologist Conrad Phillip Kottak (1979) has summarized the political-economic function of the potlatch:

> A village enjoying an especially good year had a surplus of items in the subsistence sphere, which it could then exchange for wealth items. Among the Salish, potlatch sponsors, drawing on their own wealth and contributions from other members of their communities, gave away food and wealth to people from other communities who needed it. In return, sponsors and their communities were attributed prestige. The decision to potlatch was related to the economic situation of the community in the year the blowout was given. If there had been a surplus of subsistence items and, thereby, a build-up of

wealth over several good years, it could afford a potlatch converting food and wealth into prestige. (Kottak 1979, p. 179).

Anthropologist John Pfeiffer (1969, 1977) estimates that the world's total hominid population five million years ago consisted of about twenty-five thousand individuals. "At an annual growth rate of one per thousand that figure would have increased to about ten million persons by 10,000 B.C., several hundred thousand bands foraging in the wilderness of Europe, Asia, Australia and the Americas as well as Africa" (Pfeiffer 1969, pp. 67–68).

Probably few permanent settlements were established at this time; rather, bands of about twenty-five in number still lived as hunter-gatherers, needing perhaps two to four hours a day to gather enough to supply their needs.

Early hunting and gathering bands could not grow too large, because a large size would necessitate ranging over an impractically large area given the amount of land needed to feed a single individual. As bands increased in size, therefore, they tended to split off, with the new band moving to a new territory. Eventually, the number of bands grew to the point where increased contact was inevitable. As the land filled up, and as technology improved and the supply of food became more reliable, permanent settlements developed. Nomadic hunting and gathering as the dominant form of society began to decline about ten thousand years ago.

The Coming of Permanent Settlements (7500 B.C.–3000 B.C.)

As the ice age came to an end, old methods of obtaining food were no longer reliable, and a shift from hunting and gathering to **horticulture** (the cultivation of small gardens) took place. This shift was due to other factors in addition to climatic change. As the population of hunters and gatherers grew, the supply of large game was depleted. Thus, the environment became less amenable to a nomadic existence and required a more intensive technology. Increased understanding of the relation between the seasons and growth cycles, combined with technological inventions and the domestication of animals, made permanent settlement possible. Recurrent food shortages and increased contact among roaming peoples provided the incentive to put this new knowledge to work. As Lenski points out (1974, p. 144), "for the first time in history, people were producing their own food."

With permanent settlements came an increase in group size. This increase may have been due to the effect of relative permanence on fertility as well as to the increased food supplies. With larger groups, no longer was it possible to know all members of the group by sight. Since one was likely to run into members of neighboring groups, the ability to quickly recognize group members became important. Personal adornment was useful for this purpose. As groups grew to more than 500 members, personal adornment became necessary for purposes of identification within the tribe as well (see Pfeiffer 1977, pp. 54–55).

The need emerged to hold people together with a loyalty based on principles other than those of blood and kin, since loyalty had to extend over a larger territory. Formal religion served this purpose by associating the power of gods with the power of rulers. Trade emerged as a means of controlling intergroup conflict since it could improve people's material position at a consistently lower cost than fighting for each other's possessions.

Another result of the passing of nomadism was the intensification of the division of labor between the sexes. The work of gardening was often split, with men preparing the land while women sowed and reaped. During this period women contributed many important advances, such as the development of devices for carrying food and water.

The increase of both absolute numbers and density led to other societal changes. Hierarchies with established rights and duties developed. Fences became necessary to keep domesticated animals out of the home. Since people no longer traveled continually, the need

for limiting possessions disappeared. With permanent, private space, the notion of personal possessions came into existence. The "haves" and the "have nots" arrived. The unequal distribution and possession of goods, based on social position, may have been the beginning of important status and power differences. Increased differences in power and possession led, in turn, to increased tensions and to the need for more effective mechanisms of social control (Pfeiffer 1977, pp. 79–100).

The Rise of the City and the Emergence of Kings (3000 B.C.–600 B.C.)

Increased size and density of societies, as well as an increasingly favorable climate, led to the move from the horticultural garden to the agrarian field, from the small village to the first great city, and from the headless band to the first bureaucratic empires and the divine-right kings and pharaohs.

The changing relationship between people and their environment resulted in the rise of the city. The first city was probably Ur, in the Fertile Crescent (today Iraq), which achieved city size around 3100 B.C. (Adams 1966). The growth of settlements into cities depended on a favorable relationship to the sea, to the mountains, and to the soil and on harbors, transportation, and communication. Urban sociologist John Palen (1975) notes that the cost of transporting goods ten miles by camel from Athens was more than 40 percent of the value of the goods. A Greek ship, however, could carry 7,000 pounds of grain sixty-five nautical miles at one-tenth the cost of land transportation. Trade encouraged the growth of cities at sites favored by land and sea routes, by a fertile hinterland, and by natural protection from enemies.

Once the first settlements were established, developing a surplus became essential in order to provide for periods of famine. The ability to produce a surplus released some group members from the direct quest for food. The production of surplus also created the necessity for storage, which in turn raised the question of equitable distribution. The surplus was used, in part, to support nonagricultural workers. The surplus, exacted by the priests and stored in the temples, became the basis of taxation and of capital accumulation. Temples served not only as granaries, office buildings, and places of worship but also as the first monumental buildings that came to symbolize the community. The division of labor became more complex. Accounting became necessary to keep track of the source, amount, and type of stored material. Specialized priests served as accountants and administrators. The granaries made long-term planning possible (Sjoberg 1965).

Urban elites fostered intellectual and cultural pursuits. Record keeping became necessary for storing information, arithmetic for accounting purposes, geometry for land measurement, and astronomy for prediction of changes in the seasons. Writing became essentially a state language allowing for the extension of bureaucratic control. Predictive sciences became necessary in order to know when to be ready to plant and how much to plant, as well as when to harvest, thus ensuring the most efficient harvest.

Permanent location and storage of goods required the ability to withstand external attack. The strongest members of the community were selected as warriors and warrior leaders in times of external threat. The warriors were able to trade this protection for food and services. In time, the warrior class gained ascendancy at the expense of the priests. The growth of the military led to such technological developments as metallurgy for weapons and the design of chariots and more efficient ships.

Kings and dynasties emerged, and with the shift from temple to palace, economic and social stratification became more pronounced. In time, inequality was based not only on the distribution of goods and services but on hereditary titles and land ownership. The demands of the rising aristocracy for ornaments and luxuries gave rise to a class of artisans and craftsmen. These artisans extended the more primitive methods of adornment by producing clothes and jewelry that would adorn and distinguish the various occupations and classes. In addition, changes in the system of stratification were reflected in graves, tombs, and grave offerings. The physical design of the city included a military acropolis, or fortified hill, surrounded by defensible walls, containing temples and major buildings. The upper classes lived close to the center of the city and the lower classes at the periphery, farther from the protection of the city walls.

Cities attracted new residents because they offered mutual aid and protection. Residence replaced kinship as the basis for membership in the community. Gradually, the principle of common worship and the right to worship at the same shrine were extended from the family to the entire community.

Religion thus served as a basis for group loyalty. Variations in religion depend on the type of society and on how religion and the polity interrelate. Hunters and foragers generally worship gods whom they see in animals or plants or gods located in such natural phenomena as the sun, the streams, or the stars. The different relation to nature involved in food production rather than hunting, foraging, or gathering, leads to the appearance of more "human" gods to whom great, superhuman powers are attributed. They are believed to forge alliances with the government. In societies with state religions, such as Egypt, the political and religious leaders become one, and, in fact, the pharaoh becomes the god. As the complexity of society increases, the number of gods decreases (see Swanson 1960).

The rise of city-states signified a major advance over the less complex orders of the past. Although city-states had existed in various parts of the Near East since the fourth millennium B.C., they reached the height of their development in Greece in the fifth century B.C.

Sparta and Athens are the best known of the Greek city-states. Sparta was a military state run by a small elite. The famous Spartan military regime was based on discipline, self-denial, and sacrifice. Today the term *Spartan* has come to mean "austere."

If fear was the basis of government in Sparta, democracy was the basis for Athenian government. Basic principles included administration by the many, not the few; equal justice under the law; and the responsibility of citizens to participate in the affairs of the state.

In Athens, the responsibilities for legislation lay with the entire citizenry (that is, native-born free males), who met in an open-air assembly at least ten times a year and at times every ten days. The powers of the executive lay in the elected Council of Five Hundred. Since no one could serve on the council for more than ten years, the odds were high that every citizen would eventually serve. Each council member had an opportunity to serve for one day as "president of Athens," a nominal headship in which the chief duty was to serve as chair of whatever committee was working that day. With the exception of the military, the job of administering the state was carried out by "amateurs, ordinary citizens, rather than by a permanent staff of professional bureaucrats" (Brinton et al. 1967, p. 65). Justice, also, was administered by citizens. Judges were elected each year, and on days when cases were to be heard, judges for the day were chosen by lot.

The Golden Age of Athens came to an end with its defeat during the Peloponnesian Wars of 431–404 B.C. The following period, however, was not one of unmitigated decline; this was the time of Socrates, Plato, and Aristotle.

Political Thought Among the Greeks

Until the rise of the Greek city-state, political philosophy was for the most part indistinct from religion. Political philosophy was the invention of the Greeks. The notion of the polity, and much of our political terminology, came from Greece. In ancient Greece, city-states such as Athens were called *polis*. The term *poleteuin* meant a citizen, one who is a member of the city and as such engages in political activity,

that is, in activity related to government. The English word *police* also derives from Greek and means, interestingly enough, to govern. Thus, citizens (polites) lived in the city (polis) and engaged in the conduct of government (politics). The term *citizen* itself comes from the Latin word *civitas*, meaning one who resides in the city and has both the right to worship there and the obligations of citizenship.

Political thought often flourishes during periods of major social upheavals, of destruction and decline followed by new beginnings. In Athens, during the Peloponnesian Wars (ca. 431–404 B.C.) and their aftermath, political thought reached its greatest heights in the works of Socrates (ca. 470–399 B.C.), Plato (ca. 428–347 B.C.), and Aristotle (ca. 384–322 B.C.).

Socrates' methods of questioning and analysis challenged the conventional wisdom of his time and constituted a radical departure in human thought. The Socratic revolution created new logical concepts and definitions based on what he considered timeless principles. Unlike earlier philosophers, who had sought wisdom and truth in nature and the universe, Socrates shifted the focus of his concerns to humanity; his motto was "know thyself." Politically, he defended aristocracy, believing that government should be conducted by an elite of the wise and the moral. Socrates committed suicide to avoid execution for disrespect to the gods and for allegedly corrupting the morals of youth. His acquiescence to the judgment of the court showed his sense of loyalty to the polis.

Socrates' teachings had a profound effect upon his student Plato. For Plato, actions have their source in either passion, emotion, or knowledge. The highest form of action is one based on knowledge of the most important virtue, justice. A well-run state rests on a division of labor between three social classes: workers, warriors, and philosopher-kings. Each person should be properly educated for his or her place.

Plato's *Republic* is an early classic in political thought. Among other things, it deals with conflict between people within society. Plato spoke of the *bellum omnium frontra omnes* (war of all against all), which later became the foundation for the thought of the English political philosopher Hobbes (see page 28).

While Plato was concerned with what ought to be, his pupil Aristotle was concerned with what is. Aristotle's philosophy is not only logical but also empirical, that is, based on observation. Aristotle believed that humans are political animals; they attain fulfillment only through participation in the community. The aim of the individual, as well as of the community, is the pursuit of the good. For individuals, the good translates into individual happiness; for governments, into social happiness and justice. Both the individual and the collective good can be pursued best through moderation.

Since the state is the highest form of community, the aim of the state must be the highest good. The interests of the state take precedence over the interests of individuals (for a contrary view, see Burton 1982, 1984). The best type of state, however, is one guided by moderation; a state, like a ship, should neither grow too large nor be governed by extremists. Governments are classified into three types depending on the number of rulers, with a moderate and an extreme form of each type. Government by one person may be monarchy or tyranny; government by a few persons may be aristocracy or oligarchy; and government by the majority may be constitutional government (orderly popular rule) or democracy (disorderly mob rule). The best governments are monarchy and aristocracy, which lie between the extremes of *despo* and *demo*.

Aristotle's contribution to modern political philosophy includes the discussion of which forms of government work best under different conditions and what causes "the ruin and preservation of states." Not only does he raise the question of how order and stability are possible, but he also discusses "the causes of revolutions and how they can be avoided" (Bowles 1961, p. 58).

Another important Aristotelian notion refers to the question of how the goods of a society

are to be distributed and, more important, how they are to be distributed justly. "The most specific sense that Aristotle gives to justice, and from which the most familiar formulations derive, is that of refraining from *pleonexia*, that is, from gaining some advantage for oneself by seizing what belongs to another, his property, his reward, his office and the like, or by denying that which is due to him" (Rawls 1971, p. 10).

Aristotle's ideas, like those of the other Greek philosophers, were taken up in modern times by such political thinkers as Hobbes (1588–1679) and Montesquieu (1689–1755).

Political Thought in the Seventeenth and Eighteenth Centuries

Historical Overview

During the Middle Ages, the Catholic Church was the major regulatory institution in Europe, while monarchs were weak and nation-states fragmented. The gradual dissolution of the medieval unity of empire and church began with the rise of the absolutist state in the late 1400s and ended with the French Revolution and the Napoleonic wars (1789–1815). At the dawn of the modern era, absolute monarchs consolidated their rule and claimed legitimacy by divine right.

In ancient Greece, no distinction existed between *man* and *citizen*; they were a single concept. In the Middle Ages and during the reign of absolutism that followed, the rights of individuals were subordinated to those of church, state, or community, and obedience to authority was rarely questioned. This situation changed in the wake of the economic and political crises that shook Europe and North America in the seventeenth and eighteenth centuries, including the Protestant Reformation, the industrial revolution, and the French and American revolutions. In the aftermath of these upheavals, people increasingly questioned the authority of the government. Political philosophers defended the rights of individuals vis-à-vis the state. In England, the United States, and France, rebels overthrew absolutist governments in the name of freedom. Political leaders wrote constitutions that spelled out citizens' rights and limited the state's powers. As political sociologist Seymour Martin Lipset notes, "The breakdown of a traditional society exposed . . . for the first time the difference between society and the state" (1981, p. 2). This was the birth of modern political thought.

A profound revolution took place in science as well. The Greek astronomer Ptolemy had written that the earth was the center of the universe, an idea sanctioned by the Catholic Church until the sixteenth century. But now, seemingly immutable scientific verities, as well as political and economic ones, began to crumble. Copernicus (1473–1543) argued that the sun, not the earth, was the center of the universe. Kepler (1571–1630) proved Copernicus right but qualified his theory with the idea that the earth's orbit was elliptical rather than circular. Galileo (1564–1642) was the first astronomer to use the telescope. And Newton (1642–1727) formulated the law of universal attraction or gravity. Science was progressing in giant strides, and people's confidence in their ability to solve all human problems by the application of reason and observation grew. In the seventeenth century, reason began to replace faith as the basis for human thought; in the eighteenth century, reason, backed by observation, came to dominate the social and political realms (see Singer 1959).

Thomas Hobbes (1588–1679)

The publication of *Leviathan* by Thomas Hobbes in 1651 marked the emergence of ideas that were to resonate over the next three hundred years. Hobbes is remembered for asking the question How is social order possible? That is, how can people unite to form enduring societies? He answered this question by using deductive logic, which he had learned from the astronomer Galileo while in political exile in France. Following Galileo, Hobbes believed that if univer-

sal assumptions or axioms concerning the nature of the individual could be established, deducing statements about the nature of society would be possible. His fundamental assumption about human nature was that behavior is determined by passions or urges common to all people, the major ones being gain, glory, and fear. The objects of passions are randomly distributed; that is, no laws determine that two or more people should have a strong desire for the same thing at the same time. But when people do desire the same thing at the same time and supplies are limited, they perceive each other as either aids or obstacles to the achievement of their passions. It follows that individuals are motivated to use or subdue others and, if necessary, to destroy them.

Hobbes reasoned that people are essentially equal. No person is so strong that others, in combination, cannot bring him or her down. People are equal because they are equally capable of causing death. Given the previous assumptions about passions, it follows that the most effective way to achieve one's end or desire is through fraud or force. Since we are governed by our passions or desires, which are randomly distributed, at any given moment we may come into conflict with others who desire the same things. Unless we give way because of fear or satisfy our desires through fraud, we enter into conflict over the desired goods. Such conflict is frequent, and life is therefore nasty, brutish, and short.

However, in addition to our passions, we have the capacity to be rational. Rational people, by definition, desire a life of peace and security. Thus, our forebears tried to devise a peaceful and orderly society. The principle that our passions are limitless and can be checked only by fear of death becomes the basis on which the social order is formulated. However, if the power over death is given to more than one person, conflict is still possible. The only way to ensure peace in society is to formulate a social contract that gives the power of death to a sole individual, an absolute monarch, under whom all will be subjects, sharing in an equality of fear. This, then, is how social order is possible. If we give up the absolute monarchy, we will of necessity return to the state of nature in which life is nasty, brutish, and short; the bloody English Civil War was evidence of this consequence.

Hobbes's work is an important landmark in intellectual history. He introduced the notions of an inevitable conflict of interest among people and of the need for an absolute monarch legitimated not by divine right but by a social contract. Hobbes's logic justified the role of absolute authority as an end in itself. Unfortunately for his logic, the times were changing, and an absolute ruler, whether legitimated by divine right or by a social contract, was no longer what the people wanted. Later thinkers, however, including Locke, had to confront the Hobbesian defense of absolute monarchy in order to produce an intellectual justification for constitutional monarchy (see Sabine and Thorson 1973).

John Locke (1632–1704)

Another Englishman, John Locke, wrote a few decades after Hobbes in the context of the Glorious Revolution of 1688. While Hobbes argued for absolute force to ensure order, Locke argued that when the mischief caused by obedience to the government is greater than the mischief of revolt against it, citizens have the right to resist the authority of government.

Like Hobbes, Locke believed that the basis of governmental legitimacy is the social contract and that before the social contract was instituted, people lived in the state of nature. However, Locke's assumptions about human nature, and hence his conception of the social contract, are radically different from those of Hobbes.

Unlike Hobbes, Locke believed that people are guided by Reason writ large, not passions, and that Reason enjoins them to respect each other's rights. Furthermore, rational self-interest leads people to engage in peaceable relations of exchange with one another. These rela-

tions in turn lead to commerce, specialization, and a division of labor beneficial to all. The interests of each individual harmonize with the interests of all rather than conflicting with them as Hobbes believed.

If life in the state of nature is as benevolent as Locke described it, why do individuals band together to form a social contract? People institute governments, and hand over some of their rights to them, for mutual convenience, not physical protection. In the state of nature, there is no one to referee disputes and enforce the laws of reason. The role of government, then, is that of a referee or police officer—to ensure that the laws are observed. Government is legitimate only if it protects individual liberty, property, and the pursuit of happiness. Because the state of nature precedes the social contract, individuals' rights supersede those of government. If the government violates their rights, individuals have the right to dissolve it and to institute another.

Locke's *Two Treatises on Civil Government*, written in exile during the last turbulent years before the Glorious Revolution (1688), were intended to justify the fight of the English people against royal absolutism. A century later, his ideas were incorporated into the American Declaration of Independence, which proclaims:

> The unanimous declaration of the thirteen United States of America: When, in the course of human events, it becomes necessary for one people to dissolve the political bands which have connected them with another, and to assume among the powers of the earth the separate and equal station to which the laws of nature and of nature's God entitle them, a decent respect to the opinions of mankind requires that they should declare the causes which impel them to the separation.
>
> We hold these truths to be self-evident, that all men are created equal, that they are endowed by their Creator with certain unalienable rights, that among these are life, liberty, and the pursuit of happiness. That to secure these rights, governments are instituted among men, deriving their just powers

from the consent of the governed. That whenever any form of government becomes destructive of these ends, it is the right of the people to alter or to abolish it, and to institute new government, laying its foundation on such principles and organizing its powers in such form, as to them shall seem most likely to effect their safety and happiness.

Locke's main contribution to political thought lies in the doctrine of harmony of interests. His belief that individuals' pursuit of self-interest enhances the welfare and prosperity of all fundamentally differs from Hobbes's assumption of a built-in conflict of interest. Today, the issue of harmony versus conflict of interests still polemicizes political sociology (see chapter 7).

The Enlightenment: The Eighteenth Century

Eighteenth-century French thinkers, known as *philosophes*, carried the rationalism of the seventeenth century to its extreme. Writers such as Montesquieu, Rousseau, and Voltaire believed that if reason and scientific methods could uncover the laws that govern the natural universe, comparable laws could be discovered to explain and govern society and all human affairs. "They pictured themselves as the Newtons of statecraft, justice, and economics who would reduce the most intricate institutions to formulas as neat as Sir Isaac's own mathematical laws and principles" (Brinton et al. 1967, p. 45).

Not only could natural laws, once discovered through the application of reason, be used to explain all historical and social phenomena, but they could be used to change them, to fashion a new and perfect society where humankind could attain happiness at last. This idea culminated in the American Declaration of Independence, which listed "the pursuit of happiness" as a fundamental human right along with life and liberty. The future seemed one of boundless hope and optimism; progress seemed assured.

A major corollary of eighteenth-century rationalism was **individualism**. Rousseau, Montesquieu, Voltaire, Adam Smith, and Jefferson called for the liberation of individuals from the tyranny of medieval associations—from estate, guild, church, and the patriarchal family. "Not the group but the individual was the heir of historical development; not the guild but the entrepreneur; not the class or estate but the citizen; not corporate or liturgical tradition but individual reason" (Nisbet 1966, p. 43).

The idea of individualism was translated into two leading theories of the eighteenth century—the economic theory of laissez-faire and the political theory of the social contract. Although both these theories had their roots in the seventeenth century, they were not fully developed until the eighteenth.

The theory of **laissez-faire** has been a dominant force in economics for nearly two centuries. This theory envisioned individuals, working in a free market and without governmental interference, seeking to maximize their own profit on the basis of their efforts and intelligence. In political thought, the belief in the sanctity of individual liberty was translated into a call for **democracy**, government by popular sovereignty. For the first time since ancient Greece, tyranny on the basis of divine right or hereditary monarchy was believed contrary to the laws of nature. Rousseau and Montesquieu, like Locke, believed that only free individuals, coming together voluntarily and basing their decisions on reason and knowledge, could form a legitimate government. Such a government, based on a social contract, derived its authority solely from the consent of the governed. All individuals, regardless of hereditary privilege, were to share in the government and were equal before the law. Thus, the ideas of democracy and egalitarianism were derived from the principles of reason, individualism, and natural law.

These ideas, which must have appeared dangerously radical in the eighteenth century, were to have a major impact on subsequent history. Not only did they help legitimate two revolutions, the American and the French, and shape the new societies constituted in their wake, but they also encouraged and catalyzed the development of modern sociological and political thought.

To be sure, the unbounded optimism and the faith in reason, individualism, and progress that characterized the eighteenth century soon gave way to disillusionment. Contrary to expectations, wars did not end but intensified. The French Revolution itself degenerated into terror and anarchy. As early as the end of the eighteenth century, and much more consistently in the nineteenth century, we note a distrust of the power of reason alone to solve all human problems and a deep fear of the consequences of extreme individualism. Perceptive nineteenth-century thinkers such as Comte, Ferdinand Tönnies, Durkheim, and Weber, while extolling the virtues of progress and rationality, also warned about their consequences—alienation, rootlessness, anomie, and possibly a new totalitarianism. By the twentieth century, the voices of pessimism became a chorus (see chapters 3 and 6).

Montesquieu (1689–1755)

Montesquieu was so impressed by the British system of government that he paid it the ultimate compliment of his age: He said that it "might have been invented by Locke, Newton, or Archimedes" (Brinton et al. 1967, p. 52). In England, he believed, the combination of constitutional monarchy and aristocracy prevented democracy from degenerating into the tyranny of mass rule, and the system of checks and balances guaranteed moderation and individual liberties.

Montesquieu rejected Hobbes's conception of the state of nature. Rather than existing in a state of war of all against all, Montesquieu pictured "primordial man as a timid creature . . . guided only by the elementary instincts of self-preservation and reproduction" (Becker and Barnes 1952, vol. 2, p. 446). Montesquieu was anxious to refute Hobbes because "if war and

inequality are linked to the essence of society and not to the essence of man, the aim of politics will be, not to eliminate war and inequality, which are inseparable from collective life, but to mitigate or moderate them" (Aron 1970, vol. 1, p. 51).

Montesquieu's major work was the *Spirit of the Laws*. The central thesis of this book is that humans are influenced by climate, religion, laws, maxims of government, precedents, morals, and customs. Collectively, these influences form the spirit of the nation.

The *Spirit of the Laws* includes Montesquieu's important attempt to relate types of government to types of society (see Figure 2.1). Montesquieu, taking his cue from Aristotle, developed a typology of government consisting of republics, monarchies, and despotism. Republics may be of two subtypes—democratic and aristocratic—defined with reference to the nature of government and the dominant spirit of the nation. The nature of government has two dimensions, the number of people who possess sovereign power and the exercise of sovereignty either in accordance with fixed and established laws or in accordance with personal whim. The nature of government thus involves the question of whether all people share power, some people share power, or a single individual wields power. The spirit of the nation may consist of equality of universal participation, equality of fear, or inequality. In addition to nature of government and spirit of the nation, republics are distinguished by size, principle of government, stability, and degree of moderation in the exercise of power.

In democratic republics, the nature of government is that all people share power. The principle of government involves two dimensions: respect for the law and the dedication of the individual to the welfare of the group. Democracies tend to be small and to stress equality of universal participation. They also tend to be unstable and immoderate in the exercise of power.

In aristocratic republics, as in democratic republics, the principle of government is respect

	Republic		Monarchy	Despotism
	Democracy	Aristocracy		
Nature of Government (number of people who hold sovereignty)	All of the people share power	Some of the people share power	Power in hands of one person	Power in hands of one person
Principle of Government	Respect for law, individual's dedication to the welfare of the group	Respect for law, individual's dedication to the welfare of the group	Individual's respect for what he owes to rank	Fear
Size	Small	Small	Moderate	Large
Spirit of the Nation	Equality of universal participation	Equality of universal participation	Discrimination and inequality	Equality of fear, impotence, and nonparticipation
Degree of Stability Plus Moderation	Unstable and immoderate in exercise of power	Could guarantee both moderate use of force and liberty for people	Unstable and immoderate in use of power	Unstable and immoderate in use of power

Figure 2.1   Montesquieu's Comparison of Types of Government

for the law and the dedication of the individual to group welfare. Aristocracies are also small and based on equality of participation among the elite. The major difference between aristocracies and democracies is that in the former, only a few share power; in other words, they differ in the nature of government. Unlike democracy, the aristocratic form of government is relatively stable and moderate in its use of force. Also, it allows liberty for the people. This liberty comes from the struggle between various interest groups that, Montesquieu assumed, results in a balance of power.

Size is a key variable for Montesquieu. Democracies, he felt, could exist only under conditions similar to those of the Greek city-states, whose average population was about ten thousand. As societies grow from a small to a moderate size, the republican forms of government, whether democratic or aristocratic, cease to be effective and monarchy develops. In monarchies, power rests in the hands of one individual. The principle of government is the

respect of the citizens for the perquisites of rank. The nature of society is discrimination and inequality.

A further increase in size from moderate to large societies results in despotism. In **despotism**, as in monarchy, the nature of government places sovereignty and power in the hands of one person. The principle of government is fear, and equality of fear is accompanied by a sense of impotence. People do not participate in government. Despotic governments tend to be unstable and immoderate in the use of force.

As we have seen above, size is a critical variable in shaping the nature of society and of government. Like Plato and Aristotle, Montesquieu recognized the effects of size and believed that society should not grow too large lest immoderate government result.

A key variable in addition to size is the mode of production. Montesquieu believed that population size is limited by the potential of agriculture, that is, by the number of nonfarm people that the farmer can feed. The amount of surplus the farmer can produce depends on the efficiency of cultivation. But one condition of efficiency is the willingness of farmers to produce a surplus. Why should they want to produce more than they need?

Montesquieu's answer is very important for understanding the political process and the history of political thought. It provides an explanation for the prehistoric development of agriculture discussed above, as well as for contemporary phenomena. According to Montesquieu, the farmers' motivation to produce more than they need is based on a desire to exchange their produce for goods produced by artisans in the city. This desire for luxury items leads to technological inventions, which in turn increase productivity. Increased agricultural productivity leads to mass unemployment in the countryside at the same time as new industrial jobs are created in the city. Thus, industrialization gathers momentum (see Aron 1970).

Montesquieu lived too close to the beginning of the era of industrialism and representative democracy to provide an analysis of the coming age. But no greater appreciation of the value of Montesquieu's work exists, perhaps, than that of Auguste Comte. Of Montesquieu's work, Comte, the father of modern sociology, was to say:

> The great strength of this memorable work appears to me to lie in its tendency to regard political phenomena as subject to invariable laws, like all other phenomena. For the first time in the history of the human mind, the general idea of law is directly defined, in relation to all, even to political subjects, in the same sense in which it is applied in the simplest positive investigations.[3] (Quoted in Martineau 1896, p. 98)

Jean-Jacques Rousseau (1712–1778)

While Hobbes argued that almost any government was better than the state of nature, Rousseau argued in favor of an almost biblical view that life in the state of nature ensured human happiness as long as one did not eat from the tree of knowledge. Rousseau argued that hunger for knowledge led Adam and Eve out of the Garden of Eden, where all their economic wants were taken care of by nature. In the state of nature, people were noble, pure, and happy. This view opposes the Hobbesian notion of a state of nature where life is nasty, brutish, and short. Indeed, it was Rousseau who invented the idea of the "noble savage," which immediately became the rage in Europe. It accounted for the Europeans' adoration of the "wild American ambassador" Benjamin Franklin, as well as for the recurrent "back to the land" urge that periodically has driven people to seek a better life on the farm.

Like Montesquieu, Rousseau viewed inequality and human suffering as stemming not from nature but from civilization. "Montesquieu, for whom the state of nature does not serve as a criterion, confined himself to stating that inequalities spring from society," while "Rousseau referred to a state of nature, conceived by human reason, which serves as a kind of criterion for society. By employing this criterion of what should be, he arrived at a conception of the absolute sovereignty of the people" (Aron 1970, vol. 1, p. 51).

Rousseau divided knowledge into two parts: the arts and the sciences. He argued that art and science lead to luxury, which undermines the simple and essential virtues by breeding inequalities and distinctions of class and wealth. Such distinctions are the root of economic and social evil, the great breeders of human unhappiness—ills that Rousseau assumed were minimal or absent in traditional society.

Under these new conditions, the talented differentiated themselves from the mediocre, the strong from the weak, and the rich from the poor. Soon sympathy gave way to self-aggrandizement, and the strong and the rich became dominant and organized society for the purpose of eternally keeping themselves on top and the weak and the poor in servitude.

Following this social diagnosis, Rousseau suggested how society ought to develop in order

3. By "positive investigations" Comte means essentially what we mean by science.

to minimize the evils of inequality. Legislation is required to preserve liberty and equality while maintaining social order. According to Rousseau, society is founded by individuals who associate for the purpose of offsetting, as far as possible, the evil consequences of the fall of humanity from its primitive perfection. The effectiveness of this social contract depends on the exercise of power to enforce it. This power is lodged in the body politic, the sovereign. While Hobbes had argued for a single absolute sovereign, Rousseau declared that sovereignty resides in, and is inalienable from, the people as a whole. It cannot be divided or portioned out. Law is the expression of the common will of the sovereign people with regard to matters of common interest.

Ideally, the sovereign people should legislate as a whole and not through elected representatives, since representative government curtails popular liberty. True democracy must take the form of the Athenian *ecclesia* (assembly), where the whole people gathers and legislates directly. However, such government is possible only in a small community, and therefore Rousseau, recalling Plato and Aristotle, limits the ideal state to ten thousand people.

Even in larger states, where direct government is impossible, the people remain sovereign; the power of the governing agent is derived solely from the consent of the governed and may be exercised only for their convenience. Since the device of representative government under a temporarily elected parliament is excluded by Rousseau as a subterfuge, the agent can be only a monarch or an aristocracy. Monarchy has too many disadvantages; hence, the best agent of the sovereign people in larger states is an aristocracy. It should not be hereditary, however, because the moment any governmental agency ceases to register the will of the sovereign people and begins to aggregate sovereignty to itself, it should be overthrown. The right of the people to change the form of government at will, the right to revolution, is as inalienable as their sovereignty.

Rousseau's contribution to modern political thought is twofold: first, the notion of the social contract as the basis of governmental legitimacy and second, the emphasis on the absolute sovereignty of the people. Montesquieu, like Plato and Aristotle, had favored aristocracy; Rousseau, democracy. This idea of the sovereignty of the people was unprecedented and controversial. It quickly achieved wide popularity among the reading public in Europe and the American colonies.

Summary

History may be divided into stages on the basis of the changing relation of people to their environment. Each change in the population size and density and in the basic economic systems results in changes in the distributive systems. The different economic systems give rise to corresponding differences in the nature of the political system, of the family, of religion, of the educational system, and of political philosophy.

We have seen how the economic, social, and intellectual conditions of the seventeenth and eighteenth centuries led to the development of deductive reasoning and the rise of science. In the eighteenth century, thinkers such as Montesquieu began to apply the principles of science to the study of human society. Although the concerns of political sociology were foreshadowed in seventeenth- and eighteenth-century political theory, sociology as a discipline arose only in the nineteenth century, and political sociology as a subdiscipline did not appear until the twentieth century. Political sociology builds on the distinction between the political order and the social order, between society and the state. It deals with the relation between type of government and type of society. Chapter 3 traces the emergence of political sociology from political philosophy.

CHAPTER THREE

──────

From Social Philosophy
to Social Science

Preview

Chapter 2 traced the changing nature of socio-political systems and the emergence of political thought through the end of the eighteenth century. Chapter 3 covers the social and political changes and related theoretical schemes that have emerged during the past two centuries. We will discuss the contributions of Auguste Comte (1798–1857), Alexis de Tocqueville (1805–1859), Karl Marx (1818–1883), Emile Durkheim (1858–1917), and Max Weber (1864–1920). These social scientists stand on this side of the time line that divides the agricultural, rural world of peasant, serf, and slave from the industrial, urban world of the wage and salary earner. The collapse of traditional agricultural society led people to attempt to understand the world from the perspective of social science.

Common Themes

Social Change

All five sociologists discussed in this chapter were concerned with the nature of social change. Social change in the seventeenth, eighteenth, and nineteenth centuries included the increased movement from farm to city, from agricultural work to industrial and commercial work, and from feudal relations to wage labor and bureaucratic administration. Political changes included the French, American, and English revolutions. Drawing on the perspective of their location in history and building on the work of earlier theorists, Comte, Marx, Tocqueville, Durkheim, and Weber continued to analyze the changes in people's relation to their environment and their position in the social and political order.

Human Nature

The idea of the individual has achieved unprecedented importance in the modern capitalist, democratic state. In many non-Western cultures, the concept of "self" does not even exist. Although the idea of the individual arose during the Protestant Reformation in the sixteenth century, not until the French Revolution in 1789 did the distinction between the individual and citizen or subject and between society and the state become clearly delineated (Lipset 1981, p. 3). The individual has come to be seen not only as a subject of the state but as a discrete unit with inherent rights. The notions of individual freedom and governmental accountability to the people served the same function in a later age as the divine right of kings served earlier: It legitimated a new form of government. The notion of individual rights helped make the change from monarchy to democracy possible. These notions resulted in part from changes in economic structure, specifically, from the rise of capitalism, which replaced the family with the individual as the wage-earning unit. As the individual came to be more than a subject, the state came to be seen as only one institution among several, including the religious, economic, familial, and educational institutions. The interests of individuals and groups within the state, not the interests of the state itself, are seen as supreme in modern capitalist states (see Burton 1982).

The debate over the nature of the individual in the field of sociology is between those who see individuals as free agents creating the circumstances of their lives and those who see individuals largely as products of outside forces. The classical utilitarian position, which relies on the works of Hobbes and Locke, among others, holds that individuals are free agents endowed with reason and are responsible for their own success or failure. From this viewpoint, therefore, understanding the nature of the individual is the starting point for understanding society. On the other hand, the sociological positivists, including Comte and Durkheim, believe that individual behavior is largely influenced by external factors such as institutions and population density. For the positivist, intentions and motives are not as important in understanding human behavior as are these external factors.

Social scientists since 1820 have rejected the extreme individualism of Hobbes and Locke. They have either combined individualism and positivism or emphasized external aspects of society as foremost in shaping human thought, feeling, and action. Thus, Marx saw the economic system as being of primary importance; Comte and Durkheim emphasized the division of labor; Tocqueville emphasized mediating institutions; and Weber emphasized values as well as institutions such as bureaucracy. Although sociologists have disputed the relative importance of these variables for more than a hundred years, today we tend to see them all as contributing to our understanding of how political systems operate.

The Social Scientists

Auguste Comte (1798–1857)

Comte, like Socrates, lived in a time of great social change that influenced his ideas. Troubled by the destruction wrought by the French Revolution, the Napoleonic Wars, rapid industrialization, and the diminished effectiveness of traditional values, Comte attempted to understand the basis of social order and social change through scientific inquiry. He believed that the science of society—sociology—would produce laws that society should then accept as mandatory. That new society, free of the irrationalities of the past, would be guided by reason and would guarantee human happiness to its members.

Comte's work can be briefly summarized as follows: (a) The most critical factor in the history of humanity is the increasing division of labor and specialization. Comte believed that special dispositions are inherent in different individuals. Some are disposed toward command while others are disposed toward obedience. The disposition toward command in some, affirmed by the obedience of others, results in a tendency toward government in human societies. (b) The most important specialists in any age are those representing knowledge and values. Thus, scientists and intellectuals are the elite of the modern age. (c) History has gone through three major periods. In the first period, the theological stage, the ruling elites were composed of religious and military leaders; in the second period, the metaphysical stage, the ruling elites were composed of philosophers; and in the third, or scientific, period, the ruling elites are the scientists and the industrialists. Comte called this exposition the law of the three stages.

Comte based his work on Montesquieu's *Spirit of the Laws*, whose great strength according to Comte was its "tendency to regard political phenomena as subject to invariable laws. . . . For the first time in the history of the human mind, the general idea of law is directly defined" and applied to human political phenomena (Comte 1854, 1896, p. 198). Comte's view of sociology as a science was based on the philosophy of positivism. **Positivists** believe that, just as in the case of the natural and physical sciences, laws govern individuals and can be discovered through the use of reasoning and observation.

Montesquieu's major contribution had been to attribute political evil to the correlation between type of society and the corresponding type of political institutions. Comte, on the other hand, believed that political evil resulted not from political institutions such as absolute monarchy but from "ideas and social manners" (Comte 1854, 1896, vol. II, book VI, p. 78). In making this distinction, Comte was working toward a modern definition of culture. He had seen from the French Revolution that a change in government did not necessarily result in a great change in society. Comte felt that social problems or evils resulted from the fact that the traditional ideas, values, and manners were no longer appropriate and a new set of manners and traditions had not yet been worked out by scientific means.

Unlike Hobbes, who emphasized the necessity of force in maintaining social order, or Locke, who saw order as based on a natural identity of interest, Comte became interested in the variations of institutions or agreements that help regulate human life. In this respect, he was closer to Rousseau than to Hobbes or Locke, but Comte went beyond Rousseau by asserting that these institutions varied in relation to changes in the division of labor, as the law of the three stages indicates.

Alexis de Tocqueville (1805–1859)

While Comte was concerned primarily with the decline in values resulting from industrialization, Tocqueville was concerned primarily with political institutions, particularly democratic ones. Tocqueville, like Montesquieu, saw as a central problem the relationship between various types of societies and their corresponding political systems. He explored variations of a single type of political system—democracy.

Tocqueville compared France under the aristocratic monarchy with France after the French Revolution of 1789 as well as with England and with the United States. On the basis of this comparison, Tocqueville concluded that democracy could exist in different forms ranging from liberal to despotic. By his definition, democracy included both a growing equality of conditions and liberty or freedom.

Equality implies the sovereignty of all members of society. Democracy also includes participation in the choice of political leaders and in the exercise of authority. The goal of democratic societies is the peace, prosperity, and well-being of the majority. (This may, of course, be the goal of other forms of government as well,

including an enlightened tyranny.) Tocqueville believed that political, but not economic, inequality had disappeared with the overthrow of the French monarchy and of the old aristocratic nobility.

As far back as Aristotle, philosophers have sought to define democracy and to determine the conditions under which democracy can exist. One of the oldest, and most frequent, variables considered was size. Montesquieu believed that liberty could be protected either in small republics or in large monarchies. Since monarchies and aristocracies precluded equality of condition, democracy was not fully possible under either system. Yet the ancients had thought it impossible to govern a large territory other than by monarchy. Since modern societies are obviously large, the question becomes: How is democracy possible in these large societies?

Montesquieu wrote prior to the French Revolution, Tocqueville in its aftermath. In the words of commentator Raymond Aron, Tocqueville "could not imagine that for moderns the foundation and guarantee of liberty is inequality of conditions for the simple reason that inequality of conditions had disappeared, at least in his eyes. It would be senseless to wish to restore the authority and privileges of an aristocracy which was destroyed by revolution" (Aron 1968, vol. I, pp. 188–89).

Liberty involves protection against arbitrary government and assurance that power is exercised only according to law. Since people (including those composing the governing elite) are neither trustworthy nor virtuous, liberty rests in modern society on representative government and on a balance of powers.

A basic problem in Tocqueville's work "is that of the compatibility of equality and liberty" (Aron 1968, vol. I, p. 190). Rousseau had argued that if individuals in capitalist society are absolutely free in their pursuit of scarce resources, the few will end up with a great deal, while the many will end up with little. By definition, this is inequality of condition. And if one assumes that political power rests on the economic resources one commands, then it is also political inequality.

Democracy is defined in terms of both liberty and equality. Since the conditions that permit total freedom also limit equality, democracy under these conditions is impossible. The opposite is also logically valid. As we approach the limits of total equality, economic freedom is diminished, and under the same definitions, where freedom is diminished, democracy does not exist. Thus, the problem of democracy is to find conditions under which equality and liberty are in balance.

For Tocqueville, America was a country where this balance between equality and liberty was possible. One factor that encouraged American democracy was the accident of geography. In a country without powerful neighbors and with no scarcity of land, the necessity for a landed aristocracy did not exist. The absence of belligerent neighbors negated the need for a strong military and for a social mechanism to accumulate the wealth to support them. A related geographic factor was physical size. Democracy requires a country large enough and powerful enough to provide security but small enough for legislation to be tailored to the locality. Another condition favoring democracy was that the land was settled by people with an advanced technology.

An additional factor that facilitates democracy is law. Freedom includes the ability to move freely within the society and to transport or transfer one's goods, property, and capital; these freedoms are specified and protected by law. Since people in a democracy are liable to get carried away by their emotional responses, it is necessary to avoid control of the legislature by an emotional electorate. At the same time, concentration of too much power in the legislature must be avoided. Mutual checks, on both rulers and masses, are accomplished in the United States by a bicameral (two-house) legislature, which lessens the possibility that either house will get carried away by its emotions. Other mutual checks include a president whose power is circumscribed by the constitution and

a two-party system based on differences in interest rather than of principle. This system guarantees that the parties will be more inclined to compromise than to maintain extremist positions (see chapter 9).

Karl Marx (1818–1883)

Marx's famous *Communist Manifesto*, first published in 1848, opens with the ominous sentence "a spectre is haunting Europe—the spectre of Communism." It closes equally resoundingly with the call: "The proletarians have nothing to lose but their chains. They have a world to win. Working men of all countries, unite!" Although Marx's call for a world revolution is more famous, his theoretical work has made him a major figure in the development of political sociology.

Marx believed that work shapes both people's own lives and their relations to others. The individual's relationship to the **means of production** (that is, resources such as land or machinery that are used to produce other goods) determines the class to which he or she belongs. A social class consists of all the persons who perform the same function in a productive system, such as farming or trade. Each social class occupies a different place in the social structure.

Every age or epoch is distinguished by its major productive or economic system (hunting and gathering, horticulture, agriculture, industry), and each age has a class structure that corresponds to its economic system. The class structure is composed of two principal classes—a dominant class of owners and a subjected class of toilers. There may be other classes, such as artisans in feudal society or farmers in capitalist society, but they are marginal to the major mode of production. According to Marx, two exceptions to the universality of class conflict exist. The first is prehistoric hunting and gathering societies, whose resources were more or less equally distributed. The second is the communist society, which will succeed capitalism and which, presumably, will be truly classless. For most of history, however, "freeman and slave, patrician and plebian, lord and serf, guild-master and journeyman, in a word, oppressor and oppressed, stood in constant opposition to each other." In present-day capitalist society, the class structure has been simplified into "two great hostile camps: bourgeoisie and proletariat, or capitalists and workers." The **bourgeoisie** are the owners of the means of production, that is, of factories and machines, and the **proletariat** are the laborers. Marx wrote in *The Communist Manifesto* that class antagonisms are so fundamental and pervasive that "the history of all hitherto existing society is the history of class struggle" (Marx 1956, p. 200).

Oppression and class conflict are inherent in all societies to date. In order to produce, a small elite must exist (masters, landlords, or capitalists) that controls the means of production and manages production for its own benefit. Masses must also exist (slaves, serfs, or proletarians) who toil to enrich not themselves, but the owning class. While the dominant class prospers, the laborer sinks deeper and deeper into misery. The laboring classes are impoverished not only materially but psychologically as well, for they must sell the most fundamentally human aspect of themselves, their labor, in order to subsist. Under the conditions of modern industry, work, instead of leading to self-fulfillment, is profoundly alienating.

> Owing to the extensive use of machinery and to division of labor, the work of the proletarians has lost all individual character, and, consequently, all charm for the workman. He becomes an appendage of the machine, and it is only the most simple, most monotonous, and most easily acquired knack, that is required of him. . . .
>
> In what does this alienation of labor consist? First, that the work is *external* to the worker, that it is not a part of his nature, that consequently he does not fulfill himself in his work but denies himself, has a feeling of misery, not of well-being, does not develop

freely a physical and mental energy, but is physically exhausted and mentally debased. The worker therefore feels himself at home only during his leisure, whereas at work he feels homeless. His work is not voluntary but imposed, *forced labor.* It is not the satisfaction of a need, but only a means for satisfying other needs. . . . It is not his work but work for someone else, in work he does not belong to himself but to another person. . . . It is another's activity, and a loss of his own spontaneity. (*Communist Manifesto* and *Economic and Philosophic Manuscripts of 1844*, in Marx 1956, pp. 169–70)

As the exploitation of the proletariat worsens and the rift between the classes deepens, revolution becomes more likely. However, objective conditions alone, that is, oppression and exploitation, are not enough to bring about the revolution. Before the oppressed workers can revolt, they must become subjectively aware of their true class interest. They must realize that their misery stems from the nature of private property, that the capitalists are their class enemies, and that class solidarity must override individual interests and petty competition. Through repeated industrial conflict, the members of the proletariat, assisted by revolutionary intellectuals such as Marx, forge themselves into a "class for itself," a unified revolutionary force.

In the process of liberating itself, the proletariat will abolish the conditions of all class oppression, that is, private property. A new proletariat society will arise that will not spell just another system of class exploitation. Unlike past systems, collective ownership of the means of production under the new communist society will bring about the end of class antagonism and alienation. In this society, government or politics will be unnecessary, because the age-old problems of production and distribution will be solved. Compulsion and force, which are the very reason for the existence of the state, will be replaced by free will. Individuals will produce not because they are forced to but for the simple joy of creating and sharing; work will become fulfilling, not alienating. The present system of distribution according to class position will be replaced by a humane principle of "from each according to his ability, to each according to his needs." In the new communist society, individuals will finally realize their full potential as human beings, enjoying true freedom in their work and their humanity.

Marx believed that because social classes are based on the most fundamental aspect of society—the relations of production—classes constitute the most important division in society. In their power to shape human consciousness and play a role in historical events, classes supersede all other divisions, including ethnic and racial distinctions, religion, sex, geographic location, and even national boundaries.

If humans create their own life through their means of production, and if the fundamental social divisions (classes) are based on the economic organization of production, it follows that to understand the nature of any society we must understand its technical and economic base. "The mode of production of material life determines the general character of the social, political, and spiritual processes of life. It is not the consciousness of men that determines their being, but on the contrary, their social being determines their consciousness" (Marx 1956, p. 51). This is Marx's principal contribution to the sociology of knowledge.

Marx believed that the "mental productions" of any society—its art, culture, and social and political thought—can be understood only in relation to its technical and economic structure. Art, science, and even democracy are no longer plain art, science, and democracy but bourgeois art, bourgeois science, and bourgeois democracy, just as the proletarian society of the future will produce its own forms of thought and its own institutions.

Marx believed that the state, far from being a neutral policeman safeguarding the rights of individuals, reflects the economic realities of the class system. The state is, in fact, ruled either directly or indirectly by the economic elite. In capitalist society, "the executive of the modern state is but a committee for managing the common affairs of the whole bourgeoisie" (*The Communist Manifesto,* in Drennen 1972, p. 148; see also chapter 9).

Marx's contribution to political sociology is so extensive and his influence so pervasive that it is almost impossible to imagine a contemporary understanding of society without his ideas. One major contribution is the notion that any attempt to understand society, government, or forms of political expression must start with an analysis of economic institutions. Another contribution is the notion that society (at least all known past and present societies) is based not on harmony but on perpetual conflict. A related point is that society is characterized not by stability but by relentless change. Stability, where it exists, is illusory and momentary, for the forces of change, in the form of new technological and economic developments, are always at work, either openly or beneath the surface. Eventually, the new technological and economic conditions are no longer compatible with the old political and social order, and they become "so many fetters" that must be "burst asunder" so that a new epoch may dawn (*The Communist Manifesto,* in Drennen 1972, pp. 150, 152). Finally, while earlier writers had viewed change as gradual, unilinear, and evolutionary, Marx viewed change as abrupt, cataclysmic, and violent: "Force is the midwife of every old society pregnant with a new one" (*Das Kapital,* in Marx 1956, p. 227). (For a contemporary critique of Marx's theory of dialectical change from an evolutionary perspective, see Boulding 1981a, 1981b.)

Emile Durkheim (1858–1917)

Durkheim, like Comte and Marx, was concerned with the dysfunctions produced by industrial society and with the causes and effects of social change. Taking seriously Comte's notion of empirically testing theories about the world, Durkheim developed his ideas by studying traditional societies and analyzing available statistics. He became one of the first sociologists to attempt a positive or empirical examination of social questions. Durkheim demonstrated that there are **social facts** outside individuals that influence the way they think, act, and feel. These social facts include the norms, or "the collective consciousness," of a society (for example, the norm of monogamy in marriage), structural features (such as the extent to which members are integrated into society), and social rates (such as suicide and divorce rates).

Like Comte, Durkheim distinguished earlier traditional societies from modern industrial ones. Preindustrial societies were held together by **mechanical solidarity,** a form of integration based on similarities of individual activities and shared beliefs in a common set of rules. But as the number and density of people increase, the division of labor becomes more complex and the strength of traditional bonds declines. Changes occur in the means of communication and transportation, as well as in energy sources and technology.

Producers who hold to traditional means of manufacturing or sales cannot compete with those who are expanding their markets and improving their technology. Entrepreneurs realize that traditional means of maintaining their business and making a profit are no longer adequate. The need to compete in new ways puts pressure on individuals to think things through, and thus reasoning increases. As Durkheim put it: "In general, the more subject to change the environment is, the greater the part intelligence plays in life, for it alone can have new conditions of equilibrium continually broken, and yet restore it. Cerebral life develops, then, at the same time as competition becomes keener and to the same degree" (1949, pp. 272–73). Heightened intelligence and new sensibilities lead, in turn, to new needs.

The struggle for existence need not mean a fight to the finish but an opportunity to coexist.

Under a complex division of labor, no one is self-sufficient. We depend on each other to meet needs that we cannot provide for ourselves and hence must cooperate and compete peacefully. The knowledge of our interdependence provides a basis for orderly competition, a concept different from Marxian analysis, which predicts unremitting conflict for scarce resources in modern as well as ancient societies.

Durkheim believed that in complex societies, where the division of labor is extensive, social order is based on **organic solidarity,** which rests on differences and reciprocal relationships rather than on similarities. Simply put, one person makes the nails to make shoes; someone else drives milk from the plant to the supermarket; a third person makes or repairs watches. Yet we all wear shoes, drink milk, and tell time from watches that have been made by others. Under the condition of an advanced division of labor, specialization becomes more important. Each specialized occupation influences the personality of the occupation's incumbent in a special way. Each individual makes a contribution that no one else can make.

That does not mean that specialized societies have no need for shared norms and sentiments. On the contrary, as the division of labor increases in societies with a large geographical area and large numbers of people, the collective consciousness "is itself obliged to rise above all local diversities, to dominate more space, and consequently to become more abstract" (Durkheim 1949, p. 287). Social solidarity is enhanced to the extent that the individual is able both to perceive the interdependent relations between the parts of society and to recognize that his or her own cooperation and contribution serve the common ends of society.

Collective consciousness and the perception of interdependence, however, are not sufficient to maintain social order. In addition, a specialized agency within society is required that represents the inherent unity caused by the increased division of labor and serves as a focus of collective ideas, sentiments, and interests. This entity is the state. The primary function of the state is to encourage in the members of society feelings of unity and sentiments of common solidarity (Durkheim 1949, pp. 358–59). It does this by utilizing unifying symbols such as the national flag.

Legislative and judicial functions are special functions of the state. Rousseau had recognized that complex society is based on agreements (the social contract). Durkheim realized that many of these agreements are formalized into law or written into legally binding contracts. But who enforces laws and contracts? What happens if one partner decides to back out without fulfilling his or her obligations? The contract is not just an agreement between the parties. State-imposed sanctions against violations of the contract (or the threat of such sanctions) are a very strong mechanism of social control. Behind the agreement and the enforcement by the state is a moral, not physical, force that Durkheim called the precontractual element of contract. "Every contract . . . supposes that behind the parties implicated in it there is a society very ready to intervene in order to gain respect for the engagements which have been made" (Durkheim 1949, p. 114). Social order is maintained when the members of the society agree about the right and proper procedures to be used if norms are violated. In Durkheim's terms, social order is maintained when there is agreement about the norms within the collective consciousness.

The function of the state is to maintain this normative structure or, in other words, to prevent anomie (normlessness). When violations of the norms occur, the function of the state is to impose sanctions in order to reestablish equilibrium. The application of sanctions is intended not so much to punish the transgression as to reestablish the importance of the norm in the collective consciousness. Thus, the backbone of social order is not physical punishment for transgression but the underlying agreement on the norms that exists in the collective consciousness.

Durkheim argues that the process of reestablishing equilibrium through the interven-

tion of the state is effective only with regard to normal course of the division of labor. There are three exceptional, or abnormal, forms of the division of labor where the state cannot successfully intervene, including anomie and the forced division of labor. Anomie, or the absence of binding norms and values, results when the rapid transformation from mechanical to organic solidarity causes a weakening of values and norms. Anomie may lead to increased rates of depression and suicide. The solution to anomie, Durkheim believed, is to strengthen intermediary structures such as the family, religion, and occupational groupings in order to provide an alternative source of integration in place of the old values and loyalties.

Another malfunction, or social problem, derives from what Durkheim calls the forced division of labor. Here the problem is not that there are no rules but that the rules are not accepted as legitimate. For a complex society to have social order, it must guarantee "equality in the external conditions of conflict." In other words, individuals must have an equal chance of achieving unequal positions, and the resultant inequality must be based on individual merit, not on accidents of birth. Equality in the conditions of conflict does not mean an unstratified or classless society in the Marxian sense but a stratified society where opportunities abound. A historical problem arises, however, in the class struggle between labor and capital. As noted above, increased division of labor leads to an increase in both intelligence and needs. This is true for the lower classes as well as for the upper class. Being born rich or poor means that there are inequalities in the external conditions of conflict. Lower-class people are likely to end up in lower positions than their natural aptitude qualifies them for, a condition that produces dissatisfaction and conflict. The divisive effects of the forced division of labor can be minimized when individuals are in positions congruent with their abilities that satisfy their needs. Under these conditions, people view the social system as legitimate, and regulation by society is validated on a moral basis—

people accept society's right to regulate their lives. Where this moral basis is missing, regulation can be validated only through force (Durkheim 1949, p. 377).

Equality, however, is defined not only by opportunities for upward mobility but also by what Durkheim called equality of exchange. In its juridical form, this is equality of contract. "In a given society each object of exchange has, at each moment, a determined value which we might call its social value. It represents the quantity of useful labor which it contains. . . . [A] contract is fully consented to only if the services exchanged have an equivalent social value" (Durkheim 1949, pp. 382–83). Thus, equality of exchange means that the exchange is freely desired by both parties. But it means more than that; the exchange must also be just. Durkheim argues that "there cannot be rich and poor at birth without there being unjust contracts" (1949, p. 384). Inequality of external conditions renders equality of exchange impossible. Durkheim's solution is simple: While people should be allowed to accumulate unequal fortunes and attain unequal positions, the inheritance of wealth and privilege should be abolished. This would end the "forced division of labor."

Durkheim, then, agrees with Tocqueville about the impossibility of achieving both equality and freedom simultaneously. Freedom or liberty had previously been thought of as the absence of external restraints, such as the state and the law, in order that the individual might do as he or she pleases. But to Durkheim, liberty is "subordination of external forces to social forces." Man can escape nature only "by creating another world where he dominates nature. That world is society. . . . The task of the most advanced society is, then, a work of justice. . . . [O]ur ideal is to make social relations always more equitable, so as to assure the free development of all our socially useful forces" (Durkheim 1949, p. 387). Unless regulated by societal norms and institutions, the individual is not free but a slave to his or her own passions (see Durkheim 1966, pp. 248–49, 270–71).

Durkheim's ideas represent a major contribution to our understanding of the state and society. He identifies the forces of society and examines them in a theoretical and empirical manner. He shows the division of labor as a dynamic force in history and explores its effects on various institutions, including the government. He explains the functions of government (especially the creation, administration, and adjudication of law) that emphasize and reinforce the collective consciousness. Further, he shows that politics and government cannot create social order in and of themselves; there must be an underlying social agreement, a precontractual element of the contract, a consensus of norms or a collective consciousness. Durkheim recognizes certain abnormal forms of the division of labor that create problems not amenable to the intervention of the state. His work stands as an antidote to the reification of the independent, totally autonomous individual as well as to theories that postulate a single cause of historical development.

Max Weber (1864–1920)

Weber, Marx, and Durkheim all attempted to account for the rise of the modern industrial state. Weber was particularly interested in the rise of rationality as an aspect of modernity. Two forms of rationality were basic to Weber's concern: bureaucratic organization, in which specialization and the division of labor reached their apotheosis, and, at the individual level, rational thinking and behavior. The development of rationality received a major impetus as a result of the Protestant Reformation.

The Protestant Ethic. Weber called attention to the role played by the values and behaviors embodied in the Protestant ethic in the transformation of medieval society into modern capitalist society. The new value system, Weber argued, was necessary in order for capitalist institutions to take hold. In this regard, Weber took issue with Marx, who had argued that value systems resulted from economic forces. Essentially, Weber's thesis is as follows: Many of the conditions necessary for industrial capitalism—science and technology, an economy based on money rather than on barter as a means of exchange, free (that is, not slave or serf) labor, and accessible markets—already existed in Europe at the close of the Middle Ages. Indeed, these conditions had existed in other places and at other times. Yet one more condition was necessary before capitalism could take off—the presence of **capital,** that is, money to obtain land, labor, and supplies. Where did the initial capital come from that made the transition from feudalism to capitalism possible? Weber's answer was that the accumulated capital was an unanticipated consequence of the Protestant Reformation.

The spirit of capitalism involves more than the pursuit of profit, for the profit motive itself is as old as humanity. What was new at the dawn of the age of capitalism was "the pursuit of profit . . . by means of continuous, rational, capitalistic enterprise" (Weber 1958b, p. 17) rather than by conquest or adventure. The capitalist entrepreneur, unlike earlier, more adventurous fortune seekers, systematically utilized available resources to his or her best advantage, carefully calculating profits and losses: "Everything is done in terms of balances" (Weber 1958b, p. 18). Far from being ruled by avarice (as Marx had stated), the seventeenth and eighteenth-century capitalist regarded the accumulation of wealth as a duty. Further, the early capitalist avoided all ostentation and self-indulgence, leading a life of industry, frugality, and punctuality. Work was treated as a religious calling and wealth as a trust to be passed on rather than spent.

Where did this ethos, this way of thinking and behaving, come from? Certainly not from the teachings of the medieval Catholic church, which had condemned the pursuit of profit as a moral weakness and a sin. The spirit of cap-

italism arose from the teachings of Protestantism, especially from the Calvinist doctrine of predestination.

Protestant leader John Calvin (1509–1564) scorned the Catholic notion that humans can achieve salvation by confession, the sacraments, and absolution. God, Calvin wrote, could not be swayed by trifling human action or thought. "To apply earthly standards of justice to His sovereign decrees is meaningless and an insult to His Majesty, since He and He alone is free, i.e., is subject to no law" (Weber 1958b, pp. 103–4).

For the believing Protestant of the sixteenth or seventeenth century who was deeply concerned about eternal salvation, Calvin's doctrine resulted in "a feeling of unprecedented inner loneliness. . . . He was forced to follow his path alone to meet a destiny which had been decreed for him from eternity. No one could help him. No priest . . . no sacraments . . . no Church . . . Finally, even no God. For even Christ had died only for the elect" (Weber 1958b, p. 104).

To relieve that terrible anxiety, the individual must believe herself saved and follow God's commandments to the best of her ability. However, "the question, Am I one of the elect? must sooner or later have arisen for every believer and have forced all other interests into the background. And how can I be sure of this state of grace?" (Weber 1958b, p. 110). With this question begins the search for signs of grace. Good works, however useless as a means of attaining salvation, become a sign of election. So does material success, for God, far from frowning on worldly success, bestows it on the elect.

A profound spiritual transformation had taken place. Salvation could no longer be attained by magic, that is, by the miracle of transubstantiation. Instead, salvation was predicated upon a life of unrelenting self-control, a constant suppression of emotion, spontaneity, and enjoyment. The Catholic emphasis on otherworldliness was replaced by a call for constant worldly activity for the glory of God. Rationality triumphed in practical life as well as in religion.

According to Weber, this ethos is the essence of the spirit of capitalism. Required to work hard at their worldly callings for the glory of God, Protestants soon accumulated wealth. Forbidden to enjoy their wealth, they had no choice but to save it and reinvest it. "When the limitation of consumption is combined with this release of acquisitive activity, the inevitable practical result is obvious: accumulation of capital. The restraints which were imposed upon the consumption of wealth naturally served to increase it by making possible the productive investment of capital" (Weber 1958b, p. 172). The result of this Protestant ethic, unintended and unanticipated, was the development of a capitalist economy.

Eventually, wealth had a secularizing influence on its owners. The religious legitimation of worldly success waned, "giving way to utilitarian worldliness" (Weber 1958b, p. 176). The religious props were no longer required; capitalism had triumphed. Without the encumbrance of religious scruples, "material goods have gained an increasing and finally an inexorable power over the lives of men." Materialism has become "an iron cage"; the sons and daughters of the new age have become "specialists without spirit, sensualists without heart" (Weber 1958b, pp. 181–82).

The State. Another major contribution by Weber to political sociology is his definition of politics as the leadership, or influence on the leadership, "of a political association, hence today, of a state" (Weber 1958a, p. 77).

The state is one type of ruling organization. A ruling organization is political

> insofar as its existence and order is continuously safeguarded within a given territorial area by the threat and application of physical force on the part of the administrative staff. A compulsory political organization with continuous operations . . . will be called a

'state' insofar as its administrative staff successfully upholds the claim to the monopoly of the legitimate use of physical force in the enforcement of its order. Social action, especially organized action, will be spoken of as 'politically oriented' if it aims at exerting influence on the government of a political organization; especially at the appropriation, expropriation, redistribution or allocation of the powers of government. (Weber 1978, p. 54)

Weber's conceptualization of the basic units of political sociology is so clear that it merits an extended quotation:

> 1. It goes without saying that the use of physical force . . . is neither the sole, nor even the most usual, method of administration of political organizations. On the contrary, their heads have employed all conceivable means to bring about their ends. But, at the same time, the threat of force, and in the case of need its actual use, is the method which is specific to political organizations and is always the last resort when others have failed. Conversely, physical force is by no means limited to political groups even as a legitimate method of enforcement. It has been freely used by kinship groups, household groups, consociations and, in the Middle Ages, under certain circumstances by all those entitled to bear arms. In addition to the fact that it uses, among other means, physical force to enforce its system of order, the political organization is further characterized by the fact that the authority of its administrative staff is claimed as binding within a territorial area and this claim is upheld by force. Whenever organizations which make use of force are also characterized by the claim to territorial jurisdiction, such as village communities or even some household groups, federations of guilds or of workers' associations ("soviets"), they are by definition to that extent political organizations.
>
> 2. It is not possible to define a political organization, including the state, in terms of the end to which its action is devoted. All

the way from provision for subsistence to the patronage of art, there is no conceivable end which some political association has not at some time pursued. And from the protection of personal security to the administration of justice, there is none which all have recognized. Thus it is possible to define the "political" character of an organization only in terms of the means peculiar to it, the use of force. This means is, however, in the above sense specific and is indispensable to its character. It is even, under certain circumstances, elevated into an end in itself. (Weber 1978, pp. 54–55)

Thus, Weber argues that political associations cannot be defined in terms of their ends, goals, or functions but in terms of their unique means—the actual or threatened use of force. But we must remember the critical term *"legitimate* use of physical force" (italics added).

Forms of Legitimacy. Using physical force as the only means of maintaining social order is inherently unstable. Legitimate orders are much more stable. By legitimacy, Weber meant the belief of the people that the government is operating according to approved principles. This belief does not have to be universal for the government to be effective or valid. People obey, and government is valid, both because disobedience may have disadvantageous consequences and because it may violate the sense of duty that, to a greater or lesser extent, is an absolute value to the citizen.

Weber identified three kinds of legitimacy: rational-legal, traditional, and charismatic.

Rational-legal legitimacy, the most recent type, is exemplified in Weber's Germany and in the contemporary United States. Such legitimacy rests "on a belief in the legality of enacted rules and the right of those elevated to authority under such rules to issue commands" (Weber 1978, p. 215).

Traditional legitimacy rests on "an established belief in the sanctity of immemorial traditions and the legitimacy of those exercising authority under them" (Weber 1978, p. 215). Contemporary examples include the House of Saud in Saudi Arabia and the Hashemite dynasty in Jordan. Both of these royal houses claim descent from the Prophet Mohammed and base their claim to authority on that descent.

Charismatic legitimacy tends to arise when rational-legal or traditional legitimacy breaks down. The charismatic grounds for claiming legitimacy rest "on devotion to the exceptional sanctity, heroism or exemplary character of an individual person, and of the normative patterns of order revealed or ordained by him" (Weber 1978, p. 215). Leaders who claim charismatic authority have included Jesus, Mohammed, Hitler, Gandhi, and the Ayatollah Khomeini.

The three types of domination hold up three different objects of obedience:

> [Under rational-legal domination] obedience is owed to the legally established impersonal order. It extends to the persons exercising the authority of office under it by virtue of the formal legality of their commands and only within the scope of authority of the office. In the case of traditional authority, obedience is owed to the person of the chief who occupies the traditionally sanctioned position of authority and who is (within its sphere) bound by tradition. . . . In the case of charismatic authority, it is the charismatically qualified leader as such who is obeyed by virtue of personal trust in his revelation, his heroism or his exemplary qualities so far as they fall within the scope of the individual's belief in his charisma. (Weber 1978, pp. 215–16)

Legitimacy, then, refers to the basis on which authority is claimed. When the claim of legitimacy is based on rational-legal authority, obedience is owed to the position of leadership; when it is based on traditions, obedience is owed to accustomed obligations; and when it is based on charisma, obedience is owed to the individual.

Differences also emerge in the type of administrative staff prevalent under different types of authority. Under rational authority, the staff is organized according to bureaucratic criteria that include impersonality, a hierarchy of authority, and a complex division of labor. Bureaucratic authority is exercised on the basis of written rules and regulations. Under traditional authority, the administrative staff is composed of the personal retinue of the chief. The traditional chief exercises authority on the basis of commands by interpreting and invoking the proper traditions. Charismatic leaders operate with the help of disciples who are neither appointed nor dismissed; they have no career, only a calling. Charismatic authority is exercised on a personal basis between the leader who claims supernatural powers or revealed knowledge and his or her followers.

The Environment and the Social Structure. Weber's empirical studies are embodied in many works, including *Ancient Judaism, The Religion of China,* and *The Religion of India.* In his empirical studies, his conceptual scheme was put to use, as illustrated by an example taken from *Ancient Judaism.*

Weber noted that climate, physical geography, and political geography are important independent variables that limit the workings of political and economic forces. Climate, for example, has played an important role in political and economic development in the Middle East. The central and northern regions have a relative abundance of water, while the areas of the south and east are much more sterile and the steppes are a marginal area. These conditions of the natural environment were one factor in the development of cities in the central and northern regions and of nomadic Bedouin society in the desert regions.

The absence of rain in the desert has led the nomadic Bedouins to develop a social organization based on the family. The nuclear family consists of father, mother, and unmarried children. These nomadic families live in tent communities headed by a leader called the mukhtar. For the most part, the tent community is bound by ties of marriage and patrilineal descent going back five to seven generations.

Above the level of the tent community is the sib. The sib is a group composed of a number of tent communities who trace their descent to a common ancestor through seven or more generations. The head of the sib is a sheik. The sib is a permanent, closely knit association (Weber 1952, p. 11).

Above the level of social organization of the sib are tribes, communities composed of a number of sibs. The tribe, rarely larger than a few thousand people, has a permanent leader who "through feats of warfare or judicial wisdom, has gained such distinction that by virtue of his charisma he is recognized as a *sayid.* As hereditary charisma, his prestige can then be transferred to the respective sheik of his sib." The sayid is "only *primus inter pares,*" that is, only first among equals. As such he "presides over the tribal palavers . . . and he has the decisive voice whenever opinion hangs in the balance. He sets the time for the departure of the march and determines the camp site. Like the sheik . . . he lacks all power of coercion. His example and verdict will be honored by the sibs only so long as he proves his charisma" (Weber 1952, p. 11). Among Bedouins, political participation in wars and other endeavors is voluntary. Participation is only indirectly enforced through ridicule and shame. Thus, the society operates not through law but through custom.

The single sib is the most stable unit of Bedouin society. Sibs separate from tribes at will. However, the tribe can become a relatively stable structure if the "charismatic prince succeeds in securing for himself and his sib a position of permanent military authority" (Weber 1952, p. 12). Gaining permanent military authority depends on a fixed income for the warlord, which can come from "ground rent and tribute from the intensively cultivated oases or from tolls and convoy fees from the caravans. . . . His income allows him to maintain a personal following in his mountain castles"

(Weber 1952, p. 12). Thus, even though authority may be initially gained by charisma, it is maintained only when routinized as traditional authority.

The tribal structure of the Bedouins is still an important form of political structure in the Middle East. Saudi Arabia, for example, is still run by a large sib of about four thousand people. Weber's analysis of Bedouin society illustrates the impact of the physical environment on the social and political system, as well as the integration of different types of authority in the same society.

Summary

In chapters 2 and 3, we have explored changes in politics, economics, society, and culture that have influenced writers from Aristotle to Weber. We have discussed the thoughts of these writers on questions of social order, social change, and the relation of the individual to society.

Tracing the development of political thought from social philosophy to social science illustrates a number of points. First, ideas emerge under particular conditions, and understanding the relationship between ideas and the conditions that gave rise to them is important. Second, ideas linger on well past the time when they are structurally relevant. Such ideas can contribute to a distortion of reality as well as to enhanced understanding, and it is useful to be able to recognize a fossil when one is encountered. We review below the major issues encountered in studying the transition from social philosophy to social science.

The role of the leader and of the led is a perennial question. The basis of leadership varies according to type of society and political system. The questions of why people obey and under what conditions they rebel have been addressed by Plato, Weber, Durkheim, Marx, Hobbes, and Locke. We will continue to explore these issues when we discuss the work of modern theorists.

The role of rationality and emotions in political life is central to the works of Weber, Durkheim, Hobbes, Locke, and Marx. Do people have the capacity to recognize their own interests and act upon them? Under what conditions is the irrationality of the masses a danger to democracy? From Tocqueville on, these questions have been central to an understanding of political processes.

Other questions include: What is the basis of social order? How important is legitimacy? When, as Locke put it, is the mischief of obedience greater than the mischief of rebellion? Which is a more accurate picture of the world, Weber's idea that stable government depends on the consensus of the masses or Marx's view of the domination of the lower classes by the upper class?

Having summarized the intellectual heritage that informs contemporary political sociology, we turn now to analyzing the social bases upon which political institutions and ideas rest. As we will see, these social bases consist, first and foremost, of social stratification.

2

The Social Bases
of Politics

Dimensions of Cleavage: Stratification

*Political sociology is concerned with power
in its social context.*

Tom Bottomore, *Political Sociology* (1979)

Preview

Stratification is concerned with social inequality, that is, with differences of such attributes as income, education, and occupational prestige. These distributional differences, in turn, hinge on differences in structural position, that is, in one's location within the political and economic structure of society. The distributional and structural differences that make up the stratification system profoundly affect political behavior and policy outcomes. When we discuss political issues such as welfare and taxation or racial discrimination and affirmative action programs, our concern is the impact of the state on groups located at different places in the stratification system. When we discuss political ideologies, voting patterns, and social movements, our concern is the effects of stratification on political participation. In short, the interface between the political institution and the social structure, particularly the class system, is vital to political sociology. Because stratification is intimately linked with political power to the extent that theories and research in the two fields overlap, we explore it in some detail.

This chapter deals with the realities and myths of social classes in the United States and examines the relevance of those realities and myths for the political order. The first part of the chapter presents theories of stratification, the second part briefly describes the characteristics of the various classes in the United States, and the last part explores facts and myths about social mobility. This chapter builds the foundation for later discussion of political behavior and institutions.

Dimensions of Stratification: Class and Status

Marx and the Analysis of Class

Modern stratification theory began with Karl Marx. To Marx, as we saw in chapter 3, the fundamental groups that make up society and shape the character of historical conflict are classes. **Classes** are groups of people defined, and at times defining themselves, in terms of their relationship to the means of production. The means of production are the economic resources or capital goods used to generate other goods; they include land, human labor, factories, and machinery.

At different periods in history, the chief means of production and the nature of the superordinate and subordinate classes have varied. In ancient times, when the means of production was slave labor, the dominant class consisted of slave owners and the subordinate class of slaves. In the Middle Ages, when the primary means of production was land, the principal classes were land owners (feudal aristocrats) and serfs. In the modern capitalist age, the most important means of production is capital, whether in the form of investment money, factories, or machines. Hence, the principal classes are the capitalists (owners of capital) and the proletariat (working class). Other classes, such as craftspersons and small shopkeepers (known as the "petty bourgeoisie"), are marginal to the means of production and do not play a major role in the drama of historical change. Thus, in every age the classes are distinguished not on the basis of income, education, life-style, or anything else that we deem relevant today but on the basis of their relationship to the means of production. In this system of owners versus nonowners, the former are the exploiters and the latter are the exploited. The former uphold the political order; the latter potentially seek to change it. This conceptualization of classes has been called *structural* or *relational,* since classes pertain to the social relations of production (see Szymanski 1983; Marsden 1985; Wright 1985).

Marx realized that a shared relationship to the means of production alone does not make a class politically effective, or, as he called it, a **class for itself.** To be politically effective, members of an oppressed class must communicate with each other, learn to recognize the true cause of their misery (exploitation by the dominant class), transcend their petty individual interests, and unite for such collective action as boycotts, strikes, or revolutions. These conditions occur when the working class in a given country organizes a political movement that effectively represents its interests, a phenomenon largely absent in the United States (see chapter 11). In contrast to workers, peasants, who are traditionally isolated and often accept their poverty as God-given, are usually capable of being only a **class in itself** (see Marx 1852). Phrased differently, peasants lack true **class consciousness.** The dominant class, in order to preserve its rule, attempts to keep the subordinate class in a state of **false consciousness** through control of the mass media, public education, and other mechanisms of **ideological hegemony** (see chapter 5).

Weber and the Analysis of Status

Max Weber, in an essay titled "Class, Status, Party," modified Marx's approach by the addition of factors he felt Marx had overlooked. In addition to the economic factor (class), Weber emphasized the social factor (status), the legal or biological factor (caste), and the political factor (power).

Weber clearly differentiates among the four. He defines class in terms of the market situation, that is, the ability to buy and sell skills and commodities. "We may speak of a 'class'

when (1) a number of people have in common a specific causal component of their life chances . . . (2) this component is represented exclusively by economic interests," such as income or consumer goods, and (3) this component is influenced by the market forces of supply and demand (Weber 1958a, p. 181). Factory workers, for example, constitute a class in the objective sense that their "life chances" are defined by being propertyless, by possessing a trade or a skill, and by earning wages. Their wages, in turn, are based on the supply of and demand for their skill. Class is an objective economic phenomenon that may or may not be accompanied by subjective awareness. Thus, factory workers may or may not be aware of their common interests; they may or may not form a cohesive community capable of political action.

Unlike classes, **status groups** typically form cohesive communities. "In contrast to the purely economically determined 'class situation,' we wish to designate as 'status situation' every typical component of the life fate of men that is determined by a specific, positive or negative, social estimation of honor" (Weber 1958a, pp. 186–87). By honor Weber meant prestige or esteem, a subjective dimension that exists in the minds of a group's members as well as in the minds of outsiders. For example, in Weber's nineteenth-century Germany, titled landowners descended from medieval aristocracy enjoyed high prestige, even though their financial situation was often quite modest. Industrial magnates, by comparison, although often wealthier than the hereditary aristocracy, ranked lower in prestige. In America, equivalent examples include the First Families of Virginia and the Boston Brahmins.

Status groups share not only a specific amount of prestige or honor but a similar lifestyle (a term coined by Weber). They prefer to interact with their own kind and try to limit interaction with nonmembers they feel are "beneath" them. Thus, members of a privileged status group may frequent swank clubs closed to "commoners" and may confine marriages to people within the status group. As Weber emphasizes, wealth alone does not qualify a person for admission into an exclusive status group; indeed, economic activity may even disqualify him or her.

> Precisely because of the rigorous reactions against the claims of property *per se*, the "parvenu" [that is, newly arrived] is never accepted, personally and without reservation, by the privileged status groups, no matter how completely his style of life has been adjusted to theirs. They will only accept his descendants who have been educated in the conventions of their status group and who have never besmirched its honor by their own economic labor. . . . Everywhere some status groups, and usually the most influential, consider almost any kind of overt participation in economic acquisition as absolutely stigmatizing. (Weber 1958a, pp. 192–93)

Where status groups are defined by distinct ethnic or racial differences, castes may emerge. A **caste system,** originally found in India, refers to a series of completely segregated communities that "believe in blood relationship and exclude exogamous [out-group] marriage and social intercourse" (Weber 1958a, p. 189). These restrictions, unlike those of status groups, are absolute and are legally enforced. Some castes are perceived as pariah peoples, ethnic or racial groups believed to be spiritually or biologically inferior. They are shunned socially, discriminated against economically, and barely tolerated legally. Historically, the Jews in Europe's ghettos and the blacks in the American South constituted such pariah groups. Both groups were defined by blood relationships and treated as distinctly inferior. Yet both groups, however despised by outside society, developed what Weber calls "a sense of dignity, " a feeling of their own worth based on their spiritual or religious beliefs.

In addition to the economic, social, and caste pyramids, Weber turned his attention to a fourth one: the political pyramid. In Weber's terminology, parties are groups that seek to acquire power in order to influence public policy on their own behalf. Power may be exercised by the acquisition of elected or appointed office or, more commonly, by influence over public officials behind the scenes. The pyramids of class, status, caste, and power do not necessarily coincide; groups may rank high in one pyramid but low in the others. For example, black professionals, although high in class, may be treated as socially inferior. The consequences of **status inconsistency** for the affected group or individual range from mental stress to frustration with the existing system and an impatient desire for change.

Today, the study of stratification is divided between adherents of the status-attainment school and adherents of the conflict or structural school. The status-attainment school (see Blau and Duncan 1967; Kohn 1969; Cullen and Novick 1979; Kerckhoff et al. 1982) emphasizes multiple factors, imperfect overlapping, and the continuous rather than dichotomous nature of the hierarchy. Followers of this research tradition view the strata as merging into one another, not as discrete and structurally determined. They concentrate on those dimensions that are easiest to observe and quantify, primarily studying income, education, and occupation but also considering race, ethnicity, sex, age, and religion. They exclude analysis of the possession of capital wealth and the exercise of political power (particularly the behind-the-scenes variety), which are harder to observe.

Researchers who follow the structural or Marxist tradition focus on political power and economic resources as the overriding criteria of stratification (see, for example, Wright 1979, 1985; Dahrendorf 1959). These writers see society as divided into an economically or politically based dominant class and a relatively powerless working class. Additional classes, such as self-employed or salaried professionals and small business owners, are analyzed along the same principles. The different perspectives are examined below.

Socioeconomic Status

Three factors often used to measure inequality are the distribution of income, educational attainment, and occupational prestige. These three factors may be combined to form a composite index of socioeconomic status (SES). Individuals are assigned a score for each factor, and the combined SES score is used to place them in the appropriate stratum. SES scores are useful beyond the simple classification of individuals. They can also be used to explain differences in life-style, personality, and values, to estimate the amount of social mobility, and to predict political behavior (see, for example, Kohn 1969; Kohn and Schooler 1982; Bruce-Briggs 1979; Coleman and Rainwater 1978; Kessler 1982).

Income

Of all the criteria of inequality, income is intuitively the most acceptable. All of us place individuals and families we know into different social strata on the basis of their income. It should be remembered, however, that inequality of wealth, that is, of net assets possessed by families and individuals, considerably exceeds inequality of income and translates more readily into political influence.

The income distribution of families in the United States for the year 1984 is given in Table 4.1. As the table shows, in 1984, with a median family income of $26,430, 5 percent of all families earned less than $5,000. If we combine the first two rows, we find that 14 percent earned less than $10,000; combining the first three rows shows that 25 percent earned less than $15,000. At the upper end of the scale, 34 percent of all families had incomes of over $35,000, but only 16 percent earned over $50,000. (These figures pertain only to families, not to unattached individuals. Because families often comprise two or more wage earners, the income figures for families are higher than those for all households.)

These numbers make more sense when viewed from the perspective of what percentage of the aggregate income is received by each segment of the population. As Table 4.2 shows, the poorest fifth of all families receives only 5 percent of the aggregate income. The richest fifth, by contrast, receives a full 43 percent of the aggregate income, while the top 5 percent of all families receives 16 percent of the aggregate income—three times their proportion in the population. These numbers would be even more pronounced if the table showed wealth (that is, net assets) rather than income.

Race exacerbates economic inequality. The median income of black families is about 56

Table 4.1 The Distribution of Income of Families in the United States, 1984

Income	Families	
	Approximate Number	*Percent Distribution*
Total	62,000,000	100.0
Under $5,000	3,600,000	5.0
$5,000 to $10,000	6,300,000	9.4
$10,000 to $15,000	7,200,000	10.8
$15,000 to $20,000	7,300,000	10.8
$20,000 to $25,000	7,100,000	10.7
$25,000 to $35,000	12,100,000	19.0
$35,000 to $50,000	10,500,000	18.4
$50,000 and over	7,800,000	15.8

SOURCE: Adapted from U.S. Bureau of the Census, 1986, *Statistical Abstracts of the United States*, Table 751, p. 450, and Table 757, p. 453.

Table 4.2 Percent of Aggregate Income Received by Each Fifth and the Top 5 Percent of American Families in 1984	
Group	Percent of Aggregate Income
All families	100.0
Lowest fifth	4.7
Second fifth	11.0
Third fifth	17.0
Fourth fifth	24.4
Highest fifth	42.9
Top 5 percent	16.0

SOURCE: Adapted from U.S. Bureau of the Census, 1986, *Statistical Abstracts of the United States*, Table 754, p. 452.

at the bottom of the chart, are the Communist-bloc countries of Europe. In East Germany, for example, the top 10 percent receives only 17 percent of the income, compared to 27 percent in the United States. Also ahead of the United States in equality of distribution are Canada, New Zealand, Australia, the United Kingdom, and the Scandinavian countries. We may conclude from the table that the industrialized countries display less inequality than the non-industrialized ones. Within the industrialized world, however, capitalist countries display greater inequality than socialist and mixed-economy countries. This result agrees with the conflict theories of stratification.

percent that of whites, and the median income of Hispanic families is 66 percent that of whites. The percentage of black families earning under $5,000 is nearly four times that of whites, while the percentage of Hispanics in that income category is about twice that of whites (U.S. Bureau of the Census 1986, p. 451).

Gender has a similar effect on income. In 1983, the median income of families headed by a married couple was $27,300, that of single-headed families headed by a male, $21,800, and that of single-headed families headed by a female $11,800 (U.S. Bureau of the Census 1986, p. 453).

Comparing the distribution of income in the United States with that of other countries is also of interest. Table 4.3 ranks selected countries by their inequality of income distribution. It shows that Zimbabwe has the greatest inequality, with the top 10 percent of the population earning a full 57 percent of the income, nearly six times its share, while the bottom 40 percent earns only 8 percent, or one-fifth its share (note that the data from Zimbabwe are for 1968, when that African country, then named Rhodesia, was ruled by a white minority). In general, the countries with the highest inequality are the poorest Third World nations. While no nation even comes close to complete equality, the most egalitarian countries, those

Education

Income alone does not determine one's socio-economic status. Education plays a role as well. Two individuals with the same incomes may behave very differently if one is a high school dropout who drives a truck while the other is a social worker with a master's degree. Conversely, two individuals with the same amount of education may earn very different incomes. Clearly, education and income are imperfectly correlated, yet both are important in shaping one's life-style, values, and, most important for our analysis, political clout. Thus, college graduates tend to vote more heavily than those with lower levels of education, and the rich have a disproportionate effect on public policy (see chapters 9 and 10).

The distribution of educational attainment in the United States is summarized in Table 4.4. As we can see, about 14 percent of the population twenty-five years old and older have an elementary school education or less (the first three columns combined), another 51 percent have completed between one and four years of high school (the fourth and fifth columns combined), 35 percent have at least some college education (the sixth and seventh columns combined), and 19 percent are college graduates. The median number of school years completed is 12.6.

Table 4.3 Distribution of Income in Sixty-nine Countries

Rank	Country	Percent of Total Income Going to Given Percent of Population			
		Top 10 Percent	Top 20 Percent	Bottom 40 Percent	Date
1	Zimbabwe	56.9	69.2	8.1	1968
2	Ecuador	56.6	72.0	5.2	1970
3	Kenya	54.9	66.9	9.5	1969
4	Gabon	54.7	67.5	8.5	1968
5	Brazil	50.6	66.6	7.0	1972
6	Honduras	50.0	67.8	7.3	1967
7	Iraq	49.8	66.9	6.5	1956
8	Madagascar	48.6	60.1	13.0	1960
9	Senegal	47.8	62.5	9.4	1960
10	Lebanon	45.1	59.4	12.3	1958
11	Colombia	44.4	59.5	10.0	1970
12	Zambia	44.0	58.2	13.0	1959
13	Jamaica	43.8	61.2	8.2	1958
14	Peru	42.9	61.0	7.0	1970
15	Thailand	42.6	57.5	13.2	1962
16	Botswana	42.1	60.3	7.6	1971
17	Tanzania	41.6	55.7	13.5	1967
18	Ivory Coast	41.5	58.5	10.6	1970
19	South Africa	40.9	62.0	6.7	1965
20.5	Turkey	40.7	56.5	11.4	1973
20.5	Indonesia	40.7	52.0	17.3	1971
22	Malaysia	39.6	56.6	10.6	1970
23	Costa Rica	39.5	54.8	12.0	1971
24	Benin	39.3	51.7	15.8	1970
25	Malawi	38.9	52.9	15.0	1969
26	Tunisia	37.3	55.5	11.4	1970
27	Philippines	37.1	53.9	11.9	1971
28	Mexico	36.7	54.4	10.3	1977
29	Venezuela	35.7	54.0	10.3	1970
30.5	Argentina	35.2	50.3	14.1	1970
30.5	India	35.2	48.9	17.2	1965
32	Chile	34.8	51.4	13.4	1968
33	Hong Kong	33.7	49.0	15.6	1971
34	Puerto Rico	33.6	50.4	13.7	1963
35	El Salvador	33.0	50.8	12.4	1969
36.5	Bahamas	32.9	50.6	12.2	1970
36.5	Finland	32.9	50.4	11.7	1962
38	Panama	32.2	47.4	15.2	1970
39	Egypt	31.1	48.4	14.1	1964
40	Italy	30.9	46.5	15.6	1969
41.5	Uganda	30.7	46.6	16.6	1970
41.5	Chad	30.7	44.8	19.3	1958
43.5	Uruguay	30.4	47.5	14.2	1967

(continued)

			Percent of Total Income Going to Given Percent of Population		
Rank	*Country*	*Top 10 Percent*	*Top 20 Percent*	*Bottom 40 Percent*	*Date*
43.5	France	30.4	46.9	14.1	1970
45	West Germany	30.3	46.2	16.8	1973
46	Barbados	29.3	44.0	18.6	1969
47	Sri Lanka	28.2	43.4	19.2	1970
48	Netherlands	27.7	42.9	18.1	1967
49	Korea, South	27.5	45.3	16.9	1976
50	Suriname	27.3	42.0	21.3	1962
51	Japan	27.2	41.0	21.0	1969
52	Pakistan	26.8	41.5	20.6	1970
53.5	Bangladesh	26.7	42.3	19.6	1966
53.5	Spain	26.7	42.2	17.8	1974
55	United States	26.6	42.8	15.2	1972
56	Denmark	25.5	42.2	16.9	1966
57	New Zealand	25.4	41.3	17.8	1971
58	Canada	25.1	41.0	16.8	1969
59	Taiwan	24.7	39.2	21.9	1971
60	Australia	23.7	38.8	20.1	1967
61	United Kingdom	23.5	38.8	18.9	1963
62	Yugoslavia	22.5	40.0	18.4	1973
63	Norway	22.2	37.3	19.2	1970
64	Sweden	21.3	37.0	19.7	1972
65	Poland	21.2	36.1	23.4	1964
66	Hungary	19.1	33.4	24.1	1969
67	Bulgaria	18.8	32.4	26.6	1962
68	Czechoslovakia	17.4	31.1	27.4	1964
69	East Germany	16.9	30.7	26.3	1970

Table 4.3 Distribution of Income in Sixty-nine Countries *(continued)*

SOURCE: Charles Lewis Taylor and David Jodice, *World Handbook of Political and Social Indicators*, 1983, Table 4.1, pp. 134–35. © Yale University Press, 1983. Reprinted by permission.

Women and blacks fare better in educational attainment than in income. As Table 4.4 shows, while the median number of years completed by all adults twenty-five years old and older is 12.6, the median for blacks is 12.2. Men and women have roughly the same median level of education. However, the gap between blacks and whites, which historically has been narrowing, recently has widened, since the stagnation in federal student-aid programs affects blacks disproportionately (see Darling-Hammond 1985).

Occupational Prestige

Another aspect of stratification is occupational prestige, the amount of prestige a given occupation commands in the eyes of society. This factor is more subjective than either income or education. As Weber noted (1958a), members of a particular occupation share a given amount of "honor" or prestige and hence constitute a status group. Of course, occupational prestige is largely a function of the educational requirements of the occupation as well as of the amount

	Table 4.4 Years of School Completed by Persons Twenty-five Years Old and Over, 1984						

Percent of Population Completing:

Race and Gender	Elementary School			High School		College and Graduate School		Median School Years Completed
	0–4 Years	*5–7 Years*	*8 Years*	*1–3 Years*	*4 Years*	*1–3 Years*	*4 Years or More*	
All races	2.8	5.0	6.6	12.4	38.4	15.8	19.1	12.6
Males	2.9	5.1	6.5	11.8	34.6	16.1	22.9	12.7
Females	2.6	4.9	6.6	12.9	41.8	15.6	15.7	12.6
Blacks	7.0	8.7	6.7	19.0	34.3	13.8	10.4	12.2
Hispanics	13.9	15.9	8.5	14.6	27.3	11.6	8.2	11.3

SOURCE: Adapted from U.S. Bureau of the Census, 1986, *Statistical Abstracts of the United States,* Table 218, p. 134.

of income earned. Thus, physicians, with high levels of both education and income, have high occupational prestige as well. Yet the correlation is far from perfect. For example, dentists have roughly the same education and income as physicians, yet they rank lower in prestige, and engineers and airline pilots have more prestige than teachers and newspaper columnists. Thus, the scale of occupational prestige is somewhat independent of the scales of income and education. It is also fairly stable over the years and in different industrialized societies.

Sociologist Robert Hodge and his colleagues at the National Opinion Research Center of the University of Chicago have measured the prestige of different occupations by asking a cross section of Americans to assign a rating from "excellent" to "poor" to each occupation. In their study, respondents gave the highest ranking to justices of the Supreme Court, followed by physicians. After these two categories, the most prestigious occupations are holders of high political office, such as state governors, followed by college professors, lawyers, bankers, and scientists. Skilled workers such as electricians and plumbers are in the middle of the prestige hierarchy, and unskilled laborers such as janitors, garbage collectors, and farmhands are at the bottom (for a listing of the ratings, see Hodge et al. 1964).

As we have seen, the components of socioeconomic status (SES) include income, education, and occupational prestige, and the distribution of these three factors is highly unequal. Two questions must now be asked: What are the causes of stratification? What are its implications for the political sphere? It is to these questions that we now turn our attention as we examine the theories of stratification.

The Functional Theory of Stratification Davis & Moore.

The functional theory of stratification has been at the center of sociological controversy for several decades. First articulated by sociologists Kingsley Davis and Wilbert Moore in 1945, the theory states that stratification—of positions, not of individuals—is necessary if society is to survive and to have its vital tasks performed. Davis and Moore observe that stratification is all but universal; in all societies, different positions carry different rewards. The rewards need not be material to be effective. In fact, they may be of three kinds: (a) "sustenance and comfort," meaning money or its equivalent, (b) "humor and diversion," meaning intrinsically enjoyable activities, and (c) "self-respect and ego expansion," meaning prestige and esteem. Rewards may also be a combination of the three.

Having ascertained that no society rewards all positions equally, Davis and Moore attempt to establish which positions carry the highest rewards. "In general," they note, "those positions convey the best reward, and hence have the highest rank, which (a) have the greatest importance for society, (b) require the greatest training or talent" (Davis and Moore 1945, p. 243). Society must allocate sufficient rewards to ensure that the tasks vital to its survival are carried out and to motivate an adequate number of people to undertake the arduous training necessary for demanding positions.

Which positions have the most importance for society or require the greatest amount of talent and training and hence convey the highest rewards? Davis and Moore note that the answer to this question varies from society to society, depending on which values each society holds most important and on the specific conditions of supply and demand. Thus, in every society religion (the repository of values) plays a major role in integrating the social fabric and in guiding and controlling human behavior. In all societies, religious leaders enjoy high material or nonmaterial rewards, such as reverence. The more religious the society, the higher the rewards accorded religious positions. In medieval European countries and in some contemporary Islamic countries, religious leaders enjoy not only spiritual rewards but considerable political and economic power as well. By contrast, in predominantly secular and technologically oriented societies such as the United States, the highest rewards accrue to positions of political, economic, and scientific leadership. These are the positions charged with formulating society's goals (including foreign and economic policy), devising the means for attaining these goals, and articulating the symbols that legitimate the social order. The high occupational prestige of Supreme Court justices thus reflects the fact that they are the interpreters of the Constitution, while the high prestige of physicians reflects the importance of health in our scheme of values. The high prestige and salary attached to these positions also reflect the scarce talent and arduous training they require.

Although the functional theory of stratification has received some support (see, for example, Cullen and Novick 1979), it has been vehemently criticized on theoretical, empirical, and moral grounds. Its major shortcomings are outlined below (this summary is based on Tumin 1953 and Jenkins 1981).

- How are we to decide objectively which positions are more functionally important and should carry higher rewards than others? Davis and Moore, like other functional theorists, seem to reason backward from the fact that some positions (such as lawyers) carry higher rewards than others (such as garbage collectors) to conclude that the former must be more important. Such reasoning is tautological or circular. The reader can imagine which would be more intolerable, a lawyers' strike or a garbage collectors' strike.

- Stratification, far from motivating talented individuals to develop their talents for the benefit of society, actually discourages them. Talent found in the underprivileged strata of society, where access to education and good jobs is limited, often remains undeveloped. Stratification thus blocks equal opportunity rather than promoting it.

- Rewards are not allocated proportionately to training and ability. Physicians and teachers, for example, undergo similar amounts of training, yet the former are remunerated much more handsomely. Even the laws of supply and demand do not explain the difference, because supply and demand do not just happen—they are made. Physicians have some control over the supply of manpower (by restricting the number of places in medical schools) and over the demand for services (by performing operations that may be unnecessary and requiring checkups that may be excessively frequent). It is plausible to assume that the power of an occupation rather than its functional importance or the scarcity of talent determines the rewards apportioned to that occupation.

- Even if we concede that some degree of inequality is necessary to motivate people, we must ask how much inequality is enough. Physicians earn approximately ten times more than nurses, business executives twenty times more than secretaries. Wouldn't physicians, business executives, and others in important positions be adequately compensated by a more modest salary differential, for example, 20 or 50 percent, instead of 1,000 percent? And what about the highly touted nonmaterial rewards, such as intrinsic job satisfaction and service to others, that are presumably adequate compensation for nurses but not for doctors? Thus, even if we are convinced that stratification is functional and inevitable, the range of inequality could be considerably narrowed and the allocation of rewards handled on a more equitable basis.

- Finally, stratification can be seriously dysfunctional in that it produces feelings of alienation and oppression on the part of those at the bottom of the scale. Stratification is responsible for a host of problems that afflict the lower strata disproportionately: lower health and nutritional levels, higher crime and delinquency rates, and higher rates of mental retardation and other birth defects. Stratification increases the risk of disruptive race riots and extremist social movements. The cost of poverty is borne not only by the poor but by all segments of society. Instead of unifying and integrating society around common goals, stratification is potentially divisive and polarizing.

Conflict Theories of Stratification

In contrast to the functionalists, who emphasize the needs and values of society as a whole, conflict theorists emphasize the divergent values and interests of different subgroups. Sociologist Gerhard Lenski summarized the difference between the theories as follows:

> Conflict theorists, as their name suggests, see social inequality as arising out of the struggle for valued goods and services in short supply. Where the functionalists emphasize the common interests shared by the members of a society, conflict theorists emphasize the interests which divide. Where functionalists stress the common advantages which accrue from social relationships, conflict theorists emphasize the elements of domination and exploitation. Where functionalists emphasize consensus as the basis of social unity, conflict theorists emphasize coercion. (Lenski 1966, pp. 16–17)

The conflict or structural perspective on stratification, which today arguably dominates the field, gathered impetus in the 1960s and 1970s. During those decades, when Western societies seemed increasingly polarized, several landmark books appeared that presented alternatives to the prevalent functionalist and status-attainment theories of stratification. One book was *Class and Class Conflict in Industrial Society* by Ralf Dahrendorf (1959); another was *Power and Privilege* by Gerhard Lenski (1966). More recent works on the conflict view of stratification include those by Parkin (1971), Giddens (1973), Anderson (1974), Collins (1975), Vanfossen (1979), Korpi (1983), Robinson and Kelley (1979), Domhoff (1983), Marsden (1985), Szymanski (1983), Wright (1979, 1985), Krause (1982), and others.

Dahrendorf (1959), modifying Marx's social class theory, argues that the major cleavage in societies and associations lies not between the propertied and the propertyless but between the powerful and the powerless. Those who hold official positions of authority in industry, the government, and voluntary associations are able to allocate to themselves a disproportionate share of material and nonmaterial rewards such as money, prestige, and work satisfaction.

Furthermore, the dominant class generates and enforces the norms and values that govern all classes. Since its members make up the rules of the game, they can legitimate their staying in power and award themselves society's highest rewards. "Power and power structure logically precede the structures of social stratification" (Dahrendorf 1968, p. 173). The functional theory of stratification, despite its claims of universal fairness and functionality, is a part of the ruling class's ideology and of the ruled class's false consciousness.

In spite of pervasive ideological manipulation, however, the two fundamental classes—the rulers and the subordinates—hold diametrically opposed interests. The ruling group would like to stay in power; the subordinate group would like to usurp power. This struggle may be carried on by either violent means (for example, revolution) or nonviolent means (for example, elections or collective bargaining). The main points of Dahrendorf's theory are that all societies and associations are characterized by a cleavage between the dominant and the subordinate groups, that the interests of these two groups are diametrically opposed, and that society is held together by coercion and false consciousness, not by a commonality of goals.[1]

Lenski (1966) defines stratification as society's collective answer to the question Who gets what and why? or as the process of distributing scarce goods and services. So long as society totters on the brink of subsistence, people will voluntarily share the products of their labor to assure collective survival. By definition, societies living at subsistence level, particularly hunting and gathering societies, must practice equality of distribution. However, once productivity increases enough to generate a surplus, as in horticultural and agricultural societies, the surplus is distributed unequally (see chapter 2).

How is the surplus distributed? Lenski makes two assumptions: (a) "that in important decisions human action is motivated almost entirely by self-interest or partisan group interests" and (b) "that many of the things men most desire are in short supply." Consequently, "this surplus will inevitably give rise to conflicts and struggles aimed at its control: If, following Weber, we define power as the probability of persons or groups carrying out their will even when opposed by others, then it follows that *power will determine the distribution of nearly all the surplus possessed by society*" (Lenski 1966, p. 44).

The more technologically advanced the society, the larger the surplus and the more unequal the distribution of goods and services will be. An important exception to this rule occurs in modern industrial societies: Rather than increasing with the size of the surplus, inequality decreases because several factors cause power to become more decentralized. First, political power is more widely diffused among the citizenry as a result of greater democratization. Second, military power, and with it control over the means of violence, is widely distributed as a result of broadly based military service. And third, technological power is widely distributed as a result of the diffusion of education and the need for experts to run the sophisticated technology. In short, power is no longer completely monopolized by a tiny elite and can no longer be used by that elite as a basis for allocating to itself the preponderant share of society's goods and services. To be sure, the elite still enjoys a large absolute amount of wealth, larger than in any previous society. However, because the total size of the national

1. Recently, Dahrendorf, modifying his earlier deterministic views, has proposed a theory of "life chances" (Weber's term) as a function of two major factors: "options" (opportunities) and "ligatures" (attachments or bonds that link individuals to society, for example, attachments to religion, country, and community). The ligatures lend meaning and social cohesion, while the options make possible ever-greater freedom of choice for individuals. Modernization, he argues, has led to an extension of choices (opportunities for choosing one's occupation, community of residence, political preference, and life-style), but at a heavy cost: "the reduction, and ultimately destruction of bonds. . . . From this point onward choices begin to lose their meaning," and the alienation of modern individuals pervades (Dahrendorf 1979, p. 31). For another view, see Turner 1984.

economic pie has become so enormous, the elite's proportional share is smaller than in the past and the masses' share is larger. Thus, in effect, everybody is better off than before. This theory is supported by Table 4.3, which shows that inequality decreases in industrialized countries and is lowest in those countries where labor has a greater participation in government. ✱Combining Marxist theory with empirical research, sociologist Erik Olin Wright and his colleagues (1978, 1979, 1982, 1985) have attempted to demonstrate empirically that "class✱ matters." Defining class in terms of "common positions within the social relations of production," Wright (1979, p. 17) provides a conceptual map of classes in advanced capitalist societies. This map includes (1) the bourgeoisie, those who own their work organizations and employ others in their service, (2) managers and supervisors, who do not own their work organizations yet control the work lives of others, (3) semiautonomous employees, who have a high degree of autonomy on the job but no control over other people, (4) petty bourgeoisie, who own their means of production (that is, are self-employed) but employ no one, and (5) the "real" working class, including most wage earners and lower-level salary earners. This last class is by far the most numerous, constituting about half of the labor force. Wright and his colleagues argue that

> class and occupation are different dimensions of the social structure. . . . Occupation broadly designates the technical content of jobs; class designates the social relations of domination and appropriation within which those technical activities are performed. . . . A carpenter, for example, could easily be a worker, a semiautonomous employee, a manager or a petty bourgeois artisan. In each of these cases the technical content of the job remains largely the same (transforming lumber into buildings or whatever), but the social relational content changes. (Wright et al. 1982, p. 719)

Wright demonstrates that class has a strong effect on income regardless of occupational sta-

tus. Thus, within each occupation, employers and managers receive greater income than workers, a difference Wright attributes to exploitation. When income differences between whites and blacks and between men and women are considered, Wright finds that the differences are largely reduced when one compares the groups within a particular social class. Thus, he concludes, sex and race interact with class to produce income inequality. Racial and sexual discrimination occur largely in the process of allocating members of different groups to different classes, with the result that women and blacks are severely underrepresented in the bourgeois and managerial classes and overrepresented in the working class. While "the American working class is predominantly composed of women and minorities. . . . white males are, in class terms, a highly privileged category," comprising more than their share of the top two classes (Wright et al. 1982, p. 724). Other research, however, shows that even within the same class, women's income is considerably lower than men's (see Robinson and Kelley 1979).

✱Wright, then, demonstrates that even if one does not accept Marxist theory, one must incorporate measures of class, as defined by the social relations of production, in order to fully understand social inequality.

Other structural factors besides class affect the distribution of income. Several researchers (Beck, Horan, and Tolbert 1978; Baron and Bielby 1980, 1984) note that good jobs and opportunities for advancement are not distributed uniformly throughout the economy. Rather, opportunities—and hence income—vary by industry or economic sector. The core sector of the economy is composed of large corporations and manufacturing enterprises whose labor force is highly skilled, largely unionized, and composed disproportionately of white males. The peripheral sector consists of smaller firms in agriculture, nondurable goods manufacturing (such as food and clothing), retail trade, and services. The labor force in these organizations is unskilled and disproportionately female, black, and nonunionized. In general, jobs, incomes, and opportunities for advancement are better in the core sector than in the peripheral sector, regardless of the qualifications of employees.

In the last two sections, we have seen that the conflict theory of stratification differs from the functional theory in several important respects. Functional theory views inequality as arising from society's common goals, from the need to implement these goals, and from the scarcity of competent personnel to fill important jobs. The emphasis of functional theory is on the commonality of norms and values and the distribution of rewards on the basis of merit. Conflict theory, on the other hand, emphasizes the struggle between groups for scarce economic or political resources. In this view, the rewards accrue not to the most deserving but to those who have somehow managed to acquire control of critical resources. According to the conflict perspective, society is characterized by a clash of interests, norms, and values, although the antagonisms may at times be masked by a superficial consensus. Before we examine theories that attempt a synthesis of the two views, we will consider briefly another area of inequality: gender.

Sexual Stratification

Studies of stratification, whether they center on class or on status, often exclude women. Since the family or household forms the basic unit of consumption, the status of women and children is assumed to be derived from that of men. This situation has prompted sociologist Joan Acker (1980, p. 25) to complain that "the male is still taken to be the general human being—the general societal-wide system of inequality is viewed as essentially a system of male inequality."

Several recent theories of gender stratification have been proposed in an attempt to fill the void. Researchers Peggy Reeves Sanday

(1981) and Janet Saltzman Chafetz (1984), for example, rejecting the position of some anthropologists that the subordination of women to men is universal, have examined variations in female power and male dominance in different societies. Sanday argues that in tribal societies, sexual inequality reflects each society's myths of creation and, ultimately, its ecological environment. She finds that societies worship feminine gods of fertility when the supply of food depends on gathering plants and hunting small game (tasks in which women traditionally participate) and the forces of nature appear benevolent. Such societies often demonstrate a high degree of equality between the sexes, friendly relations between men and women, and male participation in child rearing. On the other hand, societies living in harsher environments, such as those that depend on the unpredictable hunting of large game, worship male gods and emphasize male-centered symbols. Such societies often segregate women and subordinate them to men.

Chafetz (1984) argues that sexual stratification is a function of various factors: (1) the nature of the society's organization of work (that is, the extent to which women participate in productive activities and control important resources), (2) the type of family structure (whether maternal lineage and female ties are emphasized), (3) the degree of ideological or religious support for sexual inequality, and (4) the extent to which the culture believes male and female personalities to be different. These factors, in turn, are influenced by such variables as the average proportion of the female life cycle devoted to having and raising children, the degree of separation of home and work sites, the relative importance of physical strength in production, and the relative societal emphasis on the production of subsistence versus surplus goods. Ultimately, then, sexual stratification in a society is shaped by underlying structural forces such as the pressure of population on resources, the level and type of technology, and the degree of environmental harshness.

Stratification Theory: A Synthesis

Several sociologists have attempted to integrate the theories of Marx and Weber, combining the structural and the subjective elements of stratification. Anthony Giddens (1973), for example, uses the concept of **class structuration** to describe the process by which economic relationships are translated into noneconomic social groupings (which may overlap with status groups). Class structuration is a function of the following forces: (1) the relative absence of social mobility, which stabilizes the composition of each class from one generation to the next and homogenizes life experiences within classes; (2) the division of labor within enterprises, which creates homogeneous occupational groupings; and (3) the existence of "distributive groupings," that is, common patterns of consumption such as those reflected in residential or neighborhood segregation. In general, "to the extent to which the various bases of . . . class structuration overlap, classes will exist as distinguishable formations" (Giddens 1973, p. 110). Three major classes may be distinguished in industrial capitalist societies: an upper class based on ownership of property, a middle class based on education and know-how, and a working class based on manual labor.

Vanfossen (1979) utilizes a somewhat different theoretical synthesis as a starting point for an empirical analysis of the various social classes. She starts with two basic assumptions: (a) Given a choice, individuals and groups will tend to act in accordance with their own interests. These interests, although they may happen to coincide with the central values emphasized by society (such as patriotism or conservation), usually include the pursuit of scarce and valued goods and services. (b) In technologically advanced societies, the economy, not the state, the educational system, or the church, shapes the basic form of social stratification. The economy determines the occupational division of labor, the level of productivity and surplus, and the distribution of wealth and income. "The accumulation of its products—goods, services and wealth—provides tools of power, manipulation and influence" (Vanfossen 1979, p. 53). However, the economic system is not the only determinant of stratification. Political power is another. The political elite joins forces with the economic elite in molding the stratification system by trying to prevent a redistribution of wealth and income in favor of lower strata (see chapter 9).

Vanfossen points out that not only is the stratification system shaped by the political and economic elites, but other major institutions—the family, religion, the law, the mass media, and the educational system—support and reinforce the system. The law and the police keep the poor in their place, if necessary through the threat of force. More pervasive and usually more potent, however, is the support provided by the religious, familial, educational, and mass communication institutions, which socialize the poor as well as the rich to accept the norms and values perpetuated by the elite (such as the value of free enterprise) and to acquiesce to the existent distribution of money and influence. The educational system plays an important additional role by screening individuals and allocating them to different slots in the stratification system.

Social stability, Vanfossen contends, occurs when the various institutions that support stratification are successful in their socialization and enforcement efforts. Thus, the nearly universal acceptance of the capitalist doctrine of free enterprise contributes to stability. Social change comes about when subordinated groups gain greater access to resources, thereby threatening the access of other groups. For example, affirmative action programs, which increase the access of minorities and women to educational and work opportunities, are perceived as threatening to white males.

The analyses of Giddens and Vanfossen converge in pointing out that different classes, strata, or status groups become meaningful groups when individuals identify and associate with others on the basis of income, occupation, education, religious and ethnic affiliation, family background, or sex. No longer constituting merely statistical aggregates of individuals with similar characteristics, members of different socioeconomic groups interact with each other more frequently than they do with outsiders. This identification and interaction form the basis for united political action and for social change. That the different status groups or classes form distinct communities with their own unique norms, behavioral patterns, and political identities will become clear in the next section, which examines the realities of social class in America.

Classes in American Society

Americans sometimes belittle the salience of social class in their own lives. After all, some people point out, mass consumption has equalized life-styles across classes. Such consumption patterns as owning a home, patronizing fast-food restaurants, and watching spectator sports have become nearly universal. More important, others argue, the American dream requires that members of all ranks of society have an equal opportunity to rise to the top, and political democracy assures that all citizens have an equal say in government. So inequality, even if it exists, doesn't much matter. This denial of our own class structure has prompted social commentator Judith Martin (1979) to remark, tongue in cheek, that only three social classes exist in America: upper middle class, middle class, and lower middle class. She has never heard, she claims, "of an American owning up to being in any other class."

How do the myths of classlessness, equal opportunity, and the equality of political influence compare with the realities of social class? In this section we address this question as we examine the major classes in American society.

The Upper Class

The upper class comprises, according to various estimates, from 0.5 to 1 percent of the American population (see Scimecca 1981). The major attribute that distinguishes the upper class from the rest of the population is its control over vast amounts of wealth and power. Studies indicate that just 0.5 percent of all Americans own from 20 to 25 percent of all the wealth, a figure largely unchanged throughout the century (see Domhoff 1983). Membership in the upper class is largely hereditary. Owners of great wealth and holders of top positions in business, and to a lesser extent in other spheres, usually did not start at the bottom, or even at the middle, but had the "foresight" to be born into the right families. One study shows that among 884 directors of the top banks, insurance companies, and industrial companies in the United States, 53 percent came from upper-class families (Domhoff 1983). Another study has found that in Philadelphia 75 percent of the most prominent bankers, 51 percent of the most prominent lawyers, and significant though lower proportions of other top-ranking professionals and business executives were drawn from upper-class families (Baltzell 1958). If we remember that such families comprise a tiny fraction of the population, we can see that a person from upper-class origins is fifty to a hundred times more likely to end up at the top than is the average individual.

The transmission of privilege is not coincidental, of course. Members of the upper class tend to be concerned with maintaining the prominence and leadership of their families and thus socialize their children appropriately. Children—particularly sons—are sent to prestigious preparatory schools such as Choate and Phillips Exeter and to elite private colleges such as Yale and Princeton. In these schools, their parents hope, they will not only acquire the skills and credentials necessary to carry on the family's business but also absorb the proper attitudes and motivations, establish the right connections, and choose the right marital partners.

Aristocratic traditions are perpetuated by prestigious private clubs such as the Knickerbocker and the Links in New York and the Bohemian Club in San Francisco. Many of these clubs have traditionally excluded blacks, Jews, and women, although some of these restrictions are breaking down. Upper-class solidarity is fostered not only through restricted-membership clubs but also through cohesive extended kinship ties, exclusive residential locations and leisure resorts, and other forms of primary group interaction (Domhoff 1983).

To the extent possible in a society that idealizes romantic love, upper-class families try to assure that their children marry the right mates, that is, scions of other old families or at least of very rich ones. Wives are not expected to have independent careers. However, upper-class women, as sociologist Susan Ostrander (1984) points out, are not simply pampered ladies of leisure. Rather, they work hard, usually without pay, to preserve and legitimate upper-class power and privilege by providing leadership and raising funds for charitable, educational, cultural, and philanthropic organizations; by using the social contacts gained through volunteer work and club membership to advance both their husbands' careers and their children's opportunities; and by managing their children's educations. Quite consciously, upper-class women "organize and interpret their activities primarily through the framework of class" (Ostrander 1984, p. 153), and their work contributes to the perpetuation of their class.

Members of the upper class have distinct values and attitudes. They tend to value Republican politics, conservatism, tradition, "good breeding," and discretion. They shy away from conspicuous consumption and untoward publicity, unlike their more flamboyant grandparents in the nineteenth century (immortalized in the book *The Theory of the Leisure Class* by Thorstein Veblen and in the movie *Citizen Kane*). They often manifest a strong sense of "noblesse oblige." They feel obliged to contribute to society, whether through business, political, philanthropic, or cultural leadership. This contribution helps to legitimate extreme wealth both in the eyes of the wealthy themselves and in the eyes of the rest of society. Not surprisingly, the wealthy come to possess a feeling of entitlement, a conviction that they deserve their good fortunes because of their ability, dedication, and willingness to assume leadership roles. Through these and other mechanisms, the position of the aristocracy is both preserved and legitimated.

The Upper Middle Class

The upper middle class, which comprises about 12 or 13 percent of the population, consists of college-educated managers and professionals. While the upper class, by virtue of its position at the pinnacle of private and public institutions, makes the ultimate decisions about the goals of these institutions, the upper middle class is responsible for the means by which these goals are carried out. High-level managers, engineers, lawyers, and scientists provide the knowledge and expertise necessary for political, educational, and economic organizations to function. They are handsomely rewarded for their expertise with generous salaries, considerable job security, good benefits, high prestige, and interesting and satisfying jobs.

Position in the upper middle class rests not on inherited wealth or family status but on educational and occupational achievement, yet evidence shows that membership in this class, too, is largely hereditary. Census figures show that about 60 percent of the sons of upper middle class professionals and managers enter similar high-level occupations, while only 14 percent of the sons of laborers enter these occupations (see Vanfossen 1979, p. 185). An even more striking study by Sewell and Shah (1967) indicates that one-third of males with low I.Q. from upper-middle-class families actually graduated from college, compared to only one-fifth of males with high I.Q. from lower-class families. A follow-up study of those who graduated found that seven years later 60 percent of the low-intelligence sons of upper-middle-class families had attained middle-class or upper-middle-class positions (reported in Hamilton 1972). Thus, parental socioeconomic status seems to count more than intelligence in determining one's life chances.

Since education is the key to position in the upper middle class, it is heavily stressed in the socialization of children. Children are expected to attend good colleges and, in many cases, professional and graduate schools. Younger children are taught to value academic achievement, to participate in extracurricular activities that will look good on their college applications, and to develop habits of independence and self-motivation. Upper-middle-class families thus equip their children with a considerable head start in the competition for privileged positions: motivation, skills, ambition, and connections, in addition to the quality education available to those with money (see Kohn 1969).

Another major theme in the life of upper-middle-class adults is the importance of men's careers. Men derive a great deal of income, prestige, and intrinsic gratification from their careers and identify strongly with their jobs. Women may pursue careers of their own, but they are generally expected to subordinate their own career demands to the needs of their husbands and children and to provide psychic and logistical support for the activities and interests of their families. Men and women alike tend to be active in civic, political, religious and recreational associations. Indeed, although American society has been labeled a society of joiners, studies show that participation, and particularly leadership, in voluntary associations is more common in the upper middle class than in other classes (see chapter 7).

The politics of the upper middle class tends to be conservative and Republican. A minority, however, particularly well-educated professionals, is seen as liberal. This stratum has been referred to as a "new class" of "knowledge workers" whose values or interests, some observers claim, pit them against members of the conservative managerial upper and upper middle class (see Gouldner 1979; see also chapter 5).

Sociologist Steven Brint (1984) argues that the liberalism of the "new class" has been exag-gerated. A relatively small segment of this class—young "cultural and social specialists," that is, university professors, social scientists outside academia, professionals in arts and culture, clergy, architects, and doctors and lawyers employed in the public and nonprofit sector—is indeed consistently more liberal than the rest of the upper middle class. But the dominant tendency is conservative. "Conservative and conventional attitudes [are] much more widespread in the professional and managerial strata than [are] liberal and dissenting attitudes. . . . This conservatism [is] particularly pronounced among those who [are] older and employed in the numerically preponderant private-sector technical and managerial categories" (Brint 1984, p. 58). The conservatism of the upper middle class has been confirmed in recent elections (see chapter 10).

The upper middle class, unlike the lower classes, has the capacity to translate ideology into political power. Its members participate disproportionately in voting and political office holding and are involved in local decision-making bodies such as chambers of commerce and school boards. Overwhelmingly, members of federal, state, and local government bodies, from Congress on down, come from upper-middle-class backgrounds (see chapter 9). This class, then, constitutes one of the major upholders and legitimators of the power structure (see Vanfossen 1979, p. 314).

The Lower Middle Class: White Collar

Sociologist Lloyd Warner and his colleagues (1949), pioneers in the empirical study of social stratification, considered the lower middle class to be at the top of the Common Person category, the Average American. The distinction between the lower middle class and the upper lower or working class, however, has become increasingly blurred. Skilled blue-collar workers often surpass semiprofessional and clerical workers in income, work satisfaction, and even prestige. Moreover, skilled blue-collar workers often consider themselves middle class, just as clerical workers might refer to themselves as working class. Yet empirical studies reveal important cultural differences between these two groups, including the emphasis on education, women's equality, and leisure patterns.

The lower middle class, which comprises about 35 percent of the population, is composed of sales personnel; clerical workers; semiprofessionals such as teachers, librarians, and social workers; and small business proprietors. This occupational grouping, however, is not at all clear-cut. Some authorities, including the U.S. Census Bureau, regard teachers, social workers, librarians, and computer programmers, along with physicians and lawyers, as "professional, technical and kindred workers," thus including them in the upper middle class. Others, such as sociologist Robert Rothman (1978), include semiprofessionals in the lower middle class but prefer to regard small proprietors as a separate class.

Common to all these occupational groups is some degree of economic insecurity. Incomes often barely cover basic needs. With the exception of small business proprietors, members of this class also tend to experience frustration at the lack of opportunities for upward mobility in their fields and dissatisfaction with the lack of autonomy and decision-making authority in their jobs.

Because work does not serve as a major source of gratification or as a focus of interest as it does in the upper middle class, lower-middle-class subculture tends to revolve more around family, home, and church. Wives often work to help support the family; marriages tend to be egalitarian and to emphasize companionship. Child-rearing patterns are more permissive and less authoritarian than in the blue-collar working class. Children are socialized to value education, hard work, and stability and to get along with other people.

The lower middle class is believed by some sociologists to be a bastion of conservatism (see Lipset 1981). Together with the upper lower class, it constitutes the backbone of the conservative revival of the 1980s. There is some evidence, however, that despite its conservative reputation, the lower middle class is more liberal than the upper middle class (see Hamilton 1972).

The Working Class: Blue Collar

The working class, some 35 percent of the population, includes skilled and semiskilled blue-collar workers such as mechanics, bricklayers, and machine operators, as well as some service workers such as waiters and gas station attendants. Its members make up the bulk of the industrial work force, the proletariat to whom Marx addressed his call "Workers of the world, unite!"

How does Marx's notion of the working class stand up today, a hundred and forty years after *The Communist Manifesto* was published? Are its members as impoverished, dehumanized, and angry as Marx described them, a revolutionary cinderbox ready to ignite, or are they satisfied partakers of the American dream?

Clearly, the working class has come a long way since the early days of capitalism. The eight-hour day, a guaranteed minimum wage, old-age pensions, the right to collective bargaining, and the abolition of child labor have long been taken for granted (but not in all jobs—migrant workers do not enjoy any of these rights). In spite of substantial improvements, however, most working-class members remain vulnerable to the insecurities of periodic layoffs, plant shutdowns, and loss of jobs to automation and foreign competition. When they are employed, their wages are barely adequate. Despite a common belief that blue-collar workers often outearn white-collar workers, most blue-collar families, even those with two wage earners, earn but a modest income. The median family income for all but the most skilled blue-collar workers is below the level considered by the U.S. Department of Labor as the minimum necessary for a moderate standard of living. There are exceptions, of course, which we will discuss presently.

Inadequate wages and low job security are not the only problems faced by the working class. Job alienation, or the "blue-collar blues," is a major complaint. Work tends to be repetitive, brainless, tedious, and unpleasant. Tasks are so fragmented and oversimplified that workers feel no relationship to the total product. They have little control over the content or pace of their work and little opportunity to form gratifying primary-group relationships with coworkers, and they are constantly subject to demeaning authority and supervision. This state is particularly characteristic of assembly-line jobs, which are at the heart of blue-collar work (see Blauner 1964).

The exceptions are those highly skilled craftsmen whose abilities are much in demand, such as construction workers and mechanics. Members of these occupations were dubbed "working class aristocracy" by Lenin, the leader of the Russian Revolution, who realized in disgust that in England, at least, such workers were becoming too affluent to start a revolution. Today, some skilled blue-collar workers enjoy wages above those of white-collar employees, live comfortably, and above all find their jobs interesting and satisfying. Possession of highly valued skills gives them control over the nature and pace of their work, freedom from hierarchical authority, and pride in the products of their craft (see LeMasters 1975).

The majority of the working class, however, find no satisfaction in their work and have low self-esteem. In a society that values occupational achievement and insists that achievement is based on merit, those at the bottom of the occupational prestige scale regard themselves as failures and often blame themselves for their position. This poor self-image of the working class is one of the most painful costs of stratification (see Sennet and Cobb 1972).

More often than members of other classes, members of the working class live in ethnically homogeneous neighborhoods, often in close proximity to their extended families. Familial, religious, and community bonds are intense (see Gans 1962). Members of the working class tend to marry and have children at a young age. They do not place a high value on formal education and are likely to drop out of school before or right after graduation from high school. The

low regard for education, combined with the lack of role models and guidance for upward mobility, tends to inhibit any chances they or their children might have for moving into the middle class. Position in the working class, as in the other classes, is therefore largely handed down from generation to generation (see Rubin 1976; Kohn 1969).

Sex-role socialization in working-class families is more traditional than in middle-class ones, with girls socialized to marry and raise children rather than to pursue careers. The fact that women frequently work outside their homes to help support their families is viewed as a necessary evil rather than a desirable choice; the ideal is full-time homemaking. Blue-collar marriages are characterized by more role divergence and less companionship between the sexes than are white-collar marriages. Women and men have different interests and associate more with members of their own sex than with each other (see Komarovsky 1962).

The working class traditionally has supported the Democratic party. Even during the Republican landslides of 1980 and 1984, the working class gave less support to the Republican party than did the higher classes (see chapter 10). Although in Britain, Germany, and Scandinavia blue-collar workers have historically favored democratic socialism, in the United States they have almost without exception supported the capitalist system. Despite economic and psychological insecurity, the working class in America evidently believes it has a strong stake in the existing economic and political system.

The Poor

What is it like to be poor in America? The lifestyles and subcultural patterns associated with poverty have been widely documented.

> The universe of the underclass is often a junk heap of rotting housing, broken furniture, crummy food, alcohol and drugs. . . . Its members are victims and victimizers in the culture of the street hustle, the quick fix,

the rip-off, and not least, violent crime. . . . Streets are unsafe to walk at night—and, often, so are halls. Nobody starves, but many people are malnourished on a diet of hot dogs [and other junk food]. . . . Alcoholism abounds; heroin is a favorite route of escape. Another road to fantasy is the TV set. On it dance the images of the good life in middle-class America, visions that inspire envy and frustration. (*Time Magazine* 1977)

Defining poverty is an elusive task. In 1984, when the median income for all families was $26,430, the U.S. Census Bureau considered an income of $10,610 for a family of four to be the poverty line. The poverty line "is based on the amount needed by families of different size and type to purchase a nutritionally adequate diet on the assumption that no more than a third of the family's income is used for food," according to Mollie Oshansky, who developed the definition (1969, p. 38). It should be remembered, however, that this figure represents the ceiling of poverty. Poor families, by definition, do not earn enough to meet their basic needs without some kind of assistance.

The number of people living in poverty has increased steadily since the mid-1970s. While in 1973 11 percent of all Americans, or 23 million people, were living below the poverty line, by 1984 this figure had risen to 14 percent, or 34 million people (see Figure 4.1). Several factors are responsible for the increase, including the recessions of the late 1970s and early 1980s and the elimination or reduction of many antipoverty programs by the Reagan administration.

Who are the poor? Several facts regarding them are inescapable. First, they are disproportionately members of minority groups. In 1984, 12 percent of all whites were below the poverty line, compared with 34 percent of all blacks and 28 percent of all Hispanics (U.S. Bureau of the Census 1986). Second, "poverty is increasingly linked to the matriarchal family. . . . One in three families headed by women is poor, compared with only one in ten headed by men and only one in nineteen headed by

two parents. . . . Perhaps the single greatest change in American poverty is that it has been feminized" (Auletta 1982, p. 69). Third, and most tragically, "children make up the largest block of poor people in the United States. . . . Over the past generation, children have replaced the aged as the most impoverished group in the nation" (Rich 1984b). In 1984, 22 percent of all children were poor compared to 13 percent of all adults; the figure for black children under 6 years of age was 51 percent (Rich 1985b). The reasons for the rise in poverty among children, according to a Congressional Budget Office analysis, are the same as those responsible for the general rise in the poverty rate: the increase in female-headed households, the recessions of the late 1970s and early 1980s, and the reductions in governmental income-maintenance programs.

Contrary to popular image, however, not all—or even most—of the poor fit the stereotype of inner-city, female-headed families locked into long-term welfare dependence and a culture of poverty. According to a fifteen-year study of 5,000 families by the University of Michigan's Institute for Social Research, only about 2 percent of the population remain permanently poor. By contrast, as many as 25 percent of all Americans live in poverty at one time or another. For most, poverty is a short-term spell caused by adverse familial events such as unemployment or divorce. A full four-fifths of the children who live in poverty will eventually move out of it (Duncan and Coe 1984). Thus, while these data are consistent with the statistics about the feminization of poverty and the increasing proportions of children who are poor, they hardly point to shiftlessness, apathy, and irresponsible behavior as the causes of poverty. Rather, they suggest that poverty is largely a matter of bad luck.

The theory of the culture of poverty persists, however. This theory, first expressed in Oscar Lewis's famous book *Five Families* (1959), describes a cluster of self-defeating attitudes and behaviors believed to be transmitted from generation to generation and to perpetuate pov-

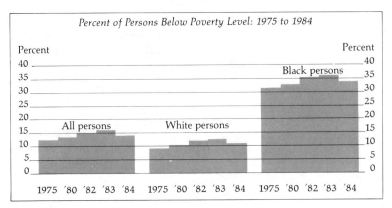

Figure 4.1   Percent of Persons Below Poverty Level, 1975–1984. SOURCE: *U.S. Bureau of the Census, 1986,* Statistical Abstracts of the United States, *p. 430.*

erty. These attitudes and behaviors include an emphasis on immediate gratification, an inability to plan for the future, irresponsible sexual behavior, a disdain for education and work, a tendency toward interpersonal violence, and, above all, apathy, fatalism, and hopelessness (see Miller 1958; Rainwater 1966). This theory implies (and sometimes explicitly states) that the poor are responsible for their own plight. Such an approach, which in effect blames the victim, is in tandem with the functional theory of stratification. Efforts to reduce poverty accordingly call for resocializing the poor to change their negative psychological and behavioral traits. Thus, black leaders call on the poor to help themselves out of the morass. A black Harvard professor, Glenn C. Loury, for example, has written that "the next frontier for the [civil rights] movement should be a concerted effort to grapple directly with the difficult, internal problems which lower-class blacks face." If poverty is to be eliminated, Loury believes, the "values, social norms and personal behaviors often observed among the poorest members of the black community" will have to change (quoted in Raspberry 1985).

Conflict theorists, on the other hand, point out that so long as the structural conditions underlying the American political economy remain unchanged, poverty cannot be elimi-

nated. These conditions include (a) the continued discrimination against minorities and women in education and employment; (b) the changing character of American industry, particularly the demise of many entry-level unskilled and semiskilled jobs and the exodus of manufacturing firms from the inner cities; (c) the various mechanisms used by the dominant elite to keep the poor in their place, such as the use of welfare to appease the poor, the perpetuation of an inequitable and oppressive tax system, and the use of ideologies and myths, such as the myth of equal opportunity, that legitimate inequality (see Piven and Cloward 1971).

A synthesis of various theories of poverty is offered by analyst Ken Auletta (1982). He notes that while some of the poor are victims of capitalist exploitation, racism, and sexism, others are victims of the negativistic values and self-defeating behaviors of the culture of poverty. Solutions, he insists, must be as complex as the problem. They must encompass self-help as well as help from community-based nonprofit organizations, the private sector, and the federal government.

In sum, the class structure may be said to consist of five classes: the upper class, made up of the corporate elite and others who control the top reaches of economic and political institutions; the upper middle class, which administers these institutions; and the three classes whose lives are shaped by these institutions—the lower middle class, the working class, and the poor. The classes differ not only in the material well-being and value patterns of their members, but also in their place in the political economy and hence in their relationship to the power structure.

Social Mobility and the Structure of Opportunity

Stratification studies portray the social structure as static; they offer "snapshots" of the distribution of rewards at a given point in time. Stratification is, however, a dynamic concept: Individuals move up and down the social structure. Advancement to a higher position on the socioeconomic scale is referred to as upward social mobility. The rate of upward mobility is defined as the proportion of people who attain occupations that rank higher in prestige, income, and educational characteristics than those of their parents (Blau and Duncan 1967). Studies of upward mobility, like other stratification studies, usually exclude women.

What determines who moves ahead? Status-attainment theorists emphasize the pivotal role of education in upward mobility. Conflict theorists, however, point to the role of parental background, that is, the material and cultural advantages or disadvantages conferred by parents on their children. The complete picture, of course, includes both, as well as factors outside the family's purview, such as the character of the economy at a given time and place.

＊Sociologist Christopher Jencks, in a book titled *Who Gets Ahead?* (1979), reviews the research data about the effects of four groups of variables on the attainment of economic success in the United States: family background, education, cognitive skills, and noncognitive personality traits. The data show that family background looms larger than has been rec-

ognized previously, accounting for perhaps half of the variation in the results. Next in importance is education. However, the economic returns for education are proportionately larger for each degree completed than for each year completed, prompting the authors to speculate that credentialism rather than the acquisition of skills makes the difference. Cognitive ability and noncognitive personality traits such as industriousness and leadership qualities play a smaller role in economic success. Overall, this book reveals "a class-ridden America in which being born into the right family looms large" (Yankelovich 1979, p. 28).

The inheritance of inequality from one generation to the next has been corroborated by many studies (see, for example, Broom et al. 1980; Goldthorpe 1980). This does not mean that upward mobility does not exist, but rather that it is more circumscribed than most people realize. Where upward mobility does occur, it is likely to span adjacent strata rather than large distances. As Vanfossen (1979, p. 180) summarized it, most people "end up in occupations and life styles very similar to those of their parents."

Further, such upward mobility as has existed has been predominantly structural, that is, it has resulted from rapid economic growth and an increase in the number of positions in the middle and at the top of the occupational hierarchy. Any future decline in economic growth, technological innovation, or demographic expansion could narrow the opportunity system considerably and create a potentially explosive, static class system (see Thurow 1980; Blumberg 1980).

The transmission of inequality from generation to generation is even more evident when class is defined in structural or relational terms, that is, in terms of its relation to the means of production or to authority. Using Erik Olin Wright's conceptualization of classes (see p. 65), sociologist Robert Robinson (1984) finds that capitalist and petty-bourgeois fathers are able to transmit to their sons the ownership of the means of production (and hence the ability to hire labor) either by handing over the family business or by giving their sons money to start their own business. The sons' educational attainment is irrelevant to this process. Fathers in the managerial class (that is, the class that does not own the means of production but controls the labor of others) cannot directly pass on their positions to their sons, but they are usually able to see that their sons receive a good education. This education significantly increases the sons' chances of securing managerial positions. Workers' sons, by contrast, are likely to become workers. Thus, not only is the class structure itself perpetuated, but "the relative positions of individuals or families in the class structure is maintained . . . from generation to generation" (Robinson 1984, p. 182). The reproduction of class relations holds true for both capitalist Western nations and Third World countries.

Given the gap between the widespread belief in equal opportunity and the reality of limited mobility, what enables the stratification system to survive? The stability of the political and economic system hinges in large part on its ideological legitimacy. The legitimation of inequality rests on the belief that mobility is widespread and that it is, in fact, based on individual merit.

Advancement and success are important values to Americans. Equal opportunity is supposed to guarantee everyone, regardless of race, class, or sex, access to top positions in the social structure. The egalitarian ethic, which grew out of the ideals of the American Revolution and the Protestant Reformation,

> holds that social and economic status of individuals should be determined not by descent, but by achievement. It also asserts that there is great opportunity for social mobility, that anyone can succeed if he or she tries hard enough, that people get what they deserve, and that one can move from the bottom to the top of the class structure if only he or she has the ambition and the talent. (Vanfossen 1979, p. 202)

Conflict theorists point out that the belief in equal opportunity, unrealistic though it may be, fulfills important functions for society. By justifying success and rationalizing away failure, this belief upholds the legitimacy of the stratification system. Many people, both rich and poor, assume that success is the reward of merit. The rich, whether self-made or hereditary, congratulate themselves for "having what it takes" to succeed. The poor blame not the lack of access to opportunities but themselves (or sometimes their hard luck) for their failure to advance. Thus, the legitimation of inequality depends in large measure on the congruence between the actual distribution of resources and self-evaluation. The rich and the powerful view themselves, and come to be viewed by others, as actually superior, while the poor and the powerless attribute to themselves relative inferiority (see Della Fave 1980; Stolte 1983). Additionally, the poor find it easier to accept their fate by channeling their hopes and ambitions for upward mobility into the lives of their children. The belief in upward mobility, complemented by the strong individualistic streak of American ideology, diverts attention from structural inequalities and buttresses the existing political and economic system. The role of socialization in inculcating these beliefs is examined in chapter 5.

Summary

The study of stratification is crucial in order to understand political sociology because political sociology deals with the relationship between the social structure and the political order.

Societies are stratified both in the distribution of rewards and in their underlying structural or relational forces. Marx defined social classes in terms of ownership or nonownership of the means of production. Weber stressed the imperfect overlapping of economic class, social status, caste, and political power. Today, sociologists in the Marxian tradition focus on relational or structural aspects of stratification, while those in the status-attainment tradition focus on the distributional aspects. The index of socioeconomic status, which consists of a combined score of levels of individual income, educational attainment, and occupational prestige, is widely used both to describe stratification and to predict political (and nonpolitical) behavior.

In explaining the reasons for inequality, the functional theory of stratification stresses the need for inequality of rewards in order to motivate people to enter vital and demanding occupations. Conflict theory, on the other hand, stresses unequal access to key resources and group self-interest as the keys to stratification.

American society may be viewed as consisting of five major classes, including the upper class, those who control business, government, and nonprofit institutions; the upper middle class, the professionals and managers who run these institutions; the lower middle class, relatively powerless semiprofessional and white-collar employees; the upper lower or working class, or blue-collar workers; and the poor.

Studies of upward mobility show that mobility is in fact less common than is generally believed. Social position, whether defined in terms of the status-attainment model or in terms of the class model, is largely inherited. Despite the limits on upward mobility, however, the belief in equal opportunity for success plays an important role in reinforcing the political order.

CHAPTER FIVE

Political Identity: The Effects of Socialization and External Constraints

Preview

This chapter examines the processes that influence the way we think and act politically. To what extent are we products of early childhood influences, such as our parents' values and child-rearing practices, and to what extent are we products of current situational constraints, such as the values and norms prevalent in our occupational community? Do behavioral and thought patterns, once set, persist through life, or do they vary according to the situation? What is the role of socialization in transmitting the dominant values and ideology of a society? Does socialization uphold the power structure, or does it foster political change?

Political thought, feelings, and action are influenced by the social structure and by culture. What we do, think, or feel at any moment is both the result of previous experience and a response to external stimuli. Some (Hyman 1969) maintain that early socialization is the principal determinant of later political attitudes. Others (Jennings and Niemi 1981) argue that adaptive response is more important and that people are capable of adapting to changing social conditions throughout the life cycle.

Generally, the effects of early socialization are more likely to persist under conditions of stability than during times of rapid and continuous change. The less deeply set values, beliefs, norms, and behavioral patterns are shattered by world changes, the more early socialization will explain political and social behavior. Conversely, the greater the extent to which change acts to shatter these internalized gyroscopes, the greater the probability that the individual will react to a new situation in novel, unprogrammed ways. Mature individuals in modern society are governed by the values, beliefs, and norms passed on by their parents only as long as those values, beliefs, and norms remain relevant to the situation (see Riesman, Denney, and Glazer 1953; Whyte 1956; Gouldner 1979).

Such individuals assess the world as it affects them, though perhaps not always accurately.

What we learn in the process of socialization is often contradictory. For example, Americans are socialized to value both individual achievement and social equality, although the freedom to achieve one's potential clearly implies an inequality of rewards. The ego of each individual must integrate experience. The power of the ego is the power to make choices, for example, to support a decrease in taxes or an increase in social services.

Choice makes possible deviance and change as well as conformity and stability, but choice is influenced by external variables. Durkheim was only partially correct in his analysis of the external constraints affecting people (see chapter 3). His limited perspective accounted for the degree of normative and structural integration without sufficiently considering adaptation to change and personality development. Durkheim failed to consider the concept of substantive rationality introduced by Mannheim (1936), the sociological imagination introduced by Mills (1959), or Gouldner's (1979) concept of subrelativity. These concepts embody the notion that to the extent that individuals can understand the nature of the social circumstances in which they live, they become capable of living with anomie, lack of integration, or cognitive dissonance.

Instead of relying on the primary model of the socialized individual, we suggest the notion of the **modular individual**. This term refers to the capacity to live out a role within a particular time frame, for example, as an undergraduate student, then to shift to a whole new set of roles as a graduate student and later a young professional. Change also occurs when individuals in isolated, static, and "primitive" societies are brought into the "modern" world. The opposite of the individual open to change is the individual closed to change. The professional athlete who continues in the role too long is an example of the individual closed to change. Obviously, some of the old values, attitudes, and skills are carried from module to module, but not always as much is brought along as we used to think (see Jennings and Niemi 1981). Philosophically, at issue is the extent to which the individual either has free will or is constrained by various forces.

There are several theories about the degree to which individuals are constrained or influenced by forces over which they have little control. First is the "oversocialized view" (see Wrong 1961), whose supporters argue that people internalize values, beliefs, and norms that become so real that they speak in a voice of their own (conscience or superego). Another persistent view of human nature is the sociobiological school, whose proponents believe that we are controlled by genetic processes (see Caplan 1978). A third view, stemming from the work of social psychologist George Herbert Mead, is based on the observation that we sometimes perform an act exactly as one of our parents did. Those who hold this view argue that we incorporate (literally take into the body) action patterns of others. This process is called role taking.

We reject all of these theories as total explanations of human behavior because action patterns or habits can be unlearned, the superego can be ignored, and values and behaviors can change. People and cultures do change, and people behave differently under different circumstances, both because of variations in role expectations and because of the uniqueness of each individual. In the following section we examine the implications of these general ideas for political sociology.

Theoretical Perspectives on Socialization

Political sociologists are interested in the relationship of the individual to the political system. Central to this issue are the questions of identity: Who am I? What are the obligations of citizenship? How do family, education, work,

politics, religion, and the mass media shape our view of the political system and our role in it? The answers to these questions depend on the domain assumptions with which one starts.

Freud and the Structural-Functional (Cultural) View

Just a few years ago, the Freudian view that personality was set for life from an early age was taken as incontrovertible truth, and the Parsonian structural-functional perspective (see chapter 1), which held that beliefs and values were the engine that ran society, was commonly accepted among sociologists. These two ideas were mutually supporting. Structural-functional theory holds that people are socialized into the beliefs and values of their society and that these values, beliefs, and norms operate as internal gyroscopes assuring that people act in consistency with their values.

This approach to political socialization is based on the following argument. Democracy requires citizens who are knowledgeable about the issues, tolerate dissent, and have a clear ideological preference. In addition to making sound political judgments, citizens in a democracy must possess enough resources to influence governmental decisions. Thus, the key elements of a democratic personality include knowledge of and interest in politics as well as a sense of competence and efficacy. These personality traits are transmitted through childhood socialization. Democratic socialization takes place in schools that teach loyalty to the nation and to its political system and tolerance of minority views and in families that emphasize participatory decision making as well as loyalty to a given political party. These early influences, in turn, shape adult voting behavior and political attitudes.

The Power Perspective

The power perspective holds that our position in the social structure (for example, whether we are among the privileged elite or the powerless masses) shapes our political values. The

Italian neo-Marxist Antonio Gramsci, for example, believes that elites utilize ideological hegemony and false consciousness to maintain social control (see chapters 8 and 9). Marxists hold that those in positions of power use their control of the basic institutions of society to promote false beliefs that maintain their own positions within the social order. Following this perspective, sociologist Claus Mueller (1973) believes that the elite's position of domination is maintained through the use of power and the manipulation of legitimacy. Language and communication are an important part of this process. Mueller's argument will be examined below.

The Sociology of Knowledge Approach

Proponents of the sociology of knowledge approach (Mannheim 1936) deny the causal priority of either cultural or structural variables. Rather, they view both culture and social structure as important and as mutually reinforcing. The question of causal order is decided on the basis of empirical evidence rather than as an a priori theoretical position.

Political order or disorder depends, in part, on shared meaning. Shared meaning depends both on the ability to communicate and on shared values, beliefs, and norms. What we do at any particular moment is influenced by our past experiences, current external forces, and our ability to know who we are and to understand our circumstances.

Socialization and Change

Consciously and unconsciously, we learn general attitudes or predispositions to action. We also learn how to play the roles expected of us, such as husband, voter, and job holder. Such learning is called socialization by sociologists and enculturation by anthropologists (see Williams 1983). Both terms refer to the processes by which norms, values, beliefs, customs, patterns of behavior, and appropriate ways of feeling in a particular situation are passed on from one generation to the next.

Political sociologist David Segal defines political socialization as the acquisition of "a set of internalized acts, attitudes, and orientations that persist throughout the life cycle." Segal asserts that learning "goes on through the life cycle" (Segal 1974, p. 136).

✳Since learning is lifelong, Segal argues that we need to "refer to the effect of these processes as 'influence' rather than 'socialization' " because there is "no evidence on how deeply the defined appropriate behaviors are internalized, rather than simply responses to felt social pressures" (Segal 1974, pp. 136–37). People's thoughts, feelings, and actions are influenced by family, friends, coworkers, and communities, that is, by the expectations and sanctions of the groups to which they currently belong.

Early Socialization and Its Persistence

Learning Political Thought. The structural-functional perspective, with its emphasis on early socialization and the empirical approach, is evident in the earliest inventory of research on political socialization. Sociologist Herbert Hyman, viewing socialization a psychological process, searched the literature for "psychological studies which will establish the beginnings of political behavior in pre-adult life" (Hyman 1969, p. 18). His main points are that "political behavior is *learned* behavior" and that *"humans must learn their political behavior early and well and persist in it.* Otherwise there would be no regularity—perhaps even chaos" (Hyman 1969, pp. 9–10). Without early socialization into society's political culture, Hyman believes, social order or regularity breaks down.

The evidence is contradictory, but the finding that seems to stand up best is that party loyalty is learned early and tends to persist. Hyman cites evidence that underlying cognitive processes tend to tie new issues to old issues, thus sustaining the effect of early socialization and providing a degree of continuity and political stability.

To Hyman, party affiliation and loyalty are important because political parties differ in their political philosophies. Thus, "insofar as the individual has developed an abiding loyalty to some political party, it would constitute an organizing principle for these issues. The party, rather than the inherent connections between new and old issues, would define the correct position. Thus crucial to socialization as a mechanism of preparation for confronting political issues is socialization into party" (Hyman 1969, p. 35). However, later evidence shows that there is less party loyalty today than there once was (see Jennings and Niemi 1981 and chapter 10).

✳Hyman finds a gradual taking on of ideological perspectives, with the primary agent of political socialization being the family. Differences exist among families at various socioeconomic levels. For example, a male child from a higher socioeconomic background is more likely than a male child from a lower socioeconomic background to be tolerant of differing political orientations. The sex of the child is also an important variable.✳Segal finds that "when disagreements occurred, daughters were more likely to be influenced by their mothers, and sons were as likely to agree with their mothers as with their fathers" (Segal 1974, p. 124). Neither parent is clearly dominant, but in case of a disagreement, the mother tends to be more influential for children of both sexes.

Political communication is tied to general cognitive ability, and both increase with age. Prior to age five, while general socialization takes place, little occurs specific to political socialization. That is, little if any cognitive awareness of governmental or political roles is evident at this age level. The preadult years may be divided into three age spans: "(1) early childhood (roughly ages five to nine), (2) late childhood (approximately ages nine to thirteen), and (3) adolescence (roughly ages thirteen to eighteen)" (Dawson, Prewitt, and Dawson 1977, p. 50).

In early childhood, children develop identity and attachments in terms of age, sex, class, race, and nationality. They learn to look at political figures positively as being people of power and importance who are benevolent and responsible for doing good. They begin to be aware of various positions such as mayor, police chief, and president.

In late childhood, children's knowledge becomes less affective and more abstract. Children in this age group develop a more detailed knowledge of political roles, responsibilities, and processes. By the eighth grade they may be able to identify the leaders of both parties. They may either increase their attachment to politics or develop a distrust for political institutions. They are able to distinguish government and politics from other social realms.

Dramatic changes occur in early to middle adolescence. Children become less dependent on parents, while peers play an increasingly important role. Standards of judgment and political skills become more sophisticated, and political identification and attachments become well established. Early idealized portraits of the role of law and political leaders give way to more realistic ones. The possibility that law can be morally wrong or that leaders can act for their own self-interest, rather than for the collective good, becomes more apparent. It becomes clear that adults can make mistakes.

During this time, the **generalized other** (the ability to understand our role in relation to others within the overall social context) continues to develop, and with it grows a sense of community. Cognitive ability increases, and concepts of authority, liberty, equity, and representative government become more sophisticated. Hypothetical-descriptive reasoning becomes more powerful, and a greater tendency to follow political events may develop. Adolescents demonstrate a greater interest in both the past and the future.

Just how generalizable these patterns are across lines of race, social class, and gender is unclear. All children seem to move from positive and idealized notions to more concrete ones and to lose the sense of politics as necessarily benevolent. Young blacks, however, tend to view themselves as less powerful than young whites and persist longer in viewing the political process as benevolent. Higher-class children are more likely to engage in discussion about politics than are lower-class children. Girls, in general, see politics as more benevolent than boys and are less well informed about the political process.

Sociologists Richard Dawson, Kenneth Prewitt, and Karen Dawson argue that the shifts in the degree of trust and respect for government among adult Americans "cannot be explained very well by psychodynamic or cognitive-developmental models, i.e., the model that stresses the extent to which the child is egocentric and able to deal with abstractions. Such change can be understood best by a model that stresses stimuli in the environment" (Dawson, Prewitt, and Dawson 1977, p. 72). Evidence on this point is provided by the decrease in trust and respect for government in the 1960s and 1970s and the increase since 1980.

Learning Political Behavior. Political socialization involves not only learning political thought and ideology but also acquiring a level of political participation or involvement. Participation ranges from high to low (see chapter 10) and is related to the availability of role models, that is, of significant others engaged in the political process. Political involvement also seems to be related to differences in class, age, sex, and interest.

Hyman's findings show "gradual growth of political participation with age" (Hyman 1969, p. 43). Interest in politics develops through social interaction. By the third and fourth grades, children are increasingly talking about politics with their families. With increasing age, the peer group becomes more important. Political interest is considerable by age thirteen and "mounts regularly through the high school years" (Hyman 1969, p. 41). Hyman argues that "the beginnings of participation must be sought in relatively early childhood years for already by age 16, the phenomenon appears to be well formed" (Hyman 1969, p. 43). Attention to news and identification are used as crude indicators of participation. Segal (1974, p. 133) argues that

political orientations and behavior are learned not only within the institution of politics but also outside the political context. Thus, while children are not involved directly in politics, they can become members or leaders of political clubs and civic groups. They can also become involved in a variety of voluntary organizations, including student government. Formal civic training appears to be less important in forming political involvement than the roles and relationships students experience within the school system.

Segal concludes that adolescents have a political life. He reports that a surprisingly high percentage of high school seniors surveyed, nearly 57 percent, have been elected or appointed officers of a club or team. Some are even more active. "About 2 percent of the high school senior sample were active in four or five different political arenas, and an additional 12.5 percent were active in three arenas" (Segal 1974, p. 122). Adolescents tend to either support the same party as their parents or to have made no choice, but while children tend to take on the party preference of their parents, they seek reasons for that preference in their own social worlds. "Each generation grows up in a world that is different" (Segal 1974, p. 124), and these differences are reflected in different political ideologies, such as socialism or conservatism.

Political socialization research as described above ignores the following basic questions: Why are Americans in general so apolitical? Why do so few Americans vote? Why is politics not often a topic of general discussion? What explains Americans' minimal sense of political history? Why is there so little in-depth knowledge about important issues? Why are people more concerned with the delivery of services than with the political process? We will address these questions below.

Change over the Life Cycle

Hyman's work is entirely within the Freudian/structural-functional paradigm, which emphasizes early socialization. Segal also develops his findings primarily within this paradigm, but his conclusions can be interpreted within the emerging paradigm of human adaptability throughout the life cycle. Segal notes that Hyman's assertion that "the family is the foremost agency of political socialization" has been qualified and that peers, school, voluntary associations, and the political climate of the community become increasingly important as the child grows older (Segal 1974, p. 132).

Individuals build their political ideologies on the basis of available alternatives, namely, the range of candidates running for office and the issues these candidates represent. Alternatives vary by generation. Each new generation "experiences social institutions and institutional arrangements that did not exist before" (Segal 1974, pp. 126–27). Age cohorts (people born in the same period) are influenced similarly by major events. Thus, we may speak of the Vietnam or Watergate generation, because each carries a lasting political legacy, such as a tradition of political activism or distrust of political institutions, generated by the times in which it lives.

The first major longitudinal study of political socialization followed a cohort of youth and their parents over a number of years. Jennings and Niemi (1981) find not only a good deal of change but also a great potential for change throughout the life cycle. In the past, the authors argue, "older adults have to a large extent been viewed as being beyond the state at which transformation in the political and personal landscapes has a major impact. They have already made whatever adjustments are needed in their lives" (Jennings and Niemi 1981, pp. 380–81). Change among the young, according to earlier studies, is more predictable than for older people because the stimuli the young are responding to are more clustered. For example, they are leaving home, forming families, and taking a first job within a short time span. "Changes in mature adults are less likely to find a simple pattern" and therefore are less easily discernible (Jennings and Niemi 1981, p. 388). Jennings and Niemi, however, find mixed evidence for this view. Adults "in their forties

and fifties are less subject to fluctuations than are new adults: but even the middle-aged are responsive to changes in their personal and political worlds" (1981, p. 381). This finding holds true at both the individual and the aggregate level. Not only do individuals undergo change, but so does each generation as a whole. Changes occur over a wide number of indicators, including political knowledge and degree of political trust. Given the importance traditionally assigned to party identification as a stabilizing principle that lends consistency to political beliefs over time, we might expect to find little change in that area. But even here Jennings and Niemi find much movement. In their studies, most movement was between a given party and nonaffiliation (that is, a former Republican or Democrat describes herself as an independent), but there was also considerable movement between parties (see chapter 10). "The main point . . . is not the limited degree of continuity even at its extreme, but the fact that significant amounts of instability occurred everywhere—in people's involvement in politics, in their resources and participation, in their preferences and attitudes, and in comparable nonpolitical domains" (Jennings and Niemi 1981, p. 382). Further, change was not restricted to any particular educational level; people with low levels of education changed as much as highly educated people.

Equally interesting is the conclusion that "in virtually every comparison of the parent-offspring pairs, youths had become less like their parents than they were as high school seniors as well as less like what their parents had become in the intermediate years. Rather than regenerating parent-child continuity, later development heightened within-family discontinuity" (Jennings and Niemi 1981, p. 383). In conclusion, "Change is a characteristic pattern of adult years:

> For a time, some researchers were convinced that development of political attitudes crystallized prior to late adolescence. When that position became untenable it became fashionable to believe that development and change continued through early adulthood.

While precise limits were rarely asserted it seemed to be commonly assumed that rigidity had set in at least by age 30. We are now taking issue with even that limitation on adult changeability. Without denying that young adults change more frequently than older persons, and that the likelihood of change is less as one gets older, we argue that older adults are far from intractable. (Jennings and Niemi 1981, pp. 384, 387)

✳Change occurs throughout the life cycle in response to developments in personal and social environments. Jennings and Niemi "would even go so far as to say that sharp breaks with the past—perhaps even support for radical changes in the form of government—can occur among older adults." In fact, "rapid political change would be nearly impossible if older adults were unyielding" (Jennings and Niemi 1981, p. 389).

When early learning persists, it does so not because it is deeply ingrained but because "the political orientations of most individuals are simply not challenged very frequently" (Jennings and Niemi 1981, p. 390). When politics enters our lives, we are generally more concerned with specific policies or applications than with fundamental issues. But

> since early learning (or later learning) is not thoroughly ingrained, people are quite susceptible to challenge to what they have learned. . . . Older adults are typically more integrated into existing social and political structures and therefore have more at stake than young people in changes to that structure. Consequently, it usually takes a stronger challenge to present circumstances or contemporary beliefs to alter their current attitudes and behavior. Even older adults, however, are susceptible. [This puts the burden on political leaders] to provide the challenges that stir people out of the inertia that otherwise characterizes them. (Jennings and Niemi 1981, pp. 390–91).

Jennings and Niemi challenge the previous emphasis on primary socialization (that is, socialization during childhood and adolescence) that neglects external circumstances in adulthood. The process of socialization, they claim, is truly dialectical. While there is a strain toward consistency of personality, social structure, and culture, all are intertwined and capable of change. Jennings and Niemi's most telling point is that the reason older Americans are less changeable is because they have a stake in things as they are rather than because of the rigidity of their early socialization. This finding suggests that older adults would be more changeable if they had more of a stake in change. Jennings and Niemi's overall conclusion is that a great potential for political change exists that has not been adequately recognized or dealt with.

In sum, primacy theories of socialization argue that early childhood socialization is the key variable in explaining adult political behavior. In the most extreme form of this theory, Hyman argues that if political values are not learned early, democracy is threatened and chaos is likely. However, more recent studies show that, in fact, people in later life are quite adaptable and at least as capable of being influenced by external circumstances as by prior socialization.

Some writers have argued that societal elites understand the effects of both socialization and external constraints and use both to maintain domination. We next examine the ways in which the power elite shapes the consciousness and behavior of actors in the political system, shoring up the elite's own legitimacy.

Socialization as a Means of Political Control

Hierarchy and the Shaping of Meaning

The ability to use language as a means of communication, as well as basic values, beliefs, and norms, are learned through socialization. One of the social contexts in which we operate is that of hierarchical orders of domination. Some ✳theorists believe that domination is necessary for social order to exist. Domination is based on both power and legitimacy. Legitimacy may be based on false or true consciousness, while power may be used to create false consciousness[1] (see chapter 7).

✳Political consciousness is related to cognitive ability. Humans process data by linking concepts, symbols, and reality. Without concepts and symbols, we might miss pieces of reality. Cognitive ability is tied to the number and quality of concepts and symbols that are part of our experience and that form the codes (shared language) with which we can interpret (decode) experience. These codes are linguistic and are learned through socialization. Not only is socialization culture-specific, but it varies within a culture according to generation, sex, and ethnic, religious, and social background. For example, Catholic working-class girls are socialized differently from boys of their own religion and social class, from upper-class girls of the same religion, and from their own mothers. Thus, to understand the politics of communication, we must understand differences in the socialization experiences that shape people's shared conceptions and their ability to understand themselves and their social world.

✳Awareness of social reality depends on effective and undistorted communication. Distorted communication precludes full discussion of the issues. Sociologist Claus Mueller's (1973) concept of distorted communication can be best understood by contrasting it with its ideal polar type: nondistorted communication.

With open and nondistorted communication, partners share a basic vocabulary, words have the same meaning, and the words are ordered by shared rules. Thus, cognitive differences are minimal. Attitudes, values, and expectations are shared, and aspirations and deprivations can be publicly discussed. Open

communication is not distorted by vested interests. Rules are flexible, and new information can be integrated into a shared view of the world. Mueller states (1973, p. 20) that where communications are open, messages about basic underlying assumptions of the political system exist, and it is therefore possible to reformulate assumptions as required. All channels of communication are equally accessible to all groups.

Two forms of distorted communication identified by Mueller are directed and arrested communication. **Directed communication** "results from governmental policy to structure language and communication." Governments and elites that view open communication as threatening to the political status quo may try to direct communication by controlling the terms used to describe conditions and politics. For example, such labels as "terrorism," "pacification program," and "fire-free zone" help define attitudes people will take toward a particular group, as does the policy of a government (such as that of South Africa) to limit television and photographic press coverage of popular insurrection and police suppression (Mueller 1973, pp. 19–24). For a case study of directed communication see Box 5.1.

Arrested communication is "the limited capacity of individuals and groups to engage in political communication because of the nature of their linguistic environment (a restricted speech code) and not because of any apparent political intervention" (Mueller 1973, p. 19). Arrested communication is illustrated by the American belief in upward mobility through individual effort. Because each of us is socialized into believing that we have access to opportunities for education and career advancement and that taking advantage of these opportunities is our responsibility, we are limited in our capacity to understand the impact of economic and societal forces in our lives. This carries over into our political debate over the role of government in the economy.

The ability to perceive alternative meanings requires an ability to see the world in a synthetic, analytic, and problem-solving mode. This

---

1. True or false consciousness is linked to the issue of whether or not people have objective knowledge of what their own interests are and are both willing and able to act in their self-interest. It is thus critical to both Marxist theory and the classical theory of liberal democracy.

ability is differentially fostered in different social locations (see Bernstein 1971).

Since most people stay within the social class in which they are born and since upward social mobility, even when it does occur, is mostly within that class (see chapter 4), people retain the speech code used in their primary group. "Class-specific differences in the acquisition and handling of language have been found among children as young as twelve months. . . . The higher the socioeconomic position of the parents, the more likely is language development to take place at an early age. Higher class children have larger vocabularies and speak in longer sentences" (Mueller 1973, p. 46). The correlation between SES (socioeconomic status) and language is even greater than that between race and language (Deutsch et al. 1967, p. 218). This statement holds true for such linguistic skills as verbal identification, use of classificatory concepts, general knowledge, and recognition of grammatical forms.

The language of the hard-core poor (Cohen et al. 1968, p.24) is descriptive rather than analytic. Objects and groups are personalized, and distinct categories such as cause and effect or means and ends are collapsed. People respond to the concrete rather than to the abstract. Other characteristics are that time is discontinuous, importance is derived from the group, and only the immediate is relevant. Therefore, the language of the hard-core poor is a restricted speech code. "It cannot be used in an instrumental, reflective way" (Mueller 1973, p. 55). Because such language does not permit abstract analysis, it precludes alternatives. The elaborated code of the middle class is more complex, richer, and more analytic. But most important, the elaborated code speaker is aware of the existence of the codes being used.

Although little research has been done on the relation between language codes and differential socialization practices, at least one key variable has been identified. That variable is the relative absence of dinnertime conversation in low-SES households. Ruesh (1958, p. 358) argues that the development of language requires deriving intention from a child's articulations or actions and providing verbal feedback. Simply put, the use of language develops from the parents' ability to understand the child, to help the child verbalize his or her thoughts and feelings, and to be able to engage in meaningful interchange. "Meager feedback and the inability of parents to respond to the child's intentions frustrate the child, thereby undermining his sense of autonomy and emotional stability" (Mueller 1973, p. 59).

Middle-class parents use moral instruction, not power, to teach children internal control and to make them aware of the consequences of their actions. Lower-class parents, on the other hand, are more prone to use authority. An example of these differences is the mother in a supermarket who explains to the child why she should not take things off the shelf as opposed to the parent who orders the child not to take things from the shelf or simply punishes her when she does (Hess and Chipman 1965; Hoffman and Saltzstein 1967). Sociologist Melvin L. Kohn (1969) also finds that working-class parents tend to punish children for their actions without taking their intentions into account, while middle-class parents often ask their children to explain their behavior before deciding on disciplinary action.

The result of these differences in socialization practices is less opportunity for self-development and autonomy among the lower classes. Members of the lower classes are less able to tolerate role conflict and ambiguity. Therefore, lower-class children are less likely to develop a sociological imagination, to independently assess their political world, and to take autonomous political action. Social scientist Roy Beasely (in personal communication) states that the lower classes do more running than problem solving. A problem solver is one who sees the reason for a problem, figures out alternative ways around the problem, and takes appropriate action. The runner cannot develop such insight and, not understanding, is unable to verbalize the nature of the problem. The

---

▄▄▄ BOX 5.1 ▄▄▄

Covering the Falklands War:
A Case of Directed Communication

The following excerpts from a column titled "How Britain Managed the News" by Leonard Downie, Jr. in the *Washington Post* (August 20, 1982) about the 1982 war between Britain and Argentina over the Falkland or Malvinas Islands illustrate how even democratic governments limit and distort the information that reaches the public.

In a recent parliamentary inquiry, British officials for the first time acknowledged misleading the media about British intentions, strengths and weaknesses on numerous occasions during the war. . . .

"We aimed throughout not to lie," testified Sir Frank Cooper, the civil servant who runs Britain's defense ministry. "But there were occasions when we did not tell the whole truth and did not correct things that were being misread."

Hours before 5,000 British troops were landed at San Carlos Bay on East Falkland Island in a massive amphibious operation, Sir Frank himself confided to British newsmen in a restricted background briefing that there were "no plans" for a "D-Day type invasion." This was not really a lie, he recently told the parliamentary inquiry, because the allies' World War II invasion on D-Day was "an opposed land-

ing," while few Argentine defenders were expected or encountered in the British landing at San Carlos.

He and other officials also left uncorrected a number of news reports, based on speculative leaks from inside the British government, that made it appear the Royal Navy had significantly more ships, submarines and aircraft around the Falklands than it actually did at various times. A nuclear powered hunter-killer submarine widely reported to be enforcing the original British naval blockade around the Falklands was later found in port in Scotland.

Good news was sometimes released prematurely, with the British recapture of Port Darwin and Goose Green announced a half-day before the Argentine defenders actually surrendered. Bad news, from accidental crashes of British warplanes and helicopters to the number of casualties inflicted by Argentine air strikes, often was held up for days. . . .

Television networks were prevented from broadcasting live from the Royal Navy's Falklands task force, and their film of events in the South Atlantic took weeks to reach London by ship and plane. So the war was nearly over before Britons saw dramatic scenes of the destruction of

---

runner, therefore, avoids, retreats, or withdraws from the situation.

✳ Mannheim (1936) argued that education is a process in which an individual is confronted with a variety of differing perspectives. Seeing the world from multiple perspectives, a faculty that is developed either by occupying a number of differentiated roles or by education, provides the ability to stand back from any role and judge it objectively. The inability to achieve

different perspectives tends to make less educated, lower-class people outer-directed, more conforming to external rules, and less self-reliant.

Not only past experiences (education and family patterns) but also current conditions mold our personality and affect our political thinking. The patterns discussed above tend to be linked to differences in working-class and middle-class occupations. Since these differ-

some of their warships or heard emotional interviews with survivors. Still photographs of burning British warships, transmitted more quickly to London, were blocked from publication by military censors for days and sometimes weeks. . . .

For an American correspondent in London, none of this should be really surprising. In normal times, the British press accepts a far greater amount of government secrecy and news manipulation than American or foreign newsmen would put up with in Washington. . . .

More insidious, however, is a practice that most British journalists agree to voluntarily and even help to protect. Most of their contacts with politicians and government officials are kept completely off the record through what is called the "lobby"—named for an area in the House of Commons where many of these contacts take place, although every government agency has its own lobby arrangement with newsmen covering it. Newsmen participating in "lobby" briefings and conversations are obligated to keep secret all their sources, all direct quotes, and even the times and locations of such contacts. They are sometimes forbidden by their sources to publish important information revealed in these contacts.

This system enables the British government to manage much of what is reported by the national newspapers and television and radio networks and to escape responsibility for planting information—true or false—that newsmen must report only on an "it is understood" basis. This was the system used by the British defense ministry to control through the lobby of defense correspondents most information about the Falklands war. Only these correspondents were allowed into secret briefings held throughout the war, while the rest of the large body of newsmen covering the conflict from London were told little in public statements and press conferences. . . .

Even after the Falklands war ended, only a few British journalists questioned whether such pervasive news management, in peace or war, was good for the country. One of them, Charles Wintour, writing in the *Sunday Observer*, emphasized that "the hidden attitudes of many people in authority toward the media have been exposed. They think the public should be told as little as possible. They don't object to deception on matters both large and small. They dislike reporters. And they prefer that ruling circles should be left to run the state without being bothered by troublesome disclosures and unpleasant truths."

"In fact," Wintour concluded, "some of them don't really care much for democracy either."

ences in socialization lead to differences in the degree to which people accept regulation from above, they may lead to variations in autonomy, in the ability to give or receive orders, and in the capacity for dealing with symbols (see Kohn 1969).

Thus, we can see that people bring their past experience to the moment of the act. But they are also capable of changing in response to new conditions and of pressuring for social change.

The Theory of Hegemony and the New Class

Mueller (1973) argues that the dominant ideology reflects the interests of elite groups and that this ideology is transmitted to subordinates by educational institutions and the mass media. But Mueller also finds that the dominant ideology is less important than it used to be. Change has become too rapid for ideologies to keep up with new developments without a threat to their plausibility. In the past few decades the United States has been, for this and other reasons, without an ideology (see Sherman and Femminella 1984). During this period, Mueller can identify no ascendant class producing a new ideology.

If the function of ideology is to maintain legitimate domination by the power elite, when no such ideology exists it becomes necessary to look for functional alternatives, that is, other ways of maintaining domination. Mueller identifies what he calls para-ideologies—ideologies that lack an ethical base (that is, a "should" component, a vision of the good life in the good society).

⨳The key para-ideology since the 1960s has been rational administration, a belief in science and technology that is not class-specific. Examples include the efforts by previous Secretary of Defense Robert McNamara (1961–1968) to take management strategies from the Ford Motor Company and use them at the Pentagon and New York Mayor John Lindsay's (1965–1973) attempt to use the same techniques to govern New York City. Evidence of this para-ideology is seen today in attempts to manage through the techniques of policy "science" or decision "science." This para-ideology promotes what Weber and Mannheim referred to as functional rather than substantive rationality (see chapter 1).

Contemporary political stability is maintained by more than the para-ideology of scientism or rational administration. The dissent of either the working class or the middle class would clearly pose a problem for political stability. But dissent is likely only under special conditions. The upper middle class and the upper class are bound to contemporary political arrangements by their stake in them. The lower class's attempts to change those arrangements are politically ineffective because its members lack the language ability and political symbols necessary for understanding how their daily living conditions are tied to the nature of

advanced technological society. The socialization practices of the lower class tend to produce restrictive codes (Mueller 1973). However, conflict requires the attachment of symbols to conditions. With no explicit ideology to give coherence to their concerns, the workers tend to concentrate on bread-and-butter issues (such as wages and fringe benefits) and to acquiesce to the political system. The opaque nature of working-class symbolism makes it impossible for workers in America to link their situation to a counterideology, that is, an ideology that calls for radical political change. As Mueller puts it, "neither linguistic ability nor interpretative schemes permit the articulation of conflict. Without labels to identify the nature of their situations, targets for political action are not available" (Mueller 1973, p. 115).

⨳Mueller believes that governmental efficiency is another source of legitimacy (see also Margolis 1979). The government's efficiency is judged by its ability to maintain a high level of economic development. Members of the working class judge governmental efficiency in terms of their own level of material well-being. Since the government can affect the level of well-being by such means as high defense spending, which promotes employment and spending power, it has the capacity to deliver a reasonably high level of material well-being to most people (the plight of those displaced by technological developments, the homeless, and others notwithstanding). Therefore, government can use the para-ideology of a rational bureaucracy capable of meeting people's needs.

Neither socialization nor the efficiency of government is ordinarily sufficient in itself to maintain the stability of the political structure. A higher principle of legitimation, such as the belief in the divine right of kings or the doctrine of popular sovereignty, is required. The function of legitimacy is to induce acceptance of domination. In addition to creating legitimacy through efficiency and through the perception that it is working to foster well-being, government can create legitimacy in other ways, such as withholding information, misleading the public, and suppressing evidence in order to deflect dissent.

Mueller notes that some writers argue that the real role of government is to preserve the economic system—not to represent the populace. According to this argument, efficiency of decision making requires that government eliminate as much as possible those factors that complicate decision making. One complicating factor is the limitation of the government's pragmatic options by people's values, for example, when citizens argue that covert CIA attempts to topple foreign governments violate the sovereign rights of countries. Another complicating factor is static (public dissent) from outside the government. Such static, for example, interferes with covert U.S. activities against socialist regimes and movements in Central America and elsewhere. Static from outside the government can be reduced by a governmental policy to limit public information and public debate.

Such situations require constrained political communication. When its legitimacy is in jeopardy, the government can focus its public relations efforts not on higher principles but on convincing the public that government policy will produce greater safety or material well-being. Thus, an effort may be made to convince the public that science and technology are required to solve problems in today's complicated world and that to keep a competitive edge much of this science and technology must remain secret. In this way, public opinion favorable to governmental policies is established while information and knowledge are withheld.

✳Sociologist Alvin Gouldner claims that the para-ideology of rational efficiency gives rise to a new class of technocrats. Paradoxically, this is also the class most likely to challenge the government's legitimacy. "The new ideology holds that productivity depends primarily on science and technology and that society's problems are solvable on a technological basis, and

with the use of educationally acquired technical competence. While this ideology de-politicizes the public realm, and, in part, *because* it does, it cannot be understood simply as legitimating the *status quo*, for the ideology of the autonomous technological process delegitimates all other social classes than the new class"(Gouldner 1979, p. 24). Gouldner conceptualizes this new class as a speech community.

Gouldner sees these professionals and intellectuals as part of a class that has been emerging since the end of the feudal period. Some of the events that mark the rise of this class are the end of scholars' bonds to the medieval church, the rise of vernacular languages to replace Latin as the language of intellectual discourse, the rise of the nuclear family, the emergence of the mass media, differentiated educational systems relatively free from family and church influence, the increase in literacy, and the development of situation-free languages.

The primary characteristic of the language code of intellectuals is that assertions need to be justified on grounds other than authority. This language code exists within a "culture of critical discourse" (CDC). Intellectuals' speech is relatively situation-free, complex, and not only descriptive but also explanatory or interpretive. Most important, speakers recognize that language claims may be mistaken, and parties to the communication mutually look for proper grounds of justification. Thus, this group is important in maintaining the potential for undistorted communication.

Gouldner argues that, compared to members of other classes, intellectuals are more concerned with ultimate values and that their thinking is less person- and situation-bound (see also Shils 1960). Further, intellectuals tend to be concerned with alternative realities. Gouldner asks how it is that revolutionaries such as Marx become alienated from the existing social and political order. He argues that this situation stems from many causes: the culture of critical discourse, which supports the intellectuals' self-reflexive and critical abilities; the intellectuals' blocked upward mobility; the disparity between their meager income and power on one hand and their considerable cultural capital and self-esteem on the other; "their commitment to the social totality"; and, finally, blockage of their technical interests (Gouldner 1979, p. 58).

The disparity between income or power and cultural capital may be perceived by the cultural stratum as inequality. Since inequality is accepted by subordinates only when domination is legitimated, loss of belief in governmental statements or actions that provide legitimacy, including the government's ability to provide the people with material well-being, leads to delegitimation unless that belief is replaced by another basis of legitimacy, such as the para-ideology of efficiency. Delegitimation without an alternative ideology leads to an increasing possibility of political conflict. In the absence of a legitimating ideology, the power structure of society becomes demystified, open to question, and therefore substantially weakened.

In sum, reflection requires distance between subject and object, which is supplied by elaborated language codes. Given their elaborated codes, the cultural stratum is least vulnerable to constraints on communication. The socialization strategies, values, and language codes necessary for professional work have the side effect of making upper-middle-class political opposition possible. However, potential opposition and the development of an effective counterideology within the new class may be forestalled by situational constraints, as we will see below.

Occupation and Political Socialization

Language and childhood socialization are not the only factors affecting the relationship between socialization and political action in advanced industrial societies. Socialization by one's occupation in adult life is another. Sociologist Diane Margolis (1979) has studied the

political consequences of occupational socialization among male middle-level managers in one Fortune "100" corporation. These managers are, for the most part, sons of the upper working class or the lower middle class. The first college-educated generation in their families, they tended to get their degrees from second- or third-line colleges and universities.

These middle-level managers are uninvolved in politics—they never question the system. Margolis argues that this political apathy results in interest only in the quality of government services, not in the political process itself. In this regard, middle managers share the para-ideology of material benefits described by Mueller. The question is how much of their lack of interest and participation comes from childhood socialization and how much is in response to the conditions under which they live. The importance of this question lies partly in the fact that this segment of the population is growing. Margolis argues that the apathy is created by corporate policy.

Although these people from blue-collar origins are not destined to become chief executives, in order to rise within the corporation they must assume corporate interests as their own. The first step in the production of political apathy stems from corporate transfer policy. The first transfer, right out of college, separates the young manager from family and childhood friends in order for him to undergo early training. The family of orientation may be proud of the child's success, but family members may also resent that success. The transfer not only separates the young from their past but teaches them "that they can live successfully without the old people and communities which nurtured them." They become dependent not on friends, family, and community but on the corporation and each other. "Subsequent transfers serve to prevent the man and his family from developing extra-corporate relationships" (Margolis 1979, pp. 53–54).

Promotions, higher salaries, and comfortable offices tend to fill people's need for recognition and self-esteem. Careers are competitive, and survival depends on promotion. Uncertainty of success is a powerful motivator. Corporate members come to depend on the corporation and to have faith in its benevolence. Overwork lowers the novice's resistance and makes him submissive to corporate authority, while long hours create conflict between the corporation and the family that tests the manager's loyalty to both. Even when home, he may have brought work with him and ask not to be bothered with family concerns. "By turning the manager into a father and husband who is there but not available, the corporation can create a subtle wall of rejection between the man and his family that will strain family relationships. Then, the corporation can become the most satisfying world to him and all other worlds can lose their importance" (Margolis 1979, p. 66).

Wives of managers cater to their husbands. They accept the work loads, moves, and lack of time together without complaint, thus putting the husband in their debt. The husband then works harder to provide more material rewards in order to pay this debt. The money is spent on consumer goods rather than saved. This interlocking cycle further subjects the couple to corporate domination.

A key resource controlled by the corporation is money (salary). In addition, the jobs are intrinsically satisfying, since problem solving brings its own rewards. Overtime pay and fringe benefits tie the individual more closely to the corporation. All these things, plus corporate image, convey status, identity, and a sense of self-worth. A certain security is achieved from upward movement while one's peers stagnate in their careers or cut loose. This enhances self-esteem. But the manager has no real base of power or independence. He is replaceable; oversupply of talent allows competition among personnel. Managers have "no exclusive control of a resource necessary to the corporation." A search for alternative employment is also blocked by "inertia, fear, and the assumption that theirs is the optimal employer" (Margolis 1979, pp. 85–94), so managers become iso-

lated. Fear, ignorance of alternatives, and subjective bonds to the corporation combine to curtail their exploration of alternative employment. This absence of alternatives limits both their power and their independence. Faith in the corporation is, in a limited sense, equivalent to loyalty to the political system. Dependency deepens with continued affiliation.

The corporation impedes "the formation of deep or enduring relationships outside of the family unit." Managers display the lower-class badges of identity: "They display not the thrift of the middle class, but the instantaneous spending characteristics of the poor. Managers enjoy large incomes but small wealth" (Margolis 1979, p. 143).

A key element of the American belief system is that upward mobility is assured by the ability to delay gratification and by an orientation to the future. This goal implies planning for the future, but these people do not plan. Margolis argues that "if you don't actively plan, if you don't actively find out what is available and make choices based on *your* preferences, you will be carried along" (Margolis 1979, p. 163). Middle-level managers are passive, accepting opportunity without exploring options.

Transients need easily understandable worlds. They require creature comfort to provide a sense of stability as well as uncomplicated social relationships where "identity and status are easily read" (Margolis 1979, p. 196). Transiency also limits the managers' ties to their communities and to community politics. When they relocate, they look for neighborhoods with people of their age and income level and with children of the same age. The ability to sell the house quickly at a profit is also important. Thus, they tend to buy in areas of high turnover. Isolated from the permanent residents, they do not participate in community affairs.

A community is "a place where people expect to see each other everyday without making special plans" (Margolis 1979, p. 203). These shared experiences produce emotional bonds. "Community exists when there are many connections between individuals so that every interaction builds upon those that went before and also prepares for the next" (Margolis 1979, p. 205). Yet the permanent residents do not acknowledge the transients quickly as members of the community. The transients can find no way to get to the core of the community, and they turn away in frustration and anger. Their closest friends consist of neighbors and other corporate members.

The locals, on the other hand, are tied into the community. They see "themselves as creators; by their very activities on their town committees they were using their energies to shape the town" (Margolis 1979, p. 220). People are brought into local politics by friends already connected to the political system. This process takes at least two years from the time one moves into town. Being enmeshed in town life gives importance to local issues that can seem petty from the outside. The managers do not share in the town's collective memory. They tend not to vote in local elections except when their interests are directly involved or a friend asks for their support. However, because they can be mobilized and are politically unpredictable, they intensify the instability of local governments (see also chapter 10).

The corporation's selection of middle managers from working-class and lower-middle-class backgrounds and its transfer policies affect the way managers think, act, and feel in regard to family, friends, community, and politics. These are not people who exhibit the Protestant ethic, that is, a future orientation and the ability to delay gratification. They are not separate and autonomous individuals who run their lives on the basis of values and beliefs instilled in them at an early age. They are unreflective. Their community and political involvement shows none of the evidence of reflection expected of the upper middle class on the basis of Mueller and Gouldner's analysis of elaborated codes. Rather, these are people who bring with them past experience but who become selected, molded, and adjusted into a system of positive and negative reinforcements that determines their day-to-day acts, thoughts, and feelings.

Summary

Just as politics cannot be understood alone, individuals cannot be understood outside of their structural and cultural context. Socialization and internalization alone are not ordinarily sufficient to create autonomous individuals. Values, beliefs, and norms are bolstered by the societal schedule of reinforcements. When social conditions change, values, beliefs, and norms change with them.

Theory and research in political socialization have been subject to the law of the hammer: If you give a child a hammer, he will discover that everything in sight needs nailing. Sociologists try to understand highly complex phenomena from the perspective of their own particular theory. Many theories, as Gouldner has pointed out, are deeply embedded in ideological premises. Political socialization and its role in maintaining social equilibrium have been treated from the perspective of pluralist or structural-functional theory. But this perspective makes the understanding of social change problematic. Conflict theory, on the other hand, stresses the relation between political consciousness and the social, political, and economic forces that shape it.

A basic premise of the dominant American belief system is that the individual is capable of great autonomy. We have been socialized to see the individual as one-dimensional and as cut off from the structural and cultural contexts in which he or she is embedded. Cultural beliefs, values, and norms do not by themselves determine human behavior but are tied to actual patterns of human association and are bolstered by the system of stratification, that is, the schedule of social and economic reinforcements.

CHAPTER SIX

Political Thinking: Ideologies and Utopias

Preview

In the first two decades after World War II, many observers heralded the end of ideology, at least in industrialized countries (see, for example, Bell 1961; Waxman 1968). Implicitly identifying ideology with extremism, they predicted that as affluence and meaningful political participation increased, extremist movements would lose their appeal and politics would become increasingly pragmatic and nonideological. The upheavals of the late 1960s, however, showed that the death knells were premature. Recently, social scientists have been more inclined to assume that all political thinking and expression are ideological, including those that proclaim the end of ideology in general or the ideological neutrality of the writer in particular (see Haber 1968).[1]

This chapter demonstrates the usefulness of applying the term "ideology" to political thinking of various shades, including our own, and the importance of acknowledging the socioeconomic bases of political thought. We begin with a general discussion of the meaning, uses, and origins of ideology and then analyze several ideologies. We do not attempt an exhaustive analysis of all ideologies, not even of all major ones, but instead examine a sample of some of the major ideological approaches to the problems faced by Western societies.

What Is Ideology?

"America's Classrooms Becoming an Ideological Battleground," proclaims a recent headline in the *Washington Post* (June 29, 1985). The *Post* reports that an ideological tug of war is being fought for influence over "the hearts and minds of the next generation." The war is being waged by New Right education groups such as the National Council for Better Education and Eagle Forum (led by Phyllis Schlafly, the conservative activist). These groups have attacked the National Education Association (NEA), the nation's largest teachers' union, as being "a propaganda front of the radical left." They criticize the NEA for allegedly "supporting abortion, homosexual rights, evolutionism, a nuclear-arms freeze, and affirmative action" and, more generally, for upholding "the forces of permissiveness and Godless communism." The NEA, in its counterattack, charges that "these extremist groups . . . want to impose a new political, religious and social order on our nation, an order that unquestioningly accepts ultra-conservative views on everything from foreign policy to the textbooks in our classrooms."

In popular parlance, ideology is often considered synonymous with extreme or dogmatic political opinion and is usually attributed to the adversary's views, not to one's own. Sociologically, however, ideology refers to any set of relatively coherent, well-integrated political beliefs—not only extreme ones—that influence political views and actions. Ideologies aren't merely free products of the mind; they reflect the social and economic circumstances of their bearers. In turn, ideologies shape political

---

1. In this chapter, we follow the common sociological usage of the term *ideology*. Technically, however, according to the founder of the theory of ideology, Karl Mannheim, *ideology* should be distinguished from *utopia*. Both *ideology* and *utopia* refer to a state of mind that is "incongruous with the state of reality within which it occurs" (Mannheim 1936, p. 192). Ideological thinking is grounded in the way things were; it is basically conservative thought. Utopian thought is not tied to the past but based on a wish to move forward to a new future. Utopian thought is capable of the revolutionary transformation of society. A third mode of thought, diagnostic or relational thinking, transcends the single limiting perspective of ideology or utopia, combining the various perspectives while recognizing the limitations of each (see chapter 1).

behavior and political institutions. Ideology, then, may be viewed as the intervening variable between social and economic forces on one hand and the political order on the other.

What Ideology Is Not

Ideologies are clearly different from political opinions or attitudes. A person who supports the Equal Rights Amendment as an isolated issue, for example, is expressing a political opinion, while one who is committed to feminism, with its complex array of theories and issues, is supporting an ideology. An ideology is a *system* of interrelated ideas and beliefs, usually distinguished by its relative coherence, articulation, and internal consistency. An ideology also contains a statement of desired ends to be attained or defended (such as a classless society or the political equality of women) and assumptions about the nature of human beings and the kind of society that best suits them.

Ideologies are not necessarily highly articulated. Studies indicate that few people subscribe to a well-articulated belief system with major ideas and attitudes that are consistent (see Converse 1964; Abercrombie et al. 1980). As we will see below, such belief systems are usually spelled out by intellectuals, while other people vary in the consistency, completeness, and intensity of their beliefs.

What Ideologies Contain

Ideologies contain an interpretation of the world and how it arrived at its present shape. Thus, Karl Marx wrote in 1859 in his famous *Preface to a Contribution to the Critique of Political Economy*: "The mode of production of material life determines the general character of the social, political, and spiritual processes of life" (1956, p. 51). More importantly, however, ideologies contain a set of political values, a cluster of ultimate or sacred meanings, that are capable of evoking strong emotional responses in intended audiences. Words such as *blood, exploitation, soil, free enterprise, un-American,*

motherland, the toiling masses, democracy, struggle, or *colonialism,* make ideologies more intellectually satisfying, emotionally stirring, and politically potent than either isolated political opinions or factual interpretations of events (see Dowse and Hughes 1972; Shils 1968). Human beings react to what the eye sees or the ear hears from the perspective of pre-established categories. For example, the ear hears that "free enterprise is the only economic system that makes sense," but the Russian mind and the American mind process the same words in different ways because of differences in the conceptual categories that make up their differing ideologies.

What Ideologies Are Used For

History shows that highly ideological regimes and movements, such as Communist regimes and national liberation movements, make conscious and sophisticated use of symbols (both verbal and nonverbal, such as flags) to appeal to people's hearts and minds. Symbols are potent because they are capable of moving people to action. "Not criticism but revolution is the driving force of history. . . . The philosophers have only *interpreted* the world in different ways; the point is to *change* it" (Marx 1956, pp. 54, 69). In the words of sociologist Daniel Bell (1961, p. 394), ideology is "the conversion of ideas into social levers." Not only do ideologies provide explanations for the present sorry state of society and for human suffering, but they are capable of inspiring a baffled, demoralized and disunited public with solidarity, a sense of mission, and a readiness for action. One example is the myth of the general strike, an ultimate Armageddon that will bring down capitalism, that is a central theme of anarchist ideology (see Sorel 1950). Another example is the African ideology of negritude, which seeks to restore "black values in their truth and excellence" and to overthrow European values and institutions (see Feuer 1975, p. 8). In both cases, the ideology is not meant to be taken literally but to be used as a symbol for rallying the disunited European working class or the African masses.

An ideology may call for the preservation of an existing society against real or imaginary challenges. Both the United States and the Soviet Union rally their respective peoples around the flag to protect, in one case, democratic capitalism and, in the other case, communism. An ideology may also call for political and social change through either revolutionary or peaceful means. Often the ideology will call for the liberation of an oppressed nation, class, or minority group, which will then set an example and lead the way for the emancipation of all humanity (see Feuer 1975). Thus, Marx believed that through the emancipation of the proletariat humanity would be liberated. Today, some feminists claim that women's liberation will liberate men as well, and civil rights leaders assert that freedom for blacks is a precondition for freedom for all Americans. Because of their emphasis on the liberation of an oppressed group and eventually of humanity, some ideologies have been said to contain a "Mosaic myth" (Feuer 1975), after Moses, the liberator of the biblical Hebrews. Ideologies thus contain both particularistic and universalistic messages, that is, a message both for one special group and for all humankind.

How Ideologies Come About

Ideologies appeal to particular groups because they are born out of the historical experiences of those groups. Karl Marx was probably the first writer to call attention to the fact that all social and political thought is grounded in the material conditions of existence and, most importantly, in individuals' class position. "The totality of these relations of production constitutes the economic structure of society. . . . to which definite forms of social consciousness correspond. It is not the consciousness of men that determines their being, but on the contrary, their social being determines their consciousness" (Marx 1956, p. 51).

Marx did not distinguish between political ideology and all other ideas or forms of social consciousness—moral, religious, philosophical, or legal. In contemporary terms, these "forms of social consciousness" might include such diverse phenomena as the right-to-life or antiabortion movement, disco music, and analytic philosophy. All are ideological manifestations, and all are grounded in economic conditions.

According to Marx, the ideas of the economically dominant class will be the ruling ideas of the age. In capitalist societies, although two major classes—the bourgeoisie and the proletariat—contend for power, the bourgeoisie dominates. Not coincidentally, bourgeois ideas, such as the importance of free enterprise, are nearly universally accepted because the ruling class controls the means of disseminating ideas (such as the schools and the press) and can manipulate members of other classes into adopting its particular ideology (see Abercrombie et al. 1980; see also chapter 5).

Marx believed that while the ideas of his adversaries, the bourgeoisie, were ideologically distorted, the ideas of the working class (namely, Marxism) were universally valid. According to Marx, the bourgeoisie represented a mode of consciousness that no longer corresponded to the changing economic and social realities. The proletariat, on the other hand, represented the wave of the future and the true course of humankind, not just the narrow interests of one class (for a critique of this contradiction, see Gouldner 1980).

It remained for sociologist Karl Mannheim (1893–1945) to analyze more even-handedly the questions of ideology, bias, and objective truth (see Sherman 1976). In his famous book *Ideology and Utopia*, published in 1936, Mannheim explained that ideology was originally a derogatory epithet used to discredit ideas by discounting the motives of an adversary. The first to use the term *ideology* in this sense was the Emperor Napoleon, who, wishing to discredit those who opposed his imperial ambitions, labeled them *ideologists*. Thus, the term *ideological* came to signify positions that were narrowly and viciously dogmatic (Mannheim 1936, p. 72). Gradually, not conscious distortion but unconscious bias came to be attributed to the adversary. In any case, ideas opposed to one's own were not to be taken at face value but rather were to be interpreted as witting or unwitting reflections of the socioeconomic circumstances of their proponents.

Mannheim's ingenious contribution was to treat all forms of political consciousness, not only that of the adversary, as a product of the concrete social and economic forces—historical period, nation, class, or ethnic group—that shaped them. To be sure, he never specified the exact nature of that shaping, for example, whether it implies a one-to-one correspondence between socioeconomic circumstances and ideas or a loose influence of the former on the latter (see Merton 1968). In any case, the focus now shifts from trading epithets and denouncing motives to examining the relationships between ideas and their social contexts. When the relativity of all knowledge is thus acknowledged, ideology gives place to the sociology of knowledge. Modern sociologists accept the notion that all knowledge, and particularly political ideology, is shaped by the socioeconomic circumstances of a given group of people.

Among the circumstances that give rise to ideologies are those of nation and class. In the early nineteenth century, Mannheim writes, the nation became the focus of attention not only to historians and publicists but to politicians, musicians, and painters as well. The historical experiences of nations were believed to have given rise to ideas, outlooks, and values (in short, to consciousness). Nationalist ideologies were born, as well as nationalist art, music, and literature. Tchaikovsky's *1812 Overture* is an example of nationalism in music; Garibaldi's wars to unify Italy are an example of nationalism in politics.

As the nineteenth century progressed, class replaced nation as the bearer of historical consciousness. While the best-known example of class-based ideology is Marxism, the ideology of the working class, other examples abound. Political sociologist Seymour Martin Lipset prefaces his analysis of ideologies with a statement about the "logical relationships between ideology and social base" in democratic countries:

> The socialist left derives its strength from manual workers and the poorer rural strata; the conservative right is backed by the rather well-to-do elements—owners of large industry and farms, the managerial and free professional strata—and those segments of the less privileged groups who have remained involved in traditional institutions, particularly the church. The democratic center is backed by the middle classes, especially small businessmen, white-collar workers and the anticlerical sections of the professional classes. (Lipset 1981, p. 129)

Mannheim believed that just as social-structural divisions give rise to ideas, ideas could shape the social structure, that is, the social conditions of our lives. To disbelieve this would make the concept of democracy an absurdity, and Mannheim was not only a fierce opponent of the absurd—he was also an ardent democrat (Sherman and Scimecca 1984).

The Role of the Intellectuals

Mannheim made yet another major contribution to the understanding of ideology. While ascribing different ideologies to different socioeconomic or national groups, he called attention to the unique role of one particular group, the intelligentsia (loosely translated as the intellectuals). Intellectuals, more than most people, travel through different social circles and thus gain a broader perspective on many issues. Also, they study at universities, where they have a better opportunity to have their ideas challenged. As a result of these two processes, they are more likely to become marginal to their own class. Because they are déclassé, that is, the alienated descendants of varied social groups, and because their education and social situation enable them to transcend the narrow boundaries of their upbringing, intellectuals may escape socioeconomic determination. Not only do they sometimes become the self-appointed ideologues of other classes or groups, but they are likely to be more arduous, more articulate, and more dogmatic than the members of those groups themselves (see Mannheim 1936).

⚡A generation after Mannheim's *Ideology and Utopia* was published, the power of intellectuals to transcend the limitations of private circumstances and "to understand the larger historical scene" was heralded by C. Wright Mills (1959) as the essence of the sociological imagination. Others, however, consider intellectuals to be a social class like all others and to hold ideas that are neither less biased nor less motivated by self-interest than those of other groups (see Gouldner 1979). In either case, there is no doubt that the intellectuals are the most articulate and most influential proponents of any ideology.

Ideas that are well articulated, properly timed, and delivered by recognizable authorities are powerful when legitimated by their intended audience. Because ideologies formulated by intellectual elites resonate at least as loudly as public opinion polls in the halls of power, men and women of ideas have enjoyed considerable political influence. As one observer of both the intellectual and the political scenes notes, "intellectuals serve as advisers to office holders and political candidates, write speeches, propose programs, draft legislation, serve on special commissions. The mass media amplify their ideas to a wider public, though not without considerable distortion. . . . They enjoy dinners at the White House, their advice is both solicited and volunteered on government programs and campaign positions" (Steinfels 1979, p. 9).

Even if they do not actually hold positions of power, the influence of intellectuals is considerable. If they are within the political mainstream, they are called on to place both their specialized expertise and their general ideas in the service of power holders. As "traffickers in symbols," they propose agendas for public policy, legitimate actual or proposed courses of action by linking them with society's values and symbols, and sound the alarm when their cherished values (such as the Protestant work ethic, the merit principle, or the nuclear family) are being threatened. If they are for a time at the fringes of the mainstream or even outside it, they still influence considerable numbers of people and eventually may see their ideas win wide acceptance.

Presidential candidates rely heavily on "idea collectors" or "issue managers," who are charged with keeping up with the ideas of other intellectuals and conveying them to the candidate. As political reporter Richard Reeves notes:

> Ideas have always been important in campaigns, but in recent years they have often dominated elections, essentially replacing party identification as the banners under which candidates run. As the words "Republican" and "Democrat" have come to mean less to voters, and "conservative" and "liberal" labels have been rejected by candidates, politicians . . . have tried to associate themselves not with traditional labels but with a set of ideas, usually presented as new. (Reeves 1984, p. 28)

Irving Kristol, editor of *The Public Interest*, a journal whose avowed aim is to inject ideas into public policy debates, claims that "the political system became more and more sensitive to ideas as party discipline became weaker. . . . This is an intellectually turbulent time in politics. The decay of the old consensus—the liberal consensus—was bound to generate ideas. At the same time, since World War II, there was a spectacular rise in media that were hungry for anything 'new.' So you have politicians desperately searching to find new ideas" (quoted in Reeves 1984, p. 28). Among the new ideas picked up by politicians in the 1980s were supply-side economics and industrial policy.

People exert more power when they form groups that are backed by substantial resources than when they act alone, and intellectuals are no exception. Several "think tanks"—centers for policy research and analysis—have influenced public policy in recent years. Among the better-known ones are the Hoover Institution, the American Enterprise Institute, the Heritage Foundation, the Brookings Institution, and the Institute for Policy Studies. So many of these think tanks are concentrated in the nation's capital that sociologist Amitai Etzioni (1985) has referred to the capital as "Washington Metropolitan University."

We turn now to an examination of some major ideologies, the historical circumstances that gave rise to them, and their role in today's politics.

Conservatism

The label *conservatism* covers such diverse, often inconsistent points of view that it can be described only with difficulty as a single integrated ideology. Conservatives often point out gleefully that their ideas defy precise labels. One conservative writes proudly:

> I doubt that there is any single satisfactory, all-encompassing definition of the complex phenomenon called conservatism, the content of which varies enormously with time and place. It may even be true that conservatism is inherently resistant to precise definition. Many right-wingers, in fact, have argued that conservatism is not an elaborate ideology at all. (Nash 1976, pp. xiv–xv)

Conservative thought spans two centuries and at least two continents, Europe and America. Two major strands of conservative thought can be distinguished: (1) classical and aristocratic and (2) contemporary and democratic. We contend that, despite their differences, these strands share an overriding similarity—a passionate defense of existing social arrangements and traditional values against unwarranted change.

Aristocratic Conservatism: The Defense of Authority

Karl Mannheim analyzed classical European conservatism in his 1927 essay "Conservative Thought" (Mannheim 1971, 1985; see also Kettler et al. 1984). According to his account, conservatism arose in Germany, France, and England in the late eighteenth and the nine-

teenth centuries as a response of the old order to the economic, political, and ideological blows of the Enlightenment, the French Revolution, and the industrial revolution.

What was the nature of the new forces that threatened the old order? Newly emergent social classes, namely, businessmen, industrialists, and factory workers, were gaining economic and political ascendancy. New institutions were also emerging: commercial agriculture, factories, international trade, and democratic governments. These developments were justified and supported by powerful ideas: the belief in the dignity and importance of the individual; in the power of science and industry to solve age-old ills such as disease, war, ignorance, and oppression; and in the right of all people to govern themselves. Rising against these revolutionary realities were the groups that had the largest stake in the old order: the monarchy, the feudal aristocracy, and the church. They were joined by socially unattached intelligentsia, the philosophers, artists, and poets of the day. Concomitantly with the conservative movement in political thought, the intellectuals and artists of the late eighteenth and early nineteenth century developed the romantic movement in art. In painting, music, and poetry, the romantics emphasized feeling over reason, passion over rigid form, religious and national themes over moral or aesthetic ones.

Initially, conservatism was viewed by its proponents not as an articulated ideology but as a way of life accepted and unquestioned from time immemorial. Conservatism emerges as a conscious, articulate political ideology only "when other ways of life and thought appear on the scene, against which it is compelled to take up arms in the ideological struggle" (Mannheim 1971, p. 173). Conservatives typically deny that their system is "ideological," that is, based on abstract rational principles. To the rationality of progressive thought they oppose "the irrationality of reality," and they extoll "the external praise of practice as opposed to theory. . . . The conservatives replace Reason with concepts such as History, Life, the Nation" (Mannheim 1971, pp. 175, 199).

While progressive thought posits "what could be" or "what should be" as criteria for evaluating present institutions and transforming them, conservative thought staunchly defends "what is." Institutions that have evolved organically through the centuries, particularly the state, the church, the family, and the aristocratic order, are viewed not only as workable but as superior. In the words of F. J. C. Hearnshaw (1869–1946), a British conservative:

> The conservative reveres the past, not for its own sake, but for the sake of the present, and the future. He feels instinctively that the accumulated wisdom and experience of the countless generations gone is more likely to be right than the passing fashion of the moment. He believes that . . . a long process of trial and rejection has purified [past] creations from error and made them fit for their appointed work. He realizes, moreover, that it is much easier to destroy than to construct; that a cathedral that took a century to build can be burned down in a night; that an institution that has evolved during a thousand years can be ruined by a single injudicious reform. He stands for the universal and permanent things of life; for the ancient traditions of the race; for the fundamental laws of his people; for established customs; for the family; for property; for the church; for the constitution; for the great heritage of Christian civilization in general. (Hearnshaw 1933, p. 22)

Religion plays a key role in conservative thought; it legitimates authority and upholds order, two things very dear to the hearts of conservatives. In fact, for classical conservatives, the "good old days" refer above all to the Middle Ages, before secularism, modernity, and democracy spoiled things forever.

> Those were lovely, glorious times when Europe was a Christian country; when *one* Christendom inhabited this human corner of the world; when *one* great bond of common interest joined the remotest provinces of this far-flung spiritual realm. (Novalis, "Christendom or Europe," quoted in Mannheim 1971, p. 198)

Before modern times, the community, not the individual, was the source of rights and freedoms, the focus of history, the sacred embodiment of authority. "Individuals are to be understood only as parts of wider whole. . . . The conservative thinks in terms of 'We' when the liberal thinks in terms of 'I' " (Mannheim 1971, p. 170). The community may be an estate, a corporation, a family, a nation, or a church. All organic communities are rooted in the soil, which is not only the basic form of property and the major means of production but the basis of individual identity, of rights and privileges, including the right to participate in government.

Conservatives insist that human beings "are essentially *unequal*, unequal in their gifts and abilities, and unequal to the very core of their beings. Freedom, therefore, can only consist in the ability of each man to develop without let or hindrance according to the law and principle of his own personality. . . . Nothing could be more inimical to freedom . . . than the concept of an external equality" (Mannheim 1971, p. 164).

From the assumption of inherent inequality to the advocacy of aristocratic rule is but a short step. The British writer and politician Edmund Burke (1729–1797), whose book *Reflections on the Revolution in France* (1790) is considered the beginning of conservative thought, emphasized the superior qualities of the "natural aristocracy," such as good breeding, innate wisdom, and the habit of commanding, and insisted that the aristocracy must lead and enlighten the weaker, less fortunate, and more ignorant masses. Such views of natural inequality are fundamentally opposed to democratic ideals and institutions. Indeed, Burke was passionately opposed to the democratic influences of the French Revolution.

Democratic Conservatism: The Defense of Inequality

Classical conservatism, although a major force in European politics, has been largely absent in America. One explanation for its absence is that the social class most likely to support such an outlook, the feudal aristocracy, has never existed in this country (Hartz 1955). The institutions and principles that conservative intellectuals in America have felt compelled to defend are liberal institutions and principles, including laissez-faire capitalism, a constitutional government, protection of individual rights and liberties, social innovation, and a commitment to technological progress and rational problem solving (Wolin 1976; Weisman 1980). As Peter Viereck, a contemporary conservative, has noted, "Conservative continuity with our liberal past simply means that you cannot escape from history; history has provided America with a shared liberal-conservative base more liberal than European Continental conservatives, more conservative than European Continental liberals" (Viereck 1964, p. 188). Today, however, an important part of the liberal-conservative consensus, namely, the acceptance of the welfare state, is breaking down.

If anything links American conservatives with those of other times and places and at the same time distinguishes them from liberals, it is their passionate defense of the existing order against proposed or recently implemented change. Conservatives, from Edmund Burke to William F. Buckley, consciously prefer the evils of the known to the terrors of the unknown. Conservative sociologist Edward Shils (1981), for example, argues that progressivism has gone too far in condemning all tradition as an obstacle to progress, in attempting to impose rational, abstract principles on all aspects of life, and in using these principles as guidelines for social change. Shils advocates a return to traditions and sees them as valid guides for the present. Traditions, he believes, represent a complex array of events and actions that have become incorporated into such institutions as the family, the church, political parties, art, science, and technology. Because they represent the accumulated wisdom of the ages and have been arrived at by the trial and error of many generations, they must not be tampered with

unthinkingly. In place of what he views as the excessive individualism of modern societies, Shils would like to see a return to "moderate individualism" backed by the best traditions of the past.

Beyond a simple defense of the existing social order, contemporary conservatives share similar views on many issues and subscribe to common principles. First, conservatives share a strong belief that the United States must regain its position of leadership in the world to counterbalance the intensifying Communist threat. Reverting to the anti-Communist rhetoric of the Cold War, many writers call for higher military spending and a more interventionist foreign policy. They denounce what they see as the evils of communism, including foreign imperialism, political repression, and economic inefficiency, and often oppose arms limitation agreements.

Second, conservatives advocate reducing the role of government wherever possible. They label the Great Society programs of the 1960s and even the New Deal programs of the 1930s a "liberal megalomania" and blame both "excessive public demands" and "bureaucratic arrogance" for governmental overspending. The term *excessive public demands* refers to an alleged feeling on the part of many segments of the population (particularly minorities and welfare recipients) that they are entitled to public benefits (including welfare, medical care, or a college education) regardless of merit or effort on their part. "Bureaucratic arrogance" refers to the alleged overconfidence of public officials that, given enough money and programs, the government can solve all social problems, from cultural deprivation among preschoolers to job discrimination. Thus, in the conservative view, excessive public demands combine with bureaucratic arrogance to produce governmental overspending. The governmental overload fuels the deficit, undermines the government's credibility, and stifles individual initiative.

From the point of view of democratic conservatism, governmental intervention is doomed to failure not only because it promises too much but also because it is wrong in principle. Poverty, discrimination, and inequality have been a part of human society since time immemorial and cannot be eradicated by governmental edict. Furthermore, inequality—the chance to do better than one's parents or neighbors—is an indispensable incentive to hard work and an essential ingredient of the American dream. Thus, welfare payments reduce the incentive to work and encourage the poor to have more children than they can support. In general, conservatives warn that egalitarian government programs undermine the nation's moral fiber (see Gilder 1981; Murray 1984). In the words of William J. Baroody, Jr., former president of the American Enterprise Institute (AEI), "For 40 years public policy had been dominated by a single idea: Whatever the individual cannot do for himself or herself it is the responsibility and social obligation of the government to do. . . . We set out to challenge that consensus." Among the conclusions of the AEI: "Alternative mechanisms to the federal government are possible to provide welfare-state services. Neighborhood. Church. Voluntary Association" (quoted in Reeves 1984, p. 29).

This position has been criticized on several grounds. Analysts have shown that the rise in the number of families on welfare has coincided with an erosion in the real value of welfare benefits. It is unlikely, therefore, that economic incentives—governmental payments—encourage individuals to go on welfare. In fact, the percentage of the population below the poverty line declined during the Great Society years and has risen since the late 1970s in direct proportion to the cutbacks in governmental spending (see Harrington 1984; see also chapter 4).

The Moral Majority and the New Right

The conservative resurgence of the 1980s has resulted in the rise of new conservative organizations and alliances, known collectively as

the New Right. The so-called New Right shares with its predecessor (now known as the Old Right) a defense of tradition, a desire to reduce the role of government in the economy and in social programs, anticommunism, and support for a strong American defense posture. It departs from the Old Right in its views on the role of religion in American society. Such New Right organizations as the Moral Majority, founded by Reverend Jerry Falwell and renamed the Liberty Federation in 1986, seek to imbue political and educational institutions with Christian values. Although the precise content of beliefs varies, many New Right supporters would like to see abortion outlawed, creation taught along with evolution in the public schools, and homosexuals denied civil rights—all positions presumably grounded in biblical authority.

Some analysts claim that the New Right represents a cultural transformation comparable to the "great awakening" religious movements that have swept America in the past (see Liebman and Wuthnow 1983). Despite the claims of the Moral Majority to have broad-based support in all reaches of the population, however, there is evidence that its support is exaggerated and comes disproportionately from fundamentalist Christian circles (see Shupe and Stacey 1982).

Whatever the magnitude of its constituency, the New Right has had an undeniable influence on American government in the 1980s. This influence is buttressed by an array of conservative think tanks supported by major corporations and private financiers such as Exxon, Dow, Chase Manhattan, and Joseph Coors (see Reeves 1984). Thus, the populist elements of the New Right are galvanized and fostered by a powerful array of elite-backed institutions (see chapter 9).

Contemporary conservatism absorbed much from early liberalism. The defense of individual liberties, free enterprise, and limited government lies at the heart of classical liberal doctrine. Today, while liberals have moved beyond this doctrine to advocate more governmental intervention and more equality, contemporary conservatives advocate a reduction in governmental programs and a return to unbridled free enterprise. Many writers feel that the mainstream American political heritage is relatively consensual and that both conservatives and liberals are defending the same institutions. As we will see in the next section, however, the principles behind conservative and liberal positions and the policies derived from them diverge widely.

Liberalism

First articulated by English thinkers in the seventeenth and eighteenth centuries, liberalism developed in its most unimpeded, most complete form in the United States. Like conservatives, liberals often claim that their thinking is not ideological but pragmatic. Indeed, liberal formulations are so diverse in emphasis and tone that one modern commentator asks, "Will the real Liberalism please stand up?" (Bluhm 1974, p. 61). Nevertheless, there are many similarities between the two major strands of liberalism: classical European liberalism and twentieth-century American liberalism.

Classical Liberalism: The Defense of Limited Government

Classical liberalism has been described as the ideological weapon of the capitalist class that in the seventeenth and eighteenth centuries transformed Europe and the American colonies from agrarian to industrial societies (see Girvetz 1963). Yet the early proponents of liberalism claimed that its principles were universal and that its validity transcended class or national lines.

Early liberals emphasized above all the importance of individual freedom. Individualism was, in fact, the "metaphysical core" of liberalism (Arblaster 1984, p. 15). Liberal thinkers agreed that individual freedom presumes pluralism, a system in which a range of different values is allowed to flourish so long as none of them seeks to exclude the others (see Seidman 1983). Freedom of religion, freedom of expression, and freedom of trade thus emerged as leading themes. Following Locke (see chapter 2), liberals called for limiting the authority of government, which in the previous centuries had been absolute, to the role of a night watchman who merely protects individuals against transgressors. Life, liberty, and the right to property were believed to be natural human rights that had existed in the state of nature before the beginnings of government. The principal purpose for which governments were instituted was to protect these rights, and any government that arbitrarily failed to do so forfeited its legitimacy and needed to be replaced. As John Stuart Mill (1806–1873), an eloquent proponent of classical liberalism, wrote in 1859:

> This, then, is the appropriate region of human liberty. It comprises, first, the inward domain of consciousness, demanding liberty of conscience in the most comprehensive sense, liberty of thought and feeling, absolute freedom of opinion and sentiment on all subjects. The liberty of expressing and publishing opinions . . . is practically inseparable from [liberty of thought]. Secondly, the principle requires liberty of tastes and pursuits, of framing the plan of our lives to suit our own character, of doing as we like, subject to such consequences as may follow, without impediment from our fellow creatures, so long as what we do does not harm them. . . . Thirdly, the liberty . . . of combination among individuals; freedom to unite for any purpose not involving harm to others. . . . No society in which these liberties are not, on the whole, respected, is free, whatever may be its form of government. (Mill 1956, p. 16)

Mill specified very strict limits for governmental intervention:

> The sole end for which mankind are war-
> ranted, individually or collectively, in inter-
> fering with the liberty of action of any of
> their number is self-protection. . . . The only
> purpose for which power can be rightfully
> exercised over any member of a civilized
> community, against his will, is to prevent
> harm to others. His own good, either physi-
> cal or moral, is not a sufficient warrant. (Mill
> 1956, p. 13)

Alcohol and drug laws provide an illustration
of Mill's thesis. According to Mill, the government may not prohibit or even regulate the sale
of alcohol or drugs—even useless, adulterated
or narcotic drugs—to any persons of legal age.
That such restrictions are for people's own good
is not a valid argument. Only if the drunken
or drugged person is endangering others, for
example, when driving, may society intervene.

Like the *philosophes* of the eighteenth century (see chapter 2), classical liberals believed
that individuals could and should govern
themselves through reason and not be governed by fear or external coercion. Unlike early
conservatives, whose view of human nature was
fundamentally pessimistic, liberals believed in
the essential goodness and perfectibility of
human beings. Thomas Jefferson wrote in 1816:
"I sincerely believe . . . that morality, compassion, generosity, are innate elements of the
human constitution" (Padover 1939, p. 18).

Liberals extend their optimism about human
nature to society as a whole and view change
as progress. Peaceful change in all spheres—
technological, social, educational, economic,
and political—is viewed as leading to improvements in well-being, to an enhancement of
human dignity, and eventually to a triumph
over such old enemies of humanity as disease,
war, and poverty (for a history of the idea of
progress, see Nisbet 1980).

Coupled with the political doctrine of limited government is the economic doctrine of
laissez-faire capitalism. In the absence of all
external restrictions and regulations, early liberals argued, individuals would be motivated

to pursue their own profits, thus incidentally
maximizing the wealth of society as a whole.
Since unhampered free enterprise worked to
the benefit of one and all, the rational interests
of individuals were seen as ultimately compatible with the welfare of society as a whole.

To guarantee individual liberty and freedom
from arbitrary authority, liberals sought to limit
the powers of government through various legal
devices. Governments were to be elected by
the people, held accountable to them, and regulated by an elaborate system of checks and
balances. Constitutions and bills of rights were
enacted to protect individuals from governmental encroachment. The principles of classical liberalism led to modern democratic governments in the United States, in England, and
briefly in France after the French Revolution.
Elsewhere in Europe, however, liberal reforms
failed to take hold until the late nineteenth or
even the twentieth century.

Nowhere did classical liberalism flourish
more vigorously than in the United States. Several writers have called attention to the fact that
the chief tenets of liberalism—free enterprise,
limited government, and individual freedom
—have become so embedded both in our consciousness and in our institutions that we have
often taken them for granted (see Tocqueville
1951; Trilling 1954; Boorstin 1953; Hartz 1955;
and Bell 1961). These writers claim that our ideological consensus has been so pervasive that
even American conservatives, from Senator
Barry Goldwater to Nobel Prize–winning economist Milton Friedman, have claimed to be the
true heirs of the liberal traditions of Jefferson
and Adams. Despite similar origins, however,
contemporary liberals are distinctly different
from their conservative counterparts.

Modern Liberalism: The Defense of the Welfare State

The limitations of classical liberalism became
glaringly obvious in the late-nineteenth century and even more so in the twentieth century

(see Sherman and Femminella 1984). In industrialized democracies such as England and the United States, giant private corporations ascended to positions of unprecedented power and replaced tyrannical government as the chief perceived threat to individual freedom. Far from diminishing in the wake of the new industrial order, violence and misery seemed to increase, particularly in the ranks of the new urban working classes. The earlier naive faith in the ultimate reason and resourcefulness of all men and women and in their ability to take care of themselves with minimal interference by the government now seemed unjustified. The poor and the working class proved incapable of defending their own interests in the unequal struggle against industrial magnates. Free enterprise and the night-watchman state apparently provided conditions not for the maximum well-being of all but for the exploitation of the many by the few, the creation of powerful monopolies, and the periodic devastation of the business cycle. It became clear that in the age of the mighty private corporation, the doctrines of extreme individualism and the night-watchman state would have to be either abandoned or modified.

The contemporary liberal recognizes the role of government in restraining the exploiting tendencies of big business and in protecting individual welfare and thus favors governmental intervention and regulation of big business. "The new Liberal puts less emphasis on property rights than did the Classical Liberal. . . . He emphasizes human rights over property rights and supports programs of social security designed to alleviate the economic hazards of illness, accident and old age. He champions the right of every man to employment commensurate with his abilities and insists on the right to equal education for all" (Bluhm 1974, p. 64). The contemporary liberal also recognizes the need for associations such as labor unions and consumer organizations to protect the rights of individuals, because individuals cannot protect their own rights vis-à-vis big

business on their own. In short, modern liberals view government intervention as indispensable if the major tenets of classical liberalism—individual dignity and freedom—are to be preserved in the modern world.

Some expressions of liberalism overlap democratic socialism. As long ago as 1911, political philosopher L. T. Hobhouse, in a short treatise titled *Liberalism*, argued that the welfare state is a necessary precondition of true individualism. Hobhouse (1964) extols liberalism as the force of life and history, the clearing of obstruction so that human dignity can flow spontaneously. Not merely technological progress but the progressive liberation of the human spirit, the idea of growth, is at the heart of Hobhouse's conception of liberalism. Not the right of one person to be left alone by the other but the right of all people to be treated with decency and dignity is the real liberty.

The role of the state, Hobhouse continues, is to create the conditions necessary for personal growth and self-fulfillment, including freedom from external compulsion, whether public (governmental) or private (capitalist). But more than that, these conditions include protection from extreme want and a guaranteed base upon which the individual can build a decent standard of living. The state should provide not only free education but also free health care, old age pensions, and unemployment insurance. Freedom from economic insecurity is necessary in order for individuals to take care of their own needs. This cushion does not stifle motivation but provides incentive for self-help. It is not charity but justice, because all members of society have a right to share in the resources that are ultimately created by society, even if this entails taxing away some of the profits of corporations and wealthy individuals.

Hobhouse, then, argues that the welfare state is necessary if the liberal democratic state is to survive. The welfare state provides the foundation for personal growth, well-being, and self-government for all people and enables individuals to compete as equals in the free market economy by partially compensating for the initial disadvantages faced by the poor.

More recent liberals, from British economist John Maynard Keynes (1883–1946) to American economist John Kenneth Galbraith, have reiterated these themes. They emphasize that, aside from those needs that individuals who are motivated by the pursuit of profit can best provide for themselves, the government must provide for needs that will otherwise go unmet. These social needs range from the central collection and dissemination of economic data to the regulation of industrial pollution and the guarantee of a minimum standard of living for the needy. An enlightened social policy, they stress, far from undermining the foundations of capitalism, is necessary for capitalism to survive. It does not weaken but reinvigorates the free market economy (see Keynes 1936; Galbraith 1978).

Thus, contemporary liberals adhere to the same principles of individual self-fulfillment and self-management as their predecessors, but their view of the conditions required to support these principles has changed. They now believe that limited capitalism and the welfare state, not complete laissez-faire and government noninterference, comprise the best society.

Liberalism has been criticized for the alleged irrelevance of its ideas to the problems of the 1980s—limited economic growth and the dislocations caused by the transition from an economy based on heavy industry to one based on communications and high technology. After decades of ascendancy followed by a decline, liberalism is again undergoing a transformation. The so-called new liberalism or neoliberalism of the 1980s has emerged out of a background of popular disenchantment with governmental programs and regulations. While maintaining the traditional goals of social justice and equal opportunity, liberals today emphasize economic growth, not government programs, as the key to achieving these goals. In an economy based on information and new

technologies rather than on mass-production industries, the new liberal program emphasizes three major themes: public and private investment designed to promote technological innovation and employment in high-tech industries; reliance on the free market rather than on government intervention to guide economic growth; and cooperation among labor, management, and government instead of the traditional interest-group conflicts. Politically, this agenda translates into a call for an industrial policy, a simplified tax structure designed to encourage investment, a more cost-effective defense system, and a Japanese model of labor-management cooperation (see Rothenberg 1984).

Traditional liberalism has been criticized not only for supporting extravagant governmental programs but also for allegedly championing the interests of some segments of society (particularly the poor, the working class, and minority groups) at the expense of the white middle and upper classes. The new liberalism, on the other hand, has been criticized for neglecting the interests of minorities and the poor as well as those of another traditionally liberal constituency, organized labor. Some critics charge that the new liberalism uses the guise of universal economic principles and the national interest to promote the special interests of the very class that has shaped it, the professional upper middle class. Clearly, the new liberalism, like other ideologies, is class-based.

Liberalism, both old and new, has been criticized from the left by socialists and other radicals and from the right by conservatives. Radicals claim that liberals, while paying lip service to the ideals of social justice and equality, accept the capitalist system and wish merely to clean up some of its most flagrant injustices and inequalities. Radicals, on the other hand, hold injustice and inequality to be inherent in the very structure of capitalism and wish to replace the whole economic system with one more conducive to human well-being. The radical position is examined below.

Socialism: Old and New Left

In the 1980s, the fiery speeches, mass demonstrations, draft card burnings, and seething rage that characterized the New Left in the 1960s are a distant, almost forgotten thunder. Whether the Movement, as the New Left came to be called, will be revived in the future remains to be seen. Although the Old Left, comprised of democratic socialist parties as well as Communist parties, time and again has been pronounced dead in the United States, it has continued to thrive in Europe, Asia, and Latin America. In the United States today, several small socialist and Communist parties continue to provide a left-wing alternative to traditional politics.

Democratic Socialism

Modern socialism emerged in the early nineteenth century, when idealistic, highly educated men and women in France, England, the United States, and even Russia were proposing blueprints for utopian societies. They thought that all that was needed to usher in the perfect society of the future was a sufficient number of highly motivated volunteers and generous financial backing. The proposed utopias differed in specific details but agreed on overall objectives—nothing less than the eternal peace, happiness, and prosperity of humankind. Some utopian societies were to be based on an equal distribution of wealth; others would preserve inequality but guarantee to all a fair share in the midst of abundance. Some were opposed to all religion; others incorporated religion into their vision of the good society. Some planned to abolish the nuclear family as an exploitative, outdated institution; others preferred to preserve traditional marriage but rear all children communally. At least one utopian community, Oneida in central New York State, successfully substituted "complex marriage" (free love), coupled with communal child rearing, for the detested conventional nuclear family.

Typical of the utopian socialists were the Welshman Robert Owen (1771–1858) and the Frenchman Charles Fourier (1772–1837). On July 4, 1826, the semicentennial anniversary of the United States, Owen issued "A Declaration of Mental Independence" from the three oppressors of humanity: private property, religion, and marriage. Fourier was even more radical a dreamer. He believed that his utopian communities, known as "phalanges," would produce such a perfect society that its members would live to a healthy 140 years of age and need only five hours of sleep a night (see Wilson 1953). A few of these dreamers, including Owen, lived to implement their ideas and form actual socialist communes, most of which were short-lived. Today, the socialist dream survives in a much more down-to-earth form both in communes scattered around the United States and in the Israeli kibbutz (collective settlement), an amalgam of utopian socialism, Marxism, and Zionism.

In the mid-nineteenth century, Karl Marx and Friedrich Engels transformed socialism from "utopian" to "scientific" form (their terms). Instead of blaming misguided human nature and wrong-headed ideas for evils past and present, they emphasized the iron laws of economics: the historical expropriation of the means of production by the owning class and the consequent exploitation of the working class. Instead of the harmonious interests of individuals in society, they spoke of class conflict. Instead of peaceful solutions to human misery, they predicted a revolution. During the revolution, they claimed, the working class would seize the means of production, abolish private property (and with it the exploitation of the masses by the few), and eventually, after a transitional "dictatorship of the proletariat," usher in a classless society. In this society, unprecedented economic abundance, social justice, the collective ownership of property, and international peace would make possible at last a true flowering of human nature and the well-being of all society's members (see Marx 1956; see also chapter 3).

Marxism gave rise to several brands of socialism, including Leninism, Maoism, anarcho-syndicalism, and democratic socialism, all claiming more or less direct allegiance to the master. Leninism's contributions to Marxist doctrine were twofold. First, Lenin forged a revolutionary party based on a nucleus of professional revolutionaries drawn from the intelligentsia rather than on a mass working-class following. Second, by successfully fomenting a revolution in Russia, a precapitalist, nonindustrialized country, he demonstrated that voluntary human intervention can change the laws of history. Maoism's contribution was to base the revolutionary movement on the peasantry rather than on the industrial proletariat. Maoism is viewed by some as more applicable than orthodox Marxism to Third World nations, which are overwhelmingly rural (for more on peasant revolutions, see chapter 13). The anarcho-syndicalists believed in direct action by the workers, to culminate in a spontaneous general strike that would bring down the government and free labor from the yoke of capitalism (see Sorel 1950). The democratic socialist alternative is embodied in socialist parties in Europe and the United States.

In Europe, Social Democratic parties grew in numbers and in strength throughout the nineteenth and twentieth centuries. Although they varied in specific details, all emphasized the following themes: public ownership of the means of production so profits can accrue to the workers rather than to the capitalists, cooperative rather than competitive social organization, a social policy that provides a minimum standard of living through universal social services such as housing and medical care, and the right to full employment through government planning of the economy.

Over the years, realizing that they could achieve most of their aims through peaceful democratic means, Social Democratic parties gradually abandoned their revolutionary rhetoric and settled for a reformist approach to politics. They also largely abandoned their quest for complete public ownership of industry, concentrating instead on other, more moderate means of equalizing income, such as progressive taxation. Accepted as a legitimate part of the political spectrum since World War I, Social Democratic parties have held power for various durations in England, Germany, Austria, and Scandinavia (see Denitch 1981; Stephens 1980; Lindemann 1983).

Organized socialism first came to the United States in the 1870s. The first movement, the Socialist Labor party, was too dogmatic and too narrowly Marxist to attract much following in this country outside the foreign-born community. Its successor, the Socialist party, founded in 1901, proved much more successful. Led by such highly respected established Americans as Norman Thomas and Eugene V. Debs, it was an organic outgrowth of the American democratic tradition. The Socialist party, which at its height in 1932 attracted nearly a million votes, appealed widely to native-born Americans, although a significant proportion of its membership was still foreign-born, comprised particularly of Jews and Finns (see Liebman 1979).

The Socialist party's program called for a wide array of social and economic reforms, including public control of utility companies and other basic industries, collective bargaining and the legal recognition of unions, publicly subsidized housing, national health insurance, minimum wage laws, and public assistance to the old, the needy, and the unemployed. In more recent times, realizing the overwhelming strength of capitalism in the United States and not wishing to make more enemies, the Socialist party has disavowed any intention of overthrowing capitalism and has become thoroughly reformist and democratic.

Many of the reforms called for by the Socialist party have been incorporated into the platform of the Democratic party and eventually into government programs. These reforms include the right to collective bargaining, minimum wage laws, and Medicare, among others. The incorporation of much of the socialist platform into mainstream politics, the harsh anti-Left sentiment of the Cold War and the

McCarthy years, and, more recently, the American public's swing to the right have accounted for the decline of the Socialist party and other left-wing movements in the United States.

Decline has not meant demise, however. In 1982, the Democratic Socialists of America (DSA), heir to the Socialist party, was organized by veteran socialist Michael Harrington and others. The DSA's program goes beyond support for the liberal welfare state. According to a recent political statement, its vision is one of "a humane social order based on popular control of resources and production, economic planning, equitable distribution, feminism, racial equality, and non-oppressive relationships." A broad vision of socialism, the DSA claims, goes beyond economic redistribution to reshape "the relationships between men and women, between whites and minorities, and between all of us and our environment." The DSA opposes "the claim of Communist countries to be socialist, [and is] committed to democracy as the only political means to achieve the economic and social power of the people." Although its long-term goal is to "create a majoritarian movement for democratic socialism," the DSA recognizes that in the near future it must concentrate on "the left wing of the possible," working for the most part within the confines of the Democratic party. A socialist movement, if it is to take root in the United States, "must grow out of existing traditions and institutions, building on what is positive in our heritage and on what is accessible in our political process" ("Where We Stand," 1982; Harrington 1972).

While, historically, support for socialism has come primarily from the industrial working class, in the United States this class has shown a strong allegiance to the capitalist system. One explanation for the absence of a socialist working-class movement in the United States is that the working class, although still victimized by recurring unemployment and demeaning jobs, has bought into the dominant capitalist ideology: laissez-faire, rugged individualism, and consumerism. Other observers claim that not the false consciousness of industrial workers but their economic dependence on capitalism, coupled with the pragmatic realization of the limits of political action, has led to acceptance of the present system (see Abercrombie et al. 1980; Hochschild 1981; Kann 1982; see also chapters 5, 9, and 11). Although socialists have followed the lead of the Republican and Democratic parties in appealing to a broad coalition of interests, including minority groups and women, socialist support comes disproportionately from the highly educated segments of the U.S. population.

The New Left

The New Left was born in the middle 1960s out of the civil rights movement, the Berkeley Free Speech Movement, and the anti–Vietnam War movement and declined with the general decrease of social activism in the 1970s. Centered loosely around such organizations as the Students for a Democratic Society (SDS) and the Student Nonviolent Coordinating Committee (SNCC), the New Left deliberately shunned ideology. "They wanted to have nothing to do with elaborate, highly unified, and rationalized schemes of utopian reform . . . which explain the whole of society" (Bluhm 1974, p. 180). Instead, they called for action. Depending on the beliefs of the particular member, "action" ranged from a peaceful transformation to a violent overthrow of the capitalist system. The New Left refused to specify the details of the society that would succeed capitalism, emphasizing instead the corrupt aspects of the present system and the fact that it had to go.

"The New Left is properly so called because in order to exist it had to overcome the memories, the certitudes, and the promises of the Old Left" (Oglesby 1969, p. 15). The New Left wanted to avoid the divorce of theory from action that they believed accounted for the deterioration into futility of the Old Left. "The instinct from the beginning was to discover the street, and there was nothing at all anti-intellectual about this. It embodied rather a refusal to tolerate the further separation of thought from its consequences; books argued with each other and lied and in any case did not make much of a difference; only direct experience was incontrovertible" (Oglesby 1969, p. 16).

The essence of the New Left was negation—the denunciation of the present ills of Western society. In addition to the burning issues of the day, the Vietnam War and racial discrimination, the New Left emphasized a theme from the early writings of Marx and Engels: the alienation of the individual in modern industrial society. To be sure, in the United States the working masses are no longer languishing in abject poverty as they were in Marx's day, but a new form of exploitation has come about. The people, deprived of real power to control their own lives and denied real freedom of thought or expression, are bribed into acquiescence by a false sense of economic security. The freedom to make consumer choices has replaced any genuine freedom to participate in decisions affecting one's life (see chapter 5). The individual is reduced to a powerless cog in the workplace, at school, and even during leisure time. This was the message embodied in philosopher Herbert Marcuse's celebrated book *One-Dimensional Man* (1964), a best-seller that stimulated and informed much of the student activism of the 1960s.

According to the thinking of the New Left, the process of bureaucratic dehumanization has overtaken all industrial societies, including the Soviet Union. Motivated by a desire to avoid the pitfalls of the Old Left (and especially of the Communist party), the New Left emphatically refused to idealize the Soviet Union or the dogmas of orthodox Marxism. Instead, it called for an entirely new society where self-fulfillment would replace technological efficiency as the supreme objective, genuine human relationships would replace racism and sexism, and participatory democracy would replace governmental repression. "Behind all this is the awareness, the feeling that one can live as a human being without running in the rat race, without performing dehumanizing jobs, the awareness of the repressive and destructive impact of the 'Consumer Society' " (Marcuse, in Gould and Truitt 1973, p. 335).

A major difference between the Old Left and the New Left concerns the question of who will bring about the new socialist order. The Marxist Old Left has always concentrated on the proletariat or working class as the agent of historical change. According to Marxism, the working class, the chief victim of capitalism, is expected to bring about the socialist revolution and create the classless society of the future. The New Left, however, inspired by the writings of C. Wright Mills as well as those of Marcuse, acknowledged that the working class was no longer a revolutionary class and looked instead to student activists, joined by oppressed groups such as racial minorities and the poor, for leadership in ushering in the new age.

As the 1960s drew to a close, the New Left splintered and countersplintered. Ironically, having deliberately shunned all theory as ideological, many elements of the movement now embraced ideologies that were largely inapplicable to American society, such as Maoism. The factions engaged in sectarian polemics that appeared sterile and trivial to many. More menacing than dogmatic sectarianism, however, were the increasingly violent tactics of some segments of the movement, notably the Weatherman faction of SDS. No longer satisfied with merely talking about the revolution, this group turned to bombings, burnings, and occasional killings in the name of the revolution. This development shocked and alienated many members of the movement. The beautiful dream had soured.

In 1970, the United States military invaded Cambodia, a peaceful country previously uninvolved in the Vietnam War. The protest demonstrations that ensued in this country were unprecedented in their scope and sense of outrage. At Kent State University in Ohio and at Jackson State University in Mississippi, unarmed students were killed by the National

Guard. This and other acts by the administration convinced many in the protest movement that the American government was too powerful to be overthrown by a handful of radical idealists. Shocked and disappointed, many gave up the cause as futile.

Other changes were taking place as the 1970s unfolded. The Vietnam War slowly wound down, the American economy entered a recession, and the job market tightened. Many young people turned their attention inward, to the task of finding a job or pursuing other personal concerns, and left to their elders the conduct of world affairs. All these changes—the increasing dogmatism and violence of segments of the New Left, the growing awareness of the intractability of the power structure, the end of the war, and the tightening job market—combined to speed the New Left into decline. The concerns of the 1970s and 1980s, it seems, left the rhetoric and tactics of the 1960s behind. Some observers, however, believe that the tradition of radical dissent is not dead; it reasserts itself today in protests against nuclear power and against apartheid in South Africa.

Who were the adherents of the New Left? All accounts agree that the New Left was predominantly campus-based, although there were sympathetic ripples throughout society. Overwhelmingly, the movement's members were college students, particularly students at elite east- and west-coast universities. Students with highly educated, middle-class parents were overrepresented, as were students with good academic standing, Jewish students, and students with no religion. Underrepresented were Catholics, students from working-class or poor backgrounds, and those attending commuter colleges. Disproportionate numbers of the New Left had parents whose politics were liberal or even radical (see Bluhm 1974; Liebman 1979).

The socioeconomic and political background of members of the New Left gives us important insights into the nature of the movement. First, the New Left was by no means a fringe movement whose followers were personally maladjusted or discontented, as many

of its detractors alleged, but a mainstream and often irresistible phenomenon on many campuses. Second, the members were scarcely engaging in adolescent rebellion against parental authority, as some critics claimed. In fact, they frequently had warm, loving relationships with their parents that were not disrupted by the students' unconventional politics. Third, far from formulating their own entirely new political beliefs, many of the leaders of the New Left had been socialized into left-wing politics by parents who were socialists or Communists. These were the so-called "red diaper babies" of the 1940s and 1950s. While the tactics and rhetoric differed from those of their parents, the basic political objectives and, above all, the humanitarian sentiments were the same. Although after the movement had gathered momentum most new members came from mainstream political backgrounds and were socialized by peers, the initial impetus revealed a great deal more continuity with the ideologies and politics of the recent past than either the New Left or the Old Left cared to admit (see Liebman 1979).

Fascism

Strictly speaking, the term *fascism* applies only to the movement that was founded by Benito Mussolini in 1919 and held power in Italy from 1922 to 1943. The term has been extended to include the Nazi regime in Germany from 1933 to 1945. It may be broadened even further to refer to the regimes of Francisco Franco in Spain (1939–1975) and Antonio Salazar in Portugal (1932–1968), as well as to several other regimes in central Europe before World War II. Movements adhering to fascist ideology have existed in both democratic and nondemocratic countries. In the United States, the German-American Bund in the 1930s and the National Socialist White People's party today have espoused fascist principles. However, applying the term *fascist* indiscriminately to any authoritarian regime or undemocratic action is a serious disservice both to the tragedies of recent history and to our clarity of thinking. Also, communist and fascist regimes must not be considered indistinguishable on the grounds that both are totalitarian. Fascism is a historical phenomenon unique not only in the amount of devastation it has wreaked but also in its antihumanitarian intentions.

Fascism glorifies the state as the embodiment of the nation and of life itself, as the supreme good. In the words of one fascist writer, "The Nation State is gifted with an organic life of its own, which far transcends in meaning the life of the individual" (Palmieri, in Gould and Truitt 1973, pp. 110–11). The state is not the sum total of individuals' interests and wills but a separate, higher entity; thus, majority vote and parliamentary democracy are meaningless concepts. Only the führer or leader embodies the genuine will of the entire people. The leader possesses charismatic authority in Weber's sense of the term; he or she derives legitimacy not from popular vote or constitutional powers but from a mystical union with the people's unconscious feelings. "The authority of the Führer is not limited by checks and controls . . . but is . . . all-inclusive and unlimited" (Huber, in Gould and Truitt 1973, p. 125).

According to fascism, the leader embodies the spiritual will of the people and their historic destiny. Mussolini believed that his and Italy's destiny was to restore the glory of the ancient Roman Empire, and Hitler proclaimed a German empire, called the Third Reich, that would last a thousand years. Claiming a historic mission to dominate the world, both leaders set out on a campaign of foreign conquest and annexation. As a result, in 1945 not only Italy and Germany but the rest of Europe and much of Asia and Africa as well lay in ruins. Hitler's Thousand-Year Reich lasted twelve years; Mussolini's empire, twenty-one.

The glorification of the state in fascist ideology is accompanied by a denial of the importance, dignity, and rights of the individual. "Compared to this personality of the State, with its characteristics of transcendent values and its problems of momentous magnitude, the personality of the single individual loses all of that importance which it has assumed in modern times" (Palmieri, in Gould and Truitt 1973, pp. 110–11). If the state is everything, the individual is nothing. Fascism is fundamentally opposed to liberal ideology. In the words of Mussolini, "Liberalism denied the State in the interests of the particular individual; Fascism reaffirms the State as the true reality of the individual. . . . Outside history man is nothing" (quoted in Gould and Truitt 1973, p. 104). In short, fascists believe, as Hitler put it, that "humanitarianism is nonsense." Not the individual but organic units such as the family, the occupational group or syndicate, and, above all, the nation have a meaningful existence.

If the purpose of man is to serve the state through subordination to the demands of the leader, the purpose of woman is to bear children for the state and to serve her family. Fascism's opposition to women's rights is consistent with the overall philosophy that life is meant to be harsh and austere, that human happiness is a meaningless goal, and that only self-sacrifice in the service of the leader is worthwhile. Also consistent with this philosophy is the repression of all dissent, the abolition of freedom of speech, and the annihilation of all political opposition. One of the first acts of both the fascist regime in Italy and the Nazi regime in Germany was the dismantling of the democratic mechanisms of government and society.

Perhaps the most sinister fascist doctrine of all is racism. Racism, a doctrine invented in the late-nineteenth century, is more characteristic of Nazism than of Italian fascism. In fact, Mussolini did not adopt anti-Semitism as a systematic policy until his alliance with Hitler forced him to do so. Nazism views history as a violent and ruthless struggle for domination among biologically distinct races. According to Nazi doctrine, the Aryan or Nordic race, composed of blond-haired, blue-eyed "supermen," is destined to rule over all others. However, its supremacy is increasingly threatened. Inferior races, which include first and most dangerously Jews but also blacks, Slavs, and others, undermine the purity of Aryan blood, Aryan culture, and Aryan political interests.

Jews assumed for the Nazis diabolical proportions and were held responsible for all of Germany's and the world's troubles. They are "carriers of decay and pollute every national culture, they exploit the human and material resources of their hosts, they destroy all faith and spread materialism and liberalism. . . . They are a poison for us and must be treated as such" (quoted in Bluhm 1974, p. 258). With the world standing idly by, Hitler embarked upon the systematic murder of 6 million Jews and 5 million Gypsies, Slavs, and other "undesirables." Today, the American Nazi party singles out blacks for its campaign of hatred.

Fascist ideology represents the culmination of the revolt against reason. Fascists glorify irrationality, force, and brutality as means toward restoring national greatness, ridding the nation of racial undesirables, and ennobling the Nordic race: "Yes, we are barbarians! We want to be barbarians. It is an honorable title. We shall rejuvenate the world. . . . We must shake off all sentimentality and be hard" (Rausching, quoted in Bluhm 1974, p. 214). Fascism is similar to other ideologies in denying its own ideological character, but it is unique among the ideologies (with the possible exception of classical conservatism) in elevating irrationality to a virtue.

The social roots of fascism are still being debated among scholars. Some believe that persons who manifest authoritarian personality patterns are particularly vulnerable to the appeal of fascism. These psychopathological patterns include intolerance of dissent, prejudice toward minority groups, an inability to deal with complex and subtle issues, and a tendency toward violence in interpersonal relations (see Adorno et al. 1950). Other scholars emphasize the rootlessness and anomie that resulted from economic and political upheavals in nineteenth-century Germany and Italy. The conditions of mass society, they claim, gave rise to a powerful yearning for national roots,

cultural unity, and a charismatic leader. In this atmosphere, Hitler and Mussolini found ready followings (see Mosse 1964; see also chapter 7). Still others claim that fascism appeals particularly to those strata in the population most threatened by the increasing bureaucratization and centralization of industrial society. These strata are, interestingly, not the lower classes but the middle class, particularly its marginal segment, the lower middle class (petty bourgeoisie). According to this theory, the middle class supports liberalism under stable conditions but is vulnerable to fascist appeals during periods of economic and political upheaval (see Lipset 1981).

More recent studies challenge the theories of the authoritarian personality, mass society, and petty bourgeois origins of fascism. On the basis of voting data, researcher Richard Hamilton (1982) concludes that, in the countryside, electoral support for the Nazis was stronger among Protestant than among Catholic peasants, perhaps because of Nazism's anti-Catholic stand. This finding points to religion rather than class as a basis of fascist support. In the cities, not the lower middle class but the privileged strata gave Hitler his strongest electoral support, while upper- and upper-middle-class institutions such as the press gave him another kind of support, legitimation through favorable coverage. The motivations for Nazi support were not anomie and psychological insecurity, Hamilton claims, but fear of communism and the impact of the Depression. Similarly, an analysis of the socioeconomic backgrounds of members and leaders of the Nazi party (Kater 1983) shows that both the rank-and-file membership and the leading elite of the Nazi party came from every walk of German society, from rural as well as urban areas and from all social classes. Thus, the Nazi party cannot be considered a class-based movement. Hamilton and Kater agree that the secret of the Nazis' success lay in their superb organizing ability, which enabled them to attract substantial support among every stratum of the population. Both authors downgrade the importance of social-psychological and socioeconomic factors in favor of a political explanation for the appeal of Nazism. (For an analysis of other social movements, see chapters 12 and 13.)

Ideologies: An Integration

Our discussion has covered such diverse ideologies as conservatism, liberalism, socialism, and fascism. It has left out for lack of space other important ideologies, including feminism, libertarianism, anarchism, populism, and communism.

Several commonalities among ideologies are apparent. First, it is intellectuals who formulate, advocate, and defend ideologies. Most people who subscribe to ideologies do so with some detachment and much inconsistency. For a coherent and publicly accessible statement of the ideas in question, we must go to those who formulated them—the intellectuals. While this might sound obvious, it is a point worth making because of the common preoccupation with the class or group to which a given ideology corresponds and from which it presumably arises.

Second, proponents of an ideology commonly shun the use of the term *ideology* when describing their own beliefs, although they apply it to their adversary's beliefs. In Mannheim's terms, they have a partial rather than a total perspective. They often consider their own beliefs pragmatic rather than abstract, that is, wedded to existing realities or to a concrete program for change. This may be because they consciously or subconsciously identify ideology with intransigence, because they consider "mere ideas" to be ineffectual and arid, or simply because they lack an understanding of human society as an integrated social system. Whatever the reason, we have seen that proponents of various ideologies deny having an ideological base. Conservatives claim they are not ideological since they wish only to defend existing institutions. Liberals claim they favor only solutions that work, not abstract dogmas.

Democratic socialists (with the exception of nineteenth- and early-twentieth-century utopians) claim they advocate only a pragmatic, if radical, transformation of society. Marxist socialists and communists claim they are only recognizing and abetting socioeconomic forces already at work, not advocating abstract principles. New Left radicals disdain ideology as ineffectual and dogmatic, advocating instead direct action to change society. And fascists ridicule ideology as a product of reason, which they despise.

Yet all ideologies address the same fundamental issues: the causes of social change and social order, human nature, the relationship between human beings and society, and the desired ends of their actions. All the ideologies we examined deal in some fashion with the problem of change and order: What kind of future lies ahead for society? What is the best way to get there? Are we not better off sticking with the present or even going back to the past? Liberals and socialists would like to hasten change, the former advocating piecemeal change, the latter a radical transformation of society. For both liberals and socialists, however, the good society necessitates a more equitable distribution of economic resources and political power. Liberals advocate peaceful democratic tactics for change, while socialists and communists differ on whether the use of violent means is desirable or indeed inevitable. Conservatives tend to glorify the present and resist change. Fascists advocate radical change but in an antimodern direction; they glorify the primordial bonds of blood and soil that allegedly existed in a mythical barbaric past.

Different ideologies evoke different images of the nature of man and woman. Liberals, socialists, communists, and New Left radicals believe human nature to be fundamentally rational, cooperative, and capable of self-government. They locate the source of the evils of modern society in outmoded economic institutions (primarily capitalism) and would like to see those institutions modified or restructured. Classical conservatives, more pessimistic about human nature, believe that institutional restraints are necessary and should not be tampered with. Contemporary conservatives are closer to the liberal and left-wing view that individual freedom should be given priority over societal restraints, but they extend that freedom to corporations as well as to individuals. Fascists, on the other hand, glorify the irrational and the violent in human nature and call for absolute subservience to the leader.

Finally, all ideologies except fascism speak in the name of humanitarian ideals, invoking images of a society where human beings can be happy and self-fulfilled. They differ, as we have seen, on what kind of society that would be, and on what means should be used to get there. Fascists, and to some extent classical conservatives, advocate a life of misery and subjugation and, in any case, consider such an existence inevitable.

Summary

This chapter has examined both organized systems of ideas and some of the mechanisms by which these ideas are translated into political action. Ideas were dealt with not as disembodied principles but as historical movements grounded in the social and political forces of their times. The chapters that follow focus in greater detail on how ideologies shape political institutions and events by moving elites and masses to behave in particular ways.

3

Power

CHAPTER SEVEN

The Realities of Power: The Pluralist Model

Preview

Power is a contested concept; how it is defined depends on the prior values and assumptions of the analysts. Much of the debate in political sociology and political science has centered on the nature, distribution, and consequences of power. Chapters 7 through 9 examine several views of power, including the pluralist model, the classical elite model, and the contemporary elite model. This chapter begins with a theoretical analysis of the nature of power and its relationship to awareness; it then presents the pluralist model and some case studies in pluralism and concludes with critiques of pluralism.

What Is Power?

Power and Awareness

Max Weber defined *power* (*Macht*) as "the probability that one actor within a social relationship will be in a position to carry out his own will despite resistance" (Weber 1947, p. 152). Power, Weber continued, is exercised in all social relationships, from marriages to nation-states. It derives either from the use or threat of force or, more commonly, from authority (legitimate or socially approved power). Legitimacy may be claimed on the basis of one of three grounds or a combination of the three: charisma, tradition, and legality (see chapter 3).

The difficult part of Weber's definition of power, as of most other definitions, is that a person exercising power first needs to know what he or she wants and then must have the desire and the will to obtain it (see Wrong 1980). Without having both this knowledge and the will to act, one cannot intend to do anything. Rational action, that is, action that uses power as a means to satisfy some personal end, is impossible in the absence of goals or ends.

For Weber, the definition of power implicitly includes the notion of will, that is, of intentionality. Weber distinguishes between actions guided by emotions, those guided by habit or tradition, those guided by a devotion to ultimate values (*Wertrationalität*), and finally those intended as a means for attaining some end or goal (*Zweckrationalität*) (Weber 1947, p. 14). The last, truly rational type of actions has been of most interest to political sociologists. The relationship between power and rationality is that those who do not know what their interests are cannot intend to achieve them, much less endeavor to do so.

Karl Marx's definition of power also contains a component of intention. Social classes either act in their own interest or do not. If they do not, it is because they are not aware of their true interests. For Marxists, however, the basis for determining class interests is not the professed interests of the class but the material conditions of its existence.

Marx's terms *class in itself* and *class for itself* distinguish between individuals who merely happen to be in situations where they have potential interests in common and those who are aware of such interests and of the collective political or economic action necessary to pursue them. Common interests may derive from the objective condition of property ownership and a desire to maintain domination and increase profits or from the objective condition of powerlessness and a desire to increase wages or to gain control of the means of production. In either case, recognizing those interests and working for them are necessary. Only when all classes in a social system are acting as "classes for themselves" does meaningful political conflict, whether peaceful or revolutionary, manifest itself.

Marx's notion of "class in itself" combines the concepts of social structure, political thought, and political action. Social-structural conditions such as membership in a particular social class generate ideological beliefs, which may represent either true consciousness or false consciousness depending on whether they correspond to that class's objective conditions. Ideology, in turn, motivates people to act, either through institutionalized means such as voting or through extrainstitutionalized means such as civil disobedience or terrorism.

Despite their differences, the Weberian and Marxian definitions have much in common. In different ways, both attempt to account for true consciousness, intentionality, and rationality. Both state implicitly that if intention includes the ability to know what one wants, power is the ability to get it. This relationship between power and intention raises problems for the empirical sociologist who wants to study power in operation: How do you study intention? When is consciousness false and when is it true? This dilemma brings us back to some of the questions raised in connection with social diagnosis, ideology, and utopia (see chapter 1).

Power, Authority, and Resources

Sociologist Robert Bierstedt, following in the tradition of Weber, further clarifies the notion of power. Bierstedt argues that power is, in a psychological sense, "synonymous with coercion; it compels a change in the course of action of an individual or group against the wishes of the individual or group. It means the application of sanctions and elimination of alternatives to the social action of one person or group by another person or group" (Bierstedt 1974, p. 230). When people agree, power or coercion becomes unnecessary; consensus prevails.

> Power . . . is the predisposition or capacity that makes the use of force possible. Only groups that have power can threaten to use force and the threat itself is power. Power is the ability to employ force, not its actual employment, the ability to apply sanctions, not their actual application. Power is the ability to introduce force into a social situation; it is a stance, not action; it is a presentation of

the probability of force. Unlike force, incidentally, power is always successful; when it is not successful it was not, or ceases to be, power. . . . Power symbolizes the force that *may* be applied in any social situation and supports the authority that *is* applied. Power is thus neither force nor authority but it makes both force and authority possible. Without power there would be no force and without power there would be no authority. (Bierstedt 1974, p. 231)

Thus, according to Bierstedt, "power is always potential, that is, when it is used it becomes something else . . . either force or authority" (Bierstedt 1974, p. 236).

For Bierstedt, the locus of power is in the community or society rather than in the government or the state. The types of social power include political, economic, financial, industrial, and military. Various forms of power relations exist, including those of the parent over the child, the master over the slave, the teacher over the pupil, and so on. Power is a universal phenomenon: It exists in all human societies and in all social relationships. In these examples we refer to the institutional power of a parent over a child, for example. That a parent has power over a child derives from community legitimacy and sanction. Power is absent only in small primary (face-to-face) groups where personal identification is complete and in relations with polite acquaintances that are social only in the minimal sense. The locus of power is in groups, and it expresses itself in intergroup relations. Power is an attribute not only of individuals but also of positions people occupy in organizations. Since various positions generate power simultaneously, there is the possibility of conflict. Someone in a subordinate position, for example, may have such a strong and legitimate power base that superordinates cannot exercise their power. The subordinate's power may derive from incontrovertible expert knowledge, from a political constituency, or from powerful allies.

Power "supports the fundamental order of society and the social organization within it. Power stands behind every association and sustains its structure. Without power there is no organization and without power there is no order. . . . Authority itself cannot exist without the immediate support of power and the ultimate sanction of force" (Bierstedt 1974, p. 235).

Bierstedt further argues that power can be based on numbers, organization, or resources such as "money, credit, property, knowledge, skill, competence, cunning, acumen, deceit . . . armament, and . . . 'natural resources' " (Bierstedt 1974, p. 239). This position challenges the Marxian argument that power rests principally on economic resources and, more specifically, on control over the means of production.

In democracies, Bierstedt reminds us, the legitimate basis for governance is neither organization nor resources, but numbers. On the basis of the principle of one person, one vote, power belongs (at least potentially) to those who can mobilize the greatest numerical support. If nothing else, democracy claims to be government by majority rule, that is, it purports to be run by those who represent the largest number of people, not by those who possess the most money (the business elite) or the most force (the military elite). That is why voting is considered so important in democratic theory. Elections determine which candidates or parties have the most people behind them and, hence, who is eligible to hold office.

Bierstedt speaks of a majority as 51 percent or more and a minority as 49 percent or less. In political sociology, we prefer to speak of minorities not in terms of statistical numbers but in terms of lack of access to power, prestige, authority, and other scarce goods. The city-state of Athens in ancient Greece claimed to be a democracy, yet 80 percent of the population (including women, the foreign-born, and slaves) did not have a voice in the decisions of the city. Thus, for our purposes, a minority is a group, regardless of its relative size, that lacks power. Women, for example, comprise more than 50 percent of the population of the United States, yet they remain a minority group.

This perspective raises questions about what objective criteria should be used to define *democracy.* If a minority is defined as a group without power, regardless of its size, then a majority must be defined politically as a group that has power, regardless of its proportionate numbers. In societies or organizations where power is exercised by 51 percent or more of the members, we speak of a representative democracy. Where power is exercised by fewer than 50 percent of the members, we may technically speak of a power elite, although usually the term refers to rule by a very small portion of the population.

We define power as the ability to get others to do what we want, regardless of what they want. Political power is the exercise of this ability within the context of the institution of politics (see also Wrong 1980).

Power: Zero-Sum or Non-Zero-Sum?

How much power is there in a given society? Proponents of the zero-sum theory of power argue that there is only a limited amount of power and that in any society power is a scarce resource. Hence, the more power one group has the less is left for others; one group's gain is another's loss. This view of power is expressed by conflict sociologist C. Wright Mills and others, who argue that power is held by a few individuals comprising a power elite. This elite exercises power in its own interests, not in those of the masses. Thus, to empower the powerless it is seen as necessary to take power from the elite.

The non-zero-sum game position, by contrast, argues that one person or group's gaining power does not necessarily mean that someone else has lost it. In fact, an increase in power for some may well mean an increase in power for others. Power, like wealth, is a resource that renews itself and contributes greatly to effective societal functioning. This position is often taken by functionalists, such as Talcott Parsons. Power, according to Parsons, is "the capacity of [a] society to mobilize its resources in the interest of goals . . . goals that are 'affected with the public interest.' Power is also the capacity to make—and 'make stick'—decisions which are binding" (Parsons 1969, pp. 204, 240). The obligation of the leaders to act on behalf of the public interest, and of the subordinates to obey, is ultimately supported by society's value system. The amount of power a society can mobilize depends on the citizens' commitment to the value system, a commitment that results from both life-long socialization and situational factors. Thus, a war may raise the citizens' commitment, while a high-reaching scandal such as Watergate may well erode it.

Sociologist Morris Janowitz (1978) and political scientist Samuel Huntington (1981), following in the footsteps of Parsons, raise the issue of whether the United States, as an advanced industrial society, has lost the capacity to exercise enough self-regulation to achieve effective social policy. Janowitz argues that political power has become so fragmented that creating meaningful coalitions is increasingly difficult. Consequently, the participants in the political process are unable to translate their preferences into policy, and society's capacity for self-regulation is seriously undermined. Unless elites resort to coercion and repression, society is destined to drift toward an uncharted future, forever reacting rather than acting. Janowitz maintains that the concern with power as a scarce, monopolized resource (zero-sum game), without "sufficient reference to the institutional and normative elements of the social order" (Janowitz 1978, p. 45), is an oversimplification and that many of the troubles of present-day American society are attributable to the excessive dispersion of power. Huntington similarly blames the alleged excesses of egalitarianism and the dispersion of power for what he believes is the weakness of central authority in the United States.[1]

From a social constructionist position, the question of whether the distribution of possible gains and losses resembles a zero-sum or a non-zero-sum game is less a matter of the objective characteristics of the situation than of the perceptions of the players. A zero-sum perception states that if I win, you lose. A non-zero-sum perception argues that there may be ways in which both of us can achieve more by cooperating than by competing. Perceptions or social constructions of reality are powerful in their own right. In politics, as in poker, they affect the outcome of the game. The art of bluffing is based on the assumption that not the cards you have in your hand but those you can make the others believe you have determine the outcome.

One example is the debate over international disarmament. Each side has power over the other to the extent that the other side believes it will use force; furthermore, power reflects the extent to which each side has the intentions and the resources to use superior force or is perceived to have such intentions and resources. In other words, each side needs to convince the other that, should war erupt, only two outcomes are possible: Either it will win and the other will lose, or both will lose. The possibilities are shown in Figure 7.1. Neither side wants a fight, but to avoid a fight, each must make the opponent believe that it has both the will and the resources to use force. One way to demonstrate this readiness is by accelerating the arms race, which means that even without

	A	
B	*Wins*	*Loses*
Wins	*	B wins/ A loses
Loses	A wins/ B loses	Both lose

*In a zero-sum game the possibility of two winning does not exist except for a tie.

Figure 7.1   Possible Outcomes in a Zero-Sum Game

1. For a review of the debate over power as a zero-sum or non-zero-sum game, see Wrong 1980, pp. 237–247; see also Offe 1972.

war, both sides lose to the extent that resources are drained from alternative expenditures.

However, if each side trusts the intentions of the other not to employ force, both sides can curtail their defense spending. With fewer and more obsolete arms, war is both less likely and potentially less destructive, and with fewer resources allocated to guns, more can be spent on butter. From this perspective, whether at war or at peace, both sides win (see Burton 1982).

The outcomes of the conflict are thus very different depending on whether participants adopt a zero-sum (win-lose) or a non-zero-sum (win-win) perspective. The growing field of conflict management is based in part on the possibility that what is perceived as a zero-sum situation may be converted into a mixed-sum or win-win situation. The reality constructed by most political and military strategists, however, is that international power is a zero-sum game (see Burton 1984).

Who Governs? The Pluralist Model

The pluralist school of political theory has enjoyed great popularity in the United States. Although today the center of gravity of political theory has arguably shifted to the elite model (see Lukes 1979), participants in the political process still tend to conceptualize democratic government, and their individual roles in it, in pluralist terms. This is true both for high-ranking participants such as elected legislators, special-interest lobbyists, and presidential advisors and for rank-and-file citizens. The pluralist model, in other words, dominates the political thinking of many Americans.

Pluralism can refer to any aspect of diversity in society—ethnic, cultural, geographic, economic, or political. **Political pluralism** refers to a situation in which several different groups have enough resources to influence policy or, conversely, no group can monopolize enough power or resources to force its policy preference on others (see Form and Rytina 1969; Berger 1981; Riesman, Denney, and Glazer 1953).

A key element of pluralist theory is competition. Because of the competitive relationships among the diverse groups that make up the polity, many believe, power is effectively dispersed. This dispersal of power necessitates continual and shifting coalitions in order to accomplish group goals. It also necessitates compromise and pragmatism rather than ideological extremism, for no one group can hope to accomplish all its goals (see Lipset 1978; Greenstone 1982; Whitt 1979; Dahl 1982).

Pluralism: The Role of Voluntary Associations

Interest groups and their formalized structures, voluntary associations, have been of interest to political theorists for nearly a century and a half. In the 1830s, French observer Alexis de Tocqueville (see chapter 3) attempted to explain why democracy flourished in America alone among the countries of his day. One of the causes, he found, was the unique role of voluntary associations.

> Americans of all ages, all stations in life, and all types of disposition are forever forming associations. There are not only commercial and industrial associations in which all take part, but others of a thousand different types—religious, moral, serious, futile, very general and very limited, immensely large and very minute. Americans combine to give fetes, found seminaries, build churches, distribute books, and send missionaries to the antipodes. Hospitals, prisons, and schools take shape in that way. Finally, if they want to proclaim a truth or propagate some feeling by the encouragement of a great example, they form an association. In every case, at the head of any new undertaking, where in France you would find the government or in England some territorial magnate, in the United States you are sure to find an association. . . .
>
> The morals and intelligence of a democratic people would be in as much danger as its commerce and industry if ever a government usurped the place of private associations. . . .

As soon as several Americans have conceived a sentiment or an idea that they want to produce before the world, they seek each other out, and when found, they unite. Thenceforth they are no longer isolated individuals, but a power conspicuous from the distance whose actions serve as an example; when it speaks, men listen. . . .

In democratic countries knowledge of how to combine is the mother of all other forms of knowledge; on its progress depends that of all the others. (Tocqueville 1966, pp. 485–88)

Voluntary associations, in Tocqueville's view, protect minorities not only against the tyranny of the elite but also against that of the masses. Unchecked democracy is no less a danger to liberty than unmitigated dictatorship.

Emile Durkheim, writing in the 1890s, was equally adamant about the importance of a middle layer of power between the citizen and the state: "A [democratic] nation can be maintained only if, between the state and the individual, there is intercalated a whole series of secondary groups near enough to individuals to attract them strongly in their sphere of action and drag them, in this way, into the general torrent of social life" (Durkheim 1949, p. 28).

Thus, according to Tocqueville and Durkheim, voluntary associations form a critical middle level of power between the ruler (king, parliament, or president) and the masses. These associations serve the dual purpose of protecting the masses from abuse of power by the elite and providing a means of channeling citizens' input into the governing process. Balancing liberty with authority, they thus strengthen democracy (see Novak 1980).

Sociologist Arnold Rose (1967, pp. 246–51) outlines in greater detail the functions of voluntary associations in America:

- Voluntary associations, and in particular pressure groups and lobbies, serve to distribute power. "Through the voluntary association the ordinary citizen can acquire as much power in the community or the nation as his free time, ability, and inclinations permit him to. . . . The purpose of these groups is to influence legislation and executive action either directly or indirectly."

- Voluntary associations socialize citizens into the workings of the political system and provide them with means of action. Making information available to members on matters affecting them is an important role of voluntary associations; modern society is complex, and citizens have little understanding of the forces that affect their destinies. Knowledge and potential for action alleviate the frustrations of incomprehension and powerlessness. An example is furnished by trade unions, which provide workers with some control over working conditions and "a sense of economic and personal security since [the union] protects [them] from being fired arbitrarily, and even directly provides [them] some recreations, social-reform activities, and other creative opportunities."

- Voluntary associations provide the organizations and resources essential for social change. Whenever unmet needs exist within a particular group, associations emerge to draw attention to those needs, galvanize support, and pressure economic, political, and other institutions into modifying their programs or structures. Other associations may, in turn, attempt to block changes that are viewed as harmful to their members. Examples of associations that militate for social change are gay rights groups and the National Organization for Women (NOW). Examples of organizations concerned with averting change are the National Rifle Association, which has succeeded in blocking gun control legislation, and the stop-ERA movement, which has contributed to the defeat of the Equal Rights Amendment.

- Voluntary associations strengthen social cohesion. Although they tend to view themselves as conflict groups, associations whose memberships overlap serve to mitigate "the disintegrative effects of conflict." Thus, they paradoxically contribute to society's unity.

- Voluntary associations provide personal identification and combat the isolation of a mass society. Associations give each member the feeling of identification with some smaller group that he or she can fully comprehend and influence in major ways. For members, especially activists, involvement in associations helps "to give meaning and purpose to their lives."

- Voluntary associations often serve to enhance the economic gain, social status, or political careers of ambitious members. Membership in prestigious social or service clubs, such as Rotary, provides executives with business contacts and "looks good on the record" of candidates for public office.

Rose concludes that voluntary associations are important for the survival of democracy because they offer legitimate and effective opportunities for influencing societal decisions and provide the satisfaction that comes with a sense of control over one's fate. In accordance with Rose's theory, sociologist Pamela Oliver (1984) finds that leaders and active members of voluntary associations have more education than nonactive members, more interest in local issues, and more close friends or relatives in the community.

Illustrations of the role of voluntary associations abound. A historical illustration is the rise of groups defending religious nonconformity in England in the seventeenth and eighteenth centuries. Political scientist William Kornhauser describes this historical role of voluntary associations first in religion, then in politics:

Nonconformist groups not only nurtured the *idea* of individual rights . . . ; they were *training grounds* and *organized bases* for the exercise of these rights. Thus, while France contained few independent groups to translate the ideal of the "rights of man and citizen" into a living reality, England and later America overflowed with fiercely dissenting groups, jealously guarding their members from outside efforts to prevent the freedom of individual conscience, and the freedom to organize voluntarily in associations of likeminded believers. . . . More than just the

principle, the habits of free association were inculcated by religious dissent. (Kornhauser 1959, pp. 137–38; italics in original)

The situation in England and America was in marked contrast to that in France, where the revolution of 1789 swept aside all intermediate centers of power so that "nothing was left to stand between man and the State. The power of the State, unchecked by any intermediate agencies, became unlimited" (Talmon 1952, p. 250).

Contemporary examples are equally. instructive. At the heart of the Polish workers' uprising of 1980 was a demand for trade unions independent of the domination of the Polish Communist party. Unlike bread-and-butter demands such as a shorter work week, this was a demand the Soviet-backed Polish government could not allow. The ruling elite, it seems, realized that an autonomous grass-roots organization would protect individual rights and seriously compromise the elite's own power. The government proceeded to crush the Solidarity movement, jailing its leaders and proclaiming martial law (see Touraine 1983). Thus, pluralism today, as in the eighteenth and nineteenth centuries, is often viewed as the enemy of dictatorship and of domination by minority interests.[2]

However, some sociologists (Knoke 1983; Knoke and Wood 1981; Laumann and Knoke 1986; Laumann, Knoke, and Kim 1985) challenge the pluralist view that "social influence associations" are the bulwarks of democracy, the weapons of the weak against the strong. On the basis of an empirical analysis of local and national associations, they conclude that the perceived effectiveness of organizations is largely a function of their position in the power, financial, and communication networks. That is, organizations are believed to influence policy decisions only to the extent that they are connected to the right sources of funding and

2. For a case study of the role of pluralist associations in formulating national policy in the United States, see Chubb 1983.

information and to the local or national power elite. These findings lead the researchers to point out the danger that "minority special interests will triumph over wider societal values" (Knoke and Wood 1981, pp. 191–92).

Pluralism and Mass Society

The notion of pluralism is often contrasted with the concept of "mass society." Together, these concepts are evoked by pluralist writers to account for the robustness of democracy in England and the United States and for its vulnerability in France, Italy, and Germany. Specifically, contemporary writers ask: Why did democracies in Europe in the 1930s and 1940s and in some Latin American countries since World War II collapse despite the fact that several of these countries (particularly the Weimar Republic in Germany) had highly democratic constitutions? And why were other democracies, notably the United States, England, and Canada, spared this fate despite the Great Depression and periodic threats from antidemocratic extremist groups?

The answer, pluralist writers contend, lies not in clever political arrangements but in the social structure that underlies governmental institutions. The English-speaking countries have been blessed with a network of pluralist associations and therefore enjoy a stable democracy, whereas Latin American and central and southern European countries have evolved into mass societies and consequently are vulnerable to a totalitarian takeover (there are additional conditions for democratic stability, but they fall outside the scope of this chapter; see Lipset 1963).

How does a **mass society** differ from a pluralist one? According to one definition:

Mass society is a situation in which an aggregate of individuals are related to one another only by way of their relation to a common authority, especially the state. That is, individuals are not directly related to one another in a variety of independent groups. A population in this condition is not insu-lated in any way from the ruling group, nor yet from elements within itself. For insulation requires a multiplicity of independent and often conflicting forms of association, each of which is strong enough to ward off threats to the autonomy of the individual. . . . In their absence, people lack the resources to restrain their own behavior as well as that of others. Social atomization engenders strong feelings of alienation and anxiety, and therefore the disposition to engage in extreme behavior to escape from these tensions. In a mass society there is a heightened readiness to form hyper-attach-ments to symbols and leaders. . . . Total loyalty, in turn, is the psychological basis for total domination, i.e., totalitarianism. (Kornhauser 1959, p. 32).

A century after Tocqueville, Karl Mannheim, himself a refugee from Nazi Germany, attempted to explain the rise of fascism by analyzing the history and implications of mass society. According to Mannheim, the forces of urbanization and industrialization in modern Europe swept away the structures that formerly mediated between the state and the individual—church, community, estate, and guild. Unlike the situation in England and the United States, in Europe no new centers of power developed. Modernization left men and women alienated and atomized, able neither to comprehend the larger forces of society nor to cope with them. Isolated and unprepared to think and act rationally, these men and women could be easily manipulated by propaganda and thus fall prey to the appeals of charismatic leaders such as Hitler and Mussolini. The masses' penchant for violence and irrationality, which has always lurked beneath the surface but has previously been controlled by the authority structure, now erupts with the full power of destruction. In Mannheim's words, "Life among the masses . . . tends to make people much more subject to suggestions, uncontrollable outbursts of impulses and psychic regressions than those who are organically integrated and held firm in a smaller type of group" (Mannheim 1940, p. 60).

Thus, modernization creates a paradox. On one hand, the economy is ever more rationally organized, and bureaucratic organization invades ever more minute areas of social life. On the other hand, mass society "favors a great number of irrational impulses and suggestions and produces an accumulation of unsublimated psychic energies which, at every moment, threaten to smash the whole subtle machinery of social life" (Mannheim 1940, p. 61). Mannheim carefully notes that it is not large numbers in themselves that unleash irrationality but the disintegration of middle-level structures of authority. "As long as society as a whole persists in its old well-integrated form . . . it shows no symptoms of chaotic mass reactions." In well-integrated societies such as England or the United States, the intermediary groups absorb and channel the irrational and violent tendencies of the mass. Only when "the impulsive energies . . . have been set free by the disintegration of society and are seeking integration about a new object" do these energies become easily controlled and channeled by dictators toward their own purposes of self-aggrandizement and destruction. Such was the fate of Italy in the 1920s and Germany in the 1930s (Mannheim 1940, pp. 60–62).

Mannheim, then, despairs of the possibility of a lasting democracy in mass society, since in such a society individuals, unable to think or act independently, lose their autonomous rationality and become susceptible to totalitarian appeals. By contrast, where the old, organic network of integrative associations persists, or where a new one is created, democracy can flourish because a buffer then exists between the individual and society. In other words, democracy can flourish only in a pluralist society.

While Mannheim, distrusting the rationality of the common people, tended to romanticize the organic ties of preindustrial associations, pluralist writers who are more democratically inclined stress the distinctive character of modern associations. Unlike their medieval predecessors, modern associations such as trade unions, churches, and political parties are noninclusive; that is, they do not control the entire lives of their members. Thus, a Catholic woman, for example, may belong either to a manufacturers' association or to a trade union; may vote Republican, Democratic, or even Communist; and may pay dues either to the American Civil Liberties Union or to the Daughters of the American Revolution. By the same token, a trade union may have members who are Catholic, Protestant, Jewish, Moslem, or none of the above. No one group controls the whole life or claims the entire allegiance of its members.[3] By contrast, a medieval man was born into a particular social class, occupation, and locality; and these affiliations, which under normal circumstances could not be changed, determined his place in society as well as his life chances. As sociologist Georg Simmel (1956) observed, superimposed and inclusive associations maximize control; crosscutting, voluntary associations maximize freedom.

Crosscutting affiliations play an additional role: They favor societal consensus and discourage ideological polarization. When memberships overlap, no group can achieve total ideological domination over its members or consider itself totally at war with another group, because members' loyalties are tempered by their affiliations with other groups. Thus, workers and employers who confront each other as antagonists across the picket line may later find themselves in the same ideological camp, for example, as Catholics lobbying for state aid to church-affiliated schools. Such a situation contrasts with one where cleavage lines coincide. If all Catholics were workers and all Protestants employers, class conflict would spill over into religious warfare. Similarly, if members of a given political party did not have to attend to other role obligations (whether as parents, workers, or church members), they might unleash all their energies into political campaigns. Society would be polarized, and

_____

3. There are exceptions, of course. Organizations such as the military and prison, which are termed by sociologists *total institutions*, come close to total control.

bloodshed would probably ensue. Karl Marx recognized that, before the proletarian revolution could take place, all ties binding the working class to the capitalists—ties of religion, nationalism, and local tradition—would have to dissolve. He believed that this was already happening under capitalism.[4]

Polyarchy and Populism

Clearly, pluralist democracy differs substantially from the classical version of direct rule "by the people and for the people." Political scientist Robert Dahl (1970, 1982) distinguishes between populist or direct democracy and polyarchal democracy, a variant of pluralism.

Populist democracy follows the cardinal principle of majority rule: "In choosing among [policy] alternatives, the alternative preferred by the greatest number is selected." An underlying assumption of this rule, of course, is that "the preference of each member is assigned an equal vote" (Dahl 1970, p. 64).

Populism, Dahl argues, presents several problems. First, if majority rule is unchecked, who will protect minorities when the majority votes to deprive them of their rights? Second, individuals do not adhere to their views with equal intensity. "What if the minority prefers its alternative much more passionately than the majority prefers a contrary alternative? Does the majority principle still make sense?" (Dahl 1970, p. 90). Consider such issues as prohibition, abortion, prayer in the schools, and the death penalty. Is it fair to assign equal weight to the views of the relatively indifferent majority as to those of the minority whose vital interests or spiritual well-being is at stake? Third, majorities may take too long to arrive at their decisions, and, furthermore, their decisions are not always wise. "Advocates of democracy have generally supposed that the majority choice ought to be a reflective one; rational choice requires knowledge of one's own values [sub-

4. For more on the stabilizing effects of multiple cleavage lines, see Coser 1956; Lipset 1959.

stantive rationality], technical knowledge about the alternatives [technical rationality], and knowledge about the probable consequences of each alternative. Such knowledge . . . requires time for debate, discussion, hearings, and other time-consuming devices. How long a delay is compatible with the [Majority] Rule? The theory of populistic democracy provides no answer" (Dahl 1970, pp. 56–57).

No one was more aware of the dangers inherent in populist democracy than the founding fathers of the American Republic. Their answer was to insert a system of checks and balances into the Constitution. Thus, the Supreme Court, for example, may legally void a decision arrived at by a majority of Congress if that decision violates the rights of a particular minority. Indeed, minority rights are guaranteed to the extent that "the process of governmental policy-making [is] so constructed that every group of a 'significant' size will have an opportunity to veto threatened deprivations of its freedom" (Dahl 1970, p. 27). Of course, veto powers may be used to safeguard minority privilege at the expense of majority rights, as in the case of a handful of wealthy industrialists defending their right to exploit child labor. There is no easy answer to the dilemma of reconciling the rights of the majority with those of the minority. Compromises must be reached and renegotiated continually.

Constitutional guarantees of minority rights are not enough, as has long been recognized. Minority rights must be reconciled with majority rule not only on the procedural level but on the social-structural level as well. This is the essence of **polyarchal democracy.**

How can the level of intensity of different groups be measured in order to arrive at a fair policy? When passions run so high that the minority cannot abide by the majority's decision, it will express its displeasure in unambiguous terms—by seceding or taking up arms against the intolerable situation, as the American South did in 1861. Short of enforcing their preferences with guns, however, minorities in a polyarchy will engage in a variety of political activities to express their wishes, from organizing direct-mail and television campaigns to demonstrating in the streets. The more intense a group is about its views, the more likely it is to mobilize its resources (money, time, energy, and connections) for political battle. As groups with their own leadership and organizational structures proliferate and compete against each other, they become part of the political landscape of polyarchy. Hence, by definition, policy outcomes will reflect the relative intensity of preference and the relative level of political activity among competing groups.

An objection may be raised that groups and individuals do not exert equal amounts of influence. A more serious objection is that some groups are disqualified from participating altogether, either because they are denied legitimacy by the majority (such as the American Communist party) or because they are reduced to inactivity by choice, intimidation, or force (for example, immigrant aliens). Neither Dahl nor other pluralists deny the inequality of influence (see Dahl 1982, pp. 207–9). However, pluralists believe that, over time, most groups with grievances are guaranteed access to the political arena. "A central guiding thread of American constitutional development has been the evolution of a political system in which all the active and legitimate groups in the population can make themselves heard at some crucial stage in the process of decision" (Dahl 1970, p. 137).

This diversity of influence is the essence of the American political system as Dahl sees it. Governmental decisions are not reached by majority rule, as in a populist democracy; majority rule, like majority tyranny, is mostly a myth. Nor are decisions controlled by a powerful minority, as in a dictatorship. Rather, government in a polyarchy is controlled by minorities. The critical features of polyarchy are that (a) constitutional and social-structural factors enable a very large number of diverse minorities to be heard, (b) elites must respond to the needs of these minorities in the process of for-

mulating policy, and (c) policy decisions are reached by bargaining and compromise.

The continual bargaining necessitated by the fragmentation of power often results in chaos and frustration in areas where important decisions must be made, such as foreign policy. Yet for all its drawbacks, the American political system enables a large number of groups to have a say in the political process. "This is no mean thing in a political system" (Dahl 1970, p. 150).

In conclusion, Dahl points out the unique contributions of the American polyarchal system:

> Probably this strange hybrid, the normal American political system, is not for export to others. But so long as the social prerequisites of democracy are substantially intact in this country, it appears to be a relatively efficient system for reinforcing agreement, encouraging moderation, and maintaining social peace in a restless and immoderate people operating a gigantic, powerful, diversified, and incredibly complex society. (Dahl 1970, p. 151)

Critics of pluralism point out that democracy should be assessed not only on the basis of the process of policy making but on the basis of its outcomes. As long as outcomes are biased in favor of the elite, the critics argue, the pluralists' focus on the relative openness of the process is irrelevant (see, for example, Parenti 1978). The critiques of pluralism will be examined below in more detail. First, however, we will examine some empirical studies guided by pluralist theory.

Pluralism in Private Organization: The International Typographical Union

A pluralist social structure, according to some researchers, is functional for the exercise of democracy not only in national or local governments but in private organizations as well. Lipset and his colleagues, in a book titled *Union*

Democracy (1956), analyzed the dynamics of democracy in the International Typographical Union (ITU). Until recently, the democratic tradition of the ITU contrasted sharply with the political situation in other unions and, indeed, with that in most organizations of any kind. Unlike other unions, the ITU sported a viable two-party system, meaningful periodic elections, and a rank and file actively involved in union affairs. Lipset and his colleagues sought out those factors that accounted for the unique strengths of democracy in the ITU.

During the time of the study, the ITU differed from other unions not only in its political institutions but in its social structure as well. The ITU was characterized by a series of strong, independent locals whose history predated that of the international organization, with their own financial and organizational resources. It was also characterized by a vigorous **occupational community**: Numerous voluntary subassociations served members' recreational and social needs. At the local level, these subassociations included sports clubs, veterans' groups, ethnic and religious associations, benevolent societies, and fraternal lodges; at the international level, they included three sports leagues that held annual tournaments. While social and special-interest clubs abound within other unions, those within the ITU were different in that they had developed independently of the union's central bodies, and were organized by the members themselves in their spare time. In addition, printers' occupational skills being what they are, several newspapers flourished within the union. But the occupational community was by no means limited to formal organizations. Since printers worked irregular hours and possessed a great deal of pride in their occupation, they tended to associate with each other on an informal basis off the job as well as on it. The ITU thus sported a strong **informal organization** in addition to formal subassociations. The significance of the extraordinary occupational community within the ITU is clear. Although the associations were explicitly nonpolitical, they strengthened and maintained political democracy within the union in much the same way that the union, along with other voluntary associations, helped to maintain democracy in the larger society.

The occupational community encouraged democracy in several ways. First, the clubs and subassociations offered individuals a chance to participate in the union community in a nonpolitical context. By interacting informally with fellow unionists, many of whom were politically active, members increased their knowledge of union politics and often their interest and involvement as well. Second, because the clubs elected their own officers, committees, and so on, club members acquired such important democratic skills as running for office, mobilizing support, and bridging differences with others. Third, the leadership's positions on issues were discussed and debated through informal as well as formal channels. This outlet gave the leadership a means of communicating its positions to the rank and file and of getting feedback in ways less threatening than the ballot box or the wildcat strike and also gave members a chance to air out, crystallize, and gather support for opposing views. Other factors that encouraged democracy in the ITU were the low salary and prestige differentials between union officers and workers. Little status was gained in becoming an officer and little status lost in returning to the role of a worker.

As the authors of *Union Democracy* make clear, a key requirement for the effective functioning of voluntary associations in the service of democracy is that they possess sources of power independent of the central body. These sources may include economic assets, popular support, control over communication media, or strong normative traditions. As we have seen, the independent power resources that existed in the ITU were decentralized locals with their own financial and organizational bases, independent newspapers, and subassociations sponsored at the grass-roots level. The result of this unique constellation of social-structural and historical factors was that, almost alone among American trade unions, the ITU was able to sustain democratic practices and institutions, including a viable two-party system, elections in which meaningful alternatives were offered to the voters, a rotation of leaders in office, and a leadership responsive to the needs of its constituency.

While the conditions that fostered democracy in the ITU developed spontaneously, similar conditions—and a functioning democracy—may be created through deliberate action by political reform movements. On the basis of a study of the United Steelworkers of America (USWA), sociologist Philip Nyden (1985) concludes that union reformers can create an occupational community, foster the political involvement of rank-and-file members, maintain close links between the leadership and its grass-roots constituents, and develop meaningful political programs. Nyden finds that, consistent with pluralist theory, "democratic reform is most likely to occur when . . . the initial organizational structure and ideology [of the reform movement] are democratic" (Nyden 1985, p. 1192).

Marxist sociologists, however, argue that, in the long run, union democracy is thwarted by capitalism. "The starting point for any realistic analysis [of trade unions] must be the massive power imbalance between capital and labour. This derives from the very fact that the productive system is, in the main, the private property of a tiny minority of the population, and that profit is its basic dynamic" (Hyman and Fryer 1977, p. 154).

The recent history of the ITU supports this contention. Since *Union Democracy* was written, automation has eliminated many printing jobs and simplified and routinized others. While the stated goal of automation in printing, as in other industries, is cost cutting, the new technology is not value-neutral. "One consequence, intended or unintended, of the new technology was the gradual diminution of judgment and craftsmanship required of the individual worker and the transferral of control

of the labor process to management" (Wallace and Kallenberg 1982, p. 322). With the erosion in the number of jobs and in required skill level, the union has been preoccupied with a fight for its survival rather than trying to keep up its democratic tradition. It appears that external economic forces, namely, technological development and management's desire for increased profitability and control, have proved mightier than either the internal social-structural dynamics of the union or its ideological commitment to democracy.

Elite Pluralism: Politics in New Haven

Since it is unrealistic to assume that rank-and-file members of organizations will share equally in political decision making (whether on the national, state, or local level), some pluralist theorists have focused on the competition for influence among certain elites, namely, the high-level representatives of the various groups. In this view, the crucial difference between tyranny and democracy boils down to the difference between government by a single elite and government by a multiplicity of elites. In the elites' constant juggling and compromising, as well as in their ultimate responsiveness to their constituents, these pluralist theorists see the litmus test of democratic government:

> [Under pluralism] the rulers are not at all closely knit or united. They are not so much in the centre of a solar system, as in a cluster of interlocking circles, each one largely preoccupied with its own professionalism and expertise and touching others only at one edge. . . . They are not a single Establishment but a ring of Establishments, with slender connexions. The frictions and balances between the different circles are the supreme safeguard of democracy. No one man can stand in the centre, for there is no centre. (Quoted in Bottomore 1964, p. 34)

Empirical research guided by pluralist theory has documented the role of elites (as opposed to a single elite) in influencing public policy. In his book *Who Governs?*, a classic study of decisions affecting public policy in New Haven, Connecticut, Dahl found that leadership in the American community is segmented. "That is, individuals who are influential in one sector of public activity tend not to be influential in another sector; and, what is probably more significant, the social strata from which individuals in one sector tend to come are different from the social strata from which individuals in other sectors are drawn" (Dahl 1961, p. 169).

Dahl traced the decision-making process in three spheres: nominations for political office, urban redevelopment of the downtown area, and efforts to improve the public school system. In each sphere, he found a specialized elite whose influence was confined to that sphere and did not spill over into others. These elites consisted, respectively, of political party activists, business owners and managers, and public school administrators (each elite, in fact, was a coalition rather than a single agency or set of individuals). Only a few persons accountable to the electorate wielded influence in more than one sphere. In fact, the most influential person, the mayor, "was not at the peak of the pyramid but rather at the center of intersecting circles. He rarely commanded. He negotiated, cajoled, exhorted. . . . Because the mayor could not command, he had to bargain" (Dahl 1961, p. 204).

Turning his attention away from the elites and the moderately active subleaders, Dahl painted a sobering portrait of the average citizen of New Haven. He found that most people are not vitally interested in politics but rather pursue personal goals and receive gratification from work, family, personal investment, or hobbies. Only when they perceive their goals to be directly threatened by the actions or inactions of government (contemporary examples include issues of zoning or school closings) are the normally apolitical citizens motivated to use their resources in order to influence governmental actions. Occasionally, they exert their influence through the ballot box; more commonly, they utilize civic and lobbying organizations. When the threat passes, they revert to their previous

pursuits. Although the political passivity of the great majority of the people goes against the grain of democratic theory, it cannot be denied.

> In New Haven as in the United States generally one of the central facts of political life is that politics—local, state, national, or international—lies at the outer periphery of attention . . . [and] activity. At the focus of most men's lives are primary activities involving food, sex, love, family, work, play, shelter, comfort, friendship, social esteem, and the like . . . Whatever lip service citizens may pay to conventional attitudes, politics is a remote, alien, and unrewarding activity. Instead of seeking to explain why citizens are not interested . . . the task is to explain why a few citizens are. (Dahl 1961, p. 279).

Thus, the political resources available to people are only potential resources that are activated infrequently in response to a perceived threat. The use of political resources to influence public policy varies with socioeconomic status as well as with disposition. The more gregarious a person is by nature (a "joiner"), the more likely he or she is to find political activity rewarding in its own right. The higher a person's income, education, and previous political experience, the more likely the person is to find politics an effective means of attaining personal goals such as economic self-improvement. Yet the amount of slack resources available is so extensive and so widespread that "virtually no one is entirely lacking in some influence resource" that can be activated should the need arise (Dahl 1961, p. 228). If elite policies antagonize any group sufficiently, that group will mobilize in order to remove the threat to itself.

Besides the existence of slack resources at the grass-roots level, another safeguard against the elite's potential abuse of power, according to pluralist theory, is the societal consensus on basic norms and values. Whatever specific differences stem from diversity of interests and goals, nearly all Americans adhere to the basic principles of democracy: that democracy is the best form of government, that a substantial degree of majority rule must be combined with a large amount of minority freedom, that political institutions such as the presidency and the Supreme Court are legitimate, that disputes should be settled by adjudication or appeals for public support rather than by violence, and even that the American form of government, warts and all, is perhaps "the most perfect form of democracy that exists anywhere" (Dahl 1961, p. 316).

This consensus on fundamentals is produced and sustained through various means of socialization, the most important of which is the school system. Moreover, while the political beliefs and values of most people are implicit, vague, and often inconsistent, the politically active stratum, and particularly the elites, adhere to these values much more consistently and articulately. The consensus with regard to democratic principles serves two functions: It limits the choices available to elites, and it offers dissenters the possibility of appeal to the electorate. Dissent can thus find legitimate outlets, with dissenters often being eventually absorbed into the system they seek to modify.

Dahl's study of New Haven politics was but one among a group of community studies that in the 1950s and 1960s provoked a passionate debate between the advocates of the pluralist model and those of the power elite model. The New Haven study itself has been criticized on several grounds. Dahl's major findings—that elites are specialized and that power is circumscribed—have been challenged as being an artifact of his methodology. By selecting for study what he regarded as key decisions, Dahl ignored other important issues that conceivably were decided behind the scenes, kept out of the public view, or simply never placed on the agenda. Thus, in New Haven, while the redevelopment of the business district emerged as a major issue, housing for low-income residents was never discussed. Subsequent analysis of the New Haven data (see Domhoff 1983) has shown that the issues not dominated by the local power structure (namely, political nominations and improving the public schools) were in fact of little relevance to it. Political nominations are not of great concern to the elite because "there is no evidence that it makes any difference whether one person or another is nominated. . . . [In any case,] the business community had access to the mayors . . . through campaign finance and personal contact" (Domhoff 1983, p. 186). Urban school issues are irrelevant to the upper class because its members send their children either to private schools or to suburban public schools. By contrast, redevelopment, which is a crucial issue for the power structure, was unquestionably dominated by it. In fact, redevelopment is a leading issue in communities everywhere because it is perceived by the local elite as essential to economic growth, and everywhere it is dominated by the elite.

Dahl's study has also been criticized for its emphasis on the crucial role of elites in democracy and for its acceptance of mass apathy as a normal, even desirable, condition. Conflict theorists Jack Walker (1966) and Michael Parenti (1978) point out that Dahl failed to analyze the major reason for apathy: the absence of any real power on the part of the masses to change their situation through institutionalized political action. At the same time, Dahl ignored noninstitutionalized political activity (such as civil rights demonstrations) that fell outside the channels he was observing and in the 1960s revolutionized the political scene. Thus, he failed to recognize that apathy was partly illusory (confined for the most part to institutionalized participation) and partly a result of the monopolization of power by the elite.

Finally, Dahl's conceptualization of an implicit consensus on the democratic creed has been attacked. Conflict theorists William Form and Joan Rytina (1969) claim that whatever agreement on norms and values exists in our society is a sham. The consensus is meaningless partly because it results from indoctrination by the elites (false consciousness) and partly because it addresses itself only to peripheral issues such as "the rules of the game." A more accurate picture, they claim, would highlight extensive disagreements on substantive issues such as who should benefit from government programs.

Whatever the methodological and ideological pitfalls of Dahl's study, there is no question that it underscores the main elements of pluralist theory: the fragmentation of power, the competition of elites, the importance of consensus, the apathy of the average citizen, and the existence of actual and potential interest groups that seek to influence policy. It is the last element—the role of voluntary associations representing diverse interest groups—that forms the center of pluralist theory and distinguishes it from other bodies of political thought. We now turn to a critical evaluation of pluralism.

Critiques of Pluralism

Pluralist writers assume that resources, however unequal their distribution, are sufficiently widespread to guarantee nearly all groups a voice in policy making. Pluralists further assume that legitimate grievances and interests will sooner or later find a forum, that elites' actions are constrained by a consensus on fundamental values, and that policy outcomes reflect not only the distribution of political muscle but also the relative intensities of preference in the population. On the basis of research guided by these assumptions, pluralists conclude that the American political system is more than a working arrangement—it is fundamentally equitable. The assumptions, data, and conclusions of pluralism have been challenged by critics who maintain that the pluralist model does not account for the workings of the political system either empirically or theoretically.

Critics claim that the pluralists' treatment of the concept of interest and interest groups, which lies at the heart of their theory, begs the questions of rationality and intentionality (see Balbus 1971; Wrong 1980, particularly pp. 184–96). Like classical liberal ideology (see chapter 6), pluralist theory assumes that individuals are fully aware of their true interests

and are motivated to pursue those interests to the best of their ability. But what about false consciousness? A group may have a common objective interest in the Marxian sense (that is, when its life chances are affected by common external conditions or by an impending policy issue) without being aware of that interest. Critics of pluralism insist that we cannot infer a group's objective interests either from its political activity or, for that matter, from its inactivity.

According to these critics, in other words, we cannot infer the absence of a legitimate grievance from the absence of an organized lobbying effort in the pluralist arena. Thus, the movement for women's rights did not explode upon America's public consciousness until 1968 (see Freeman 1973), although women had always suffered discrimination with regard to employment, credit, and popular stereotypes. We still remember when a married or engaged female student could not be accepted in a top graduate school because she was not considered a "serious student" and when a divorced woman could not qualify for a mortgage or a credit card. A student leader of the 1960s, Mark Rudd of Columbia University, called on women to join the peace movement so they could serve coffee to the male activists. Another leader of the 1960s, Stokely Carmichael of the Student Nonviolent Coordinating Committee (SNCC), insisted that "the only position for women in SNCC is prone." Until recently, women by and large accepted their secondary role. If they chafed, they were often told by the media and even by psychiatrists that they had failed to internalize appropriate feminine role expectations and that they needed to adjust to the prevailing institutions and mores. A few women struggled alone to overcome the odds against them and achieve occupational success, but no organized movement to combat discrimination and inequality existed.

By the late 1960s, however, women schooled in the civil rights and the antiwar movements began to see sex-role equality not as a personal or psychological *trouble* but as a political and economic *issue*. They organized to lobby for changing the country's laws and institutions. In Marxian terms, women had overcome their false consciousness, which had diverted them from the political and economic struggle for equality, and had achieved true consciousness. In Mannheimian terms, they no longer held utopian or ideological views but had realistically diagnosed their social situation. In Millsian terms, they had exercised their sociological imagination. Regardless of the theoretical imagery brought to bear, these women came to know the social forces operating in their world. According to conflict theorists, this understanding is a major prerequisite for political action (other conditions necessary for the emergence of organized movements are discussed in chapters 12 and 13). In short, according to critics of pluralism, the appropriate question for political sociologists should be not how various groups attempt to influence a given public policy but under what conditions objective, structurally induced group interests can be translated into purposeful political activity.

Innumerable barriers besides false consciousness may prevent the aggrieved from voicing their opinions and mobilizing for effective action within institutionalized political channels, including lack of money, organization, education, time, energy, or political savvy; fear of retaliation by law-enforcement authorities or employers; and feelings of hopelessness and powerlessness. These barriers do not affect all segments of society equally. Like resources for participation, barriers are a function of the socioeconomic structure. The poor and minorities are relatively voiceless, while the well-to-do, the well-educated, and the well-connected exert a disproportionate influence on policy decisions. Although the United States is often described as a nation of joiners, the joiners tend to come primarily from the ranks of the upper-middle and upper classes; those at the bottom of the scale participate much less. Leadership and involvement in voluntary associations, as well as voter participation, vary with socioeconomic status. A pluralist social

structure cannot guarantee a voice to the aggrieved and the exploited. In fact, the very myth of pluralism—that all legitimate interests will sooner or later be aired—acts to perpetuate economic and political inequality (see Form and Rytina 1969).

Moreover, even if we were to assume that all interests are somehow represented by one voluntary association or another (clearly an inaccurate assumption), it cannot be denied that all associations do not carry the same weight. Organizations representing big business interests, for example, are more powerful than those representing labor, racial minority groups, or even organized religion. In the federal budget cuts of the first Reagan administration (1981–1985), programs benefiting the middle class (such as student loans, Social Security, and Medicare) were largely spared, while programs whose principal beneficiaries were the poor (such as food stamps, Aid to Dependent Children, and Medicaid) were slashed more drastically. The reason for the difference is that groups representing middle-class interests were able to exert more pressure on Congress than groups advocating the rights of the needy. Thus, pluralism, far from equalizing political influence across the socioeconomic spectrum, further distorts influence in favor of the upper strata.

Critics of pluralism also point out that crucial decisions are often made away from the publicized give-and-take of the political process. A decision made at corporate headquarters to move a plant out of a Midwestern community and into the Sunbelt may cause the destruction of jobs, loss of tax revenues, and in some instances the demise of the city. Similarly, an unpublicized decision by a governmental agency to reduce safety inspections in coal mines may affect the fortunes of the coal industry, the lives and health of miners, and the ecological and economic well-being of entire regions. Yet at no point in these decisions are those whose lives are affected given an opportunity to intervene. Moreover, powerful groups may be able to prevent an issue from being publicly debated altogether. "Political elites . . . regularly have the capacity to wield a great amount of power and authority in the form of decisions and non-decisions which significantly influence the values of a society. . . . To the extent [that elites can] prevent potentially unfavorable issues from becoming overt, the nondecision-making process is utilized" (Bachrach 1967, pp. 77–78; see also Lukes 1979). Pluralists limit their analysis to observable decisions, ignoring the agenda-setting ability of powerful groups and individuals. In focusing on public power, they overlook private power.

The elitist bias of some pluralist theorists has also come under criticism. Pluralists portray the masses as either irrational or acquiescent (see Dahl 1961; Mannheim 1940; and Kornhauser 1959). Consequently, they claim that intermediary associations are needed to shield the elites from the masses and that democracy is adequately safeguarded when *elites* enjoy freedom of competition and share a consensus on key values. This viewpoint, conflict theorist Jack Walker believes, profoundly distorts the intentions of the classical theorists of democracy.

> The heart of the classical theory was its justification of broad participation in the public affairs of the community; the aim was the production of citizens who were capable enough and responsible enough to play this role. The classical theory was not meant to describe any existing system of government; it was an outline, a set of prescriptions for the ideal polity which men should strive to create. The [pluralists], in their quest for realism, have changed this distinctive prescriptive element in democratic theory; they have substituted stability and efficiency as the prime goals of democracy. (Walker 1966, p. 289)

Furthermore, according to Walker (1966) and Parenti (1978), pluralist theory is empirically inadequate in that it fails to come to grips with the real workings of the political system. Consider the issue of the apathy of the masses. Dahl and other pluralists feel that apathy is a normal, even healthy condition of the political system for two main reasons: It implies a fundamental acquiescence, if not actual satisfac-

tion, with the way things are, and it allows elites to govern. Walker and Parenti believe that apathy reflects not acquiescence and a preference for private pursuits over public ones but powerlessness and frustration with the institutionalized political process (see also the discussion of nonvoting in chapter 10). Thus, apathy signals not the health of the political system but its disease. In fact, the masses occasionally indicate their dissatisfaction through noninstitutionalized means such as demonstrations for nuclear disarmament and against apartheid in South Africa, hunger strikes for the Equal Rights Amendment, and other actions. Grass-roots participation through noninstitutionalized means, all but ignored by the pluralists, is, according to Walker and others, a potent agent of social change and innovation.

Dahl (1982, p. 7) defends pluralism against the charge that it falls short of the ideal democracy depicted by the writers of the classical school. "The ideal criteria are so demanding that no actual regime has ever fully met them. Possibly none ever will. To deny the term *democracy* to any regime not fully democratic in the ideal sense would be equivalent to saying that no democratic regime has ever existed." Even in ancient Greek city-states, as historians have shown, political realities differed from the ideal image later attributed to them. "Their history is a tale of bitter conflicts and an almost total failure to develop effective institutions for settling political disputes by peaceful and constitutional means. . . . The outcome of political conflict was typically savage. Victors exiled or killed the losers, seized their property, and took vengeance on their kin. In this respect republics with popular governments were on the whole no better than the oligarchies and despotisms of their day" (Dahl 1982, p. 10). In modern diverse societies, much more so than in the small and relatively homogeneous city-states, government cannot be highly participatory, nor can the average citizen have much influence over societal decisions. Given the limitations inherent in numbers, Dahl argues, pluralism (or polyarchy) offers the best hope for democratic government.

Summary

The question of how power is distributed in society is answered differently by various theoretical perspectives, notably the pluralist and elite models. Pluralist theorists consider voluntary associations to be crucial for the survival of democracy. The functions of these associations include providing legitimate channels for citizens' input into the governing process, protecting the liberties of citizens against elite encroachment, and strengthening society's cohesion and stability.

Several case studies support and amplify pluralist theory. Lipset and his colleagues find grass-roots participation to be a necessary condition of democratic government. Dahl, on the other hand, portrays the American community as governed by elites, with the masses largely acquiescent. Yet Dahl claims that democracy is maintained by the fragmentation of elites and the dispersal of resources for grass-roots participation.

Critics charge that pluralists confuse the issues of subjective and objective interests and overlook the obstacles to effective political action inherent in the stratification system. Pluralists unduly emphasize the legislative political process and fail to take into account the influence of bureaucratic and corporate elites. In addition, they ignore the issue of who ultimately benefits from societal decisions. Finally, pluralists are charged with betraying the classical principles of democracy and harboring a pro-elitist bias.

In response to these criticisms, pluralists argue that no large-scale society can approximate the conditions of ideal democracy depicted by the classical writers. To hold any contemporary government to that ideal would be to deny the possibility of democracy at all. Pluralism, the defenders claim, offers the best hope of attaining even a modicum of democracy.

In chapter 8, we turn our attention to the classical elite theory of political power.

CHAPTER EIGHT

The Realities of Power: Classical Elite Theory

Preview

This chapter examines the classical formulations of elite theory, which were developed in the early part of the twentieth century, and sets the background for the discussion in chapter 9 of contemporary elite theory, which may be considered to begin with the work of C. Wright Mills in the 1950s.

Elite theory contrasts with pluralist theory in many ways: Pluralism envisions an array of independent centers of power; elite theory views power as centralized and hierarchical, as a zero-sum game (see chapter 7). Pluralism considers resources for participation in the political process to be widely distributed; elite theory documents the monopolization of resources in the hands of the few. Pluralism emphasizes the balance between consensus and conflict; elite theory stresses the antagonism between elites and masses. Finally, empirical studies guided by pluralist theory focus on the *process* of decision making in democratic societies: Who has what visible input into the legislative process? Studies guided by elite theory, on the other hand, highlight the *outcomes* of policy: Who gets what?

In the past, most elite theorists viewed elite rule not only as inevitable but also as desirable. Plato saw government by an aristocracy based on wealth and learning, headed by a philosopher-king, as the best guarantor of society's well-being. Utopian socialists Charles Fourier (1772–1837) and Henri de Saint-Simon (1760–1825) advocated rule by an industrial and scientific elite as the perfect form of government in the society of the future. The early-twentieth-century elite theorists examined in this chapter, Pareto, Mosca, and Michels, supported the fascist regime of Benito Mussolini in Italy. As we will see in chapter 9, however, contemporary elite theorists decry elite rule as undemocratic and call for greater equality of power; they may, in fact, be termed antielitist. Elite theories, then, convey an ideological stance as well as an analytical scheme.

Vilfredo Pareto (1848–1923): The Psychology of Power

Modern classical elite theory began at the turn of the twentieth century with the work of European social scientists Vilfredo Pareto, Gaetano Mosca, and Robert Michels. Pareto, an Italian aristocrat with antidemocratic tendencies, stressed in his book *The Mind and Society* (completed in 1912) the importance of psychological causes of elite rule. All societies, he insisted, including even nominally democratic ones, are governed by elites.

> Ignoring exceptions, which are few in number and of short duration, one finds everywhere a governing class of relatively few individuals that keeps itself in power partly by force and partly by the consent of the subject class, which is much more populous. The differences lie principally . . . in the relative proportions of force and consent and . . . in the manners in which the force is used and the consent obtained. (Pareto 1935, p. 1569, sec. 2244)[1]

According to Pareto, psychological properties, which he termed *sentiments* or *residues*, play a key role in elite rule. These sentiments are responsible for elevating certain individuals and families into the elite, for sustaining elites'

---

1. Pareto's work *The Mind and Society* (originally titled *Treatise on General Sociology*) contains more than two thousand pages and is divided into numbered sections from 1 to 2612. Since the section numbers are consistent across various editions, they will be used here along with page numbers to facilitate reference.

power, and for precipitating their occasional downfall. Two classes of residues are particularly important. Class I residues, "the residue of combinations," refer to the ability to take familiar elements out of their traditional context and rearrange them in new ways. This residue is responsible for innovativeness or creativity. Among scientists, the presence of Class I residues leads to the discovery of new theories out of manipulations of familiar facts. Among political leaders, it leads to revolutions and social transformations. In nonrevolutionary regimes, a preponderance of Class I residues results in a preference for peaceful policies over militaristic ones, an ethic of individualism and experimentation, economic expansion, and artistic and scientific creativity. The men and women who led the Russian Revolution and who later transformed the Soviet Union from a quasi-feudal agrarian society into a collectivized industrial one were dominated by Class I residues. In a different way, so were the captains of industry and government who in the late nineteenth century led the United States into a period of unprecedented economic expansion.

Class II residues, "the residue of the persistence of aggregates," refer to a conservative predisposition dominated by a desire to preserve the status quo. These residues are manifest in regimes that value domestic stability, nationalistic pride, and militarism. Recent examples of Class II residues are the authoritarian regimes of Francisco Franco in Spain and the Duvaliers, father and son, in Haiti.

Although individuals tend to be dominated exclusively by one class of residues or another, elites usually contain a mixture of both. In fact, in order to remain in power, elites must display the right proportion of each type. Elites, therefore, must elevate into their ranks individuals from the lower strata who manifest the requisite residues as well as purge from their ranks those who do not. "The governing class is restored not only in numbers but—and that is the more important thing—in quality, by families rising from the lower classes and bringing

with them the vigor and the proportions of residues necessary for keeping themselves in power. It is also restored by the loss of its more degenerate members. . . . In virtue of class-circulation, the governing elite is always in a state of slow and continuous transformation" (Pareto 1935, pp. 1430–31, 1435, secs. 2054, 2056).

Pareto is referring, of course, to social mobility, which he believes is necessary for the health and stability of elite rule. Where the stratification system is too rigid and social mobility is blocked, as in Czarist Russia or Imperial Germany, revolution is inevitable. Revolutions occur when elites stagnate as a result of being deprived of the invigorating qualities of new blood. At the same time, the lower strata are filled with highly capable, frustrated individuals. Those members of the lower strata willing to use force who possess the residues necessary to govern but are blocked from entry into the elite will sooner or later start a revolution. Pareto cynically observes that, although leaders of revolutions typically resort to populist slogans such as "Liberty, Equality, Fraternity" or "Power to the People" in order to win support, once the leaders acquire power they do not necessarily share it with the masses. On the contrary, revolutions merely lead to the replacement of one elite by another. Thus, the French Revolution replaced the aristocratic elite of the *ancien* (old) *regime* with the despotic rule of the Jacobins, while the Russian Revolution (which occurred five years after the completion of *The Mind and Society*), in the view of some observers, merely replaced the czarist autocracy with a Communist one. In brief, if an elite is to preserve its rule, it must possess the right combination of residues or psychological propensities. In the absence of such residues, the elite may be overthrown.

Elites are composed of two groups, an inner elite and an outer elite. The inner elite, the smaller and higher ranking of the two groups, actually governs. The outer elite, composed of the politically inactive members of the upper class, does not govern directly but nevertheless enjoys the accoutrements of power and privilege.

In order to govern, elites must use the services of members of lower strata. These servants of the elite, or subelites, are in turn divided into two groups that correspond to "the two principal instruments for holding power secure. The one group uses force, and is made up of soldiers, police of one sort or another" (Pareto 1935, pp. 1585–86, sec. 2257). The second, more important group uses persuasion. Experts of persuasion include elected officials who enact tariffs and tax laws that benefit big business, newspaper editors who write editorials that support probusiness policies, and teachers who transmit the elite's values to the young. Subelites, typically drawn from the middle class, are not themselves the ultimate beneficiaries of society's decisions, yet they are the pillars on which elite rule rests. They enact policies on its behalf, create and maintain the consensus that upholds its rule, and, when necessary, use violence to enforce its domination.

The subelites and outer elites clearly are too numerous and diverse to act in a unified, single-minded manner. But even the inner elite is far from cohesive. Critics erroneously perceive the inner elite in conspiratorial terms as a cabal, "as a person, or at least as a concrete unit, and imagine that it knows what it wants and executes by logical procedures designs which it had conceived in advance" (Pareto 1935, p. 1576, sec. 2254). Pareto cites the tendency of the anti-Semites of his day to invoke an international Jewish conspiracy and of some socialists to invoke a capitalist conspiracy.

The image of the elite as a cohesive clique rationally pursuing a strategy of aggrandizement and domination could not be further from the truth, according to Pareto. Contrary to popular perceptions, members of the inner elite "hold no meetings where they congregate to plot common designs, nor have they any other devices for reaching a common accord" (Pareto 1935, p. 1576, sec. 2254). Rather, the very powerful, like the rest of us, simply drift into major

decisions or make a series of small day-to-day decisions that have the cumulative, unforeseen effect of perpetuating the elite's domination and increasing its wealth, whatever the cost to society. At the turn of the century, arms manufacturers in Europe and the United States were making myriad discrete decisions to increase the manufacturing of arms and their sale to other nations. The motive was "not to bring on a war, but . . . to make a direct profit in each little case." At the same time, governments were striving to arm their nations and appealing to "sentiments of patriotism in the masses at large," again without "preconceived design" to make war. Pareto foresaw that as a result of all this activity a war that nobody consciously wanted would ensue: "Some day the war they have made way for but not wanted may break out; and then it will be a consequence of the past activities of the speculators [that is, the arms merchants], but not of any intent they have had" (Pareto 1935, p. 1577, sec. 2254).

Pareto was prescient. Before the manuscript of *The Mind and Society* could be brought to press, World War I broke out. Today, some observers believe, the same chilling possibility exists of a war nobody wants, a war brought about by an unwitting game of zero-sum international politics played by the ruling elites of the superpowers. Pareto's point, however, is not that militarism is dangerous but that elite rule is haphazard by nature. Because their members have been socialized by similar influences and share similar individual interests and outlooks, elites make decisions in a consistent though disorganized way (see chapters 4 and 9). Despite the absence of conscious design, therefore, elites reach decisions whose cumulative effect is to increase the collective power and profit of their members.

This does not mean that elites lack class consciousness in the Marxian sense. In fact, while the masses are governed totally by irrational sentiments or residues, elites are governed at least partly by rational interests. Specifically, the elite's interest is to consolidate its power and augment its profits. To this end, a shrewd elite will manipulate the masses into serving its own interests by appealing either to the masses' emotions or to their lofty ideals. Such manipulation creates a false consensus that allows the elite to reduce its reliance on force to maintain power.

Pareto calls the doctrines used to induce consent *derivations*, a concept akin to Marx's ruling-class ideology. Derivations include religious myths, such as the myth that the elite's rule is sanctioned by divine right, and political myths, such as the democratic fiction that real power rests with the masses. "The 'divine rights' of the prince, of the aristocracy, of the people, the proletariat, the majority—or any other divine right that might be imagined—have not the slightest experimental validity. . . . To say that not one of these 'rights' has any experimental foundation does not, of course, in any way impugn the utility to society with which it may be credited" (Pareto 1935, p. 1567, sec. 2239). The function of derivations is to persuade the masses to acquiesce to elite rule.

Persuasion alone, however, is not enough to guarantee that the elite will remain in power. Derivations must be augmented by a readiness to use force. In other words, elite rule rests on a combination of force and consent. Elites that possess Class I residues are more likely to rely on persuasion or, in Pareto's words, on chicanery and cunning. Pareto calls such elites foxes. Elites possessing Class II residues are more likely to rely on force. These elites are called lions by Pareto. Frequently, elites are transformed over the course of time from lions to foxes. Having come to power through the use of arms, they lose their militaristic qualities as more peacefully inclined industrial and commercial elements come to the fore. Lions thus become foxes, only to be overthrown by a new group of lions.

Stable elite rule requires the use of both force and persuasion in the right proportions. An elite that relies excessively on the use of force risks antagonizing the populace to the point

where revolution is inevitable. Recent examples of such regimes include the governments of Jean-Claude Duvalier in Haiti and Ferdinand Marcos in the Philippines. In both cases, the use of force to suppress the masses became increasingly costly in terms of lives, money, and worldwide public opinion; and in 1986 both governments were overthrown.

An elite whose power rests on persuasion alone is even more unstable than one that relies excessively on force. Elites that rule out the use of force, whether for misguided humanitarian reasons or for strategic reasons (that is, a belief that other means will be more effective), are easily overthrown by less squeamish counterelites. "A mere handful of citizens, so long as they are willing to use violence, can force their will upon public officials who are not inclined to meet violence with equal violence" (Pareto 1935, p. 1556, sec. 2228). In other words, when the foxes within an elite have pushed out the lions, the elite will lose its capacity to put its collective self-preservation before the individual interests of its members, to devise strategic long-term plans, and to take unpalatable action in its own defense. A counterelite is then sure to stake its claim to power.

> One might guess that if cunning, chicanery, combinations were all there was to government, the dominion of the class in which Class I residues by far predominate would last over a very long period. . . . But governing is also a matter of force, and as Class I residues grow stronger and Class II residues weaker, the individuals in power become less and less capable of using force, so that an unstable equilibrium results and revolutions occur, such as the Protestant revolt against the ruling classes of the renaissance, or the uprising of the French masses against their governors in 1789. (Pareto 1935, p. 1556, sec. 2228).

A more recent example is provided by events in Europe in the 1930s. Some contemporary historians believe that the "failure of nerve" of the democracies, in particular the French and

British premiers' reluctance to stand up to Hitler that culminated at the Munich Conference in 1938, left the way open for Hitler's aggression and eventually led to World War II: Had the democracies been ready to use deterrence as early as the German militarization of the Rhineland in 1936, the argument goes, perhaps World War II could have been avoided.

According to Pareto, then, in order to remain in power, elites must maintain the right balance between force and persuasion, between the qualities of lions and foxes. Since such a constellation is exceedingly rare, elites typically do not last more than a few generations. "History is the graveyard of aristocracies" (Pareto 1935, p. 1430, sec. 2053).

Most of Pareto's analysis so far has centered on aristocratic elites, and his examples have been drawn from the more or less remote past. The reader may object that Pareto's theory is not relevant to democratic countries such as the United States. But as we have seen, Pareto considers democracy no exception to the principle of elite domination. In fact, he reserves his highest scorn for the democratic self-delusion that sovereignty rests with the people. "We need not linger on the fiction of 'popular representation'—poppycock grinds no flour" (Pareto 1935, p. 1569, sec. 2244). Only the *form* of elite rule differs between democracies and aristocracies. In a democracy, power rests in the hands not of a visible elite but of a hidden one composed of the owners and managers of big business, or in Pareto's term, the plutocracy. Plutocrats always pursue a single interest—their own profits—and are quite adept at deceiving the masses into seeing themselves as the sovereigns. "King Demos, good soul, thinks he is following his own devices. In reality he is following the lead of his rulers. But that very often turns out to the advantage of his rulers only, for they, from the days of Aristotle down to our own, have made lavish use of the arts of bamboozling King Demos" (Pareto 1935, p. 1573, sec. 2253). Thus, democratic appearances notwithstanding, in reality elite rule is inescapable.

Gaetano Mosca (1858–1941): The Sociology of Power

Italian social scientist and politician Gaetano Mosca first published his classical work *Elements of Political Science* in 1896. A revised edition was published in 1923, just one year after Mussolini's rise to power in Rome. An English edition, titled *The Ruling Class*, was published in 1939.

Like his contemporary Pareto, Mosca was skeptical about the future of democracy and believed that the rule of the few over the many was inevitable. This principle, he realized, contradicted not only democratic theories of majority rule but also earlier classifications of different types of government, such as those of Aristotle and Montesquieu (see chapter 2). Indeed, Mosca insisted that all types of society and government are ruled by small elites. He differed from Pareto, however, in emphasizing the social-structural and organizational rather than the psychological roots of elite government. Mosca's theory is therefore both more sociological and more modern than Pareto's, and his pessimistic conclusions seem more inescapable.

Mosca does not mince his words regarding the inevitability of elite rule:

> In all societies—from societies that are very meagerly developed and have barely attained the dawning of civilization, down to the most advanced and powerful societies—two classes of people appear—a class that rules and a class that is ruled. The first class, always the less numerous, performs all the political functions, monopolizes power and enjoys the advantages that power brings, whereas the second, the more numerous class, is directed and controlled by the first. (Mosca 1939, p. 50)

What enables the few to consolidate and sustain their domination over the many? To be sure, the personal attributes emphasized by Pareto play a role. Members of the elite typically possess "certain intellectual qualities, such as readiness of perception and keenness of observation." They also possess such strengths of personality as "tenacity of purpose, self-confidence, and above all, activity," in other words, the capacity for hard work. It helps, of course, to be born into the upper class. "In any type of society, whether ostensibly democratic or otherwise, being born to a high station is one of the best claims a person can have to staying there" (Mosca 1939, pp. 122–23).

And yet, according to Mosca, the crucial resource the ruling class possesses is not its members' superior personal qualities but their superior organization. The minority is always better organized than the majority, and it is this talent for organization that enables the minority to prevail.

> In reality the dominion of an organized minority, obeying a single impulse, over the unorganized majority is inevitable. . . . The minority is organized for the very reason that it is a minority. A hundred men acting uniformly in concert, with a common understanding, will triumph over a thousand men who are not in accord and can therefore be dealt with one by one. Meanwhile it will be easier for the former to act in concert and have a mutual understanding simply because they are a hundred and not a thousand. (Mosca 1939, p. 53)

The significance of the concept of a ruling class, Mosca asserts, lies in the crucial role elites play in society. "The varying structure of ruling classes has a preponderant importance in determining the political type, and also the level of civilization, of the different peoples" (Mosca 1939, p. 51). Thus, for example, the brilliant civilization of France in the seventeenth and eighteenth centuries had less to do with the contributions of the common French people than with the shining qualities of the aristocracy (see Mosca 1939, p. ix).

But the relationship between elites and societies is not one-sided. Just as elites shape their societies, social forces within those societies also shape elites. The concept of social forces is cen-

tral to Mosca's theory. **Social forces** include various economic sectors such as manufacturing, agriculture, and commerce, as well as major institutional spheres such as education, religion, and the military. Each social force is associated with a specific social class—farmers, landowners, clergy, warriors, and so on. Each organized social force constitutes a special interest group headed by its own elite that vies for power in the central government. As the balance of social forces shifts, the composition of the central ruling elite changes to reflect the new balance. For example, the transition from hunting and gathering societies to settled agricultural ones gradually transforms the social structure as well as the political elite. In agrarian societies such as medieval Europe, farming is the mainstay of the economy, religious beliefs are strong, and concern with military security is high. Consequently, three major classes vie for power: farmers, priests, and warriors. Usually the warriors win the struggle, establishing themselves as the most powerful and wealthiest group.

In time, warfare declines, economic productivity increases, and society progresses from feudalism to industrialism. New social forces emerge—commerce and finance, manufacturing, and secular science. These social forces, in turn, give rise to new elites. "Wealth rather than military valor comes to be the characteristic feature of the dominant class: the people who rule are the rich rather than the brave. . . . To be rich is to become powerful" (Mosca 1939, p. 57). The feudal state has been transformed into a bureaucratic state, the feudal elite into a bureaucratic elite. An examination of the two types of elite illustrates the complex relationship between social structure and political power.

Feudal society is characterized by small, self-sufficient units of production such as the baronial manor or the craft guild. In addition to agriculture, military and religious social forces play important roles. In feudal society, the elite tends to be a hereditary ruling class, an aristocracy of birth. Power is exercised informally by those members of the ruling class with moral persuasiveness or military prowess and a willingness to use these resources. Authority is diffuse; the same individual performs several functions of government. "The medieval baron was simultaneously owner of the land, military commander, judge and administrator of his fief. . . . Sometimes religious functions also are exercised by the leader who has charge of other social activities" (Mosca 1939, pp. 81–82). The feudal elite is a cross between traditional and charismatic authority in Weber's sense. Perhaps the best-known examples of feudal societies existed in medieval Europe.

Bureaucratic society differs from feudal society in many important ways, and its political institutions reflect these differences. Bureaucratic society is characterized by very large units of production and administration. Power is centralized, and the government is strong enough to "abrogate a considerable portion of the social wealth by taxation and [use] it to maintain a military establishment and . . . to support . . . a number of public services" (Mosca 1939, p. 83). Wealth, represented by industry, capital, or other assets, becomes the most important social force, and the wealthy assume key positions of power. Unlike the feudal elite, which is essentially hereditary, the bureaucratic elite is relatively open to talented individuals from all classes. In addition, "in a bureaucratic state there is always a greater specialization in the functions of government than in the feudal state" (Mosca 1939, p. 83). Separate bureaucratic positions are created to manage judiciary, fiscal, and military affairs. Power is associated with positions, not with individuals. In Weber's term, the basis of authority is now legal-rational. Compared to the haphazard and often unstable nature of power in the feudal state, the bureaucratic state is more stable, for it "assures a far greater discipline in all grades of political, administrative, and military service." Bureaucratic elites exist in all modern societies (Mosca 1939, p. 83).

Clearly, whatever the predominant social forces in a society, elite rule is inevitable. Only the composition of the elite and its mode of organization vary. Elites may recruit new members in a number of ways. Aristocratic elites rely on a hereditary ruling class, while democratic elites recruit new members from the lower classes. A relatively open class system, which allows some (but not too much) upward mobility, serves several functions. One function is to replenish the elite with new talent while at the same time depriving the masses of strong potential leaders who might some day spearhead a revolution. The existence of upward mobility also serve the function of demonstrating that the rules of the game are fair, that those born into the lower ranks have opportunities to advance themselves, and that membership in the elite is based on merit rather than on arbitrary criteria such as high birth or political cunning. In short, a democratic system of recruitment into the elite serves to legitimate the elite's rule without changing its essentially antiegalitarian nature.

Even in so-called democracies, then, elites predominate. Consider the case of the United States, where the myth of popular sovereignty runs deep, where "all powers flow directly or indirectly from popular elections, and suffrage is equal for all men and women" (Mosca 1939, p. 57). Even here "democracy . . . does not prevent a rich man from being more influential than a poor man, since he can use pressures upon the politicians who control public administration. It does not prevent elections from being carried on to the music of clinking dollars. It does not prevent . . . congressmen from feeling the influence of powerful corporations and great financiers" (Mosca 1939, p. 58). Moreover, even in a democracy, wealth, superior education, and the skills of leadership are passed down within the same families, so that elite position becomes hereditary in fact if not in principle.

> All ruling classes tend to become hereditary in fact if not in law. . . . Wealth and military valor are easily maintained in certain families by moral tradition and by heredity. Qualifica-

tions for important office—the habit of, and to an extent the capacity for, dealing with affairs of consequence—is much more readily acquired when one has had a certain familiarity with them from childhood. Even when academic degrees, scientific training, special aptitudes as tested by examinations and competitions, open the way to public office, there is no eliminating . . . special advantage. . . . In actual fact, though examinations and competitions may be open to all, the majority never have the resources for meeting the expense of long preparation, and many others are without the connections and kinships that set an individual promptly on the right road, enabling him to avoid the gropings and blunders that are inevitable when one enters an unfamiliar environment without any guidance or support. . . . The truth is that social positions, family tradition, the habits of the class in which we live, contribute more than is commonly supposed to the greater or lesser development of the qualities [necessary for leadership]. (Mosca 1939, pp. 61–63)

Thus, while Pareto maintained that members of the elite possess innately superior qualities, Mosca argued that such qualities are a product of one's location in the social class structure rather than the cause of one's position.

Whether bureaucratic or feudal, aristocratic or democratic, elites must be willing to use force if they are to remain in power, yet no society can be ruled by force alone. "Physical force may suffice to prevent the outbreak of a violent catastrophe from day to day, but it cannot restore to the social body the moral unity essential for a stable order" (Mosca 1939, p. 320). Or, as a Mongol minister admonished his chief, the son of Genghis Khan, "Your empire was conquered on horseback, but you cannot rule it from the back of a horse" (Mosca 1939, p. 313). Like Pareto, Mosca recognized the importance of a legitimating myth or **political formula** in influencing the masses to accept elite rule. Elite rule must be justified on the basis of some universal moral principle and must appeal to the commonly held beliefs of the masses. In a deeply

religious society, the divine right of kings may be invoked as the political formula that legitimates elite rule, while in a secular democratic society such as the United States, the principle of government by the will of the people will be used. Both principles are equally fictitious. "The divine right of kings was the great superstition of past ages, and . . . the divine right of elected assemblies is the great superstition of our present age." However, no society "can hold together without one of these 'great superstitions,' for a universal illusion is . . . a social force that contributes powerfully to consolidating political organization and unifying peoples" (Mosca 1939, p. 71).

The more unified elites and masses are in their belief systems, the more effective the political formula and the more stable the government. On the other hand, where the masses are alienated from the elite's value system or where the elite has lost sight of its roots in the religion and culture of the people, revolution is likely. A recent example is the fate of the late Shah of Iran. The Shah, who ruled from 1953 to 1979, attempted to modernize his country by importing not only Western technology but also Western values such as secularism and women's equality. However, the masses, deeply religious and wedded to traditional Islamic ways of life, grew progressively alienated from the regime and more and more hostile to it. In 1979, the Shah's regime was overthrown and replaced by a militant Islamic regime headed by the Ayatollah Khomeini, a religious leader. The new regime, whose methods were no less brutal than those of the Shah (an estimated twenty thousand people were executed in Iran between 1979 and 1981), nevertheless succeeded where the previous regime had failed. The people and their leaders were now united in a common cause, the defense of Islam against alleged foreign imperialism. With an effective political formula, the regime seemed solidly entrenched.

In order to foist a political formula upon the people, the elite must make effective use of various means of persuasion or, in Mosca's terms, of propaganda. The process of inculcating the "correct" beliefs in the masses and uprooting "false" ones is often referred to as *political socialization* (see chapter 5). The means of socialization include the educational system and the mass communication media. They may also include more sinister practices such as the use of censorship to eliminate subversive ideas and the establishment of thought-reform camps. Whatever the means of socialization, the aim is to create a "thoroughgoing identification of the concept of justice and right with the given religious or political doctrine" (Mosca 1939, p. 186). When such moral justification has been established, the elite's rule is secure.

Robert Michels (1876–1936): Power in Organizations

German writer Robert Michels, who at different times in his life was a revolutionary socialist, an anarcho-syndicalist, and a fascist sympathizer (see Scaff 1981), analyzed the German Social Democratic party. It must be remembered that at the turn of the twentieth century, when much of Europe was ruled by autocratic monarchs (such as Kaiser Wilhelm and Czar Nicholas) socialist parties were deemed by many to be the best hope for genuine democracy. The German Social Democratic party was dedicated to the pursuit of democratic goals, including universal suffrage, by any means necessary, reformist or revolutionary.

Because Michels was studying what he believed to be the most democratic organization in the world, his conclusions were even more pessimistic than those of Pareto and Mosca. Inexorable laws, he believed, drive all associations, as well as all governments, into oligarchic rule: "Who says organization, says oligarchy." This conclusion has been labeled the **Iron Law of Oligarchy**. Regardless of the democratic principles that might have inspired both the leaders and the followers at the outset, "we find everywhere that the power of the elected leaders over the electing masses is almost unlimited. The oligarchic structure of the

building suffocates the basic democratic principle" (Michels 1962, p. 365). The socialists' hope for a more humane, democratic society is misguided. "Society cannot exist without a 'dominant' or 'political' class . . . The government or, if the phrase be preferred, the state, cannot be anything other than the organization of a minority. . . . The majority is thus permanently incapable of self-government. . . . The socialists might conquer, but not socialism, which would perish in the moment of its adherents' triumph" (Michels 1962, pp. 353–55).

Michels's book *Political Parties* was first published in 1911. The timing was ominous—within three years, World War I broke out. By the end of the war, the autocratic regimes of Austria-Hungary, Germany, and Russia had been swept aside. Socialist governments, promising democratization, were instituted in their place, but none of these socialist governments was to survive as a democracy. The revolutionary regime of Alexander Kerensky was overthrown pressed brutally, in Germany with the help of none other than the leadership of the Social Democratic party. In Russia, the moderate regime of Alexander Kerensky was overthrown by the Bolshevik Revolution under the leadership of Lenin and Trotsky. The Soviet Union, which as late as the 1920s was believed by many to offer the people genuine hope for a better future, evolved under Stalin into a narrowly autocratic and repressive regime. It seemed as if Michels's predictions were borne out.

What are the forces that doom democracy in the modern world? According to Michels, these forces are both psychological and structural, centering on human nature as well as on the dynamics of organizations. The structural causes of oligarchy are twofold: the impossibility of direct democracy in very large societies and the necessity for prompt and efficient action to meet external adversity. Direct democracy—the participation of all members in societal decisions—is possible only in very small societies. The classic examples of direct democracy are the *ecclesia* (assembly) in ancient Athens and the town meeting in New England (even in Athens, as we have seen, democracy fell short of the ideal in many ways). When a society or an organization reaches a very large size, however, the delegation of authority becomes unavoidable, as is the case with modern political parties. By the beginning of the twentieth century, the Social Democratic party in Berlin alone numbered ninety thousand members. Obviously, an organization of this size cannot be governed by direct democracy, with all members voting on all issues. Instead, direct democracy must give way to representative democracy, with elected delegates empowered to make collective decisions. Once power is delegated, however, democracy succumbs to elite rule. "All power thus proceeds in a natural cycle: issuing from the people, it ends by raising itself above the people" (Michels 1962, p. 75).

The contingencies of size and complexity are compounded by the organization's need to function effectively in a hostile environment. If general elections are to be fought or collective bargaining agreements won (especially in an autocratic climate such as Imperial Germany), the organization, be it a political party or a trade union, cannot afford to function as an amateurish debating society. Freedom of dissent and grass-roots participation must be curtailed in the interest of skillful and prompt decision making. Where would a modern army be, for example, if decisions to attack or retreat were subject to grass-roots debate? Thus, a fateful paradox emerges: On one hand, "democracy is inconceivable without organization. . . . Organization is the weapon of the weak in their struggle with the strong" (Michels 1962, p. 61). On the other hand, if the organization is to meet its goals, power to make decisions must be delegated to a technically skilled, full-time management. Therefore, rule by an elite (in Michels's term, oligarchy) is inevitable.

To these structural forces must be added psychological ones, including factors having to do with the psychology of the masses as well as of the leaders. The masses, Michels believes,

are both too ignorant and too apathetic to govern themselves. "There is no exaggeration in the assertion that among the citizens who enjoy political rights the number of those who have a lively interest in public affairs is insignificant. . . . [Furthermore] most people are altogether devoid of understanding of the actions and reactions between that organism we call the state and their private interests, their prosperity, and their life" (Michels 1962, p. 85). As evidence of the masses' ignorance and apathy toward government, Michels cites the low voting turnout and low attendance at political meetings of his day. Today, nearly a century later and a continent away, similar concerns have been voiced by democratic theorists such as Everett C. Ladd (1977; see also chapter 10).

Contemptuous as Michels is of the masses' ignorance and apathy, he criticizes even more severely what he perceives to be their propensity for hero worship. Among the masses, he observes, there is "a genuine cult for the leaders, who are regarded as heroes." Even before the age of electronic mass communications, leaders were endowed by the masses with such heroic qualities as "the force of will which reduces to obedience less powerful will," the persuasive strength of their convictions, impressive knowledge and expertise about the political process and about the issues of the day, the wisdom associated with superior age, and, not least, "the prestige of celebrity." Given the political immaturity of the masses and "their immense need for direction and guidance," it is no wonder that they perceive their leaders not only as heroic but as indispensable to their own struggle for self-improvement (Michels 1962, pp. 88, 100).

The leaders, for their part, possess both organizational and personal resources that help to maintain and perpetuate their power. Their personal resources include superior education and knowledge, political savvy, and oratorial skills. Even more formidable than the leaders' personal qualities, however, are the bureaucratic resources at their disposal, the very resources entrusted to them by the masses, including control over the organization's coffers, complete access to its communication media, and the legitimate authority to make decisions on the organization's behalf. These decisions might deal with issues such as whether to call a strike or to settle for an employer's wage offer, or whether to tolerate internal dissent or to muffle it in the name of the collective cause. However, "the accumulation of power in the hands of a restricted number of persons . . . necessarily gives rise to numerous abuses. The 'representative,' proud of his indispensability, readily becomes transformed from a servitor of the people into their master" (Michels 1962, p. 166).

But, an objection may be raised, is this abuse of power inevitable? Undeniably, opportunities for such abuse abound. But what about the leaders' motives? Are we to assume, perhaps without justification, that all leaders seek selfish rewards? Not so, says Michels. Democratically elected leaders, especially at the outset of their careers, may well be courageous, honest, and sincerely devoted to their constituents' cause, but once they are in office an insidious psychological transformation takes place—the "natural greed for power" grows with its possession. "He who has once attained to power will not readily be induced to return to the comparatively obscure position which he formerly occupied." Manual workers turned union officials loathe to return to manual labor, for they have grown accustomed to the soft life: "Their hands have lost the callosities of the manual toiler, and are likely to suffer only from writer's cramp. . . . The proletarian leader has ceased to be a manual worker, not solely in the material sense, but psychologically and economically as well." This process has its counterpart among scholars who accept administrative or political positions. Scientists in this situation will "find that their scientific faculties undergo a slow but progressive atrophy. Having become absorbed in the daily political round, they are dead for their discipline, for they no longer have time for the serious study of scientific problems and for the continuous development of their intellectual faculties" (Michels 1962, pp. 206–8, 279). Furthermore, the financial rewards, social prestige, and intellectual stimulation that accompany an administrative career compare very favorably with the conditions attending manual or even low-level white-collar work. No wonder, then, that leaders, whether they initially sought leadership positions out of personal ambition or out of sincere devotion to a cause, soon become enamored of power and concerned above all else with preserving it for themselves and, if possible, for their offspring.

The economic and psychological transformation of the leaders is frequently accompanied by an ideological transformation as well. Leaders who started out as fiery advocates of radical change are likely to temper their views, becoming either outright conservatives or moderate gradualists. This transformation can be traced to the change in their personal circumstances as well as to the growing weariness and cynicism that age and power bring.

> The ex-worker is apt to take pleasure in his new environment, and he tends to become indifferent and even hostile to all progressive aspirations of the democratic sense. He accommodates himself to the existing order and ultimately, weary of the struggle, becomes even reconciled to that order. What interest for them has now the dogma of the social revolution? Their own social revolution has already been effected. (Michels 1962, pp. 283–84)

Thus, even the most dedicated leaders may be co-opted by the established system and betray the interests of their constituents.

Over time, the original goals of a movement, whether better living conditions for the masses or a social revolution, are gradually abandoned in favor of a new, insidious goal—the survival and growth of the organization. This process, which has been termed *goal displacement* by sociologist Robert K. Merton, occurs when a revolutionary party realizes that hopes for a revolution "in our lifetime" are dim and that further talk of revolution will needlessly antagonize the ruling class. Revolutionary slogans may still be mouthed and the red flag of communism waved at rallies, but these symbols are now empty of all content, evoking only catharsis and nostalgia. In Germany, the "revolutionary" Social Democratic party renounced, for the sake of either convenience or survival, the use of such radical tactics as the general strike, antimilitarist agitation, and any other "aggressive action." By the turn of the century, Michels wrote, the party "carefully avoids . . . anything which might irritate the state to excess. The party doctrines are, whenever requisite, attenuated and deformed in accordance with the external needs of the organization. Organization becomes the vital essence of the party" (Michels 1962, p. 336). The leaders realize that "a bold and enterprising action," whether a strike or a revolution, would endanger the magnificent bureaucratic structure they have built, as well as their own careers.

> The work of many decades, the social existence of thousands of leaders and sub-leaders, would be compromised. For these reasons the idea of such a tactic becomes more and more distasteful. . . . It is opposed by the artist's love of the work he has created with so much labor, and also by the personal interest of thousands of honest breadwinners whose economic life is so intimately associated with the life of the party and who tremble at the thought of losing their employment and the consequences they would have to endure if the government should proceed to dissolve the party, as might readily happen in case of war. . . . Thus from a means, organization becomes an end. (Michels 1962, p. 338)

Curiously, Michels finds the most flagrant examples of organizational goal displacement and the abuse of power in the United States. Here, Michels notes sarcastically, in the "land of the almighty dollar . . . corruption is not merely exhibited upon a gigantic scale, but . . . has become a recognized institution." American labor leaders are no less corrupt than

their capitalist counterparts. While Michels concedes that many honest and capable working-class leaders exist, others, he says, are blatantly opportunistic. "Many of them shamelessly and unscrupulously exploit for personal ends the posts which they have secured through the confidence of their fellow-workmen. Taken as a whole, the American labor leaders have been described as 'stupid and cupid.'" Even more dangerous than personal corruption, however, is ideological co-optation. American as well as English labor leaders have been known to accept money from the government or from capitalist organizations to purge the more radical elements within their own ranks. As early as 1894, the American Federation of Labor, under the leadership of Samuel Gompers, repudiated the socialist program of collective ownership of the means of production, concentrating instead on achieving better conditions for the workers within the capitalist system. In the 1940s and 1950s, the AFL-CIO, responding to governmental pressures, purged Communists from its ranks. To Michels, this would have signified a complete and cynical betrayal by labor leaders of the interests of the working class. In England, he believed, similar betrayals were responsible for the moderation of the goals of the English trade union movement. As Marx and Engels said in 1906, "English socialism would certainly be far more advanced than it is today had not the capitalists been clever enough to check the movement by corrupting its leaders" (Michels 1962, pp. 287–91).

While socialist parties and trade unions in the United States and Europe have long since abandoned their radical goals in favor of working within the democratic capitalist system, revolutionary Marxist movements have continued to pursue the goal of a social revolution. Following Marx, Communist parties in the USSR and elsewhere have called for the abolition of private property and with it an end to the domination of one class by another. Yet Michels astutely foresaw that the same combination of structural and psychological factors that made political equality an impossible dream in capitalist societies would persist in socialist and communist ones. Even if private property is abolished (as was the case in the Soviet Union after 1917), bureaucracy is structurally unavoidable. "Social wealth," like privately owned wealth, "cannot be satisfactorily administered in any other manner than by the creation of an extensive bureaucracy. . . . The administration of an immeasurably large capital, above all when this capital is collective property, confers upon the administrator influence at least equal to that possessed by the private owner of capital." Marx himself envisioned a period of postrevolutionary transition marked by a temporary dictatorship of the proletariat. Eventually, however, Marx believed, the state would wither away. Michels was less optimistic: "To put the matter less euphemistically, there will exist a dictatorship in the hands of those leaders who have been sufficiently astute and sufficiently powerful to grasp the scepter of dominion in the name of socialism." Human nature—the age-old greed for power of those who possess it— would intervene to perpetuate elite rule and prevent the creation of the longed-for genuine democracy for which the revolution was waged. "It is extremely probable that a social group which had secured control of the instruments of collective power would do all that was possible to retain that control." Members of the new ruling elite would "utilize their immense influence in order to secure for their children the succession of the offices which they themselves hold." Thus, six years before the Russian Revolution, Michels predicted that the abolition of capitalism would not bring about political equality but would merely replace one elite with another, one system of oppression with another. Quoting a popular song of his time, Michels concluded, "It's not worth the bother to change the government!" (Michels 1962, pp. 347–56). For a comparison of classical elite theorists and Marx, see Table 8.1.

Summary

The three classical elite theorists we have examined—Pareto, Mosca, and Michels—promulgated their ideas in Europe in the early 1900s. Shortly after the turn of the century, the mighty aristocratic regimes of Europe—Russia, Germany, Italy, and Austria-Hungary—were replaced by floundering liberal governments or beleaguered socialist regimes. Against this background, European social scientists warned that genuine democracy, whether under capitalist or socialist conditions, was a naive dream. They claimed that the inexorable laws of history, the vicissitudes of human nature, and the dynamics of social organization made elite rule inescapable. Not surprisingly, these theories were initially rejected by American and British sociologists, who optimistically continued to espouse the pluralist model of democracy.

Elite theory has recently reemerged. It is, arguably, the dominant approach in American political sociology today. We now turn our attention to the major formulations of contemporary elite theory.

Table 8.1 A Comparison of Classical Elite Theories and Marx's Theory of Class

	Principal Divisions in Society	Factors Responsible for Elite Rule	Composition of Elites	Means Used by Elites to Retain Power	Implications for Democracy

Pareto (1848–1923)	Elites
	  Governing elites
	  Nongoverning elites
	Servants of the elite
	  Experts of force
	  Experts of persuasion
	Masses
		The psychological superiority of elites (superior residues)	"Lions" and "foxes" in different proportions; elites, although conscious of their class interests, are not homogeneous or unified	Derivations (i.e., ideologies or myths) and force	Plutocrats (i.e., the very rich) always dominate societies that are nominally democratic

Mosca (1858–1941)	Elites (ruling class) Subelites (technocrats, etc.) Masses	Superior psychological and organizational resources	Shifts to reflect balance of social forces; in feudal societies, hereditary ruling class; in industrial societies, bureaucratic elite	Political formulas (i.e., legitimating myths) and force; to be effective, political formulas must rest on a shared value system	The wealthy always enjoy disproportionate influence in democracy

(continued)

Table 8.1 A Comparison of Classical Elite Theories and Marx's Theory of Class *continued*

	Principal Divisions in Society	Factors Responsible for Elite Rule	Composition of Elites	Means Used by Elites to Retain Power	Implications for Democracy
Michels (1876–1936)	Upper class Working class Leaders (key officials in working-class organizations) Masses	The dynamics of large organizations The need to delegate power The need for expertise and efficiency Psychological forces The masses' ignorance and hero-worship The leaders' desire for self-aggrandizement The concentration of organizational resources in the leaders' hands	Working-class leaders eventually join forces with the upper class in suppressing the masses	Control over organizational resources such as money, communication media, and the authority to make decisions on members' behalf	"The Iron Law of Oligarchy": Given large organizations, elite rule is inevitable in democratic and socialist societies
Marx (1818–1883)	Owners of the means of production, e.g., landlords, capitalists The working class, e.g., serfs, proletarians	Ownership of the means of production	Depends on predominant means of production: slave-owners, landlords, capitalists	Force and ideological hegemony	With the abolition of private property, classes will be abolished; eventually economic inequality and the state would wither away

CHAPTER NINE

——

The Realities of Power: Contemporary Elite Theory

Preview

Contemporary elite theorists agree with their classical predecessors that society is ruled by an elite but disagree on the desirability of elite rule. Classical theorists insisted on the benefits of elite rule, while most contemporary theorists stress its harms. They see the masses as exploited and misled by the elites and, at the same time, as ultimately capable of governing themselves.

This chapter examines contemporary issues in elite theory, reviews empirical studies that support this theory, and explores the implications of elite theory for democracy.

Structural Reciprocities Between Elite and Society

Contemporary elite theorists emphasize the importance of elites in shaping societal trends and human destiny but reject the view that elites are all-powerful. Sociologists G. Lowell Field and John Higley (1980) utilize Mosca's framework of social forces, particularly his distinction between feudal and bureaucratic societies, to analyze the reciprocal relations between elite and society. Rejecting both the view that elites completely dominate the course of their societies and the assertion that they are completely determined by it, they argue that elites are constrained by two major factors: the developmental level of the society and the attitudes and orientations of nonelites. Within certain limits established by these conditions, elites may choose among several alternative courses of action and thus play a key role in the unfolding of historical events. Field and Higley (1980, p. 25) maintain that elites must be allowed to continue playing such a role. If they are hampered by too many demands on the part of nonelites

or by an excessive egalitarian zeal on the part of "misguided" liberals, elites will no longer be able to mediate domestic or international disputes or, ultimately, save society from disorganization and chaos.

Field and Higley view all societies as existing at one of four distinct levels of economic development, each characterized by a particular configuration of nonelite attitudes or political orientation. Each economic level and political orientation, in turn, limits the character and actions of the elite that rules that society. The relationships between developmental levels and elite characteristics are summarized in Table 9.1.

Level 1 societies are economically undeveloped. The work force is predominantly agricultural, although other primary occupations, such as hunting, are not uncommon. (Farming and hunting are called **primary occupations** because they involve extracting food directly from the land.) In these societies, which persisted in Western Europe until the sixteenth century and in Asia and Africa into the twentieth century, production is organized in small units. Each household or village runs its own enterprise. Workers are autonomous and, at least on a day-to-day basis, not subject to hierarchical supervision. Their work is determined by the natural environment, the rhythm of the seasons, and the elements rather than by managers and foremen. Consequently, workers in Level 1 societies have an egalitarian, antihierarchical orientation.[1]

1. It seems to us that the authors confuse the features of hunting and gathering societies, whose members are fiercely independent, with those of agrarian societies, which contain large subject classes. In ancient Mediterranean as well as medieval European societies, agriculture was often organized into large, centrally administered units such as manors or *latifundia* (Roman estates). Large nonagricultural enterprises existed as well. Certainly the pyramids were not built by small entrepreneurs! Most workers were not independent peasants and craftsmen but bonded serfs or slaves. Their

Table 9.1 Socioeconomic Conditions, Nonelite Orientation, Elite Characteristics, and Political Consequences

	Level 1	Level 2	Level 3	Level 4
Work force composition	Predominantly agricultural	Increasingly industrial	Predominantly industrial	10% or less agricultural; 40–50% industrial; 40–50% white collar
Units of production	Very small	Some large bureaucratic units	Predominantly large bureaucratic units	Predominantly large bureaucratic units
Nonelite orientation	Egalitarian, complacent	Egalitarian, antielitist, and volatile	Mixed: egalitarian and antiegalitarian	Managerial, nonegalitarian
Nature of elite	Hereditary aristocracy	Holders of strategic positions in bureaucratic organizations	Same as Level 2	Same as Levels 2 and 3
Prevailing conflicts in society	Subdued class conflict between nonelites and elites	Class conflict between industrial work force and elite	Class conflict between nonelites and elites, but also conflict of interest among segments of nonelites	Conflict between insiders and elites and between insiders and outsiders
Elite conflict and cohesion	Disunited elites	Disunited or, if a revolution has occurred, ideologically united (egalitarian)	Disunited or, if a revolution has occurred, ideologically united (antiegalitarian)	Consensually united
Political regimes possible or likely	Stable aristocratic rule	Leveling revolution followed by "reign of terror and virtue"	Antiegalitarian revolution followed by fascist or right-wing repression	Stable representative government

SOURCE: Based on G. Lowell Field and John Higley, *Elitism* (London: Routledge and Kegan Paul, 1980).

Having no large-scale bureaucratic organizations, Level 1 societies have no bureaucratic elites. The elite consists of a hereditary leisured aristocracy and thus is a ruling class, not a bureaucratic elite. Usually, the lower classes accept a domination they cannot hope to change. The aristocracy does not intervene directly in either production or the day-to-day lives of the lower classes as long as the latter continue to support its extravagant and leisurely life-style. However, if peaceful means of domination fail, the aristocracy secures its rule by the force of arms.

Level 2 societies are transitional societies. Although a very large sector of the work force is still agricultural, these societies are rapidly industrializing and urbanizing. England and other European nation-states, the United States, and Canada achieved this level of development in the seventeenth and eighteenth centuries, while Russia, Eastern Europe, and most other countries did not enter it until the twentieth century. In Level 2 society, factories multiply rapidly and an increasing number of rural laborers are brought together under the factory roof. The new elites, composed of the top echelons of bureaucratic organizations (from owners and managers of industrial and commercial firms to governmental ministers and police chiefs), no longer enjoy unlimited hereditary authority. Indeed, a professional, full-time bureaucracy is needed to manage both the economy and the society, since economic decisions have become infinitely more complex and the workers more rebellious. Not only are the new industrial workers, formerly fiercely independent, now subjected to the harsh discipline of foremen and supervisors, but they also find their work meaningless, authoritarian, and alienating. Radical antielitist sentiment runs high, from time to time erupting in strikes and riots or manifesting itself in movements that promise to bring about a true equality for all.

orientation was probably not one of egalitarianism but rather one of submission in the face of inevitable, immemorial, and religiously sanctioned authority.

Occasionally, such movements succeed in fomenting a leveling, or egalitarian, revolution followed by a "reign of terror and virtue" (see Brinton 1965 and Box 9.1).

In the twentieth century, industrial workers in Level 2 societies, more so than their counterparts in other societies, are susceptible to the radical appeals of communism. It is in these societies that class conflict between elites and nonelites is most pronounced and Communist-style revolutions are most likely to occur.

Level 3 societies are fully industrialized. Britain, the United States, Canada, Japan, and most of Europe had reached this level of development by 1900. Thanks to mechanized farming, only a small agricultural sector is needed to feed the population. The labor force is predominantly manual, employed in such **secondary industries** as manufacturing, mining, and transportation, while a few workers are engaged in nonmanual managerial or service jobs. Nonmanual workers tend to accept the necessity for managerial authority more readily than industrial workers; hence, their orientation may be characterized as antiegalitarian. Moreover, the industrial labor force, now large, increasingly prosperous, and well-organized in labor unions and political parties, begins to abandon radical solutions in favor of more moderate demands for economic and social improvement. While conflict between nonelites and elites still abounds, the egalitarian forces among nonelites have lost their edge. Therefore, a Communist revolution is less likely to occur. Instead, Level 3 societies are more likely to succumb to a right-wing or fascist dictatorship. With the support of some segments of the nonelites, the elite in right-wing regimes brutally suppresses egalitarian movements, as happened in Italy under Mussolini (1922–1943), in Germany under Hitler (1933–1945), and in Spain under Franco (1939–1975).

By the end of World War II, the United States, Canada, Britain, most of Europe, Australia, New Zealand, and Japan had reached the fourth level of development. In Level 4 societies, agricul-

━━━ BOX 9.1 ━━━

The Republic of Virtue

An illustration of a "reign of terror and virtue" that follows a leveling revolution is the Republic of Virtue proclaimed in France in 1792 by Maximilien Robespierre, one of the most radical leaders of the French Revolution. Under the Republic, the traditional cultural institutions and customs of the old regime, including religion, art, fashion, the calendar, and even the forms of address, were replaced by new "republican" customs and practices: Catholic churches were renamed "temples of Reason"; the ornate art and decorative style of the baroque were replaced by neoclassical imitations of Roman art and symbols; the elaborate fashions of the eighteenth century gave way to the austere *sans-culottes*, baggy, peasant-style trousers; the traditional measurements were replaced by the metric system; the Gregorian calendar was supplanted by a new, more "rational" decimal calendar; the familiar forms of address "Monsieur" and "Madame" gave way to the egalitarian "Citizen" and "Citizeness."

Even more ambitious than the cultural reforms of the Republic, although less successful, were the economic reforms. Laws were passed to ration food at affordable prices, reduce wage inequality, and redistribute aristocratic properties to landless peasants. These measures encountered stronger resistance than anticipated, however, and were never fully implemented. Yet, like the cultural reforms, they reflected the radical egalitarian motives of the postrevolutionary regime.

The Republic of Virtue was accompanied by a gruesome reign of terror. As many as twenty thousand Frenchmen and Frenchwomen, mostly aristocratic and Catholic opponents of the Revolution, were put to the guillotine or drowned.

The "reign of terror and virtue" in France, like others elsewhere, was short-lived. In 1794, Robespierre was executed and the machinery of the terror dismantled. Shortly thereafter, the reforms of the Republic of Virtue were abolished and prerevolutionary institutions restored.

Similar radical egalitarian regimes existed briefly in England under Cromwell (1648–1649) and in the Soviet Union under Lenin (1917–1921). In all cases, the society was undergoing the economic upheavals characteristic of Level 2 development and had recently emerged from a leveling revolution (see Brinton et al. 1967).

---

tural and industrial productivity soars. Only a small portion of the labor force remains employed in farming, and the proportion employed in manual industrial jobs also diminishes steadily. The remainder of the work force, as much as 50 percent, is employed in white-collar jobs in such **tertiary occupations** as computers, education, entertainment, and office work, producing not tangible goods but intangible services. The large nonindustrial work force is permeated by "a generalized bureaucratic culture" (Field and Higley 1980, p. 30). Among nonelites, a widespread acceptance of managerial authority and a strong antiegalitarian sentiment develop.

Since the service sector in Level 4 societies cannot absorb all the surplus labor force, large numbers of the population are permanently unemployed or marginally employed. The unemployed and underemployed do not come in equal proportions from all segments of the population but are disproportionately drawn from disadvantaged minority groups, youth, and women. This situation is potentially explosive because economic resentment is intensified by tensions along racial, ethnic, generational, and gender lines.

In Level 4 societies, class conflict declines and is replaced by other conflicts. Nonelite insiders—persons with good jobs—must guard against actions by the elite to diminish their pay or abolish their jobs. This possibility is a constant threat, because as productivity comes to depend more on sophisticated technology, the need for labor diminishes. Elites consequently attempt to impose salary freezes, to replace assembly-line workers with robots, or to close down unprofitable plants. At the same time, nonelite insiders seek to protect their hard-won gains against outsiders—the alienated, unemployed, and underemployed—seeking to gain access to good jobs and economic security. Outsiders seek employment either by peaceful, institutionalized means, such as lobbying for equal opportunity or affirmative action programs, or by violent extrainstitutionalized means, such as riots and terrorism.

Clearly, the nature of elites in Level 2, 3, and 4 societies differs in important ways from that in Level 1 societies. Outside Level 1, we no longer speak of a ruling class but of a bureaucratic elite. "In more developed societies it is therefore misleading to conceive of a ruling class of privileged families because privilege and power emanate not from the family itself, but from the strategic positions which one or more of its members happens to hold in complex organizations" (Field and Higley 1980, p. 33). Of course, members of bureaucratic elites in Level 2, 3, and 4 societies still wish to pass on their power and wealth to their offspring and are frequently in a position to do so. They secure expensive educations, high-level jobs, and good marriages for their children. Nevertheless, the key to power is bureaucratic position, not hereditary privilege. Unlike aristocratic elites, bureaucratic elites are limited by their legal

mandate as well as by the resources of nonelites. They no longer enjoy unrestricted power.

Level 2, 3, and 4 societies offer no alternative to rule by bureaucratic elites, and where elites exist, fundamental inequality is inevitable. "Elite persons always have more power, and they usually have more wealth, status and privilege than others have. Because of this, the existence of elites is fundamentally incompatible with any full measure of freedom and equality in society. This is why elitism, in the sense of an acceptance of elites, is . . . correctly regarded as inimical to radical libertarian and egalitarian preferences" (Field and Higley 1980, p. 69).

We have seen that the fundamental nature of the elite—hereditary or bureaucratic, militaristic or peaceful—is determined by developmental conditions and nonelite orientations. However, elites also possess considerable power to shape the conditions and destinies of nonelites. The relationship between elite and society is best conceptualized as dynamic and reciprocal rather than as deterministic. The intensity and nature of conflict among elites shapes the course of events for the whole society. Three configurations of elite conflict or unity are possible: disunity, ideological unity, and consensual unity. The societal ramifications of each configuration are examined below.

The first type, **disunited elites**, has prevailed throughout most of history, particularly in Level 1 societies, and is still common today in Level 2 and Level 3 societies. Members of the disunited aristocratic or bureaucratic elite form factions or alliances against each other, often appealing to nonelites for support. Elite conflict coupled with deliberately inflamed discontent among the nonelites may lead to chronic political instability, civil war, or revolution. An example of chronic instability is the situation in some Latin American and African countries where different factions of the elite overthrow and replace each other in a rapid succession of coups d'état without allowing nonelites a sustained voice in the process.

While disunited elites have prevailed in the

past, a growing number of elites today give the appearance of solidarity and cooperation. These elites may be unified in one of two distinct ways: Either they are committed to a common ideology or they share a loose consensus on basic principles.

Ideologically unified elites typically emerge after a revolution. The unifying ideology may be egalitarian, as in China under Mao Tse-tung, North Korea under President Kim Il Sung, and Cuba under Fidel Castro, or antiegalitarian, as in Germany under Hitler and Italy under Mussolini. In either case, these elites attempt to regulate all aspects of society and the economy according to ideological guidelines and repress all dissent. Ideologically unified elites are "committed to strictly impossible political goals, but through totalitarian organizational devices their leaderships quickly become entrenched and self perpetuating. . . . None has avoided heavy-handed repression of real or suspected dissidents, and each has been ruthless in stifling nonelite opinion and sacrificing some elite persons as scapegoats for inevitable policy failures. For these reasons, ideological unified elites are anathema from the standpoint of liberal values" (Field and Higley 1980, pp. 73–74).

Consensually unified elites, on the other hand, neither speak with a single voice nor attempt to eliminate dissension and diversity. Their consensus covers only basic underlying principles, such as the sanctity of established institutions and of democratic procedures, and does not extend to details of policy. Consensually unified elites are most common in Level 4 societies, where the ideological, class, and ethnic divisions that previously polarized both elites and nonelites have lost some of their urgency. Field and Higley stress that a stable, cohesive elite unified by consensus rather than by ideology is a prerequisite of democratic government. Because they do not exhaust themselves in internecine warfare and are secure in their own survival, consensually unified elites are able to respond in a large measure to popular concerns and wishes. They are also unique among elites in not being threatened by granting nonelites considerable freedom to participate in the political system and opportunities to voice their concerns and desires. By contrast, neither disunited elites nor ideologically unified elites are able to sustain democratic institutions for more than a short time.

Where elites are not consensually unified and where Level 4 development has not been reached, no rhetorical exhortation or constitutional reforms on the part of well-meaning liberals will secure a stable representative government. Even armed intervention by a foreign power in the cause of democracy is doomed to fail, as did American intervention in Indochina in the 1960s and 1970s. In the absence of a consensually unified elite, the extension to all segments of the population of the right to participate in government leads to impatient popular demands for social and economic reforms that cannot be fulfilled without seriously detracting from the freedom and privilege already enjoyed by the more prosperous and better-educated classes. Irreconcilable (zero-sum) conflicts of interest between the privileged and the underprivileged or between insiders and outsiders become increasingly disruptive. Political crises follow in rapid succession, only to terminate in an overthrow of the floundering representative government. Such was the fate of the democratic governments in Germany, Italy, and Spain following World War I. These governments, able neither to reconcile ideological disunities among the elites nor to satisfy public demands, eventually succumbed to dictatorships—Italy in 1922, Germany in 1933, and Spain (after a bloody civil war in which each side was backed by foreign powers) in 1939.

Level 4 societies with stable, consensually unified elites have their own share of problems. In these societies, the principal danger is not the overthrow of the elite but its paralysis. Pressures from outsiders within the society (for example, racial and ethnic minorities, women, and youth) for a larger share of the economic pie are paralleled by vociferous demands from Third World nations for a more equitable distribution of international resources. These domestic and international demands are often supported by humanitarian public opinion within the ranks of the privileged, yet they cannot be satisfied in an era of shrinking resources and limited growth. When the pie is no longer growing, the allocation of economic benefits becomes a zero-sum game: Any gain for the underprivileged detracts significantly from the well-being of the privileged, a cost that the well-to-do nations cannot afford. Their only alternative, therefore, is to accept inequality as a necessary evil, here to stay. "If the chips are down," the authors claim, "nations, classes, interest groups and individuals" must put their own interests above those of others. Hence, "a more self-consciously elitist frame of reference" is necessary "if Western elites and their supporters are to stem internal conflicts involving insiders and outsiders, as well as manage conflicts between developed and developing societies" (Field and Higley 1980, pp. 128–29). In concluding, Field and Higley call for a restoration of elitism not only as a framework for sociological analysis but as a political ideology.

Field and Higley's analysis forms a bridge between classical and contemporary elite theories. Like Mosca, they envision the relationship between elites and society as dynamic and reciprocal. Just as the structure and actions of the elite crucially affect the political and social fortunes of society, social-structural forces, namely, developmental level and nonelite orientation, limit the options available to the elite. Conversely, the nature of the elite's unity or disunity affects the stability and well-being of the entire society. Other contemporary elite theorists espouse both the notion of structural constraints on the state imposed by economic institutions and the notion of the impact of the elite's characteristics on society. However, in accepting the necessity and even the desirability of inequality, Field and Higley adopt a conservative political stance differing significantly from that of other contemporary elite theorists.

Power Elite or Ruling Class?

The Composition of the Power Elite

In the heyday of pluralist theory, when most political theorists were celebrating the strengths of American democracy, sociologist C. Wright Mills published his book *The Power Elite* (1956). This book introduced elite theory to American political analysis and voiced serious misgivings about the possibility of a genuine democracy in advanced industrial societies.

As Mills writes, while the vast majority of people are "circumscribed by the everyday worlds in which they live . . . driven by forces they can neither understand nor govern," a few persons occupy positions that "enable them to transcend the ordinary environment of ordinary men and women; they are in positions to make decisions having major consequences. . . . For they are in command of the major hierarchies and organizations of modern society. They rule the big corporations. They run the machinery of the state and claim its prerogatives. They direct the military establishment. They occupy the strategic command posts of the social structure" (Mills 1956, pp. 3–4).

Mills identifies three groups that, as he carefully documents, have had the greatest impact on American society since World War II: the political, military, and corporate elites. The **political elite** consists of the top level of the executive branch of government: the president, the members of the White House staff and of the executive office of the president, the members of the cabinet, and the heads of the major departments and agencies—some fifty-odd men and a few women. As far back as the Eisenhower administration, Mills argued that the legislative branch of the government, directly elected by the people and closest to their concerns, was steadily losing its power to the executive branch. The major conflicts of interest and contests of power, as well as the major policy initiatives, were increasingly coming to a head "in the executive chambers, and in the agencies and authorities and commissions and departments that stretch out beneath them . . . rather than in the open arena of politics," that is, Congress (Mills 1956, p. 229).

The **military elite** (below the presidentially appointed Secretary of Defense) consists of the Joint Chiefs of Staff—"a military board of directors"—as well as of the upper-echelon generals and admirals who preside over America's mighty war machine (Mills 1956, p. 187).

The **corporate elite** functions entirely outside the democratic electoral system yet wields vast power. This elite consists of the chief executive officers, major stockholders, and boards of directors of the major industrial and financial corporations. The three elites overlap, as we will see below (the second elite analyzed by Mills, the military, is often subsumed under the governmental elite).

What has happened to the array of organizations and institutions that the pluralists extoll as the wellspring of power in democratic society? According to Mills, these organizations—labor unions and churches, farm organizations and trade associations, state and local governments, and even Congress—constitute the middle level of power. It is at this level that conflicting interests and points of view vie for domination. These intermediary organizations, once truly powerful, have lost their historical influence, abdicating important decisions about war and peace, the economy, and the well-being of society to the federal government and the major corporations.

Below the intermediary level of power are the vast majority of the people, who constitute the powerless masses or **mass society** (see chapter 7). Despite its name, mass society is by no means homogeneous. It sports distinctions of religion, ethnicity, race, occupation, age, gender, and social class. Contrary to the pluralist assumption, however, these groupings and affiliations do not "serve as a basis for organization to counter the power of the elite" (Schneider 1968, p. 19). Despite the illusion of

freedom, the masses are powerless. They follow the orders of their superiors in the workplace, and their tastes and behavior in politics and in the marketplace are shaped by others. They passively support the elite in power and, when called upon, fight and die for it.

In advanced industrial societies, then, as Weber and Mosca realized, the elite consists of bureaucratic decision makers. This elite could potentially include all the people who head various institutions in the public and private sectors—the heads of the labor unions, mass communication media, churches, universities, and nonprofit foundations. In reality, however, as Mills and most contemporary elite theorists agree, the elite consists first and foremost of the people who control the government and the large industrial and financial corporations. As one observer puts it, the "elites of the state and the economy . . . head the most powerful institutions. Leaders of other institutions such as education, religion, and communications exert power in their particular realms, but it is only in the economic and governmental areas that elite decisions are of broad enough scope to affect comprehensively all members of the society" (Marger 1981, p. 211).

For Mills, as for Field and Higley (1980), the modern power elite is not an economic class in the Marxian sense of ownership of the means of production. Those who control the state apparatus do not own it, just as those who control the major corporations are not necessarily the major stockholders. Conversely, only a small portion of the upper class, perhaps those endowed with the most energy, highest sense of mission, or most gregarious disposition, choose to use their assets as a base for wielding corporate or political power. This segment of the upper class constitutes the governing or **ruling class**.

What is the socioeconomic background of the members of the power elite? Studies show that they are overwhelmingly male and drawn disproportionately from the economic upper class. In both the corporate and the government sectors, the higher the position, the more likely the incumbent is to be an upper-class man. Thus, virtually none of the top executives in the Fortune 800 corporations are women, although this situation is changing slowly (see Epstein and Coser 1980). Among 884 directors of major industrial, financial, utility, and transportation corporations, over half—53 percent—have their roots in the upper class. Among 205 members of presidential cabinets in this century, 66 percent came from the upper class, with the percentage somewhat lower among Democrats (60 percent) than among Republicans (71 percent) (Domhoff 1967, p. 51; Mintz 1975, p. 135; Freitag 1975, p. 151; Burch 1980). The remaining members of the corporate and government elites come from the upper middle class; they include managerial and professional experts, corporate lawyers, and retired military "top brass" (for more on the role of the upper middle class in maintaining the power structure, see chapter 4). In order to appreciate how truly lopsided these figures are, we must remember that the upper class accounts for less than 1 percent of the population in the United States and the upper middle class for only 5 to 10 percent (see chapter 4).

Many of the top positions in the government, corporate, and public interest sectors are filled by the same individuals, either sequentially or simultaneously. Between 1897 and 1973, 76 percent of all cabinet secretaries held positions in the corporate elite either before or after their cabinet service (Mintz 1975, p. 135; Freitag 1975, p. 151). Members of the corporate elite hold an average of eleven different elite positions over their lifetime (Dye 1976, pp. 130, 135). This does not mean that elite positions are monopolized by a conspiratorial cabal. It does mean, however, that elites overlap significantly.

Sociologists Richard Alba and Gwen Moore (1982) have investigated the ethnic origins of the American elite through an analysis of 545 holders of top positions in powerful governmental, economic, and nonprofit organizations. They find greater ethnic diversity than

was the case in the past; today, all large ethnic groups in the United States are represented in the elite. However, WASPs—white Protestants with ancestry from the British Isles (including Scotch-Irish but not Irish Catholics)—are overrepresented in most sectors of the elite with the sole exception of organized labor. Overall, WASPs constitute between 42 and 48 percent of the elite sample, compared to about 30 percent of the population as a whole. WASP overrepresentation is most pronounced in two sectors, business and Congress, where it approximates 60 percent. By contrast, minority groups, including nonwhites and persons of Hispanic ancestry, are greatly underrepresented. Alba and Moore argue that the contribution of ethnicity to one's chances of attaining an elite position is largely indirect. WASPs are more likely than members of other ethnic groups to have an upper-class or upper-middle-class background (as indicated, for example, by attendance at prestigious private schools and colleges), the pool from which members of the elite are recruited.

Studies of elites in other Western countries yield similar conclusions. In all countries studied, both capitalist and socialist, women's representation in governmental, business, and professional elites is very small. The proportion of women in national legislatures varies from one in four in Norway to one in twenty in Germany and Austria and is even lower in the United States. Women are virtually absent from top positions in business and industry, perhaps because public pressure to include them is considerably less than in the government sector (see Epstein and Coser 1980).

Elite circulation, that is, mobility into and out of the elite, has existed both in societies whose regimes have undergone changes and in societies with stable regimes. However, the turnover is counterbalanced by a large degree of continuity in elite membership, even where a change of regime has occurred. For example, the return to democracy in Italy after the fall of Mussolini and in Spain after the death of Franco triggered some changes in the composition of the ruling elites, but substantial numbers of the previous elite members stayed on. Thus, the insights of Pareto, Mosca, and Michels (see chapter 8) have been corroborated (see Czudnowski 1982, 1983).

The Cohesion of the Power Elite

As we saw in chapter 4, members of the upper class attend the same select preparatory schools and colleges, frequent the same exclusive clubs and resorts, sit on the same corporate and foundation boards and policy discussion groups, and often marry one another. Similarity of socioeconomic backgrounds and interchangeability of positions contribute to relatively unified world views and perceptions of interest among the members of the elite, disagreements on specific issues notwithstanding.

Gwen Moore (1979) has studied occupants of top positions in ten institutional sectors that exercise power in American society, ranging from Congress and the federal administration to business, labor, political parties, and the media. She finds that the different elites form several small circles centered on similar issue concerns. Some members of those specialized circles (ranging from 17 to 60 percent) are also members of a large inner circle whose concerns and membership origins are broad and inclusive. The most heavily represented groups in the central circle are the federal government and business.

The central circle comprises the core of the power elite. Its members, who are nearly equally divided between Republicans and Democrats, are overwhelmingly upper or upper middle class in origin (90 percent attended college), male (95 percent), and over fifty years old (75 percent). They have significantly more influence on policy (as measured, for example, by serving on key policy planning boards) than do the other members of the narrower outer circles. Moore concludes that, contrary to pluralist assertions,

> no fragmentation of elites in different institutions or issue areas was found. On the con-

trary, the evidence . . . indicates that considerable integration exists among elites in all major sectors of American society. The existence of a central elite circle facilitates communication and interaction both within that large, diverse group and between its members and those in more specialized elite circles and cliques. (Moore 1979, p. 689)

Similar integration has been found within the corporate world. Elite theorist Michael Useem (1983a, 1983b) asserts that both the family capitalism and the managerial capitalism of the past have given way to **institutional capitalism**, a classwide organization of the capitalist class. Useem notes that among the array of interlocking directorates within American and British corporations there is an inner circle whose members are more unified as well as more politically active than other business leaders. Members of the inner circle are able to transcend the narrow interests of single corporations or industries and represent the broad class interests of the business community as a whole. They are also able to translate those interests into political influence, as we will see below (see also Mizruchi 1982; Herman 1981; and Fidler 1981).

Elite theorist G. William Domhoff (1974, 1983) has studied exclusive social and recreational clubs where members of the upper class and the corporate and governmental elites gather informally. These clubs, one of the most prominent of which is the Bohemian Club in San Francisco, help foster the cohesiveness of the power elite as well as provide settings for informal discussions of national policy and group interest. Thus, they complement the role of more formal organizations such as policy discussion groups in forging elite consensus.

> There is reason to believe that [the social activities of the upper class] play a role both in solidifying the upper class and in maintaining the class structure. . . . Constant interaction in small-group settings leads to the social cohesion that is considered to be an important dimension of a social class. This social cohesion does not in and of itself

demonstrate that members of the upper class are able to agree among themselves on general issues of economic and governmental policy. But it is important to stress that social cohesion is one of the factors that makes it possible for policy coordination to develop. (Domhoff 1983, p. 50)

Thus, the evidence shows a considerable degree of integration and cohesion both within the corporate elite and between the corporate and governmental elites. As we discuss below, however, although interpersonal networks are important, they are not solely responsible for the tendency of the modern state to pursue policies favorable to business interests.

The Impact of the Capitalist Elite: How Autonomous Is the Modern State?

Elite theorists disagree as to whether the real power in advanced capitalist societies is wielded by the governmental elite or the top corporate leadership. Marx, in *The Communist Manifesto*, stated that all power in capitalist societies emanates ultimately from the business class: "The modern state is but a committee for managing the common affairs of the whole bourgeoisie." However, in a later work, *The Eighteenth Brumaire of Louis Bonaparte*, Marx himself rejected simple economic determinism, acknowledging the role of noneconomic causes and forces and emphasizing merely the primacy of economic factors. C. Wright Mills, on the other hand, argued that the governmental elite possesses considerable autonomy. Moreover, he believed that power in the three sectors—business, the state, and the military—rests in bureaucratic position rather than in economic assets. In other words, although members of the power elite tend to come disproportionately from the wealthy classes, wealth is not crucial to their dominion. The legitimate power of decision making vested in their position is more significant. This is consistent with the theory of Max Weber, who, as we saw in chapter 3, stressed the development of bureaucracy as an independent force in modern society, a develop-

ment that has transformed the historic relation between owners and workers.

> "Ruling class" is a badly loaded phrase. "Class" is an economic term; "rule" a political one. The phrase, "ruling class," thus contains the theory that economic class rules politically. . . . Specifically, the phrase "ruling class" . . . does not allow enough autonomy to the political order and its agents, and it says nothing about the military as such. [In fact] the higher agents of each of these three domains now often have a noticeable degree of autonomy. . . . Those are the major reasons we prefer "power elite" to "ruling class" as a characteristic phrase for the higher circles when we consider them in terms of power. (Mills 1956, p. 277)

Today, elite theorists are divided into two schools. The Millsian school (see Nordlinger 1981; Birnbaum 1982; Evans, Rueschemeyer, and Skocpol 1985) argues that the state enjoys considerable autonomy, partly as a result of conflict among social classes or interest groups. The Marxist school, on the other hand, emphasizes the primacy of corporate interests in shaping state policy. The Marxist school itself can be divided into two subschools, the instrumentalist and the structuralist.[2] **Instrumentalists** tend to see "government as a mere committee of the ruling class, directly manipulated by leading members of that class" (Domhoff 1980, p. 11; see also Poulantzas 1968). In other words, instrumentalist elite theorists emphasize the direct or indirect participation of the business elite in running the state. **Structuralists**, on the other hand, emphasize "the systematic functional interrelationships among the institutions of a society, and especially the underlying functional relationship between the

2. Some writers (for example, Useem 1983a, 1983b) include proponents of the relative autonomy of the state within the structuralist school. We have chosen to view Millsians as a separate school and to treat both the structuralists and the instrumentalists as subschools of Marxist elite theory because both structuralists and instrumentalists emphasize the overriding influence of the business elite on the state (although they differ in their explanation of the ways in which this influence operates).

economy and the state" (Domhoff 1980, p. 11; see also Therborn 1978; Block 1977). These writers stress the structural constraints within capitalism that limit the autonomy of the state.

On the Millsian side of the debate, elite theorist Eric Nordlinger believes that both Marxist and pluralist writers have underestimated the state's independent role in shaping societal preferences and policy outcomes. He asserts that state officials are able to shape policy when societal (private) and state (public) preferences diverge. Under these conditions, state officials use the opportunity "to free themselves from societal constraints and translate their preferences into authoritative actions" (Nordlinger 1981, p. 119). Additionally, state officials are sometimes able to influence societal preferences, thus bringing them into congruence with their own preferences. Similarly, elite theorist Pierre Birnbaum (1982), analyzing different periods in French history, argues that the state's autonomy varies over time and is a function of the unity or disunity of the ruling elite that runs the state's institutions. For example, in France during the Third and Fourth Republics (1870–1940 and 1945–1958), the state was able to act relatively autonomously for two reasons: the underrepresentation of the business elite in government and the conflict between politicians (whose origins were in the middle class) and top administrators (whose origins were in the upper class). During the Fifth Republic (1958–present), however, and especially in recent years, state autonomy has declined as economic power and administrative power have increasingly converged.

Marxist elite theorists reject the notion of the autonomy of the state from corporate interests, insisting that "the economic [elite] is ultimately decisive and fundamentally controlling" (Apetheker 1968, p. 160). "What we have in the United States is a ruling class with its roots deeply sunk in the 'apparatus of appropriation' which is the corporate system. To understand this ruling class—its metaphysics, its purposes, and its morals—we need to study . . . the whole system of monopoly capitalism" (Sweezy 1968, p. 129; see also Miliband 1969, 1982; Clark and Dear 1984; Block 1977; Zeitlin 1980).

Instrumentalist elite theorists point out that the capitalist upper class influences policy outcomes through such direct means as participation in the policy-making process, campaign contributions, and lobbying activities. These activities will be examined later. Structuralists point out, however, that the state's responsiveness to capitalist interests does not depend solely on direct participation by the upper class. "Even if there were no politically engaged ruling class members, there is still every reason to believe that the state and policy-making groups would advance policies that are in the interests of the ruling class" (Block 1977, pp. 13–14). According to this view, structural constraints limit the autonomy of the state, increasing the likelihood that the state will pursue policies favorable to capitalism or at least not harmful to it.

> Those who manage the state apparatus—regardless of their own political ideology—are dependent on the maintenance of some reasonable level of economic activity. This is true for two reasons. First, the capacity of the state to finance itself through taxation or borrowing depends on the state of the economy. If economic activity is in decline, the state will have difficulty maintaining its revenues at an adequate level. Second, public support for a regime will decline sharply if the regime presides over a serious drop in the level of economic activity, with a parallel rise in unemployment and shortages of key goods. Such a drop in support increases the likelihood that the state managers will be removed from power one way or another. And even if the drop is not that dramatic, it will increase the challenges to the regime and decrease the regime's political ability to take effective actions. (Block 1977, p. 15)

Thus, state agencies tend to orient their programs toward the goal of encouraging private investment (business confidence), or at least not discouraging it. In other words, the range of policy alternatives is constrained by "the contradictory requirements of the accumulation process," or by the "calculus of profitability" (Zeitlin 1980, p. 23).

In addition to the dynamic of business confidence, Block argues, another structural mechanism explains why the state's actions tend, in the long run, to favor capitalism—class struggle. "Class struggle is responsible for much of the economic dynamism of capitalism" (Block 1977, p. 21). This paradox can be seen most clearly in the struggle over wages. When workers succeed in gaining higher wages, capitalists are motivated to substitute robots or other machines for human labor. Thus, many workers lose their jobs while capitalist profits increase. Similarly, when the working class pressures the government to improve public services such as education, the content of the education will probably be geared to the needs of capitalism—the production of workers with needed skills and appropriate attitudes (namely, support for, or at least acquiescence to, the status quo). The tendency for class struggle to bolster capitalism occurs with considerable friction and unevenness. However, in the long run, "if the state managers decide to respond to [popular] pressure with concessions, they are likely to shape their concessions in a manner that will least offend business confidence and will most expand their own power. These two constraints increase the likelihood that the concessions will ultimately serve to rationalize capitalism" (Block 1977, p. 24). Thus, the ruling class needs neither class consciousness nor mechanisms of direct participation in the state in order to assure that its interests are given priority.

Elite theorist Goran Therborn (1978) argues similarly for the primacy of structural constraints over instrumentalist intervention in accounting for the power of capitalist interests in the modern state. Therborn rejects the assumption that power is to be understood in "subjectivist" terms, that is, in terms of *who* has it. He argues that power should be defined in terms of its contents and effects, not in terms of the actors who wield it. State power, according to Therborn, "is a relation between social class forces expressed in the content of state policies. The class character of these policies may be seen in their direct effects upon the forces and relations of production, upon the ideological superstructure, and upon the state apparatus," that is, the specific institutions through which state power is exercised (Therborn 1978, pp. 34–35). The characteristics of the state, including modes of political representation and processes of policy formation, take different forms in different societies, depending on the class nature of the society. To claim that a particular class is the ruling class, therefore, is to argue that state actions have the effect on society of reinforcing the dominant position of that class. It is in terms of the effects of state actions, therefore, that the capitalist class may be said to be the dominant class in advanced capitalist societies, just as the landed aristocracy was the dominant class in feudal societies.

Mechanisms of Ruling Class Domination

In addition to structural constraints on governmental policy, instrumentalist elite theorists call attention to mechanisms of direct and indirect participation by the economic elite in politics (see Domhoff 1978, 1983; Useem 1983a, 1983b; Fidler 1981; Silk and Silk 1980). These mechanisms include the special-interest process, the policy-formation process, the electoral process, and the ideological hegemony process.

The Special-Interest Process

The special-interest process is the process by which individuals, families, corporations, and business sectors within the ruling class seek governmental actions and rulings that benefit their own interests. The special-interest process manifests itself in the workings of "lobbyists, backroom super-lawyers, trade associations and advisory committees to governmental departments and agencies" (Domhoff 1978, p. 25). Desired governmental actions include tax breaks, subsidies, and favorable procedural rulings by regulatory agencies.

A recent report described in the *Washington Post* documents the extent to which health and safety regulations are influenced by powerful private groups in business and industry. Under the Reagan administration, the report points out, "health, safety, and environmental regulators routinely [granted] preferential and secret access to business regulatees" while effectively shutting out the general public. The Environmental Protection Agency (EPA), for example, instead of setting environmental standards for marketing pesticides, let the pesticide industry write its own standards by engaging in a series of informal "decision conferences" between the industry and agency representatives. Similarly, the Occupational Safety and Health Administration (OSHA), instead of using its own stringent standards for protecting the safety of workers in oil fields, adopted the less rigorous standards developed by the oil industry. OSHA officials, in meetings with representatives of 3M Company, also "agreed to relax standards governing the quality of respirators used to protect workers from airborne lead." The report further charges that the Office of Management and Budget, acting under an executive order of the president, "has provided industry . . . the legal and institutional power effectively to control what rules come out of the executive agencies protecting the public health" (quoted in Barringer 1983).

Pluralist theorists rightly point out that the organized business community is only one of many groups seeking to influence governmental decisions (see chapter 7). A closer look, however, shows that the business community is significantly more successful than other groups. Organized labor, for example, has not been nearly as successful as organized business in gaining control of governmental bureaucracies that affect its interests. While the creation of a federal Department of Labor in 1913 was a triumph for the hard-lobbying

American Federation of Labor, the labor movement's control of the new department was undermined by organized business groups such as the National Association of Manufacturers (see DiTomaso 1980). Even the National Labor Relations Board (NLRB), created during the New Deal to protect the interests of labor, has been dominated by both labor and management. In this regard, the NLRB differs from other regulatory agencies, which are dominated by their clientele (see McConnell 1966). The NLRB's probusiness bias is illustrated by its 1984 ruling that an employer does not have to bargain with a union if the union cannot show that a majority of the workers support it, even when the employer has been engaged in unfair and unlawful practices aimed at stopping union organizing. This reversal of an earlier decision (one of several during the Reagan administration) left the NLRB "powerless to deter unfair labor practices," according to a dissenting opinion on the board (*Washington Post*, May 18, 1984). Thus, although groups other than the ruling class often use the special-interest process to further their own aims, the uneven success rate reflects the underlying distribution of power.

The Policy-Formation Process

The policy-formation process differs from the special-interest process in two important ways. First, the special-interest process serves the interests of a narrow segment within the ruling class—a single industry or even a single corporation (thus, Chrysler Corporation, after intense lobbying, was bailed out of near-bankruptcy in 1979 by federal government guarantees of $1.5 billion in loans). The policy-formation process, however, transcends specialized interest groups. "It is within the organizations of the policy-planning network that the various special interests join together to forge, however slowly and gropingly, the general policies that will benefit them as a whole. It is within the policy process that the various sectors of the business community transcend their interest-group consciousness and develop an over-all class consciousness" (Domhoff 1978, p. 61).

Second, while the special-interest process is openly biased (lobbies and trade associations serve the interests of those who hire them or those who pay their membership dues), at the policy-formation level an aura of disinterest-edness prevails. "It is a world where 'expertise' and a mild disdain for the special interests are the coin of the realm. Only the 'national inter-est' is of concern. 'Nonpartisan' and 'objective' are the passwords" (Domhoff 1978, p. 62).

As political scientist Nelson Polsby (1984) shows, contrary to both popular and pluralist perceptions, new policies originate neither in the traditional political parties nor in organized interest groups such as labor and business. Rather, they originate in the policy-formation network, a network composed of corporate- and foundation-supported organizations that spe-cialize in identifying problems and inventing solutions. At the same time, ambitious politi-cians (such as members of the U.S. Senate with designs on the presidency) are constantly searching for new solutions to old or recent problems. Out of these intertwined processes—the politicians' search for new solutions and the policy entrepreneurs' invention of new alternatives—policy initiatives arise. These processes have been responsible for most of the major policy innovations since World War II, including the formation of the Peace Corps and the Atomic Energy Commission, the pas-sage of Medicare, and supply-side economics.

The policy-formation network consists of presidential commissions, policy discussion groups, and policy analysis institutes (popu-larly known as think tanks). Presidential com-missions are temporary committees made up partly of private citizens, who are assigned to gather information, deliberate, and report to the president on a topic of national impor-tance. They are intended to "suggest new pol-icy initiatives or to build support for programs the President wishes to pursue" (Domhoff 1983, p. 133). Thus, they legitimate new policies.

Policy discussion groups, such as the Coun-cil on Foreign Relations and the Business Council, provide a forum for members of the political and economic elites and experts from academia and research institutions to come together to discuss such topics as foreign aid, the population/resource problem, and the set-ting of national goals. It was the policy net-work, with its roots in the ruling class, that moved the United States from a pre–World War II isolationist stance to one favoring the inter-national cooperation of Western democracies in the cause of containing Soviet "expansionism" and protecting free enterprise at home and abroad. In these policy discussion groups, plans for Social Security, the Marshall Plan, and the World Bank were laid.

Members of policy discussion groups are frequently called on to serve in top govern-mental posts. Thus, a Harvard professor of political science, Dr. Henry Kissinger, whose book *Nuclear Weapons and Foreign Policy* grew out of a study group sponsored by the Council on Foreign Relations and received considerable attention within the political elite, was later called upon by President Nixon to serve as Sec-retary of State and National Security Advisor (see Domhoff 1978; Silk and Silk 1980).

Think tanks differ from policy discussion groups in that they are more permanent bur-eaucracies. Highly prestigious organizations, think tanks in fact supply the research data and the expert advisors for the policy discussion groups. They may be affiliated with major uni-versities, such as Georgetown University's Center for International and Strategic Studies, or they may be independent, such as the Hoo-ver Institution on War, Revolution, and Peace and the Heritage Foundation. Think tanks are financed by corporate, foundation, and per-sonal donations or by contract research that they carry out for business and governmental agencies.

The policy network is neither united in its views nor representative exclusively of the interests of the ruling upper class. Domhoff (1978, 1983) discerns three broad ideological groupings among policy discussion groups and think tanks. The first grouping, moderately conservative, includes such policy discussion groups as the Council on Foreign Relations, the Committee for Economic Development, and the Conference Board. Financial and directional support for this grouping comes from the largest corporations. Its greatest influence is on the moderate wings of both the Republican and Democratic parties, and it enjoys numerous ties to the White House no matter which party is in power. The second grouping, more staunchly conservative, includes such organizations as the National Association of Manufacturers, the Chamber of Commerce, the American Enterprise Institute, and, more recently, the Heritage Foundation. This grouping draws its financial support from smaller, more marginal corporations and has its greatest impact among ultraconservative Republicans, particularly members of Congress. Recently, as government has shifted to the right, the boundary between the two conservative groupings has been blurred. The third grouping, moderately liberal in its views, is a loosely knit coalition of organizations based in trade unions, university communities, various liberal organizations, and "the independent wealth of a few rich mavericks" (Domhoff 1978, p. 118). The liberal-labor coalition has no major stronghold within the political elite. On most major issues, the moderately conservative grouping, the pivotal center, determines the outcome of policy struggles. Clearly, then, although the policy network is ridden with conflict and diversity, the differences of opinion within it are relatively circumscribed and the different groupings unequally weighted. Furthermore, the right wing within the policy-formation network is not counterbalanced by a strong left wing.

Policies that originate in the policy-formation network are not limited, of course, to the interests of the ruling elite. Analysis of policy initiatives that have been enacted into law shows that a great many, from Social Security and Medicare to tax credits for child care for working parents, have improved the lives of Americans from many walks of life. However, "the proof of the pudding in terms of power is the ability to maintain the class system that sustains ruling-class privilege and prerogatives. On this score, the ruling class has done very well within the general policy arena" (Domhoff 1978, p. 119).

The Electoral Process

The ruling elite does not operate entirely outside the democratic process. In fact, a major mechanism of ruling elite domination—the election process—lies within the heart of the democratic system. This process, which is examined in more detail in chapters 10 and 11, will be summarized briefly here.

Both national and local electoral campaigns center on images rather than issues. According to Domhoff, "in a system where policy preferences become blurred, the emphasis on the images of individual candidates becomes very great. Individual personalities become more important than the policies of the parties. . . . It is because the candidate-selection process in the American two-party system is so individualistic and therefore dependent on name recognition and personal image, that it can be in good part dominated by members of the ruling class through . . . large campaign contributions" (Domhoff 1983, pp. 121–22). Of course, the candidate who spends the most does not always win, but a candidate without a large war chest cannot even hope to stay in the race for long. Thus, the ruling elite—the prime donors—play a direct role in selecting and promoting the candidates of their choice.

Since the campaign reform acts of the 1970s, corporate contributions have been channeled largely through political action committees (PACs) (see chapter 11). Campaign finance reform, intended to limit the impact of business interests, has in fact strengthened those interests. "The effect of the reforms, although unintended, was to corporatize campaign finance and to make political money even more directly tied to the top leaders in the corporate community" (Domhoff 1983, p. 123).

The candidate-selection process, then, provides the ruling class with yet another channel for influencing the course of government and society and complements the special-interest process and the policy-planning process. According to political scientist Michael Parenti, "ironically enough, the one institutional arrangement that is ostensibly designed to register the will of the many serves to legitimize the rule of the privileged few" (Parenti 1977, p. 215).

The Ideological Hegemony Process

The ideological hegemony process refers to the ways in which the power elite attempts to shape the political beliefs, attitudes, and opinions of the public (see chapter 5). As Weber, Pareto, and Mosca pointed out, ruling elites cannot rely solely on force or even on institutional mechanisms such as those described above. A modicum of nonelite acquiescence, if not outright support, is necessary. In fact, elite rule will be stable only if it is viewed by the masses as beneficial to themselves, basically fair (despite occasional flaws), and normal or natural. In other words, elites must forge and continually reinforce the legitimacy of their rule; this is what the process of ideological hegemony is about.

An ideology that justifies the prevailing structures of power and inequality is called a dominant ideology[3] (see chapter 5). The dominant ideology contains both economic and political aspects. The economic tenets include support for free enterprise, competition, private ownership of property, the profit motive, and minimal governmental intervention in the economy. The political tenets include government "of the people, by the people and for the people," which in practice translates into the principles of pluralism described in chapter 7. These tenets are nourished by an underlying value system that stresses individualism, or, more specifically,

> the notion that each member of society is personally responsible for his or her social lot. . . . The society's opportunity structure is pictured as open, providing equal chances for all to achieve material success or political power regardless of their social origin. This being so, each individual controls his or her placement in the social hierarchy. Social success, then, is the result of one's willingness to work hard; failure is the result of lack of ambition or desire to improve oneself. Differences in wealth and power are not denied, but they are seen as the product of individual factors rather than the workings of a class system that automatically favors success for the well-born and failure for the poor. (Marger 1981, pp. 310–11)

To be sure, there are variations (centering on such details as the proper role of government) between the conservative and the liberal versions of the dominant ideology (see chapter 6). The crucial point, however, is that there is no disagreement on the fundamentals espoused by the dominant ideology, whether conservative or liberal.

The premises of the dominant ideology are not "natural" but are inculcated in us in myriad ways, both conscious and unconscious, through the process of political socialization (see chapter 5). Political socialization, as we have seen, is transmitted through such institutions as the schools, the family, the churches, and the mass media. Among the agents of socialization, the schools play a key role. Although widely believed to be ideologically neutral, the schools teach both formally and informally the virtues of laissez-faire capitalism, competition, individual responsibility for success and failure, the fundamental fairness of the major institutions, and the supremacy of the American system over all others.

School curricula are not developed in a vacuum, however. Much of the public schools' curriculum in social studies, for example, is the product of efforts by an organization called the

---

3. The term *ideology* is used here in a different sense than in chapter 6. Here no distinction is made between liberal and conservative ideologies. Rather, an emphasis is placed on those common elements of both ideologies that support the status quo.

Joint Council on Economic Education. The council's activities, which include publishing classroom materials and training teachers, aim to promote "economic literacy," which is defined as knowledge of, and support for, the capitalist system. The council is an outgrowth of an important policy organization, the Committee for Economic Development (CED), which is backed by the major foundations and corporations (see Domhoff 1978).

While schools, churches, and families focus their socialization efforts primarily on children, the mass communication media help shape political values and attitudes throughout people's lives. As with the other means of socialization, the messages conveyed through the mass media are often implicit and unconscious. For example, juxtaposing the terms "the free world" and "the Communist world" conveys the impression that international affairs are a contest between the forces of good (Western or capitalist countries) and the forces of evil (Communist countries).

None of the agents of political socialization transmits exclusively and unquestioningly the views of the power elite. In a country where the media are relatively free, diverse views inevitably find expression. Furthermore, the ideological hegemony process is not all-pervasive in molding the political opinions and attitudes of the average citizen. Attitudes are shaped by many different sources, and people are remarkably resistant to official attempts to influence them. Yet the ideological hegemony process, incomplete as it is, complements the special-interest, policy-formation, and electoral processes in helping to forge public consensus behind the elite's decisions. More broadly, it helps maintain at least passive support for the precepts that underlie the existing structures of political and economic inequality.

Together, the four mechanisms of ruling-class influence—the special-interest process, the policy-formation process, the electoral process, and the ideological hegemony process—complement the structural constraints discussed above in assuring the continued domination of the power elite. While elite theorists hold differing opinions on the forms of the economic elite's influence on the state, in practice, the outcomes of elite domination are the same regardless of how power is exercised.

Elites in American History

American history has often been portrayed as an unfolding of the people's will, from the popular uprising against British colonial power through the triumph of such grass-roots movements as the abolitionists, the progressives, the populists, and, most recently, civil rights and women's liberation activists. However, political scientists Kenneth Prewitt and Alan Stone (1973) show that in every era of American history the ultimately controlling influence was wielded by a tiny elite of privilege, often against the true interests of the majority. Furthermore, as historian Edward Pessen (1984) points out, most American presidents, the "log cabin myth" notwithstanding, came from upper-class or upper-middle-class origins—sixteen from the upper class, six from the intersection between the upper and the upper middle class, ten from the upper middle class, three from the "true" middle class, and only four from the lower middle and upper lower classes.

The American Revolution was launched by those men who had the most to lose from British colonial power—wealthy landowners and merchants such as John Adams. The Constitutional Convention, which met in Philadelphia in 1787, was composed predominantly of wealthy gentlemen. The few among the founding fathers who were not independently wealthy, for instance, Alexander Hamilton, loyally upheld the interests of the upper class. In fact, Hamilton, James Madison, and the other founding fathers were deeply troubled by the prospect of popular rule and tried to devise a system that would protect the rights and privileges of the minority against what they regarded as excessive popular participation in government. The Federalist Papers abound with references to the dangers of "mass tyranny." To ward off this danger, the founding fathers set up stringent property qualifications for voting and office holding and successfully opposed the Bill of Rights, which they saw as protecting the rights of ordinary people against the elite. They also devised a checks-and-balances system with the intent of preventing any one branch of the government, particularly the democratically elected Congress, from gaining too much influence. Only in the decades following the Constitutional Convention was the Bill of Rights finally adopted and suffrage gradually extended (see chapters 7 and 10). The checks-and-balances system has survived as a continuous watchdog against popular "passions."

After the Civil War, a transformation of the mode of production (in Mosca's terms, of the social forces) brought about a change of ruling elites. The old agrarian economy was replaced by a bustling industrial one, and the old quasi-feudal aristocracy of plantation owners and gentleman merchants was replaced by a capitalist elite of corporate leaders. At the very same time that the classical liberal ideology of laissez-faire capitalism (see chapter 6) was at its height, an intimate relationship developed between the corporate and the political elites. For example, railroad companies openly bought off politicians, as well as using other corrupt and fraudulent means to drive out less aggressive competitors and charge the public exorbitant rates. The government, in turn, handsomely subsidized railroad and canal enterprises. By 1871, a total of 100 million acres of federal land, then worth $500 million, had been distributed to various railroad companies (Prewitt and Stone 1973).

By the beginning of the twentieth century, the era of unbridled capitalism was over. Business leaders had become convinced that adulterated products, unregulated municipal growth, cutthroat competition, and open corruption were harming their own interests. Popular indignation, too, was aroused by muckraking writers such as Upton Sinclair,

whose best-selling novel, *The Jungle*, exposed the horrendous conditions in the meat-packing industry. In a flurry of reforms, governmental regulations were imposed to ensure standards of quality in foods and drugs, and antitrust legislation was enacted to stem out unfair competition. Municipal reforms limited the influence of corrupt, but democratically elected, political machines and placed more power in the hands of professionally trained, ideologically "neutral" experts, including traffic engineers and city managers. "The public interest" and "clean government" became the watchwords of the day.

However, the influence of the corporate interests on public policy did not decline but merely changed form. Consider the history of the automobile. The deterioration of public transit in industrialized countries and its replacement by the private automobile have often been attributed to social and market forces beyond human control: the migration of urban populations to low-density suburbs, technological innovations in the automobile industry that made private cars easily and cheaply available, and the tastes and preferences of consumers. A closer look, however, reveals that "transportation technology is not some external force imposed on society, but an instance of the articulation of class power" (Yago 1980, p. 286). The specific configuration of industrial and financial interests within a capitalist class accounts for the historical development of transportation patterns in a given society. Thus, in the United States, the powerful corporate car complex—the auto-rubber-oil industries—contributed to the decline of public transit and its replacement by the automobile in the 1920s and 1930s. In Germany, by contrast, the dominance of the rail-electric-steel cartels ensured the continued prevalence of rail transit until World War II (see Yago 1984).

In the 1920s, America's corporate car complex faced a dual crisis: the persistent popularity of public transit in large cities and the saturation of the new car market. Led by General Motors, the automobile industry and its partners in the gasoline and rubber industries developed a long-term corporate strategy to defeat rival railroad interests and increase demand for new cars. Thus, General Motors and other automobile manufacturers secretly purchased rail and electric transit systems, only to convert them to gasoline-run bus lines. In addition, the automobile industry persuaded local governments to adopt transit specifications that only auto manufacturers could meet, suppressed opposition to bus conversions from both the rail industry and citizens' groups, and undermined or bought off transit employee unions. Thus, "the decline of public transit was consciously achieved . . . through the acquisition of transit companies, conversion and resale" (Yago 1980, p. 314).

> The corporate car coalition was highly successful. Every possible dimension of the transit industry was integrated into the growth complex of the auto-rubber-oil industries (such as GM licensing of repair and dealerships, financing used car purchases, and involvement in road construction through GM subsidiaries). Because future demand could be assured only insofar as auto companies monopolized transit technology, the corporate car coalition sought to eliminate technological competition from other modes. (Yago 1980, p. 316)

This corporate strategy was supported by governmental policies. Beginning with the New Deal, federal agencies such as the Bureau of Public Roads, as well as local and regional planning commissions, encouraged and financed highway construction and facilitated automobile driving, often at the expense of rail transit. Gradually, "the neglect of public transportation became institutionalized" (Yago 1980, p. 318). Not coincidentally, representatives of the corporate car coalition participated in public transportation planning bodies or sought to influence them through the increasingly effective highway lobby. At the same time, the emergent professions of urban and traffic planning added to the impression that transportation decisions were being made on technical

rather than political grounds. The state was thus made to appear as a neutral referee promoting the interests of the citizenry—orderly urban traffic and suburban growth—rather than backing the interests of one segment of the capitalist class. In this way, "the routinization [and legitimation] of the capitalist class interest within the state itself" was completed (Zeitlin 1980, p. 28). This transportation strategy achieved its greatest success during the Eisenhower administration. The Federal Highway Act of 1956 initiated the most massive government-financed road construction project in history, the interstate highway system. This system has permanently altered the face of America.

In other capitalist societies, the development of transportation has followed different patterns in response to different constellations of corporate interests. In Germany, for example, the infrastructure for capitalist expansion was laid by the railroad, shipping, mining, and steel industries in the late nineteenth century. The cartels (monopolies) that ran these industries were fully supported by both the national and the municipal governments until 1933. The national government financed the construction and maintenance of railroads and protected railroad-related industries against competition from the automobile industry. Municipal governments paid for the electrification of rail lines and subsidized fares. The German railroad-steel-coal cartels were successful in fending off serious competition from the automobile industry until the 1930s. The Nazi regime, however, believed that a strong automobile industry would strengthen its war machine (since automobile-manufacturing equipment could be easily converted to military purposes) as well as stimulate the economy. Therefore, the Nazi government allied itself with the automobile industry and began to promote motorization. This policy—and the alliance that promoted it—survived Nazism and continued after World War II in the Federal Republic of Germany. In fact, the automobile industry became one of the cornerstones of economic recovery in the postwar era. With the growing use of the automobile, public transit declined even further.

The history of transportation policy in the United States and Germany illustrates the indirect as well as direct influence of corporate interests on public policy. To be sure, the specific structure and historical circumstances of the capitalist ruling class vary from country to country. Nevertheless, corporations create the environment that constrains governmental actions, and the interests of corporations limit and skew the alternatives for public policy. In practice, corporations use both structural constraints (private investment decisions) and instrumental means (intervention in policy-making bodies) to influence policy, and the two are often inseparable.

The effectiveness of the various mechanisms of ruling-elite domination is illustrated by studies of the role of elites in local communities as well as in national policy. In the San Francisco Bay area, the urban business elite, which stood to gain an increase in property value from mass transit, united in a successful campaign for the Bay Area Rapid Transit (BART) system (see Whitt 1982). In Detroit, the interlocking power structure has thwarted rational urban planning, class integration, and racial and ethnic group assimilation (see Ewen 1978). The power structure in Atlanta has built an inhospitable urban environment for its own profit at the expense of poor blacks and whites (see Hunter 1980). And the ruling class in Boston, New York, Charleston, Chicago, and Los Angeles has similarly been able to translate wealth into political power and local influence (see Jaher 1982).

On a national level, Useem (1983a, 1983b) has investigated the role of business elites in the United States and in Great Britain in bringing about a governmental shift to the right. Useem notes that in the 1970s and 1980s the business communities in both countries were faced with new challenges—the decline of profitability (a problem endemic to both countries), the resurgence of labor socialism in Brit-

ain, and the growth of governmental intervention in the United States.

In answer to these challenges, the business communities in both Britain and the United States mobilized to strengthen their political influence. They increased their contributions to political campaigns and probusiness foundations and lobbies, cultivated better relations with influential opinion makers such as the media and academic elites, accepted invitations to defend business in the media, and in general pursued a vigorous public relations campaign to improve their image and create a favorable political climate. Useem believes that the successes of the Thatcher government and the Reagan administration in curbing social spending and expanding free enterprise are due in no small part to the successful mobilization of the business communities in Britain and the United States.

> The decline of the welfare state, the slowing of social spending, and the end of activist government in the U.S. and U.K. were thus not simply . . . a product of spontaneous disaffection with the socially interventionist state. . . . Rather, the rise of new conservative forces that were among the pillars of the Conservative and Republican governments was importantly a product of the formation . . . of informal and formal organizational networks linking together most large corporations. These networks facilitated the political mobilization of business—by helping business to identify the public policies most needed for its aggregate welfare, and by helping business to express these preferences in electoral campaigns, government lobbying, and other forms of intervention. . . . With emergence of classwide organizations, more overall planning initiative is assumed by business, less by government. Rather than having to sift through the disparate demands of a thousand chief executives, government officials are presented with an integrated vision already developed by those members of the corporate community best positioned to reconcile the competing demands. (Useem 1983a, pp. 304–5)

Another consequence of this mobilization is the strengthening of the organizational foundation of the business community. While specific issues and campaigns are ephemeral, this change (which corresponds to the rise of institutional capitalism) is permanent. "When business encounters its next crisis, whether economic or political, it will be better prepared to meet this challenge, to offer classwide answers" (Useem 1983a, p. 300).

In sum, the links between economic and political power are both instrumental and structural. While the business elite uses various modes of intervention to strengthen its influence on policy decisions, the interests of the capitalist state cannot be separated from those of the corporate elite. Both the agenda of public debate and the range of policy alternatives are defined by the requirements of capitalist accumulation. Under these conditions, Marxist elite theorists point out, "the capitalist class does not have to 'govern' in order to 'rule' " (Kautsky 1903, p. 13; Zeitlin 1980, p. 25).

Summary

In this chapter, we have seen that elite theories emphasize the critical role of elites, whether defined as bureaucratic office holders or an economically based ruling class, in shaping trends and historical events. As Prewitt and Stone, Yago, and Useem remind us, such events as the American Revolution, the debate over the Constitution, the reforms of the progressive era, the decline of public transit and the spread of the automobile, and the governmental shift to the right in the 1970s and 1980s tes-

tify to the role of elites in influencing public policy. We have also seen that the mechanisms that support elite domination are both instrumental and structural.

Contemporary elite theorists disagree with Pareto's view that elites prevail because of their psychological and intellectual superiority. Rather, they agree with Weber, Mosca, and Michels that it is the structural forces of modern society—including the rise of the bureaucratic state, the giant corporation, and institutional capitalism—that make elite rule inevitable.

Whether elite rule is viewed as beneficial to society or as exploitative depends on the writer's ideological perspective. Conservative contemporary analysts such as Lowell Field and John Higley consider elite rule necessary for economic and political stability. According to Prewitt and Stone, "the conservative sees the relationship between the rulers and ruled in terms not of privilege but of responsibility. The moral significance and material well-being of society rests on the shoulders of the elite" (Prewitt and Stone 1973, p. 19). Radical elite theorists, on the other hand, emphasize the exploitative nature of elite rule—the fact that the existing structure of political and economic inequality serves the interests of the few at the expense of the many (although usually with their acquiescence). This view is expressed by most contemporary elite theorists, including C. Wright Mills and his heirs.

In chapters 7 through 9, we have examined various theories of power. Our emphasis was on the power wielders, the elites. In the remaining chapters, we turn our attention from the elites to the masses and examine the avenues through which the masses influence political institutions and decisions.

4

Political Participation

CHAPTER TEN

Voting

Preview

Political participation links the political order with the broader socioeconomic sphere. Classical theorists of democracy, from Alexis de Tocqueville to Thomas Jefferson, believed that political participation, particularly voting, was the key to democratic government: the mechanism by which governments are held accountable to the people. Pluralist theorists, while viewing voting as important, stress the importance of interest-group activity as well (see chapter 7). Conflict theorists, on the other hand, view most forms of nonelite participation as symbolic rituals rather than rational acts of choice and consider them ineffective in controlling elite behavior (see chapter 9). Social construction theorists share with conflict theorists a concern with the symbolic meaning of political participation for the individual and for society. Despite varying points of view, however, all schools of political sociology must come to grips with the nature of the linkages between the state and society, between the political order and the social structure.

Chapters 10 and 11 discuss institutionalized forms of political participation: Chapter 10 looks at voting; chapter 11 explores political parties. Chapters 12 and 13 discuss noninstitutionalized political behavior, including mass movements, violence, and revolutions. This chapter explores in detail the following questions: Who votes? How do people vote? What effect does voting have on the political system?

Forms of Participation

What are the channels through which the masses may attempt to influence or control the government? Political participation can be divided into institutionalized and noninstitutionalized forms.

> Institutionalized forms of participation are the established and acceptable methods of citizen action, those recognized as legitimate by the prevailing political system. Voting, writing letters to political officials, working for a political party, demonstrating peacefully, and so on are institutionalized actions. Noninstitutionalized forms of mass participation are not recognized as legitimate, extending beyond the official definitions of what is appropriate citizen behavior. These might include civil disobedience, violent confrontations with authorities, and most extreme of all, actions designed to overthrow the prevailing system. (Marger 1981, p. 268)

Political scientist Lester Milbrath (1965) has developed a model of the spectrum of institutionalized political participation. This model is presented in Figure 10.1. The pyramid-shaped model of participation underscores the differences among political activities. Activities differ in the amount of individual resources (time, money, and energy) they require, in the number of people who take part in them, and in the impact they have on the political decision-making process.

> The hierarchy seems to have a kind of internal logic, a natural progression of becoming involved in active politics. Although persons engaging in the topmost behaviors are likely also to engage in those behaviors ranking lower, the obverse does not hold. Minimally involved persons confine their actions to those acts ranking low in the hierarchy. As [people] become more involved in politics, [they] engage in a wider repertoire of political acts and [move] upward in the hierarchy from the more frequent to the less frequent behaviors. (Milbrath 1965, pp. 19–20)

Borrowing a metaphor from ancient Roman games (in which, incidentally, the loser was

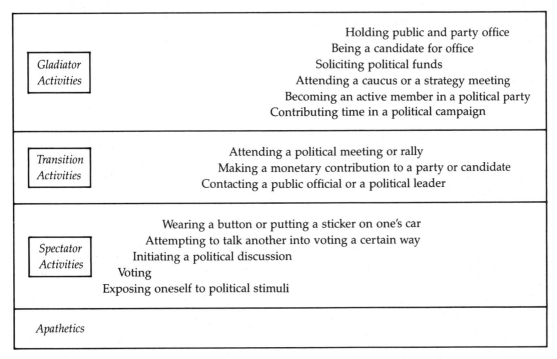

Gladiator Activities	Holding public and party office
	Being a candidate for office
	Soliciting political funds
	Attending a caucus or a strategy meeting
	Becoming an active member in a political party
	Contributing time in a political campaign
Transition Activities	Attending a political meeting or rally
	Making a monetary contribution to a party or candidate
	Contacting a public official or a political leader
Spectator Activities	Wearing a button or putting a sticker on one's car
	Attempting to talk another into voting a certain way
	Initiating a political discussion
	Voting
	Exposing oneself to political stimuli
Apathetics	

Figure 10.1   Hierarchy of Political Involvement. SOURCE: *Lester W. Milbrath,* Political Participation *(Chicago: Rand McNally, 1965), p. 18. Reprinted by permission of Houghton Mifflin Company.*

condemned to death), Milbrath divides the pyramid into three parts: gladiatorial, spectator, and transitional.

> A small band of gladiators battle fiercely to please the spectators, who have the power to decide their fates. The spectators in the stands cheer, transmit messages of advice and encouragement, and, at given periods, vote to decide who has won a particular battle (election). The apathetics do not bother to come to the stadium to watch the show. (Milbrath 1965, p. 20)

Spectator activities include exposing oneself to political stimuli (whether through the mass media or face-to-face communication), voting, "talking politics," and displaying buttons or stickers. Spectators rarely cross over to gladiatorial activities unless propelled by an unusually emotional issue or unusually strong group pressures, although they sporadically engage in **transitional activities,** which include attend-

ing rallies, contributing money, or contacting politicians. At the rarefied top of the pyramid are **gladiatorial activities:** active campaigning and lobbying, holding office, or being a candidate for office. Gladiators are distinguished from all other participants in actually exercising (or seeking to exercise) political power; they are insiders. In many countries, they are professional politicians.

What proportion of the electorate participates at the various levels? According to Milbrath, "about one-third of the American adult population can be characterized as politically apathetic or passive; in most cases, they are unaware, literally, of the political part of the world around them. Another sixty percent play largely spectator roles in the political process: they watch, they cheer, they vote, but they do not battle. In the purest sense of the word, probably one or two percent could be called gladiators" (Milbrath 1965, p. 21).

A more detailed analysis shows that in the

United States, 40 to 60 percent of the electorate vote (depending on the election), 25 to 30 percent engage in political talks and persuasion, about 15 percent display buttons and stickers, a similar percentage contact officials, and perhaps 10 percent contribute money. Only 4 or 5 percent campaign in person, and only 1 percent or fewer hold or seek office (Milbrath 1965, p. 19).

The pyramid has two serious shortcomings. First, it treats the apathetic, those who "do not bother to come to the stadium," as an uninteresting residual category (Milbrath 1965, p. 20). Yet this group, which comprises "the largest political party in America" (Reid 1980), accounts for nearly half the American electorate. Whatever the reasons for abstaining, such a large rate of nonvoting has significant implications for the political system; it cannot be dismissed simply as "apathy."

Second, the pyramid does not address the impact of different modes of participation on the societal decision-making process. It does not raise—let alone answer—the question of what difference participation makes. Yet we know that periodic electoral activity does not carry as much weight as continuous involvement in the day-to-day affairs of government. The real issues, those that affect people's daily lives, are defined, proposed, debated, and legislated between elections, often away from the limelight. Electoral campaigns are fought about generalities (such as the need to balance the budget), while legislative and executive actions center on specific, often crucial, decisions (such as the choice between raising corporate taxes and lowering Social Security benefits). In short, not all political activities carry the same weight.

Despite these shortcomings, however, Milbrath's pyramid contributes to our understanding of the political process by ranking different modes of participation in terms of the numbers of people who engage in them. A further contribution is that the pyramid permits us to proceed to the next important question, Who are the people who participate at each level?

Who Votes? The Dimensions of the Turnout

The History of Voting Rates in the United States

The percent of the American electorate who have voted in presidential elections since the adoption of universal white male suffrage is shown in Table 10.1. As the table shows, the figures have hovered around 60 percent, ranging from a high of 82 percent in 1876 to a low of 49 percent in the 1920s. In the past two decades, the turnout has comprised little more than half the electorate. One factor responsible for the fluctuations in the turnout rate is the changing composition of the electorate due to the incorporation of successive groups into the American polity.

Contrary to popular belief, the United States was not very democratic until the administration of President Andrew Jackson (1829–1837). Until then, only white male property owners could vote; only 26 percent of free adult males voted in 1824. Not until the 1830s was suffrage made universal for white males on a state-by-state basis.

Few blacks were allowed to vote before the Civil War. In 1870, the Fifteenth Amendment to the Constitution struck down voting discrimination on the basis of "race, color, or previous conditions of servitude," extending to emancipated blacks the right to vote. This right was fully exercised only during the years of Reconstruction (1865–1876), however. Southern states increasingly used such means as literacy tests, poll taxes, and grandfather clauses to prevent blacks from voting. The absence of black voters in the South after they were enfranchised by the Fifteenth Amendment depressed the national voter turnout figures for about two-thirds of a century. In Mississippi during that period, the voting turnout ranged between 9 and 25 percent, hitting the lowest point in 1920 (U.S. Bureau of the Census

Table 10.1 Voting Turnout in the United States, 1824–1984			
Year	Percent Who Voted*	Year	Percent Who Voted
1824	26	1904	65
1828	58	1908	65
1832	55	1912	59
1836	58	1916	62
1840	80	1920	49
1844	79	1924	49
1848	73	1928	57
1852	70	1932	57
1856	79	1936	61
1860	81	1940	63
1864	74	1944	56
1868	78	1948	53
1872	71	1952	63
1876	82	1956	61
1880	79	1960	64
1884	78	1964	62
1888	79	1968	61
1892	75	1972	56
1896	79	1976	55
1900	73	1980	53
		1984	53

*Percent of the eligible electorate who voted in the presidential election, compiled from reports made by each state. SOURCES: U.S. Bureau of the Census, *Historical Statistics of the United States: Colonial Times to 1970*, pp. 1071–72. U.S. Bureau of the Census, *Statistical Abstract of the United States, 1986*, p. 255.

1975). Not until the 1960s, as a result of a series of Supreme Court decisions, congressional civil rights acts, and the passage of the Twenty-fourth Amendment to the Constitution (which outlawed the poll tax), were blacks effectively incorporated into the American electorate. For another two decades, their turnout continued to be lower than that of whites (see below).

After a prolonged and bitter struggle, women were enfranchised in 1920 by the Nineteenth Amendment to the Constitution. The habit of nonparticipation and social pressures to refrain were hard to overcome and were partially responsible for the low overall turnout of women voters for the first decade and a half after women's suffrage. The national turnout did not regain its pre-1920 level until 1936.

Residents of the District of Columbia were added to the electorate (in presidential elections only) by the Twenty-third Amendment in 1961. The Twenty-sixth Amendment in 1971 extended the vote to citizens between eighteen and twenty-one years old after a decade of militant political activity and participation in the Vietnam War had made the exclusion of this age group an anachronism. This group has tended to vote less heavily than older age groups, a fact reflected in lower national turnouts since 1972.[1]

Voting Rates in Different Countries: A Comparison

How does the United States rank in comparison to other countries' voting rates? Table 10.2, which presents data on voter turnout in ninety countries, shows that the United States ranks rather low—seventy-third. The highest-ranking countries are communist countries such as Albania, Bulgaria, and the Soviet Union, where nearly 100 percent of the adult population votes. The lowest-ranking are Third World countries such as Zambia, Guatemala, Sudan, Malawi, Kuwait, and South Africa, where fewer than one-third vote.

In most of the highest-ranking countries, it should be noted, voters are presented with a single slate of candidates rather than a choice among alternatives. The reason for the phenomenal turnout in these countries is not civic consciousness but laws that make voting mandatory and levy stiff penalties for nonvoting. Mandatory voting laws exist not only in some single-party countries such as the Soviet Union but also in a few multiparty countries such as Australia. Where a single slate of candidates is presented, as in communist countries, elections still play an important role in the political process. Rather than offering a choice between

1. Actually, only about one-quarter of the drop in turnout has resulted from the eighteen-year-old vote; the rest is due to other factors (see Wolfinger and Rosenstone 1980, p. 58).

Rank	Country	Voters as Percentage of Adult Population	Date
1	Albania	100	1974
1	Bulgaria	100	1976
1	Czechoslovakia	100	1971
1	Poland	100	1976
1	Romania	100	1975
1	Gabon	100	1973
1	Cameroon	100	1973
1	Guinea	100	1974
1	Indonesia	100	1977
1	Ivory Coast	100	1975
1	Mongolia	100	1977
12	Hungary	99	1975
13	Soviet Union	98	1974
14	Kampuchea	97	1976
15	Italy	97	1976
16	Malta	96	1977
17	Portugal	96	1976
18	Burma	96	1974
19	East Germany	94	1977
20	Niger	93	1970
21	Netherlands	93	1977
22	Australia	91	1975
23	Sweden	91	1977
24	Austria	90	1975
25	Israel	89	1977
26	Iceland	89	1974
27	New Zealand	89	1975
28	Denmark	88	1975
29	Belgium	88	1974
30	West Germany	87	1977
31	Algeria	87	1975
32	Ireland	86	1977
33	Jamaica	85	1977
34	Finland	85	1975
35	Puerto Rico	85	1975
36	Yugoslavia	85	1974
37	Uruguay	84	1971
38	Dominican Republic	81	1978
39	Mauritania	81	1975
40	Greece	81	1974
41	Venezuela	80	1973
42	Spain	80	1975
43.5	Norway	79	1973
43.5	Bahamas	79	1977
45	Rwanda	79	1969

Table 10.2 Voting Turnout in Ninety Countries

(continued on following page)

Rank	Country	Voters as Percentage of Adult Population	Date
46	Chad	78	1969
47	Argentina	77	1973
48	United Kingdom	76	1974
49	Japan	75	1977
50	Morocco	73	1977
51	Madagascar	73	1970
52	Sri Lanka	71	1970
53	Paraguay	70	1973
54	Gambia	70	1977
55	Canada	68	1974
56	Tanzania	68	1975
57	Chile	67	1973
58	India	67	1977
59	Singapore	67	1977
60	France	66	1973
61	South Korea	65	1973
62	Senegal	65	1973
63	Trinidad & Tobago	64	1976
64	Fiji	63	1978
65	Mexico	63	1977
66	Tunisia	62	1974
67	Bangladesh	61	1973
68	Guinea-Bissau	61	1975
69	Turkey	59	1977
70	Cyprus	58	1973
71	Pakistan	57	1975
72	Brazil	56	1974
73	United States	54	1976
74	Thailand	50	1976
75	Honduras	47	1971
76	Switzerland	43	1975
77	Philippines	42	1969
78	Upper Volta	41	1970
79	Malaysia	41	1974
80	Laos	39	1972
81	Ghana	36	1969
82	Colombia	36	1974
83	Zambia	27	1973
84	Guatemala	23	1974
85	Sudan	23	1975
86	Egypt	21	1975
87	Bahrain	19	1973
88	Malawi	16	1978
89	South Africa	10	1974
90	Kuwait	7	1975

SOURCE: Charles Lewis Taylor and David Jodice, *World Handbook of Political and Social Indicators*, 3rd ed. (New Haven: Yale University Press, 1983), vol. 1, pp. 76–77. Reprinted by permission.

different parties, elections serve the functions of educating the masses, recruiting new leaders, fostering national unity, and rallying support behind the regime.

The low turnout in many Third World nations, on the other hand, may be explained by the high proportion of adults legally ineligible to vote. For example, blacks in South Africa and nonnatives in Kuwait are excluded by law from participation in national elections. In both cases, those excluded comprise the majority of the population. Additionally, in many Moslem countries, women are ineligible to vote. Clearly, then, both those countries with the highest turnout and those with the lowest are not true democracies. It should be noted, however, that where the citizens do not engage in institutionalized means of political participation such as voting they often partake of noninstitutionalized means such as demonstrations or terrorism (see Barnes et al. 1979). Thus, in Guatemala, where the voting turnout is low, terrorist groups have posed a serious challenge to the government.

The United States, where voting is voluntary, should not be compared with countries where it is mandatory. A more relevant comparison is that between the United States and other industrialized multiparty countries where people are exhorted but not forced to vote. Strikingly, the United States ranks lowest of all the democracies in voter turnout. Table 10.2 reveals that in Western Europe the rate of voter turnout hovers around 80 or 90 percent. In Japan, a country where universal male suffrage was not established until 1925 and where the political tradition was "one of almost complete centralization, regimentation and submission" until 1945 (Steiner 1965, p. 54; see also Shupe 1979), the turnout rate is 77 percent. In the United States, it is about 53 percent.

A major reason for the difference in voter turnout in the democracies is registration laws. In most countries, the government automatically registers all persons when they reach the age of eligibility. In the United States, however, voting requires two separate acts: registration

and voting. Registration may involve a trip to an inconveniently located office that may be open only a few hours a week. In some states, registration closes a month or more before an election, and there may be an additional residency requirement before a person can register. Moreover, Americans must reregister every time they move. Clearly, the cumbersome registration laws disenfranchise many Americans. In fact, one study has calculated that if registration were made easier the voter turnout would increase by a full 9 percent, or 12 million voters (Wolfinger and Rosenstone 1980). Even more people would vote if registration were eliminated altogether.

Yet registration laws are not the only culprit. Another technical factor that accounts for the gap between voter turnout in the United States and in other democracies is the relative difficulty of voting. Many European countries hold elections on Sundays, while election days in the United States are Tuesdays. In many states, election day is not a legal holiday; workers are expected to take time off from work in order to vote, often in polling places remote from their work site. In addition, while American voters are restricted to voting at a polling place near their homes, New Zealanders, for example, may vote anywhere in the country, including at polling places at race tracks (see Dionne 1983).

Other factors are sociopolitical. Some political scientists believe that American turnout is low because of the absence of an alliance between a trade union movement and a major party. Political parties tied to other organizations (labor parties allied with trade unions or Christian Democratic parties allied with the Catholic church, for example) often get help from these organizations in turning out the faithful (see Crewe, in Butler et al. 1981). In addition, the absence in the United States of a European-style Social Democratic party that would represent the interests of the poor and the working class and thus motivate them to vote "creates a giant hole in the electorate" (Burnham, quoted in Dionne 1983). Political scientist G. Bingham Powell, Jr., (1980) has found a strong correlation between voting turnout and the presence of parties that represent clearly defined social groups, such as economic classes and ethnic communities. Voters who are able to perceive a direct link between the interests of their own class or community and the success of a specific political party are more likely to vote in order to protect those interests. Finally, as we will see in chapter 11, "European parties cover a broader range of opinion than America's Republicans and Democrats. Countries with proportional representation—allotting seats in national legislatures even to splinter groups—thus make it more likely that a single vote will carry weight" and give people more incentive to vote (Dionne 1983, p. 4E).

A comparison of other types of participation places the United States in a more favorable light. Americans report a somewhat higher level of interest in politics and a somewhat higher frequency of political discussion than do the English and West Germans. One poll reports that 13 percent of Americans have attended party meetings or rallies compared to 10 percent of people in England. In general, the data in most democratic countries show a much lower level of participation in transitional and gladiatorial activities than in spectator activities (Dowse and Hughes 1972). In other words, Milbrath's pyramid gives a true picture of most democratic countries where participation is voluntary but generally encouraged.

There is one form of institutionalized political activity in which Americans participate significantly more heavily than do citizens of other democratic countries: writing letters to their elected officials. During one ten-day period in April, 1981, after the Reagan administration proposed cuts in the Social Security program, Senator Daniel Patrick Moynihan (D–New York) received 37,071 letters, mostly against the proposed cuts. Although senators from less populous states receive less mail, none receives fewer than seven hundred or eight hundred pieces a week. By comparison, an established parliamentary leader in England receives only about one hundred fifty letters a week, in Sweden only about thirty-five. As Elizabeth B. Moynihan, the Senator's wife, writes, "if Senator Moynihan's mail is added to that of the other 99 senators, the 435 representatives and the thousands of state legislators across the country, what quickly becomes self-evident is an involved citizenry. . . . The continuous outpouring of constituent mail in the United States seems to contradict the conventional wisdom that the American public is apathetic. . . . Far from being apathetic, millions of Americans are exercising a little-noticed democratic privilege to a remarkable degree" (Moynihan 1981, p. 165).

We now turn to an examination of variations in the turnout rate within American society. Why do some people or groups vote more than others?

The Sociological Correlates of Voting

Classical democratic theorists extolled voting as the ultimate expression of enlightened self-interest and the most important means of self-government in a democracy. The image of the voter conjured up by the writings of Jean-Jacques Rousseau, John Stuart Mill, and others is that of an educated, rational citizen actively involved in community affairs, knowledgeable about the issues, and careful to weigh the qualifications of the candidates as well as his or her own interests before casting a ballot—in short, an image of voting as a rational act. Such individual decisions, classical writers believed, should produce elected officials of the highest quality as well as national policies in the best interest of the majority.

Reality, however, has not measured up to the ideal. Empirical voting studies since the 1940s have dispelled the notion of the enlightened voter. In particular, two celebrated studies, *The People's Choice* by Lazarsfeld and his colleagues (1944) and *Voting* by Berelson and his colleagues (1965), showed that until recently people voted not on the basis of what they thought but on the basis of who they were. Voting decisions have been first and foremost a function of personal and familial tradition (for example, once a Democrat always a Democrat), secondarily a function of peer group pressures (particularly from one's spouse), and only finally a function of exposure to campaign issues and rhetoric.

Voting preference has become much more volatile over the years, of course. No longer are there traditional Republican and traditional Democratic blocs. But the basic forces behind voting turnout have remained the same. A combination of sociological and psychological attributes predisposes people to vote or to abstain from voting. Bureaucratic and political factors such as registration and voting laws and the salience of campaign issues also strongly affect voting turnouts.

The sociological correlates of voting have been explored extensively (see, for example, Campbell et al. 1960; Verba and Nie 1972; Nie et al. 1979). Lipset (1981), summarizing data from several countries, divides the factors that affect voting rates into four categories: the relevance of government policy, access to information, group pressures to vote, and cross-pressures.

- *The relevance of government policy.* Groups whose interests are affected by government policies, including government employees and old-age pensioners, tend to vote at a higher rate than the general population. Groups with strong sentiments about morality issues such as abortion or gambling turn out heavily in elections in which these issues are raised. Interestingly, national crises raise the voting rate of the entire population.

- *Access to information.* Having a personal stake in the electoral outcome is not enough; the individual must be aware of his or her stake. Traditionally, as we saw in chapter 4, the upper and middle classes have been more aware than the working class and the poor of how the government affects their lives.

As Lipset notes, "insight into complex social problems can result from education and no doubt contributes to the higher voting among the more educated groups. But it seems to depend even more on the social experiences flowing from one's work. The upper occupational groups not only have more education, their job activities continue their intellectual development. Routine clerical and manual jobs, on the other hand, allow little opportunity for acquiring such insight" (Lipsett 1981, pp. 197–98). Awareness of one's interests and of how to go about protecting them is a prerequisite of power. The distribution of awareness, like that of other resources, varies directly with socioeconomic status: It is higher among the higher classes (see chapter 8).

- *Group pressures to vote.* Many organizations, from labor unions to national lobbies, exhort their members to vote for the good of the group. Members of such organizations generally vote at a higher rate than nonmembers. By contrast, other organizations, such as radical political parties, urge their members *not* to vote as a way of registering their protest against the system. The norms of the upper and upper middle classes encourage voting, while those of the lower class and subordinate minority groups may discourage it. Feelings of frustration and powerlessness among members of the latter groups partially account for their low voting rate.

- *Cross-pressures.* When individuals are pulled in different directions, that is, pressured to vote for different parties, they may resolve the conflict by withdrawing from the electoral process altogether. This fact accounts for the low voting rate of individuals whose party preference differs from that of their family and friends. It also accounts for the frequent abstention of people who, through social or geographic mobility, have left behind one group with a particular set of norms (for example, a working-class community with a

Occupation of Respondent	Percent of Labor Force	Percent Who Vote
Table 10.3 Occupations and Voting Turnout		
Upper middle class:		
Professional and technical workers	15	86
Managers and administrators	10	79
Lower middle·class:		
Clerks and salespeople	24	75
Working class:		
Skilled workers	13	64
Semiskilled and		
unskilled workers	23	53
Nondomestic service workers	11	63
Agriculture:		
Farmers and farm managers	2	79
Farm laborers and foremen	1	46
Total	99	—

SOURCE: Raymond E. Wolfinger and Steven J. Rosenstone, *Who Votes?* (New Haven and London: Yale University Press, 1980), p. 23. Reprinted by permission.

Democratic tradition) but have not yet been completely assimilated into another (for example, a middle-class suburb with Republican norms).

These insights into the sociological correlates of voting have been confirmed by recent empirical studies of the American electorate (Wolfinger and Rosenstone 1980; Edsall 1984c). Whatever criterion is used for socioeconomic status—education, income, or occupation—we find that the higher a person is on the ladder, the more likely he or she is to vote. Thus, the very poor are underrepresented among voters by one-third, while the well-to-do are overrepresented by one-fifth (see Edsall 1984c, p. 181). The effect of income is highest at the lower end of the scale. The poor apparently need all their resources simply to survive and cannot spare time, energy, and attention for nonessentials such as politics (Wolfinger and Rosenstone 1980, pp. 20–21).

Occupation has a similar effect on voting, as Table 10.3 shows. At the bottom of the occupational prestige scale, among farm laborers, the turnout is approximately 46 percent. This figure rises to 64 percent among skilled blue-collar workers, 75 percent among nonprofessional white-collar employees, and 86 percent among professional and technical personnel (Wolfinger and Rosenstone 1980, p. 118). In general, "white-collar voters [turn] out at a rate 25 percent higher than blue-collar workers" (Edsall 1984c, p. 187).

Since voting is time-consuming, some believe that those people with the most time on their hands are most likely to vote, but this is not the case. Unemployed persons do not vote more than persons employed outside the home, for example. The explanation for the higher turnout of white collar and professional workers lies not in their having more time but in their exposure to peer pressure and their possession of the necessary skills. These skills include dealing with the bureaucratic requirements of registration and voting and translating abstract political ideas into meaningful personal action.

Two exceptions to the positive correlation of occupational prestige and voting are evident: farmers and government employees. These two occupational groups, which vote disproportionately, share a high dependence on the gov-

ernment and a direct stake in the election's outcome. The dependence of public employees on
the government is obvious. In the case of farmers, their low rank on the occupational prestige
scale would lead us to predict a low turnout.
However, their dependence on the government is high:

> Innumerable public programs give and loan
> money, limit production, buy crops, guaran-
> tee prices, regulate farm labor, give advice,
> improve land, provide water, and so on. . . .
> More than most people, farmers observe
> governmental actions whose impact on their
> prosperity is direct and easily understood.
> There is nothing esoteric or abstract about an
> embargo on wheat sales to the Soviet Union
> or the termination of a price support pro-
> gram. The perpetual uncertainty about har-
> vests and markets, combined with govern-
> mental involvement in many aspects of
> farming, raise farmers' political conscious-
> ness to a level attained by few other groups.
> (Wolfinger and Rosenstone 1980, pp. 32–33)

It seems, then, that the more people perceive
the government as relevant to their lives, the
more likely they are to vote.

The most dramatic socioeconomic factor
associated with voting is neither income nor
occupational prestige but education. As Figure
10.2 shows, only 38 percent of people with fewer
than five years of education vote, compared
with 69 percent of people with a high school
diploma, 86 percent of people with a college
diploma, and 91 percent of people with at least
one year of graduate education. The effect of
education on voting is considerable even when
the other factors are held constant. Among
people at the same income or occupational level,
the more educated are more likely to vote. Also,
at each age level, people in school vote significantly more than their peers who are not.

That education has a substantial impact on
voting should come as no surprise. In high
school and college, we learn about the political
system and about how the issues affect our lives,
are exposed to peer pressure to participate in
the political process, and acquire a sense of effi-

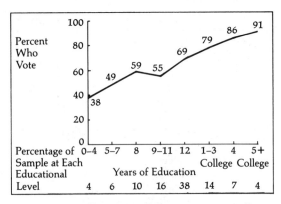

Figure 10.2   Education and Turnout. SOURCE: *Ray-
mond E. Wolfinger and Steven J. Rosenstone,* Who
Votes? *(New Haven and London: Yale University
Press, 1980), p. 17. Reprinted by permission.*

cacy, of control over our fate. All these influences predispose us to vote. The poorly educated, by contrast, are predisposed to avoid
politics because of their lack of interest in the
political process, their unawareness of its relevance to their lives, and their lack of those
skills necessary to deal with the bureaucratic
aspects of voting and registration.

Aside from socioeconomic status, other
characteristics that have been widely reported
to be correlated with voting turnout are race,
sex, and age. Blacks and Hispanics historically
have voted less than whites. In the case of
blacks, part of the reason for a lower voting
rate was the historical legacy of disenfranchisement. Before the voting rights acts and the
Supreme Court decisions of the 1960s, only 5
percent of blacks in Mississippi were registered
to vote, and only 13 percent of blacks in Ala-
bama. A comparison between black voter turnout in the South and in the rest of the country
in the 1980s, however, shows that the lingering
effects of discrimination are wearing off. While
southern blacks vote less than nonsouthern
blacks, southern whites also vote less than
nonsouthern whites. In fact, not only is the
regional difference among blacks less than
among whites, but southern whites vote less
than nonsouthern blacks. A closer analysis
reveals that differences in educational level, not

cultural heritage, are responsible for the difference in voting turnout between blacks and whites. When educational level is held constant, the differences in voting rates between blacks and whites vanish. Blacks have voted less than whites because they have tended to have less education than whites (see Wolfinger and Rosenstone 1980). However, blacks' educational attainment has been catching up with that of whites, and the gap in the voting rates can be expected to narrow as well. Furthermore, major voter registration drives have significantly increased black turnout in the 1980s, just as the gap between the South and other regions has narrowed.

Similarly, the lower turnout of Hispanics is due largely to their lower educational level. At any given level of education, blacks, whites, and Hispanics vote in roughly similar proportions. The reason for the higher turnout among Mexican-Americans than among Puerto Ricans is that the latter automatically become eligible to vote upon arriving in the continental United States, while Chicanos have to apply for citizenship. Those who become eligible by naturalization are, through self-selection, more highly motivated to participate in American politics.

Many older studies report a lower turnout for women than for men (see Verba and Nie 1972; Lipset 1981). In the 1980s, however, women's voter turnout has caught up with men's. Only very old women, those more likely to have been socialized to believe that a woman's place is at home, vote significantly less than men of the same age.

Another major group recently enfranchised, youths eighteen to twenty-one years of age, has not caught up with the rest of the population. Before passage of the Twenty-sixth Amendment, young people participated heavily in political campaigns, antiwar demonstrations, and civil rights protests. Their voting turnout in the 1980s, however, is a full fifteen percentage points lower than that of the population as a whole. Among young people, undergraduate and graduate students partici-

pate significantly more than nonstudents, a difference of some fourteen to twenty percentage points depending on age and level of schooling. Apparently, as we saw above, college attendance fosters political involvement (Wolfinger and Rosenstone 1980).

At the other end of the life cycle, aging brings with it not a decline but a gradual increase in political participation. The physical infirmities and transportation difficulties that face many aged persons are offset by a growing interest in politics motivated, perhaps, by the realization of the high stake that elderly persons have in government programs such as Social Security and housing subsidies.

Taken together, the data on voting turnout show that, in the United States, the ballot, far from equalizing differences of income, education, occupational prestige, and race, in fact reflects those differences. Whatever scale is used to measure social inequality, people at the top vote more heavily than people at the bottom. Further, while the overall turnout has declined steadily in the past two decades, the voting rate among the lower classes has fallen off more sharply than among the middle and upper classes. Thus, the class bias of voting turnout patterns has intensified (Edsall 1984c, p. 183).

Although scholars disagree on whether the class disparity in voting turnout significantly affects electoral outcomes and policy directions, political reporter Thomas B. Edsall believes that it does. "A . . . neighborhood of 10,000 blue-collar workers translates, in the mind of the astute politician, into 4,800 votes, while a white-collar community . . . of 10,000 people translates into 7,100 votes" (Edsall 1984c, p. 186). In making a choice on policy matters that affect the economic well-being of all Americans (for example, on tax reforms or the allocation of spending cuts among different federal programs), politicians are influenced by a voting constituency skewed in favor of the affluent. Further, although there is no conclusive evidence, a study of class patterns in voting turnout since 1952 shows a correlation with the subsequent bias of enacted legislation. Thus, in the 1960s, the decline in the discrepancy in voting rates between the upper and lower classes coincided with a burst of legislative activity favoring the lower and middle classes, including Medicare, Medicaid, federal aid to education, and civil rights legislation. Since 1980, however, with the discrepancy increasing, "economic, social spending, and foreign policy initiatives shifted sharply to the right," including tax legislation that favors the rich and cuts in federal programs that predominantly affect the poor (Edsall 1984c, p. 189).

Who Doesn't Vote?
Correlates of Nonvoting

"Over the Years, 'None of the Above' Got More Votes," proclaimed a headline in the *New York Times* (September 21, 1980). The article went on to explain that if nonvoters "are assumed to have preferred 'none of the above,' that category would have won every Presidential contest." This result contradicts the principle of majority rule, the theoretical underpinning of democracy. Clearly, nonvoters, who comprise nearly half the population, cannot be dismissed as an uninteresting residual category but must be analyzed separately. The phenomenon of nonvoting has been the subject of a lively debate among those who concern themselves with the strengths and weaknesses of democracy. Are the implications of nonparticipation for democracy "an unhealthy apathy and the weakening of democracy, [as] some liberal rhetoric suggests," or, alternatively, "a reflection of the stability of the system, a response to the decline of major social conflicts" (Lipset 1981, p. 185)?

Writers in the 1930s and 1940s tended to attribute the collapse of European democracies such as Germany, Italy, and Austria before World War II to massive apathy on the part of citizens. In the 1950s, however, when social psychologists using survey techniques painted a portrait of nonvoters as intolerant and authoritar-

ian, nonparticipation came to be viewed as a boon to democracy, since nonparticipants were believed to be an undemocratic element. "The apathetic's characteristics—inability to recognize personal responsibility or to examine or even to accept his own emotions and feelings . . . feelings of worry, insecurity, and threat; complete, unchallenging acceptance of constituted authority (social codes, parents, religion) and conventional values—form a self-consistent pattern: . . . passivity" (Mussen and Wyszynski 1952, pp. 78–79). By contrast, the politically active individual is characterized by "an emphasis on strivings for ego-satisfaction, independence, maturity, and personal happiness . . . self-understanding . . . sensitivity to others' feelings . . . great social consciousness and emphasis on social contribution and love-giving" (Mussen and Wyszynski 1952, pp. 78–79).

Summarizing several studies, Lipset finds that "nonvoters and those less interested in political matters are much more intolerant and xenophobic than those who vote and have political interests. The 'hard core' of 'chronic know-nothings' comes disproportionately from the less literate, lower socioeconomic groups" (Lipset 1981, p. 103). Because nonvoters come disproportionately from the ranks of the poor and the uneducated and because "economic underprivilege is psychological underprivilege," Lipset concludes that "nonvoters differ from voters in having authoritarian attitudes, cynical ideas about democracy and political parties, intolerant sentiments on deviant opinions and ethnic minorities, and in preferring strong leaders in government" (Lipset 1981, pp. 104, 228). In short, democracy is better off without such voters.

The massive dimensions of nonparticipation, however, compel us to seek a more convincing explanation than pathological personality patterns. In fact, it is tempting to regard participation (especially in gladiatorial activities) as deviant behavior in need of a psychological explanation, since participation rather than nonparticipation is distinctly a minority pattern. Perhaps the poet William Butler Yeats said it best:

> *A statesman is an easy man,*
> *He tells his lies by rote;*
> *A journalist makes up his lies*
> *And takes you by the throat;*
> *So stay at home and drink your beer*
> *And let the neighbor vote.*
>
> "The Old Stone Cross," *The Nation*, March 12, 1938. © *The Nation*. Reprinted by permission.

Another explanation for nonvoting is a lack of interest in politics and certain people's belief that they are powerless to influence political decisions. Such an orientation reflects not deep-seated personality disorders but a healthy adaptation to the reality of the unequal distribution of power in society. In other words, the causes of abstention are not psychological but social-structural. A perception of powerlessness and inefficacy is, not surprisingly, correlated with low socioeconomic status and particularly with low levels of education.

> As a matter of fact, the evidence is that such basic personality traits as rigidity, guilt, intolerance of ambiguity . . . and manifest anxiety do not correlate highly with [the absence of] political participation. . . . Other psychological traits, which owe their origin to social learning, appear to be more correlated in the aggregate with political participation than does basic personality. Amongst these learned traits the following have been researched: sense of efficacy, sense of civic responsibility, sociability, sense of alienation. (Dowse and Hughes 1972, p. 305)

We present below a typology of orientations that characterize the nonparticipant—apathy, anomie, and alienation.

Apathy, rather than being a manifestation of an authoritarian personality, simply indicates a lack of interest in matters political. It may result from a lack of exposure to political stimuli, or "the individual may feel that the subject matter of politics is not very interesting. . . . Furthermore, he may feel that political activity provides little or no immediate satisfaction and few direct results" (Rush and Althoff 1972, pp. 91–92). Apathy is the most general term of the three; the apathetic individual may also be anomic or alienated.

Anomie refers to a sense of inefficacy, of anticipated frustration. "An individual may regard political activity as futile. . . . He may feel that he is totally unable to influence the course of events and that the political forces he perceives are in any case beyond [his] control" (Rush and Althoff 1972, p. 91). This feeling of powerlessness, if it becomes extreme and extends to a sense of lack of control over life in general, constitutes anomie.[2]

Alienation goes beyond apathy and anomie. It is a feeling of active estrangement from government, a belief that the government has little or no effect on one's personal life. Worse, the government may be perceived as having malevolent consequences or as being run *"by* others *for* others according to an alien set of rules" (Lane 1962, p. 177). Hence, the alienated individual, rather than withdrawing from politics, may take up alternative forms of political action such as attempting to overthrow the government by violent means, to change it by nonviolent means, or to emigrate. Where entire classes, ethnic groups, or ideological groups share this alienation, the legitimacy of the government is undermined and the likelihood of revolution is high (see chapters 12 and 13; see also Almond and Verba 1965).

Studies of the sociological correlates of nonvoting repeatedly show that nonvoters are poorer, less educated, younger, and more likely to be unemployed than voters. Wolfinger and Rosenstone (1980) point out that the following groups are underrepresented in the voting population by at least 15 percent (and some by as much as 50 percent): people without a high

---

2. This concept of anomie differs from Durkheim's, which means normlessness rather than powerlessness. See chapter 3.

school diploma, people who make less than the median income, southerners, blacks, Hispanics, the very young, the unemployed, and people who have moved in the past year. The most underrepresented are the most disadvantaged—the poorest, the least educated, and members of minority groups.

These data lend themselves to two related conclusions. First, political participation is a function of resources and opportunities that are not equally distributed but rather are skewed toward the middle and upper rungs of the stratification system. Middle- and upper-class resources—education, money, a prestigious occupation, and involvement in various organizations—enhance many attributes that make political participation both easier and more rewarding: a sense of efficacy or control over one's fate, an ability to understand abstractions, a feeling of ease in social situations, the skills necessary for dealing with bureaucratic hurdles, and a sense of civic duty (see Dowse and Hughes 1972; Milbrath 1965; Templeton 1966; Almond and Verba 1965).

The second conclusion rests on the extent of nonvoting not only among the poor and the uneducated but among all walks of life. Nonvoting has not declined despite recent gains in education and the easing of registration laws and residency requirements. "The new nonvoters come from all walks of life, cutting almost evenly across income groups and the two sexes. They are of the middle class and working class in equal proportions. . . . As a group, they are more apt than the rest of the population to see 'no difference' between the two major parties. . . . They are more likely . . . to see the United States as being 'seriously off on the wrong track' " (Sussman 1982). While in the 1980s intensive registration drives have resulted in blacks' and union members' turning out to vote in record numbers, leading to a slight increase in the overall turnout, other people— many of them younger voters who came of age in the 1970s and 1980s—have dropped out of the voting process. This situation leads to the conclusion that a massive disaffection with

politics exists (see Balz 1985; Edsall 1984c; Broder 1980).

How Do We Vote? The Social Bases of Party Preference

In this section, we set aside the degree of involvement in politics and concern ourselves with the direction of political involvement in America: How do we vote? What accounts for the way we vote—the issues of the day, the candidates' personality and campaign style, our socioeconomic background, or plain habit? The question may be phrased more broadly as follows: What is the relationship between the political behavior of people, their ideological or political thinking, and their location in the social structure?

American political parties, unlike those of countries such as France or Germany, do not correspond clearly to social-structural cleavages. Yet even in the United States, the issues of equality versus privilege and of the status quo versus social change have dominated the political struggle. Historically, the relationship between social structure, ideology, and political preference has been reflected in the alignment of the parties from right to left. Traditionally in American politics, specific alignments of demographic groups with political parties have remained constant for a generation or two, only to be followed by a realignment (see chapter 11; see also Lazarsfeld et al. 1944; Berelson et al. 1965). Elections that give rise to a new coalition, such as the New Deal election of 1932, are called **realigning elections.** Elections that preserve the existing pattern, such as the 1948 election, are known as **maintaining elections.** Elections in which short-term factors, whether a particularly popular candidate or a volatile issue, effect a temporary shift in voting patterns are called **deviating elections.** Such was the case in 1952, when many lifelong Democrats crossed party lines to vote for Eisenhower, a popular military hero. This vote, however, did not entail a change in party pref-

Table 10.4 Percent Democratic Vote of Different Demographic Groups in Presidential Elections, 1952–1976							
		1952	*1956*	*1960*	*1964*	*1968*	*1972*	*1976*
Education:	College	27%	31%	36%	54%	37%	37%	43%
	High school	43	44	53	69	48	33	54
	Grade school	49	42	56	80	61	40	67
Income:	Top 1/20	23	23	24	54	33	18	23
	Middle 1/3	46	43	55	74	46	37	53
	Bottom 1/6	43	41	46	74	49	44	67
Sex:	Male	43	44	52	66	45	32	51
	Female	41	37	47	69	47	39	51
Race:	White	40	39	48	65	41	30	95
	Black	80	64	71	100	97	87	95
Region:	South	51	49	51	65	40	34	54
	Nonsouth	40	38	49	68	45	37	50
Union membership:	Union household	56	53	64	83	56	43	64
	Nonunion	36	36	44	62	43	33	47
Occupation:	Professional	31	33	42	54	40	34	41
	White-collar	35	37	43	66	45	37	47
	Blue-collar	56	49	63	80	54	39	66
	Unskilled	66	63	33	90	80	53	66
	Farmers	36	48	47	65	42	20	44
	Housewives	37	35	43	66	44	30	46
Religion:	Protestant	36	36	37	63	39	31	46
	Catholic	52	46	83	79	60	40	58
	Jew	72	77	89	89	93	70	72
	Other and none	54	57	60	68	65	61	62
Population as a whole		42	40	50	68	46	36	51

SOURCE: Adapted from Warren E. Miller et al., *American National Election Studies Data Sourcebook, 1952–1978* (Cambridge, Mass.: Harvard University Press, 1980), Tables 6.7–6.15, pp. 337–45. Reprinted by permission.

erence among the electorate; in fact, Congress remained Democratic throughout the 1950s. As we will see below, a lively debate exists among political analysts about whether the Republican victories in the 1980s constitute a major realignment or merely a short-term fluctuation (see Campbell et al. 1966; Sundquist 1983).

The New Deal coalition, which lasted from 1932 through the 1970s, is an illustration of a classic political alignment. "The New Deal built a Democratic majority out of the white South, Catholics (through big city party organi-zations), blacks, Jews, and union members. . . . In the 1948 election, . . . almost eighty-five percent of Truman's vote was cast by southern whites, Jews, blacks, Catholics, and union members" (Nie et al. 1979, pp. 382–83) (see Table 10.4). Prior to 1932, most of these voters had been either politically uninvolved or underaged. It was President Roosevelt who succeeded in galvanizing the young, the urban, the working class, and the children of immigrants into a lasting Democratic coalition. Today, however, new patterns are emerging.

We explore below the changing impact on

Table 10.5 Percent Democratic and Republican Vote of Different Demographic Groups in Presidential Elections, 1980–1984

	1980		1984		1980–84 Change	
	Rep.	Dem.	Rep.	Dem.	Rep.	Dem.
All (100%)	51%	41%	59%	41%	+8	05
Men (50)	53	38	63	37	+10	−1
Women (50)	49	44	56	44	+7	0
Whites (82)	56	36	67	33	+11	−3
Blacks (12)	10	86	9	91	−1	+5
Hispanics (4)	36	54	47	53	+11	−1
East (25)	47	43	59	41	+12	−2
South (28)	51	44	58	42	+7	−2
Midwest (29)	51	41	59	41	+8	0
West (18)	52	35	59	41	+7	+6
Southern whites (22)	59	36	73	27	+14	−9
Nonsouthern whites (60)	55	32	64	36	+9	+4
Protestants (62)	54	39	61	39	+7	0
Catholics (8)	47	46	59	41	+12	−5
Jews (3)	39	45	32	68	−7	+23
"Born-again" white Protestants (14)	61	34	80	20	+19	−14
Age 18–24 (13)	⟨43	43⟩	59	41	⟨+17	−3⟩
25–29 (13)			61	39		
30–39 (26)			57	43		
40–49 (17)	⟨54	38⟩	59	41	⟨+5	+3⟩
50–59 (14)			62	38		
60+ (17)	54	40	60	40	+6	0
Family income:						
−$10,000 (16)	—	—	45	55	—	—
$10–20,000 (25)	—	—	56	44	—	—
$20–30,000 (24)	—	—	61	39	—	—
$30–40,000 (18)	—	—	66	34	—	—
Over $40,000 (17)	—	—	68	32	—	—

(continued on following page)

partisan support of specific divisions within the social structure: socioeconomic status, ethnicity and religion, gender, and region of residence.

Socioeconomic Status

Of the various cleavages in the social structure, none has influenced political behavior more than class. This is true whether we measure class in terms of income, education, occupation, or relationship to the means of production, and it holds true in all industrial countries. As Lipset notes, "more than anything else the party struggle is a conflict among classes, and the most impressive single fact about political party support is that in virtually every economically developed country the lower-income groups vote mainly for parties of the left, while the

Table 10.5 Percent Democratic and Republican Vote of Different Demographic Groups in Presidential Elections, 1980–1984

	1980		1984		1980–84 Change	
	Rep.	Dem.	Rep.	Dem.	Rep.	Dem.
Didn't finish high school (8%)	45%	50%	48%	51%	+3	+1
High school grad (29)	51	43	56	44	+5	+1
Some college (29)	55	35	62	38	+7	+3
College grad (21)	⟨51	35⟩	63	37	⟨+8	+6⟩
Postgrad (14)			52	48		
Union households (30)	44	47	48	52	+4	+5
Nonunion (70)	55	35	64	36	+9	+1
Financial situation:						
Better (41)	37	53	81	19	+44	−34
Same (40)	46	46	51	49	+5	+3
Worse (19)	64	25	27	73	−37	+48
Democrats (34)	26	69	16	84	−10	+15
Independents (36)	55	29	67	33	+12	+4
Republicans (30)	86	8	97	3	+11	−5
Liberals (30)	27	57	32	68	+5	+11
Moderates (34)	48	42	59	41	+11	−1
Conservatives (36)	71	23	82	18	+11	−5
1980 vote:						
Reagan-R (45)	100	—	90	10	−10	+10
Carter-D (31)	—	100	20	80	−20	+20
Anderson-I (5)	—	—	32	68	+32	+68
Did not vote (15)	—	—	58	42	—	—
Registered:						
Before 1981 (84)	—	—	60	40	—	—
1984 (8)	—	—	61	39	—	—
1981–83 (8)	—	—	51	49	—	—

SOURCE: *National Journal*, November 10, 1984. Reprinted by permission.

higher-income groups vote mainly for parties of the right" (Lipset 1981, p. 234). In Europe, the lower and working classes have tended to vote for Socialist or Communist parties, while the middle and upper classes have supported conservative or centrist parties such as the Christian Democrats.

In the United States, the class bases of the political parties, though less clear-cut, have been similar. The lower and working classes, and in particular organized labor, have tended to vote for the Democratic party, which historically has taken a prolabor stance, while the middle and upper classes outside the South have supported the Republican party, which, in turn, has favored probusiness policies. As both Table 10.4 and Table 10.5 show, in every election the percentage of the electorate voting Democratic declines substantially and the percentage voting Republican increases as income and education rise.

Along with party preference, attitudes on political issues also vary according to socioeconomic status. People on the lower rungs have favored more governmental intervention to improve the economy, raise wages, and subsidize medical care, while those on the higher rungs have opposed such measures and have supported instead a larger role for private enterprise. Broader political philosophies encompassing the role of government vis-à-vis that of business, the makings of the good society, and the general direction society should take often underlie specific attitudes. These philosophies constitute political ideologies (see chapter 6).

The relationship between social class, ideology, partisan support, and voting patterns, however, is changing. Many political commentators have noted the decline of support for the major parties and the erosion of stable voting patterns. Some express hope that the voters, loosened from traditional partisan attachments, will be able to exercise a more rational choice based on a thoughtful consideration of the issues. Thus, political analyst Hilde Himmelweit and her colleagues propose a "consumer model" of party choice, contending that voting today is merely "one instance of decision making, no different in kind from the process whereby other decisions are reached" (Himmelweit et al. 1981, p. 12; see also Orum 1978). Others, however, fear that the volatility and unpredictability of the electorate will cause our political leadership to drift (see Ladd 1981).

In Europe, "the more explicit forms of class consciousness . . . seem to be on the decline, and class is much less important as a source of political struggle in advanced industrial society than it once was" (Lipset 1981, p. 504). In the United States among all segments of the population, including the middle and lower classes, attitudes have shifted toward the conservative end of the scale and voting for the Republican party has increased. Lipset attributes the decline

in class-based voting to the rise of postindustrial society, which, as we saw in chapter 9, has led to a decrease in the size and importance of the industrial labor force and an increase in information-based occupations. In the new postindustrial society, relationship to the means of production no longer determines either economic interests or positions on issues. Perhaps Marx was right after all: As technology has changed, so has the basis of power.

Other observers, however, maintain that, despite some crossing over at the polls, the working class has remained substantially liberal in its support for governmental programs and the upper class is still fundamentally conservative. The cross-over vote, in this view, signifies dissatisfaction with a particular candidate's performance and a rise in patriotism rather than a profound change in values. Thus, working- and lower-class voters who would otherwise vote Democratic may be drawn to the Republican party by patriotic feelings intensified by President Reagan's politics. Some observers even find an increase in class divisions between Republicans and Democrats, along with a heightened perception that the Republican party is the party of the well-to-do. The persistent relationships between class and voting preferences are shown in Table 10.5 (see also Miller 1981; Edsall 1984c; Ranney 1981).

Ethnicity and Religion

A second set of factors influencing party identification, political attitudes, and voting behavior consists of ethnicity, race, and religion. In countries where parties are not officially divided along religious lines, members of minority groups subjected to economic, political, or social discrimination tend to vote for more liberal or left-wing parties, while members of the majority group tend to vote for more conservative or right-wing parties. In the United States, blacks, Hispanics, Jews, and Catholics have voted disproportionately Democratic, while white Anglo-Saxon Protestants have disproportionately thrown their support behind the Republican party. Table 10.5 indicates that in 1984 91 percent of all blacks voted Democratic compared to 33 percent of all whites and that 68 percent of all Jews voted Democratic compared to 39 percent of all Protestants.

Of course, class and ethnicity overlap. Blacks and Hispanics as a group rank lower in socioeconomic status than whites, Catholics lower than Protestants (see chapter 4). Yet it appears that many upper- or middle-class Jews and blacks vote Democratic, while working-class WASPs vote Republican. Thus, ethnicity, race, and religion exercise an influence due to historical or cultural factors that is separate from that of economic class position.

Among blacks, particularly those who live outside the South, support for the Democratic party dates from the New Deal. Unlike other pro-Democratic groups, who were mobilized from among the ranks of the apolitical, blacks had previously been active supporters of the Republican party—the party of Abraham Lincoln and the Emancipation. "The conversion [of blacks] is a consequence of the welfare programs of Roosevelt's administration and the political recognition that his first administration accorded blacks. With Roosevelt, the pictures of Abraham Lincoln were 'turned to the wall' and a wholesale conversion of northern blacks to the Democratic party took place" (Nie et al. 1979, p. 226). In the South, however, blacks continued to support the Republican party because until the 1960s the Democrats were the party of segregation and the Republicans the party of racial moderation.

Today, blacks everywhere overwhelmingly support the Democratic party. In the 1984 election, blacks gave 91 percent of their vote to the Democratic party compared to 41 percent for the entire electorate. While the country as a whole has arguably shifted to the right on issues such as civil rights and government spending, the black population has swung to the left, prompting one observer to note: "No other group in American society is as distinctively liberal as American blacks" (Nie et al. 1979, p. 255).

Among white religious and ethnic groups, the most consistently liberal and pro-Democratic are Jews. Jewish support for the Democratic party, first mobilized during the New Deal, has remained high. With the exception of the 1980 election, when Jewish Democratic support was drained by the candidacy of liberal independent John Anderson, Jews have voted Democratic by a ratio of about 2 to 1. When asked which party they identify with (as distinct from which party they vote for), Jews who identify with the Democratic party outnumber those who identify with the Republican party by a ratio of 4 to 1 (see Tsiantar 1984). With respect to attitudes, Jews are twice as likely as non-Jews to describe themselves as liberal. On specific social issues—legal abortion, the equal rights amendment, the environment, and civil rights for minorities—Jews have remained more consistently liberal than any other white group. This fact is particularly striking when we consider that Jews tend to enjoy high socioeconomic status, a factor that among other groups is correlated with conservatism.

The persistent affinity of Jews for liberal and left-wing causes has been explained by some as stemming from a religious concern with social justice, by others as a reaction to centuries of oppression and discrimination. According to Lipset, "the Jewish ethic with its emphasis on community and family welfare may be contrasted to the Protestant ethic with its stress on individualism. . . . The former has obvious links to the principles espoused by American liberals and the Democratic party; the latter has clear relations with the values subsumed under laissez-faire competitive individualism as expressed by conservatives and the Republican party" (Lipset 1984, p. C2).

Although Jews tend to vote disproportionately, they constitute only a tiny minority of all voters—about 4 percent. More significant by far are the Catholics. Historically staunch supporters and leaders of the Democratic party, Catholics have been drifting away from it. In 1952, 52 percent of all Catholics voted Democratic; in 1984, that figure dropped to 41 percent. Much has been written about the swing to the right among Catholic voters in recent years. Catholics, primarily those who are blue-collar workers of southern and eastern European origins ("the white ethnics"), have been portrayed as angry about the rise in costly welfare programs for the poor and allegedly excessive government spending. Yet closer analysis shows that Catholics have not in fact switched camps but rather have begun to resemble the rest of the nation in voting along class lines; upper- and middle-class Catholics vote Republican slightly more often and express slightly more conservative views than they did in the past, while lower- and working-class Catholics vote even more solidly Democratic and express more liberal views than in the past. Much evidence supports the fact that economically liberal views, particularly support for government programs, are still popular among Catholics, although conservative views predominate on some social issues, such as abortion (see Nie et al. 1979).

Protestants are the largest and most diverse religious group in the United States, and they defy generalization even more than the other groups. While Protestants as a whole have always voted disproportionately Republican (see Tables 10.4 and 10.5), coherent patterns of change emerge when we look at specific Protestant groups. For now, we restrict our discussion to white Protestants living outside the South.

With respect to political attitudes, studies show that northern Protestants, like Catholics, have become increasingly differentiated along class lines, but in the opposite direction. While most Protestants, regardless of class, have remained conservative, a liberal minority exists among the well-to-do. A small number of the highly educated, professional upper middle class sees the need for government programs to aid education, subsidize medical care, and create jobs. Upper- and upper-middle-class Protestant liberalism may be interpreted as enlightened self-interest, since it enables members of this group to achieve needed reforms,

retain the loyalty of the underprivileged, and perpetuate their own positions of power (see Lipset 1981, p. 322). At the same time, the majority of all Protestants, including the business-oriented upper and upper middle class, hold conservative, antigovernment views. As Nie and his colleagues indicate, their views are particularly important because members of the ruling elite—the policy makers and the heads of political and economic institutions—are recruited primarily from this group (Nie et al. 1979, p. 263).

In sum, our review of the relationship between ethnicity and political behavior in the United States shows that for most Americans ethnic influence is diminishing. Among the major groups, only blacks and Jews are consistently liberal regardless of class. Among Catholics and white Protestants, political attitudes increasingly diverge along class lines.

Gender

Recent elections have shown significant differences between male and female voting patterns. In 1984, 56 percent of women gave their vote to the Republicans compared to 63 percent of men, and 44 percent voted Democratic compared to 37 percent of men (see Table 10.5). The gap has been even wider in congressional and state races.

Two major theories have been advanced to explain this "gender gap." One theory is that "women traditionally are concerned about questions of peace and well-being, and that Reagan's rhetoric and actions set off alarm bells by emphasizing armaments." Another explanation is that "women as a group see themselves as particularly vulnerable to Reagan's [economic] policies and are reacting against them out of self-interest. . . . Not only are women the main recipients of most of the income-linked welfare services that have been cut in Reagan's budget," but as frequent employees of human-service organizations, they see their jobs, too, as threatened by budget cuts (Broder 1983).

This support by women was not enough to win the 1980 and 1984 elections for the Democratic party, however, partly because white males have voted in unexpected numbers for the Republicans. In 1984, "Reagan won every category of white males except white Jewish males. . . . He won rich and poor, Catholic and Protestant, young and old, North and South, 'Yuppie' and blue collar. Generally he won them by overwhelming margins." This popularity among white males has been attributed to Reagan's self-assuredness, his strong defense posture, and his lukewarm support for the rights of women and minorities, which, to white men threatened by the recent gains of women and minorities in the work force, was part of Reagan's appeal (Balz 1984).

The gender gap, like the class- and race-based vote, lends support to the conflict view of politics. When people vote their interests and when men and women, blacks and whites, rich and poor compete for a greater share of the economic pie, politics may be viewed as a zero-sum game. Today, as in the past, electoral results reflect the divisions in the social structure. The haves tend to support the Republican party, the have-nots the Democratic party. This fundamental fact of American politics has not changed despite a changing economic structure and a swing to the right among all sectors of the population.

Geography

Regional loyalties also affect party support. "In many countries certain regions have developed historical loyalties to one or another political party, which have been maintained long after the specific event which gave rise to the allegiance has lost its relevance" (Lipset 1981, p. 231).

In the United States, the outstanding example of regional politics has been the once-solidly Democratic South. Southern whites, regardless of class and ethnicity, voted heavily Democratic until the 1960s as a result of the legacy of the Civil War and Reconstruction. Regionalism has also been influential elsewhere, however. Several New England states were once as solidly Republican as the South was Democratic. Besides region, other geographic factors that affect politics are a community's size, age, and rural or urban character. Inner cities and older suburbs tend to vote disproportionately Democratic, while newer suburbs, rural areas, and small towns often vote Republican.

In the 1980s, regional disparities in voting patterns are vanishing. Like whites elsewhere, southerners at the lower end of the socioeconomic scale tend to vote Democratic and those at the upper end Republican. As Table 10.5 indicates, today no significant differences are evident between the southern vote and that of the rest of the nation. Southern whites have become more conservative across class lines. In the 1984 election, the Republican party won decisively in the South even though southern blacks voted heavily Democratic (Nie et al. 1979; Cavanagh and Sundquist 1985).

Several factors account for the recent political and ideological changes in the South: the civil rights confrontations of the 1960s, economic development, and the migration of businesses, jobs, and people to the Sunbelt. Perhaps the most obvious factor is the civil rights movement, which in the 1960s convulsed and polarized the South more than the rest of the nation. The present-day conservatism and Republican support demonstrated by southern whites in all walks of life may be traced to that era. The Democratic party, once a bastion of racial segregation, has since the 1960s supported the civil rights movement and integration, while many elements within the Republican party have resisted these developments. Consequently, many southern whites turned away from the Democratic party, while the national Republican party began to court southern voters. Once it established footholds in the South, Republicanism offered many people an alternative that had previously not existed. The South, once solidly Democratic, has become like the rest of the nation—bipartisan.

Other changes have helped bring the South closer to the mainstream of American politics. As long as the South remained a rural and economically depressed region, the class conflicts that characterize industrial society remained submerged beneath the weight of historical traditions and regional loyalties. Many white southerners continued to see themselves as victims of the Civil War and Reconstruction, and their politics reflected this feeling. In the past decades, however, the South has undergone rapid industrialization, and southern politics has taken on a class rather than a regional flavor. The poor and the working class have intensified their support for the Democratic party, while the well-to-do have increasingly turned to the Republicans. In short, with economic development, class divisions have begun to supersede regionalism as the basis of political power in the South.

The demographic composition and politics of the South have also changed considerably with the migration of corporations and workers from northern states. The politics of the newcomers, however, have not reflected the politics of their places of origin. Rather, in the process of uprooting themselves from old neighborhoods, old ethnic and familial ties, and old institutions, the migrants apparently left behind their political habits as well. They have become increasingly independent, with their vote being influenced largely by short-term factors and, disconcertingly for political organizers and analysts alike, unpredictable. This change in political orientation shows the importance of situational factors as opposed to long-term socialization for political behavior (see chapter 5). For a case study of Sunbelt politics, see Box 10.1.

Realignment or Fluctuation?

In the decades since the New Deal, whenever the Republicans have won an election, political scientists have debated whether the event signaled a long-term realignment—the end of the liberal-Democratic ascendancy and the emergence of a stable conservative-Republican majority—or merely a short-term swing of the pendulum.[3] A realignment would have the following implications: the proportion of the population identifying themselves as Republican, long a minority, has increased; new issues have emerged that cut across the old cleavages; key voting blocs have switched their allegiance from the Democratic to the Republican party; and new voters, including both those who have recently come of age and those who, although eligible to vote, did not do so in the past, have begun to vote Republican in significant numbers. If past trends are an indication, these new voters may form a lifelong allegiance to the Republican party, just as the Democratic party mobilized the new voters of the New Deal generation.

The other possibility is that these voting changes are merely a response to new circumstances and will last only as long as the new conditions prevail. Some observers argue that major, long-lasting realignments are a thing of the past. The evidence shows that voters no longer make lifelong partisan commitments but change their affiliations in response to new issues, personalities, and events. Most voters do not hold consistent positions on issues or ideologies. They are suspicious of both political extremes, taking not so much a centrist position as an ambivalent position on most issues. Thus, voters want increased governmental services but not higher taxes or deficits, military strength but not military adventurism, help for the deserving poor but not for the undeserving. This ambivalence militates against lifelong commitments and stable coalitions. "Whichever party is in power, grievances accumulate as time passes. The gap widens between what the governing party offers and what the people

---

3. See Converse 1976; Knoke 1976; Ferguson and Rogers 1981; Wolfe 1981; Ranney 1981; Stockton and Wayman 1983; Sundquist 1983; Cavanagh and Sundquist 1985; Ginsberg and Shefter 1985.

■■■ BOX 10.1 ■■■

In the News: Political Change in the Sunbelt

The following case study illustrates the political changes brought about by migration to the Sunbelt. This case study contrasts two congressional districts, one in Cleveland, Ohio, the other in Pasco County, Florida. Cleveland's West Side

> was, and is, typical of much of older, urban America—a world of stable, tightly knit ethnic neighborhoods where the people worked hard, saw a better future for their children and voted Democratic.
>
> That world is diminishing. In a highly mobile society fewer and fewer Americans have chosen to stay close to their childhood roots. Over the years more and more of the children of the West Side have sought their futures elsewhere. They still work hard, but when they vote, which is less often than their parents, it is not always Democratic. (Walsh 1981a, pp. A1–2)

The people of Cleveland and other midwestern cities are moving to the outlying suburbs and farther beyond to the Sunbelt, where jobs are plentiful, taxes low, and the climate mild.

With the shift in population comes a shift in political power. In the Northeast and Midwest, the Democrats' traditional base is eroding. In Florida and other southern states the presence of the newcomers has meant a lower Democratic vote but not necessarily a higher Republican vote. The newcomers, demanding the high level of services to which they are accustomed yet rebelling against high taxes, have not found a coherent political voice. "The new residents of Pasco County tended to be former blue-collar workers, union members, many of them lifelong Democrats" (Walsh 1981b, p. A6). Today, however, according to a local political activist, they "are in large part without any loyalties to individual political figures or institutions in their new home state. 'The people don't have roots or traditions,' he said. 'It is a very volatile situation' " (Walsh 1981b, p. A6). Their voting turnout rates are lower, and when they vote they are as likely to base their decisions on the candidates' personalities or campaign styles as on long-term loyalties to parties or principles.

Thus, demographic shifts can signal changes in the bases of power. Long-standing party loyalties may give way to voting preferences based on personalities and issues.

---

expect and want—and think they voted for. At some point the electorate expresses its dissatisfaction in the only way it can: by turning to the other party. . . . The pendulum swings once more" (Cavanagh and Sundquist 1985, pp. 65–66). If this analysis is correct, short-term alternations are more likely than a long-term realignment in American politics.

Voting and Nonvoting: The Implications

Our analysis has shown a continued polarization between the parties along major cleavage lines in the social structure as well as a tendency toward volatility or short-term fluctuations in party affiliation. Other major trends are nonparticipation and **dealignment,** that is, an erosion of support for both major political parties and an increase in the number of people who identify themselves as independent.·Both nonparticipation and dealignment are disproportionately evident among the young.

What are the implications of these trends for democracy? Some writers see dealignment as a positive step. Political sociologist Anthony Orum, for example, believes that the rising salience of issues at the expense of parties reflects "a broader trend toward increasing rationality in the sphere of electoral decisions on the part of the public; responses to parties are becoming less automatic and more calculating" (Orum 1978, pp. 266–67). Political scientists Gabriel Almond and Sidney Verba claim that both nonparticipation and uninformed voting have positive functions for democracy: "Nonelites cannot themselves rule. If the political system is to be effective . . . there must be mechanisms whereby government officials are endowed with the power to make authoritative decisions" (Almond and Verba 1965, p. 341).

More common, however, is the view of political analyst Arthur Hadley, who fears that the trend toward nonvoting may in fact be dangerous for democracy. Noting that both populist heroes such as presidents Franklin D. Roosevelt and Andrew Jackson and demagogues such as Adolf Hitler built their support by mobilizing the previously uncommitted, he warns that "the refrainers sit out there, an ever-swelling, explosive mass awaiting some trigger. Until their numbers begin to gradually diminish, we can be certain of continuity in neither our politics nor our policies" (Hadley 1978, p. 84). Political scientist Evert C. Ladd similarly laments dealignment because it signifies the public's confusion about the course of government policy. "Large segments of the American public have become so ambivalent and undecided about the proper course of public policy that they are unable to give a clear endorsement to the stands of the parties" (Ladd 1981, p. 20). Furthermore, Ladd points out,

dealignment means unpredictability. "In the absence of stable party ties there is little 'memory.' This year's striking division may not be seen at all in the next election" (Ladd 1981, p. 15).

A question less frequently asked by those who study voting behavior is What difference does it make? Pluralist theorists argue that in terms of influencing policy outcomes, voting is less effective than other forms of participation such as joining interest groups and lobbying (see chapter 7). Conflict theorists argue that, regardless of how many people participate in the electoral process and how they make their decisions, elites are not responsive to the desires of nonelites (see chapter 9) because of several factors. First, the elite's upper- and upper-middle-class background tends to influence its decisions in the direction of the interests of these classes, not of its nominal constituents. Second, once the election is over, lawmakers enjoy a great deal of autonomy vis-à-vis the electorate. Third, much power is exercised by nonelected elites, such as business executives and governmental bureaucrats, whose actions are not subject to the public scrutiny of the political process.

If, as adherents of both the pluralist and the conflict perspective assert, voting is not an effective means of influencing policy or holding elites accountable, what functions does it serve in a democratic society? At best, as pluralist theorists maintain, elections allow the masses to choose their leaders from among competing slates and to convey the electorate's mood and general desires to the elite, although voting cannot influence specific decisions. At worst, as conflict theorists claim, elections give the masses the illusion that they have control over political decisions that affect their lives. "While its effectiveness in translating mass wants and needs into public policy is questionable, a major function of the electoral system is to legitimize the dominant system of political rule. . . . Voting has a palliative effect on nonelites, helping to assure them that their voices can be at least collectively heard on the society's important issues. . . . The electoral process serves . . . to deter serious noninstitutional challenges and thus maintain the status quo" (Marger 1981, p. 293).

We believe, however, that both the pluralist and the conflict perspectives underrate the importance of elections. Although a broader range of alternatives would be desirable, the two major parties offer discernibly different approaches to society's problems (see chapter 11). Furthermore, elected officials have enormous power to affect people's lives and the direction of society. Given the limitations of an imperfect democracy, voting is the closest approximation we have to the expression of the will of the people.

Elections serve another important function, according to classical theorists of democracy such as John Locke, John Stuart Mill, and Thomas Jefferson. Political participation does not just assume human reason; it promotes it.

> The most important point of excellence which any form of government can possess is to promote the virtue and intelligence of the people themselves. The first question in respect to any political institutions is how far they intend to foster in the members of the community the various desirable qualities . . . moral, intellectual, and active. (John Stuart Mill, quoted in Walker 1966, p. 288)

In other words, classical theorists of democracy emphasized not only the effects of voting on policy but the importance of individual participation for human development. "By taking part in the affairs of his society the citizen would gain in knowledge and understanding, develop a deeper sense of social responsibility, and broaden his perspective beyond the narrow confines of his private life" (Walker 1966, p. 288). The fact that lack of involvement is common, in this view, does not render the classical theory of democracy invalid. The intention of classical theory was not to give an accurate description of how people behave in a democracy but rather to be a prescription for the ideal

democratic society. As a goal, the tenets of classical theory are still valid.

Summary

Political participation by the masses may take place within the channels defined as legitimate by those in power or outside those channels. In terms of Milbrath's pyramid of institutionalized participation, voting is located at the lower end of the spectrum. Other forms of institutionalized participation include contributing money to a campaign, lobbying, and running for office. People who do not participate in institutionalized activities are considered apathetic by Milbrath and others, even though they may participate in noninstitutionalized activities.

The most striking feature of voting behavior in the United States is the low turnout rate. The turnout rate in presidential elections, which hovers around 50 percent, is lower than that of any other democracy. The reasons for this low rate are complex. The most significant reason, however, is that elections are perceived as irrelevant by large segments of the electorate.

Studies show that voting turnout is positively correlated with socioeconomic status. Nonvoting, although widespread in all walks of life, is particularly prevalent at the lower levels of the socioeconomic scale, a fact interpreted by some observers as a response to the political reality of powerlessness. Thus, voting, rather than compensating for the inequalities of the stratification system, reflects these inequalities.

Among those who vote, the following divisions within the social structure have historically been correlated with political preferences: socioeconomic class, ethnic or religious background, gender, and region of residence. To a large extent, the political party system reflects the class divisions of society, with members of the upper and upper middle classes voting disproportionately Republican and members of the lower and lower middle classes voting disproportionately Democratic. Ethnic factors include the historical preference of Protestants for the Republican party and that of Catholics, Jews, and blacks for the Democratic party. Regional factors have included until recently the predominance of the Democratic party among whites in the South. The historic relationships between ethnicity and regionalism on one hand and party preference on the other have declined, while the effects of class and gender on party affiliation have intensified.

The implications of these trends are controversial. According to some observers, the confluence of dealignment, volatility, and nonparticipation threatens to undermine the legitimacy of the political system. Other writers point out that nonparticipation contradicts the intent of the classical theorists of democracy, who saw political participation as the key to rational self-government.

In chapter 11 we examine the organizational conduit of voting behavior, political parties.

CHAPTER ELEVEN

———

Political Parties

Preview

The political party is one of the chief mechanisms linking the popular base of the political order—the voters—with the institutions of government. In addition to providing continuity and focus for voters' attitudes and preferences, political parties have traditionally played such major roles as nominating candidates for office and organizing and financing electoral campaigns.

In recent years, many observers believe, the parties' role in the political process has waned and new political structures and technologies have taken over. As we will see, however, the parties have proved resilient enough to adapt to new conditions. This chapter examines the functions and characteristics of political parties and explores the implications of recent changes in the political process for democracy.

The Origins of the American Political Parties

The Differences Between Parties and Factions

American political parties first emerged in the 1790s. Until that time, parliamentary political groupings were known as political clubs or **factions**. These groupings differed from the later parties in several important ways: They were composed of shifting alignments, they dealt with immediate issues and the personal advancement of their leaders, they lacked a formal leadership and a bureaucratic structure, and they lacked an ideology (see Chambers 1963). By contrast, parties have a stable structure and leadership, perform regular political functions, and tend to formulate a consistent ideology. These differences are examined below.

Leadership and Structure. Whereas clubs and factions consisted of shifting alignments and personal fellowships, parties have a more durable structure consisting of a stable relationship between national leaders, subleaders, active participants at the local level, and the public at large. The structure of parties does not necessarily involve a large full-time bureaucracy or formal mass membership, features largely absent in American political parties.

Political Functions. Parties develop procedures for performing key political functions such as winning office. These procedures include nominating candidates, campaigning in elections, and establishing coalitions among disparate groups, functions not performed regularly by the earlier political clubs.

In order to mobilize group interests and appeal to voters, parties develop a broad program or statement of principles that lends coherence, focus, and continuity to the party's activities. By contrast, earlier political clubs concerned themselves only with the immediate issues and the advancement of personal careers. "Indeed, the formulation of comprehensive statements of issues, positions, and policies has become almost a defining characteristic of modern parties. In pluralistic societies, such formulations . . . represent a conception of public policy broader than the claims of particular groups" (Chambers 1963, pp. 46–47).

Support Base. Unlike eighteenth-century clubs and factions, parties in a pluralistic society appeal to a wide range of groups, enjoy the support of a relatively large segment of the electorate, and have a relatively stable following. Party success partly depends, therefore, on bringing together a large number of people from all walks of life "who identify with the party, not just in a given election or on a single issue but over a period of years. . . . A party . . . depends heavily on the brokerage function and on compromise to bind disparate interests and individuals into a working coalition." By contrast, factions and cliques possessed "a narrower range of group support . . . and greater fluidity of alignments in the electorate" (Chambers 1963, p. 47).

Ideology. Parties articulate a set of perspectives that develop into an ideology. "As perspectives take on emotional or moral impact, beliefs develop into faiths, identifications emerge as loyalties, ideas of right and wrong become moral commitments. . . . [If the right leaders emerge,] attachments to revered leaders may reach charismatic intensity. . . . Party outlooks are drawn in terms of 'we' and 'they'— our rightness and their wrongness . . . the 'truth' of our doctrines and the error of theirs" (Chambers 1963, p. 48). Clubs and factions, by contrast, neither develop full-fledged ideologies nor attach emotional symbolism to leaders or issues.

The parties that emerged in the early days of the Republic represented an important departure from the politics of earlier eras. These parties articulated a set of political goals and principles and developed systematic means for translating them into governmental action. They also attempted to develop a broad base of popular support, campaigned to win elections, negotiated to meet the claims of diverse interest groups, and coordinated the functions of government. In developing new structures and functions, the party elites (although largely unaware of their own innovativeness) put into practice major features of political modernization.

Early Attitudes Toward Parties

The first political parties in the New World were the Federalists, led by Alexander Hamilton, and the Democratic Republicans, led by Thomas Jefferson. An unfamiliar feature of political life, parties were intensely disliked even by their

builders. Party leaders believed "that those with whom they differed were disloyal to the nation and to its ideals. Though vastly different in structure and function from earlier forms of political organization, the first parties were confused with factions because the modern political party was outside the range of this generation's experience as well as its historical consciousness. Federalists and Republicans alike regarded themselves not as parties, but as embodiments of the nation's will. When out of office, their duty was to recapture power from those temporarily and illegitimately exercising it; when in office, their duty was to keep it from those ready to usurp and misuse it" (Goodman 1967, p. 57).

The founding fathers at first resisted the idea of parties. As *The Federalist Paper No. 10* indicates, James Madison, confusing parties with factions, considered them dangerous to the rights of individual citizens:

> By faction I understand a number of citizens, whether amounting to a majority or minority of the whole, who are united and activated by some common impulse of passion, or of intent, adverse to the rights of other citizens, or to the permanent and aggregate interests of the community.
>
> There are two methods of curing the mischiefs of faction. The one, by removing its causes; the other, by controlling its effects. (Hacker 1972, p. 17)

Since the causes—the contentiousness of human nature and the plurality of individual interests—could not be removed, Madison and the other founding fathers concentrated on controlling the effects by devising constitutional mechanisms to foster national unity and discourage factions.

President Washington, who was elected unanimously by the Electoral College, viewed his role as that of a "patriot king"—"a leader above partisan and factional strife whose task it was to embody national unity" (Price 1984, p. 97). In his farewell address in 1796, he discouraged parties as a source of conflict and corruption:

[The spirit of parties] serves always to dis-
tract the public councils and enfeeble the
public administration. It agitates the community with ill founded jealousies and false
alarms, kindles the animosity of one part
against another, foments occasionally riot
and insurrection. It opens the door to foreign
influence and corruption, which finds a facilitated access to the government itself
through the channels of party passion.
(Washington 1940, vol. 35, pp. 223–28)

Jefferson, too, regarded political parties as divisive although temporarily expedient (especially when his own Democratic Republican
party became the majority party). In his first
inaugural address, in 1801, he struck a concil-
iatory note: "We have called by different names
brothers of the same principles. We are all
republicans; we are all federalists" (quoted in
Hofstadter 1969, p. 151). As president, however, he worked not for national reconciliation
but for the absorption of the opposition party
into his own.

Despite the misgivings of their founders,
parties did not go away. Although brief periods
of relative national consensus have invariably
been mistaken (with either relief or alarm) for
the disappearance of the two-party system,
parties have endured.

The First American Parties: Issues and Social Bases

The issues that divided the early American parties foreshadowed contemporary political issues:
the role of the federal government in the economy and America's relations with foreign
superpowers. The Federalists advocated
strengthening the role of the federal government through such means as having the government assume the debts inherited from the
Confederation period and establishing a central bank to provide for the fiscal needs of the
new republic. The Democratic Republicans,
deeply mistrustful of central authority, defended
states' sovereignty. Jefferson, an heir to the

classical liberal tradition, challenged the idea
that government should be "trusted to the rulers . . . alone." Confident of the rationality and
wisdom of the common people, he believed
that "the people themselves are [govern-
ment's] only safe depositories." At least before
becoming president, he opposed a large federal bureaucracy. "Let the general government
be reduced to foreign concerns only," he wrote,
"and our general government may be reduced
to a very simple organization and a very unex-
pensive one: a few plain duties to be performed by a few servants" (quoted in Garraty
and Gay 1981, p. 793).

Partisan passions over domestic issues were
dwarfed by those aroused by the French Revolution, which followed our own by thirteen
years. The French Revolution was seen both as
morally vindicating the American Revolution
and as placing France in an alliance with the
United States. The Democratic Republican
leadership was particularly vehement in its
support for the French Revolution and was
prepared to come to the aid of an embattled
France against the European alliance headed
by Britain. The Federalists, on the other hand,
appalled by the Reign of Terror that followed
the French Revolution (see Box 9.1), called for
either neutrality in the European wars or an
alliance with Great Britain.

Matters came to a head over the ratification
of the John Jay Treaty with Great Britain. The
Federalists argued that the Jay Treaty would
keep the United States out of war with Britain,
while the Democratic Republicans protested that
it would harm American interests and jeopar-
dize American relations with France. Eventually, the treaty was ratified and signed, but war
with England followed anyway, in 1812.

Differences over issues, as we have seen,
reflected differences in attitudes toward national
authority. They also reflected citizens' perception of their own interests and how they believed
the policies in question would affect these
interests. Thus, issue differences, then as now,
reflected divisions within the social structure.
As historian David Fischer shows, the division

between Federalists and Democratic Republicans was not between the upper and lower classes or between elites and masses, but between competing elites. "The established elites in most states were Federalists; their challengers were Jeffersonian" (Fischer 1965, p. 95). More specifically, the urban aristocracy, members of older families, and wealthy merchants (particularly those who had inherited their wealth or attained their positions of power before or during the Revolution) supported the Federalists. These people, feeling threatened by the new elites, looked to a strong, pro-British federal government for protection. "The Republicans, on the other hand, attracted persons either outside the elite or enjoying a recently acquired and insecure position in local society. They were often new men who came from rising families that had been excluded from the highest levels of influence and standing" (Fischer 1965, p. 95). These ambitious newcomers looked to the Democratic Republican party as a stronghold against entrenched privilege.

Soon after 1800, the Federalist party declined. The Democratic Republican party, having lost its opposition, appeared to have lost its élan as well. The presidency of James Monroe (1817–1825) was known as "The Era of Good Feelings," an era without strong partisan conflict. Of the many theories that attempt to account for the Federalist party's decline, one is of particular relevance to this chapter in that it stresses the importance of coalition and compromise in American politics. According to Lipset (1978) and others, the Federalists, particularly Alexander Hamilton, failed to understand the necessity for reaching out beyond the narrow core base of their support—the established urban elite—to other groups and interests, especially to the 90 percent of the electorate who were farmers. In insisting that the federal government sponsor economic development, the Federalists followed a policy that was, in retrospect, historically valid. Yet by failing to compromise their principles in order to appeal to a broader coalition, they destroyed their party.

Subsequent American Party Systems

In the 1820s, the Union appeared secure and no longer threatened by the existence of factionalism. With this change in the political climate, parties reappeared. This second party system pitted the revitalized Democratic party against the newly formed Whig party. The new Democratic leaders, Martin Van Buren and Andrew Jackson, did not share their predecessors' disdain for political parties, nor did they repeat their predecessors' mistake of eschewing coalitions. They reorganized the Democratic party, emphasizing party loyalty above ideological purity and coalitions above consistency, a legacy that has survived to this day as a characteristic of American parties. Finding the right balance between ideology and coalition, however, has proved difficult.

Another lasting legacy contributed to American politics by this second party system was "the mobilization of mass participation in elections and in politics generally" (Chambers and Burnham 1967, p. 11). At a time when Great Britain boasted an electorate of only about 650,000, the American presidential election of 1840 drew nearly 2.5 million voters, although the total population in both countries was about the same—approximately 16 or 17 million (for a discussion of voting turnouts, see chapter 10). The relatively broad participation in the United States was due in part to the egalitarian ethos of Jacksonian democracy and in part to the mass-entertainment character of American electoral campaigns (see Chambers and Burnham 1967).

The second party system lasted from the 1820s to the 1850s, when the Whigs declined and finally disappeared. The Civil War polarized the country along regional lines, with the Democratic party representing the South and the newly formed Republican party representing the North. The third party system, encompassing the Democratic and the Republican parties, lasted from the 1850s to the 1890s. This party system saw the intensification of regional politics—the emergence of the solidly Democratic South—and the rise of the urban political machine and its corrupt boss (see Box 11.1).

The fourth party system in America, which lasted from the 1890s to the 1930s, did not entail the formation of new parties. Rather, under the impact of progressive reformers, the existing parties democratized their structure and broadened their base of participation. Direct primary elections for nominating candidates were established under this system.

The fifth party system originated in the New Deal era of the 1930s and saw a massive realignment of voting blocs: a new Democratic coalition consisting of southern whites, organized labor, Catholics, and blacks on one side and a Republican coalition consisting of middle- and upper-class northern whites on the other. This party system lasted until the 1970s and 1980s, although the distinct character of southern politics had dissipated before this time. In the 1980s, many working-class whites shifted their support to the Republican party. Whether this shift is a temporary phenomenon or the beginning of a long-term realignment and the birth of a new party system only the future can tell (see chapter 10).

Conditions for the Rise of Modern Political Parties

LaPolombara + Weiner.

Given the disdain with which they were initially viewed, why did modern political parties arise? Several broad historical trends make the rise of political parties possible, including secularization, the rise of voluntary associations, and development of a communication network. First, before modern parties can arise, society must move away from the pervasive religious determinism that compelled people to accept the ruling authority as inevitable. Individuals must believe that their actions are capable of affecting the world in ways favorable to their interests. Second, people must be accustomed to working together in voluntary organizations as channels for promoting their interests. Organizational participation lies at the

very heart of modern, broad-based political parties. Third, an extensive network of communication and transportation is necessary to facilitate campaigning in elections and maintain contact between parliamentary leaders and their constituents back home (see LaPalombara and Weiner 1966).

These historical trends, which mark the transition from the Middle Ages to the modern era, are not enough, however, to bring parties into being. More specific circumstances, namely, the interrelated historical crises that occur when formerly colonial or tribal societies attempt to achieve nationhood, are necessary. These crises include a crisis of governmental legitimacy, a crisis of integration, and a crisis of mass participation.

A **crisis of legitimacy** occurs during revolutionary struggles when a colonial or another oppressive regime is overthrown and a new government is established. New grounds for legitimacy are needed in order to support the claim to power of the new government. The revolutionary party, which allegedly represents the will of the people, provides the needed legitimacy. A **crisis of national integration** refers to the need to unite diverse territorial units, tribes, or ethnic groups in a single nation. Disparate local, ethnic, or tribal loyalties must be transcended, and the new nation must become the focus of the citizens' loyalty. National parties fulfill the function of pulling together members of different ethnic groups or provinces and focusing both their energies and their sense of belonging on the central government. A **crisis of participation** occurs when demands arise for broadening the suffrage and permitting or encouraging political participation by nonelites. In modern democratic states, where rule by insulated elites is not acceptable, parties perform the important function of mobilizing and channeling nonelite participation.

America experienced some of the conditions necessary for the rise of political parties. By the time of independence, America had achieved a secular orientation, a tradition of voluntary associations, and a rudimentary transportation and communication network. However, the specific historical circumstances differed from those set forth above.

First, America experienced no crisis of legitimacy in its birth as a nation. "The new Revolutionary government in America, following the Declaration of Independence, enjoyed legitimacy from the outset without the aid of modern parties to express majority will. . . . The colonists believed they were upholding the British constitution against those who sought to subvert it" (Goodman 1967, p. 60). A crisis of legitimacy did arise a decade later over the establishment of the federal government when threats of secession by discontented elites and uprisings at the grass-roots level persisted, testifying to the fact that the legitimacy of the new government was by no means universally accepted. Despite these challenges, however, the majority quickly came to believe that the constitutional structure itself was legitimate, however "evil" the doings of particular office holders, and that peaceful change within the government was possible. This attitude was to change in the middle of the nineteenth century, when the southern states, no longer able to find redress within the political system, seceded from the Union. This event, not the founding of the nation, was America's gravest constitutional crisis.

Second, national integration had already been achieved in America by the time political parties emerged. "Long before Americanness was embodied in a sovereign state, the colonists had sensed that they shared a common nationality born of their unique experiences—the product not simply of a common language, culture, religion, or long identification with place, but of being uprooted and replanted in the wilderness. . . . When the Revolution came, Americans and their admirers abroad universalized this example as a model for mankind, defining more clearly than ever before the nature of American nationality" (Goodman 1967, pp. 62–63). The parties, then, were not needed to foster national integration at the time of the Revolution; however, they did fulfill this func-

tion during the constitutional crisis that attended the birth of the Union.

Third, independence was not attended by a crisis of participation, since the American Revolution did not result in a fundamental social and economic transformation. Existing elites (with the exception of the British rulers and loyalists who went into exile) were not overthrown, and wealth was not redistributed. "The Revolutionary leaders did not, as later ones did, need to create a party to mobilize support outside the government, because they already dominated much of the existing political structure. They were not conspirators forced to operate outside the framework of established authority, but parliamentary leaders, accustomed to exercise power and able to work through established institutions" (Goodman 1967, pp. 58–59). The suffrage, which at the time of the Revolution was limited to male white property owners, was not extended until half a century later.

The American experience, then, fits LaPalombara and Weiner's (1966) model only imperfectly. The Revolution was not attended by the crises of participation, legitimacy, and national integration that characterize the birth of other nations. Not until the constitutional debate and the establishment of the federal government in the 1790s did these crises materialize and the first modern political parties come into being. The parties then fulfilled the functions of mobilizing popular support, shoring up the government's legitimacy (as well as the legitimacy of opposition within the government), and fostering national unity.

The Characteristics of Contemporary Political Parties

Duverger

Political scientist Maurice Duverger (1967) classifies parties on the basis of their constituent units or elements and their form of membership. His classification is examined below.

■■■ BOX 11.1 ■■■

Political Machines:
An American Phenomenon

Political machines are typically associated with big-city politics, the Democratic party, control by a single ethnic group, and tight domination by an authoritarian boss. None of these generalizations, however, is entirely true. One of the most successful political machines operated in rural Louisiana under Senator Huey Long, another in Virginia under Senator Harry Byrd. In Philadelphia and a few other places, the machine was run by the Republican party. And in many cases, especially in recent years, machines have operated in a decentralized, nonauthoritarian fashion.

Political machines are a peculiarly American phenomenon that came into being in the late nineteenth and early twentieth century in response to the needs of the masses of immigrants and other urban poor inadequately served by government agencies and unable to find their way around the bureaucracy. Machines also served the needs of ambitious political leaders who saw the possibilities of accumulating political power by building political organizations that combined vote getting with social welfare. Some machines have become legends: Tammany Hall in New York (especially under Boss William Tweed) and the Democratic party organization in Chicago (most recently, from 1955 to 1976, under Mayor Richard Daley).

The classic machines are tightly organized, highly disciplined political organizations with two intertwined goals: winning elections and controlling jobs and other benefits that can be used as rewards for partisan loyalty. At the top of the hierarchy is the boss. Beneath the boss are lieutenants, and beneath them are ward

committeemen, precinct captains, and other functionaries.

At all levels of the hierarchy, producing votes is the major responsibility, and failure results in discipline, possibly loss of a job. In Chicago, Mayor Daley and his lieutenants sponsored an estimated 30,000 jobs, including many thousands of jobs in the private sector. Patronage jobs ranged from county commissioners and judges to floor sweepers in the county hospital. Holders of patronage jobs were expected to contribute a part of their salary (usually 2 percent) to the party, attend fund-raising dinners, and round up the voters on election day. According to political scientist and Chicago ward worker Milton Rakove, "a review of the performance of every committeeman in the ward is conducted by the party leadership after every primary and every election. . . . Losing the ward, or delivering a lower percentage of the vote than was estimated, can have serious consequences for the committeeman. He could lose his job. . . . Outstanding committeemen are rewarded by a significant elected office, a well-paying patronage appointment," a bank of patronage jobs to be used as rewards for their underlings, or an honorary position next to the mayor in the annual Saint Patrick's Day parade (Rakove 1975, p. 111).

How did a precinct captain deliver the vote? "Not by stressing ideology or party philosophy, not by stuffing mailboxes with party literature, not by debating issues with his constituents, but rather by ascertaining individual needs and by trying to serve those needs. Good precinct captains [knew] that most elections are won or lost, not on great national, ideological issues, but rather on the basis of small, private, individual interests and concerns" (Rakove 1975, p. 117).

What kind of services did the machine provide? In the past, when masses of impoverished immigrants filled America's cities, the ward committeeman would produce a bucket of coal for a tenement dweller or a sweater for her child. More recently, the machine's largesse was likely to consist of services rather than goods. Depending on the precinct's social class composition, services might have included free legal representation for the destitute, repair of broken street lamps and curbs, increased police patrols in a particular neighborhood, talks with the probation officer of a youngster in trouble, scholarships and summer jobs for college students, appeal of a tax assessment, or help in finding the way through the maze of government bureaucracy. According to committeeman and alderman Vito Marzullo, 77, a fifty-five year veteran of Chicago ward politics, "anybody in the 25th [Ward] needs something, needs help with his garbage, needs his street fixed, needs a lawyer for his kid who's in trouble, he goes first to the precinct captain. . . . If the captain can't deliver, that man can come to me. My house is open every day." Marzullo went to wakes, funerals, "whatever. . . . I never ask for anything in return. On election day, I tell my people, 'Let your conscience be your guide' " (Rakove 1975, pp. 118, 120).

Ward committeemen and precinct captains considered themselves "godfathers to their constituents, ministers to the wayward, and shepherds to their flock. It is true that they [expected] their pound of flesh on election day in return for their services, and rewards from the party for

their efforts" (Rakove 1975, p. 129).

The defeat of the Daley machine by Mayor Jane Byrne in 1979 and even more decisively by Mayor Harold Washington in 1983 signaled for many the end of the machine era in American politics. There are several reasons for the decline of old-style political machines: The adoption of the merit system as the basis of staffing public sector jobs has undermined the patronage system. Public and private social service agencies have taken over the responsibility of providing for the needs of the poor. Further, local party organizations have been bypassed by new national, media-based, PAC-financed campaigns.

Political scientist Samuel Eldersveld, however, argues that the machine has not disappeared from American politics but has only changed its style:

> The workings of the party in American municipalities show that many of the conditions of the classic political machine no longer exist—the intimidation, the blatant manipulation, the fraudulent control of votes, the use of the payroll to reward all party personnel, the unquestionning loyalty to a leader. But machines, in the sense of a rather cohesive group of committed partisans, inside and outside the formal organization of the party, doggedly and tirelessly performing the tasks of the party (screening candidates, raising money, recruiting workers, registering voters, getting out the vote) and being rewarded on other than purely materialistic grounds—are often a reality. . . . Where there is politics there will be machines, otherwise the work of politics would never get completed. (Eldersveld 1982, pp. 153–54)

For other fascinating accounts of the Daley machine, see (in addition to Rakove 1975) Royko 1971 and O'Connor 1975.

Table 11.1 Duverger's Classification of Political Parties According to Structural Unit			
	Basic Structural Unit		
	Caucus	*Branch*	*Cell*	*Militia*
Composition	Politicians, legislators, and business people	Elected officers and rank-and-file members	Workers in the same factory or office	Small, permanently mobilized nucleus and reservists
Class base	Usually upper or middle class	Working class	Working class and intellectuals	Uncertain
Ideology	Elitist or no ideology	Democratic	Marxist	Fascist
Goal	Winning elections	Winning elections and providing political education	Overthrowing the government	Establishing a fascist dictatorship
Example	The American political machine	European socialist parties	Communist parties	The German Nazi party and the Italian Fascist party

Basic Structural Units

According to Duverger, four basic structural units comprise political parties: the caucus, the branch, the cell, and the militia (see Table 11.1).

The Caucus. "The first characteristic of the caucus is its limited nature. It consists of a small number of members, and seeks no expansion. It does not indulge in any propaganda with a view to extending its recruitment. . . . Its strength does not depend on the numbers of its members but on their quality. . . . Moreover, the activity of the caucus is seasonal: it reaches its peak at election times and is considerably reduced in the intervals between these ballots" (Duverger 1967, p. 18).

The caucus consists of locally influential people in business and the professions as well as elected legislators and professional politicians. At the top are the party boss and his or her lieutenants. At the lower levels of the organization are precinct captains, who supervise canvassers and other volunteers. One of the purest examples of caucus-based parties is the political machine, which dominated the politics of American cities until recently (see Box 11.1). Today, the caucus, although overshadowed by national party organizations and political consultants, still serves important functions in local party organization.

Duverger regards the caucus as an archaic form of party organization because of its elitist nature. In a world in which political parties are class-based, the caucus is most suitable to upper-class or upper-middle-class parties trying to keep the masses in a passive role in order to limit their political influence. Everywhere outside the United States, he argues, the coming of mass working-class political parties has led to the replacement of the caucus with the branch or the cell as the principal constitutive unit.

The Branch. Unlike the caucus, with its small size and closed nature, the branch is open to all. Elected officers run branch meetings, draw up agendas for meetings, collect dues, and communicate with the central party headquarters. The branch tries to expand by recruiting as many members as possible. It is thus a more democratic form of party organization than the caucus. (As the "Iron Law of Oligarchy" [see chapter 8] states, however, branch democracy often breaks down in practice.)

The branch tries to keep in touch with the masses and operates at the neighborhood or block level. Unlike the caucus, which is typically inactive between elections, the branch operates on a more permanent and regular basis, holding meetings once or twice a month. "Moreover the character of the meeting is not the same as that of the caucus: it deals not only with election tactics, but also with political education. Party speakers come to talk of problems to the branch members; their lecture is usually followed by a discussion" (Duverger 1967, p. 24). Thus, the branch has additional goals besides winning elections, namely, mobilizing grass-roots support and socializing members.

The branch is an invention of European socialist parties. "The choice of the branch by Socialist parties was perfectly natural. They were the first to try and organize the masses, to give them a political education, and to recruit from them the working-class elites" (Duverger 1967, p. 25). This form of political organization has also been adopted by nonsocialist parties because of its effectiveness in attracting working-class support and its conformity with democratic principles.

The Cell. The cell has a workplace rather than a residential locus, meeting in the office, factory, or ship where its members work rather than in the neighborhood where they live. The cell is much smaller than the branch. Whereas branches typically comprise several hundred members, the optimal cell size is fifteen to twenty members, and cells composed of three to five members are not unknown.

Because of its location and size, which make it possible for officers and members to stay in continuous contact, the cell is more permanent and cohesive than the branch. The cell's activities deal with work-related problems such as working conditions and salaries. Such problems, which are of immediate consequence to the cell's members, "are an excellent point of departure for a sound political education" (Duverger 1967, p. 29). A capable cell leader will point out the connection between problems at the workplace and the larger issues of the political economy.

The cell marks an important break in the nature and purpose of political action from the caucus and the branch. The caucus and the branch operate within the political system, the former concentrating on winning elections and the latter on political socialization. The cell, on the other hand, although it does not shun parliamentary and electoral politics if these serve its purpose, has as its primary goal the overthrow of the existing government.

Cells are an invention of Communist parties. The cell is the most efficient form of organization for revolutionary parties not only because Marxist doctrine emphasizes the connection between workplace issues and the political sphere but also because the cell is ideally suited for underground or clandestine action. Where Communist parties must operate illegally, either cells can hold meetings before or after work or members can be contacted individually and word passed on without even calling a meeting. Cells are tightly disciplined, and their membership is highly loyal and dependable. "The cell system constitutes one element in the strength of the Communist parties" (Duverger 1967, p. 35). It is hardly surprising that Communist parties were almost the only organization to survive the Nazi occupation of Europe. Communist cells operated even inside Nazi concentration camps. They alone were capable of leading armed resistance movements; they alone emerged after World War II ready to resume political life in an open society.

The Militia. The break with democratic politics is even more clear-cut in the case of militia-based parties. "The militia is a kind of private army whose members are enrolled on military lines, are subjected to the same discipline and the same training as soldiers, like them wearing uniforms and badges . . . and like them ready to meet the enemy with weapons in physical combat" (Duverger 1967, p. 36). Although most members are civilians who have the status of reservists and are called upon only infrequently, a small elite nucleus is permanently mobilized. In Hitler's Nazi party, the elite—the Storm Troopers or the S.S.—were active-duty members, while most other members retained their civilian occupations.

The militia was invented by fascist parties, and its structure conforms to fascist ideology, which stresses elite rule and glorifies violence and brutality (see chapter 6). Historically, fascist militias have been used to put down working-class movements. The fascist militia in Italy, for example, was used to reestablish order in the turbulent 1920s and to put Mussolini in power. The Nazi militia in Germany was used first to wrest domination of the streets from the communists and socialists and later, after Hitler's rise to power in 1933, to intimidate and suppress the opposition.

Thus, the structure of political parties— whether the basic unit is the caucus, branch, cell, or militia—reflects their ideology (or, in some cases, their lack of it) as well as their social-class base. It should be noted that the distinction between caucuses, branches, cells, and militias is one of ideal types. With the exception of the old-style American machine, which typified the caucus in its purest form, parties are rarely based exclusively on one basic unit, containing instead mixed units.

Forms of Membership

A second dimension used by Duverger to classify political parties is their forms of membership. Based on this classification, modern political parties fall into two categories: mass parties and cadre parties (see Table 11.2).

Mass parties, typical of working-class parties in European countries, aim to recruit the largest number of members possible, for both political and financial reasons. As we have seen above, one of the branch-based party's goals is political socialization. "The members are therefore the very substance of the party, the stuff of its activity. Without members, the party would be like a teacher without pupils" (Duverger 1967, p. 63). Further, dues paid by members are the chief means of financing the party's activities. This method of campaign financing, Duverger believes, is more democratic than financing by a few big donors who tend to wield undue influence on the party.

Cadre parties, of which American political parties are an example, do not have dues-paying, card-holding members but consist instead of a group of notables who nominate candidates, raise funds, and manage campaigns. The distinction between cadre and mass parties, like the distinction between the caucus, the branch, the cell, and the militia, is one of ideal types. In reality, most parties sport mixed forms of membership, although one form usually predominates.

Cadre parties evolved at a time when the franchise was limited to property holders, parties operated almost entirely within the legislature rather than at the grass-roots level, and capitalist financing of elections raised few eyebrows. Mass parties, on the other hand, emerged after the introduction of universal suffrage. Their purpose was to mobilize the political and financial support of the masses as a resource and a means of legitimation for the pursuit of power. The ultimate purpose of mass parties was, after capturing power, to change the socioeconomic system. The question remains as to why the American working class, alone among working classes in industrialized societies, has failed to give rise to a mass-membership party that represents its interests. This question is discussed below.

Political scientist Robert H. Blank (1980) dis-

Table 11.2 Duverger's Classification of Political Parties According to Forms of Membership

	Forms of Membership	
	Mass Parties	*Cadre Parties*
Membership goal	Aim at recruiting the largest possible number of members	Emphasize quality rather than size of participation; no dues-paying members
Financing	Dues paid by members	Donations by a few big donors
Example	Working-class European parties	American parties

cerns six levels of participation in American political parties. These six levels may be visualized as a series of concentric circles (see Figure 11.1). At the center is a small group of leaders, from precinct captains to state and county chairpersons and national officers. Party leaders tend to be more ideologically sophisticated than other participants. Immediately surrounding party leaders are the party workers, the group from which future leaders will be recruited. Party workers are highly influential by virtue of their continuous participation. Next are the party members, people who have formally joined a party and subscribe to its principles. By comparison with the membership of European parties, the proportion of members in American parties is minute.

The next three levels operate, strictly speaking, outside the party organization. Primary voters are people who vote in the party primaries. Although they do not usually participate in other party activities, they are influential because the primaries serve one of the party's most important functions, nominating candidates for office. The next level, general supporters, is composed of people who vote for all, or most, of the party's candidates in the general election. The final category, identifiers, is composed of people who sympathize or identify with a given party. The last two categories have declined in recent years, a phenomenon with far-reaching implications for the American political system (see chapter 10).

Political scientist Samuel Eldersveld describes the structure of American political parties as a **co-archy,** "a structure of equal power relationships." American parties are not based on hierarchical relationships among different internal units and officers but rather are sets of "self-contained organizational subsystems, which are not subordinate to each other but separate power centers. . . . Each one of these units has a separate base for organizational power, performing different organizational functions" (Eldersveld 1982, pp. 102–4).

As Figure 11.2 shows, American parties consist of five or six basic structural units, depending on whether the parties are in power or out. For the party in power, the first unit

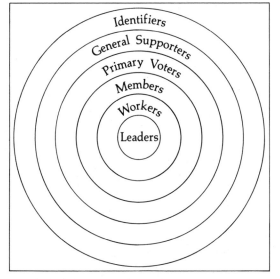

Figure 11.1 Levels of Party Involvement. Adapted from Robert H. Blank, Political Parties: An Introduction *1980, p. 31. Adapted by permission of Prentice-Hall, Englewood Cliffs, New Jersey.*

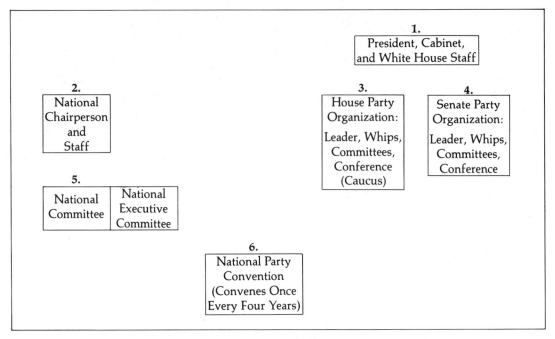

Figure 11.2   The Structure of American Parties. Reprinted from Samuel J. Eldersveld, Political Parties in American Society *(New York: Basic Books, 1982), p. 103. Reprinted by permission of the publisher.*

includes the president, the cabinet, and the White House staff. The remaining five units exist in both parties. The second unit, the managerial component, consists of the national chairperson and his or her staff. The third and fourth units, the House and Senate party organizations, provide leadership on policy matters. The fifth unit is the national committee, which provides organizational policy making and planning. The final unit, the national convention, is "the plenary body of the party symbolizing the representative component" (Eldersveld 1982, p. 104). These structural units are not linked to each other in hierarchical ways; rather, the coordination among them is based on informal communication.

American parties, then, are unique in that the caucus is their basic organizational unit and the cadre is their main form of membership. They are less ideological than their European counterparts. Below, we examine the reasons for the nonideological character of American parties.

Two-Party Systems and Multiparty Systems

The United States, along with a few other English-speaking countries, has consistently had a two-party system. Third parties occasionally emerge and may even capture major-party status, but the basic character of the two-party system remains. By contrast, most other democracies sport multiple parties that cover the ideological spectrum from left to right. In Israel, for example, twenty-six parties competed in the 1984 national election, and fifteen succeeded in capturing at least one parliamentary seat.

What accounts for the persistence of the two-party system in the United States and the multiplicity of parties in other countries, and what are the consequences of having a two-party system rather than a multiparty system? The number of parties in a given country can be explained by the interaction of two factors: social structure and electoral laws.

Social structure alone cannot account for the difference in the number of parties. The multiple cleavages—socioeconomic, ethnic, regional, and religious—that crisscross the United States characterize other postindustrial societies as well. Yet while these divisions have given rise to multiparty systems in countries such as France, they have failed to do so in the United States.

The major reason for the persistence of bipartism in the United States, according to some observers, is the nature of our electoral laws. As Duverger (1967) notes, the simple-majority, winner-take-all, single-ballot election favors the two-party system. In such an election, most voters are reluctant to vote for a third party, however attractive it might be, because they see a third-party vote as a wasted vote and thus prefer to vote for the lesser of the two evils among the major parties. A third party will endure and gain major-party status only if it has a strong regional base as well as a powerful national organization. This has happened only once in our history, in the case of the Republican party (founded in 1854).

By contrast, multiple parties flourish in countries with proportional representation. In Israel, for example, parliamentary delegates are accorded each party on the basis of its share of the national vote. Thus, many small parties are able to attract enough votes nationwide to win one or more seats in the Knesset (the Israeli parliament). Because no party achieves a clear majority, small parties are pivotal. The winning party must form a coalition in order to govern and must trade off policy concessions and attractive offices in order to woo the small parties into the coalition.

Multiple parties also flourish in countries that hold a run-off election. In France, for example,

national elections take place on two successive Sundays. In the first round, people feel free to vote their true preference, "since a vote for a candidate or a party who cannot win is costless" (Lipset 1978, pp. 442–43). For the second round, the parties, however antagonistic to each other, are pressed to form coalitions; voters thus choose basically between two candidates representing the left and the right. In a typical election, the three left-wing parties, the Socialists, Communists, and Radicals, run separately in the first ballot but join forces for the second. Similarly, the two right-wing parties, the Gaullist right and the center, oppose each other on the first ballot but come together on the second. Thus, differences in electoral laws foster different outcomes in countries with similar social structures.

The Consequences of the Two-Party System

Both consensus and conflict theorists agree that the two-party system has major consequences for the American political system, but they disagree on the desirability of the consequences. Lipset, a consensus theorist, points out that neither party stands to gain by emphasizing extreme differences of opinion with the other party. Nor do the parties have much incentive to stress the interests of their "natural" constituencies, since those groups would vote for them in any case. Instead, both parties try to appeal to the center vote, which could swing either way. Elections therefore "become occasions for seeking the broadest possible bases of support by convincing divergent groups of their common interests" (Lipset 1978, p. 449), contributing to the nonideological character of American parties. Unlike multiparty systems, which necessitate coalition building and compromise following an election, two-party systems require them before an election.

Rotation in office further encourages moderation:

The 'out' party has usually been able to realistically aspire to gain office within a few years. This tends to stifle exaggerated commitments on its part to ideal or ideological goals which may embarrass its candidates when they gain office. It also reinforces the adherence of the opposition to the 'rules of the game.' The weakness of ideology, which is inherent in two-party systems, has the further consequence of reducing intense concern with the particular issues dividing parties and sharpening the emphasis on party leaders—that is, on personality. (Lipset 1978, p. 449)

Multiparty systems, by contrast, emphasize *representation* of specific constituencies rather than *integration* of the different constituencies. Parties of representation seek to win the greatest possible electoral support from a limited base, such as a social class, an ethnic or religious minority, or some other division within the social structure. Such parties "therefore stress the interests of that base, and the cleavages which set it apart from other groups in society. . . . This enhances the ideological content" of election campaigns (Lipset 1978, p. 449).

Conflict theorist Martin Marger points out the negative consequences of the nonideological, two-party system: "In creating stability and consistency . . . the American party system has . . . frustrated any attempts at fundamental socioeconomic change through institutional means. Plainly the structure and workings of the two-party system have strongly aided the higher social classes in extending their domination of the political process" (Marger 1981, p. 282).

Historically, both parties in the United States have recognized the importance of coalition and compromise. On those occasions when one of the major parties has struck out for principle over pragmatism, that party has lost resoundingly, such as in 1964 when the Republican party nominated the right-wing Barry Goldwater, in 1972 when the Democratic party nominated the left-wing George McGovern, and again in 1984 when the Democrats nominated Walter Mondale, who appealed only to traditional Democratic constituencies. In all cases, the party lost the support of constituencies outside its narrow, "natural" base.

The Decline and Rise of Political Parties

An election-year cartoon by political cartoonist Mark Alan Stamaty depicts an apocryphal advertisement clipped from the "politicals" section of the classified pages: "Large, diverse electorate, 208 years old, seeks president to fulfill psychological and emotional needs. Dynamic speaking skills, good looks and charisma preferred. Can you keep us entertained for 4 years? If so, write: Populace, U.S.A." (*Washington Post*, February 13, 1984).

For reasons that we have discussed above, American elections have often been contests of personalities, not ideologies. Recently, this trend has been accelerated by new developments: the explosion of new campaign technologies, the increasing role of the mass media in campaigns, and the use of direct campaign financing that bypasses the parties. Ironically, many of these developments have their roots in campaign reforms that aimed to democratize the parties but instead have resulted in making the chief actors in the political process even less accountable to the masses. Despite laments from some political observers that the role of political parties has been eclipsed, however, the parties have shown remarkable resiliency in adapting to new conditions.

The Nomination Process

In hindsight, observers agree that 1968 was a pivotal year in American politics. Riots engulfed inner cities, and student demonstrations shut down college campuses. Two popular leaders, the Reverend Martin Luther King, Jr., and Senator Robert Kennedy, were assassinated. The Democratic national convention met in Chicago in the midst of violent street demonstrations, which were put down with considerable force by the Chicago police under the direction of Mayor Daley in full view of a prime-time television audience. Inside, the convention nominated Vice-President Hubert Humphrey, who was disliked by many for his association with President Johnson and his initial approval of the Vietnam War and who had not run in most of the primaries. To many people, Humphrey was the choice of smoke-filled backrooms, the product of old-style party caucuses that did not represent the will of the people (see Polsby 1983).

The violent confrontations during the 1968 Democratic convention heightened the sense of the illegitimacy of the political process for outsiders and even many insiders and accelerated the long-simmering impetus for reform. Briefly summarized, the reforms in the Democratic party after 1968 included the following:

- Primaries were to become the predominant means of selecting delegates to the national convention. The traditional system of selecting delegates by state party committees and caucuses, long entrenched in many states, was eliminated. In addition, winner-take-all primaries were abolished in favor of a modified form of proportional representation.

- Delegates were required to pledge themselves to a given candidate at the time of the primary and to adhere to that preference on the first ballot.

- The representation of minorities, women, and youth at all levels of party operation was to be assured by a series of "affirmative steps."

- The reform guidelines were considered mandatory, in contrast to similar recommendations in the past, which had been merely advisory. Compliance by state party organizations was enforced by the use of sanctions. Thus, the autonomy of the state parties was considerably reduced and the primacy of the national organization established.

Reforms in the Republican party, though less extensive than those in the Democratic party, similarly expanded the role of the national organization and encouraged candidate selection through primaries rather than caucuses. The Republican party reforms, however, remained advisory rather than mandatory; no steps were taken to enforce compliance by state organizations (for more details on the party reforms, see Price 1984).

The party reforms succeeded in broadening participation in the nomination process and thus making that process more democratic. Whereas before a few thousand people controlled the presidential nomination, now millions participate. At the same time, the reforms had the unintended consequence of removing many decision-making powers and functions from party organizations.

Further, political scientist Nelson Polsby (1983) believes that in an effort to increase the number of participants in the nomination process, the quality of participation (and of the resultant choice as well) has been transformed. The traditional process, which relied on face-to-face interaction among candidates, party activists, and voters, required a careful review of the candidate's qualifications and potential by his or her peers within the party as well as complex, multidimensional deliberation by other participants in the process. The new process, by contrast, relies more heavily on the mass media. In media-based campaigns, showmanship and image—the attributes of celebrity—have a greater impact than leadership ability, experience, or stands on issues. Another result of media-based campaigns is that candidates no longer rely on the parties for campaign funds, organization, and staff, turning instead to media specialists and fund-raising consultants, who have been labeled "the new kingmakers" for their ability to make or break campaigns (see Sabato 1981).

The demise of winner-take-all primaries has had the same consequences for the parties that proportional representation in general elections has in other countries. Runners-up, instead of being eliminated early in the primary process, are encouraged to stay in the race since they continue to amass delegates and qualify for federal campaign funds even while they are losing. While a fairer reflection of voter preferences on the convention floor results, the chances of any one candidate obtaining an early and decisive advantage are diminished and the possibility of an inconclusive outcome increased.

Another consequence of the party reforms for the nomination process is the loss of decision-making discretion by the delegates at the national convention due to the "binding" (pledging) of the delegates to a given candidate. Candidates thus exercise more power over the delegates, are placed in the center of media attention, and have fewer ties and obligations to the party. Together, the reforms have contributed to making presidential campaigns less party-centered and more candidate-centered.

New Trends in Campaign Finance

The decline of the parties' role in elections has been hastened by another major development—the post-Watergate campaign finance reforms. The major provisions of the Federal Election Campaign Act (FECA) of 1974, as amended, are as follows:

- Individual contributions are limited to $1,000 per year for each candidate for each election (primary and general) and $5,000 for each political organization.

- Qualified presidential candidates can have small private contributions matched by public funds.

- Presidential candidates who accept public funding are limited in the amount they can spend on the primary and general elections.

- There is no limit to individuals' spending their own money on their own campaigns for office.

The campaign finance reforms have had the unintended consequence of further weakening

the structure and role of the parties. There are several reasons for this: "First, most public subsidies flow to candidates rather than to parties. . . . [Second], campaign finance regulation has enhanced the role of PACs [political action committees] at the potential expense of the parties. . . . Finally, the FECA has restricted the ability of state and local parties to pursue their own campaign strategies and has created disincentives for their involvement in presidential and congressional campaigns" (Price 1984, pp. 242–45).

The goals of democratizing campaign financing and reducing the influence of special interests, however, have not been achieved. As political reporter Thomas B. Edsall points out, numerous loopholes in the FECA as well as later court decisions have made it relatively easy to circumvent the law, which has been labeled "the law of unanticipated consequences." In particular, neither "the attempt to limit the importance of money by placing a ceiling on expenditures" nor "the attempt to prevent 'special interests' from gaining excessive influence over politicians" has had the anticipated result (Edsall 1984a, p. A4). Despite the FECA's limitations on campaign spending, campaign costs have risen dramatically.

Self-financing. A major source of campaign money, especially for candidates for congressional and state offices, is self-financing. Since the Supreme Court in 1976 struck down the limits on self-financing while upholding stringent limits on outside contributions, the proportion of independently wealthy candidates and office holders has grown enormously. One example is Representative (later vice-presidential candidate) Geraldine Ferraro (D–New York), who financed her 1978 race with $130,000 received from the sale of her share of some real-estate holdings. This transaction took place after the Federal Election Commission had notified her that the loans made by her husband and children to her campaign exceeded the $1,000 limit set for individual campaign contributions. By selling her real-estate holdings to a business partner of her husband, she was able to raise enough money to pay back her loans (*Washington Post,* July 29, 1984). Thus, the law's effect has been to skew the composition of the political elite—elected public officials at all levels—more than ever before in the direction of the upper reaches of the socioeconomic scale.

Political Action Committees. Another major source of campaign finance since passage of campaign finance reforms has been political action committees (PACs). PACs are designed to allow members of different groups to donate money directly to candidates. Although PACs may be connected with different types of organizations—corporate, labor, professional, or single-issue groups—the list is dominated by corporation-established committees. By far the most influential committee is the NCPAC, the National Conservative Political Action Committee. PACs have come to be viewed by reform groups as "legally sanctioned conduits for special interests' money" (Edsall 1984a; see also Sabato 1985).

PACs differ from traditional lobbies in that they are more numerous and wealthier. Their effect on the functions and cohesion of the political parties has been far-reaching. Since 1974, many members of Congress have won office without traditional ties and obligations to the political parties and are not amenable to pressures from the congressional party leadership to vote in the interests of the national party. This does not mean, however, that they are more accountable to their grass-roots constituents. Instead, they are indebted to the single-issue groups and other PACs that helped elect them.

Among the congressional bills in 1982 whose outcome was heavily influenced by the contributions of special interests were "a resolution to kill the Federal Trade Commission requirement that used-car dealers inform consumers of known defects in cars; . . . a 'bankers' bill' requiring people, but not businesses, to pay back their debts even after declaring bank-

ruptcy; [and] a bill allowing drug companies to keep their patents for up to 24 years, which reduces competition from generic drugs and hits the elderly particularly hard. All these bills were accompanied by lavish political action committee donations from the industries that stood to benefit" (Mann 1982). The National Automobile Dealers Association, for example, had spent close to $700,000 in the 1980 congressional campaign. Of the 286 House members who voted to kill the FTC regulation, 242 had received money from the auto dealers. As one member of Congress later told political commentator Elizabeth Drew, "Of course it was money. Why else would they vote for used-car dealers?" (Drew 1983, pp. 78–79).

Pluralist theorists claim that since PACs span the entire ideological spectrum and since all interest groups are free to join in the game by raising and distributing money, "it all evens out in the end." But this premise, as Drew points out, is simply not true. Observers agree that conservative PACs have been both more successful in raising money and more influential in spending it than liberal PACs. Besides, as Senator Robert Dole (R–Kansas), chairperson of the Senate Finance Committee, has said, "There aren't any Poor PACs or Food Stamp PACs or Nutrition PACs or Medicare PACs" (Drew 1983, p. 96). Neither, for that matter, are there any Victims of Defective Brakes PACs or Victims of Smoking PACs.

The techniques used by PACs to raise money depart significantly from the traditional fund-raising techniques of political parties and candidates. Pioneered by New Right leader Richard Viguerie, the new techniques rely on direct mail and media solicitation. Direct-mail solicitations are highly effective because they use refined mailing lists of known supporters and publicize issues and candidates at the same time as they are soliciting funds. They also reach deep into the grass-roots level, thus enjoying the legitimacy that broad participation brings (see Brownstein 1985).

In order to maximize potential giving, direct mailers often use emotionally charged language aimed at raising the readers' hackles. Political scientist Larry J. Sabato (1981) characterizes direct mail as "nothing more than mass-produced and lovingly refined hate mail." In order for direct-mail appeals to work, direct mailers believe, the message must be overblown. The opponent is commonly painted as the devil incarnate. An antiabortion PAC, for example, sent out "Stop the Baby Killers" letters to 50,000 Catholic and other religious families in 1979. The letter called for the defeat of five proabortion "baby killers" in Congress. The words *baby killers* and *murder* appeared fifty-one times in the letter (Sabato 1981, pp. 241, 329).

Direct-mail letters stress both the urgency and the personal nature of the appeal. The opening sentence might read "This is the most urgent letter I have ever written in my life." The closing sentence might read "The survival of America is on the line. Let me hear from you today." Exaggeration of the opponent's financial resources and distortion of the sender's own financial situation are common (Sabato 1981, pp. 242–45).

A recent innovation is the "spouse letter," a folksy appeal for money and votes from the candidate's spouse. During the 1981 campaign of Republican George Landrith for the Virginia House of Delegates, his wife mailed to the voters a sixteen-page booklet containing family pictures, recipes, and anecdotes. She opened with a note that read in part:

> I'm Patti Landrith. My husband, George, is a candidate for the Virginia House of Delegates. . . . We have five children, and as you turn the pages you will meet them one by one. I wanted to send you this booklet so that you will have a chance to get to know our family and share some of the things that are important to us. . . .
>
> George's campaign for the House of Delegates has been truly a family effort. Each one of our children has participated. We feel strongly about our obligation to give service in our community. . . .
>
> From our home to yours—enjoy!

Although the "spouse letter" is inoffensive, many observers feel that it damages the political process by trivializing it (Sabato 1981, p. 245).

Campaign Financing by the Political Parties

The fund-raising techniques of PACs have been borrowed by the political parties. Both the Republican and the Democratic parties have hired private research firms to refine mailing lists, polish the messages conveyed in mass-media and direct-mail appeals, and utilize computer technology to solicit funds and votes. Computers are used to determine "which demographic groups—such as women, abortion opponents, Hispanics, blue collar workers—are key to the election and are 'leverageable,' meaning that significant numbers can be persuaded to change their positions" (Edsall 1984b, p. A6). The candidate's message can then hone in on issues that matter to these swing groups. More likely, since issues are considered divisive by political consultants, the message will convey a desired image rather than a stand on an issue (something akin to a corporate image that helps sell otherwise undifferentiated products).

Computer technology is also used to generate profitable mailing lists. The 1981 campaign of liberal senator Lowell P. Weicker (R–Connecticut) combined and sampled commercial as well as political mailing lists, including, among others, lists of subscribers to magazines such as *Rolling Stone* and *Psychology Today* and lists of contributors to other politicians and to liberal PACs. The campaign was able to target four groups of potential donors: feminists interested in abortion rights and the ERA, liberals interested in general liberal issues, people afraid of the growth of the New Right, and Jews. The resulting direct-mail program yielded $750,000 in contributions—two and a half times the cost and about one-third the amount of Weicker's total campaign budget. It also yielded a highly prized "house list" of 30,000 names of known givers (Ringle 1982). Since such lists can be used for further fund-raising, they are the most important asset of fund-raising organizations (Brownstein 1985).

Recently computer technology, previously accessible only to well-financed campaigns for national office, has been adapted to personal computers. The new campaign software may be used by candidates for all levels of political office to communicate with donors, organize volunteer activities, and manage finances. The relatively low cost of this technology may contribute to a democratization of election campaigns by helping candidates with limited finances (see Henderson 1986).

Thus, political campaigns are undergoing a profound transformation. Long based on clubby face-to-face appeals for money and on special-interest pragmatism, campaigns have increasingly become high-tech affairs. Today, both political parties rely on direct mail, sleek media messages, and other techniques borrowed from advertising and market research, but the Republicans are widely believed to have the edge in utilization of new technologies. The Republicans started earlier and have more money to spend on the latest and most expensive advances. While the traditional elites' influence has waned, new elites, largely outside the parties and not accountable to the voters, have moved in to fill the vacuum. A further consequence of the changes in political campaigning is that the role of money in politics is larger than ever.

The Republican and Democratic Parties Today

Although many observers believe that the role of parties in American political life has declined, the parties have in fact adapted to the new political and technological realities. Today, as throughout American history, both the Republican and the Democratic parties are struggling to balance new ideas with old, cherished ideological principles with the need to broaden their base of support. Because American parties are loosely organized coalitions rather than ideologically cohesive units on the European model, both parties constantly appear to be searching for their soul.

The Republican Party

During the Reagan presidency, the Republicans engaged in a tug of war. On one side were right-wing ideologues, including presidential advisors inside the government and lobbyists outside it, who supported a core conservative agenda regardless of the political consequences. On the other side were more pragmatic politicians and legislators who realized the need for ideological compromise in order to govern the country and win elections (see Roberts 1983; Blumenthal 1985).

The Republicans, long the minority party, were gaining support. In 1980 and 1984, the Republicans, while retaining the loyalty of the affluent, won the allegiance of such traditionally Democratic groups as Catholics, blue-collar workers, Southerners, and the professional upper middle class. In addition, they were winning the war of ideas, the battle to define the agenda for public debate. With the help of corporate-financed conservative institutions such as the Heritage Foundation and the American Enterprise Institute, they succeeded in persuading the American public that the interests of the party's core supporters, the corporate upper class, were common interests. Thus, tax cuts that benefited the wealthy were presented as benefiting the common good in the name of "supply-side economics." The Republicans appealed to Americans of all classes by elaborating a vision of a nation prosperous at home and respected abroad (see Ginsberg and Shefter 1985).

The Republican party was in good shape financially and organizationally. "The Republicans have understood, far better than the

Democrats, the changing character of political parties. As the traditional, locally based parties eroded under the hammer blows of modern life—suburbs, television, education—the G.O.P. created a whole new animal, a national party. . . . It was organized from the top down, not the bottom up, and its threads of allegiance were knotted together by computer banks, not precinct captains. Aggressive marketing techniques turned the party into a money-making machine" (Roberts 1983, p. 33).

Despite these strengths, however, the Republican party was seen by many as favoring the rich and lacking in compassion. As we saw in chapter 10, the strongest Republican support came from white males at the upper income levels, a dangerously narrow base for a mass party. The party was therefore attempting to broaden its appeal to women and minorities at the same time that the conservative elite within it was trying to preserve its ideological purity.

The Democratic Party

The Democratic party, meanwhile, was torn between traditional values and constituencies and the need to build a new agenda for the future, a conflict drawn along generational and regional lines. Older leaders emphasized the traditional values of New Deal liberalism and the importance of organized interest groups such as labor and minorities. These leaders were being challenged by younger leaders, many from the Sunbelt, who entered Congress after the reforms of the early 1970s and had few ties to organized labor or other traditional Democratic constituencies (see Broder 1984; Edsall 1984c).

Both the traditional elite and the challengers professed allegiance to Democratic values, symbolized by the word *compassion*, as well as to the neoliberal agenda, symbolized by the word *growth*. But the younger elite, reflecting the outlook of the Sunbelt, tended "to emphasize growth as the wellspring from which society can finance compassionate efforts," as Senator Gary Hart (D–Colorado) put it. One observer described the conflict between the old and new elites within the Democratic party as follows:

Traditional Democrats stress carving up the pie more equitably; the new crowd talks more of making a bigger pie, even if its slices won't always be equal. When they think of new jobs, the newcomers tend to see computers, not smokestacks. . . . They speak . . . about 'free-market capitalism.' Both sides look approvingly on an activist government, but in different ways. The post–New Deal, post–Great Society, post-Watergate, post-Vietnam lawmakers are skeptical of trying to solve domestic problems with dollars and regulations or foreign policy problems with Marines and missiles. They advocate overall fiscal restraint but are keen on spending money for research and development, education and training for jobs of the future. When possible, they would use the carrot of tax incentives more than the stick of regulation or the plum of federal aid. But they speak approvingly of long-term economic planning and of government involvement in retooling industry. . . . They aim at young, urban professional people . . . who may be up for grabs for the two parties. (Dewar 1984, p. A7)

Like the Republicans, then, the Democrats were struggling to balance the interests of their traditional constituencies with the need to broaden their appeal. They were also attempting to come to grips with the new organizational and financial realities of the 1980s. Despite the erosion of traditional political patterns, both parties retained their role as conduits of political power and as links between masses and elites.

Summary

This chapter traced the rise, decline, and transformation of political parties in America. The first political parties arose in the 1790s, as the young American republic struggled to forge a union. Although originally distrusted as divisive, parties have endured to become key political institutions linking the social and political spheres. Successful party systems have represented the interests of different elites within the context of changing demographic and economic conditions.

Unlike modern political parties in other countries, which are based on the branch as the basic unit of organization and which attempt to attract a mass, dues-paying membership, American political parties are based predominantly on the caucus and have a narrower membership called a cadre. Another difference is the persistence of a two-party system in the United States, in contrast with the multiparty system that has developed in most other democracies. As a consequence of the two-party, caucus-based system, American parties tend to

be less ideological than those found abroad. Unlike multiparty systems, the American two-party system does not clearly reflect socioeconomic cleavages in the populace. Rather, American parties are uneasy coalitions composed of diverse interest groups.

The parties are continuously trying to resolve the conflict between adhering to clear-cut ideological principles and reaching out to broaden their base of support. At the same time, they are grappling with new political and technological developments that are changing the very nature of the political process.

In chapters 12 and 13 we examine noninstitutionalized political participation—social movements, rebellions, and revolutions—and assess the chances for peaceful change in today's world.

CHAPTER TWELVE

———

Social Movements

Preview

Few areas in sociology deal with more important issues than does the field of social movements. Also, few areas exist in which the perspectives brought to the data are more critical. The sociology of knowledge perspective holds that perceptions of reality are influenced by social location and by ideas that have become reified and passed down. This chapter examines some of the classic works on social movements that have dominated the field for the past hundred years, critiques various aspects of the classical approach, and presents more recent theories and findings that set the stage for a new approach to the field of social movements.

What Is a Social Movement?

When the powerless unite in an effort to effect a redistribution of power and influence or a structural change in society, they launch a **social movement.** No widely accepted definition of social movements exists. A key feature according to many is that social movements are relatively unorganized. However, from a political process or resource mobilization perspective, such a distinction is not useful. The problem is not that movements are unorganized but that they are perceived as unorganized by those people in power who are being challenged.

A social movement is in essence the mobilization of previously unmobilized people. But previous inactivity does not preclude the availability of organization or resources for these people to utilize. Without resources and organization, in fact, mobilization may not be possible. Social movements are composed of challengers who are not members of the polity, while interest groups and lobbies are composed of people who are. Social movements are often attempts to create changes in the system, in the distribution of resources or policy, or in the composition of membership of the polity. Members of social movements no longer wish to be excluded; they seek power and influence. Thus, social movements are always efforts of out-of-power challengers to create some form of change. Efforts designed by people in power to maintain the status quo or create change in a direction that will benefit themselves, therefore, are not a social movement.

How a social movement is characterized depends on whether the observer takes the perspective of elite-conflict theory or pluralist-consensus theory. From a consensus perspective, social movements are viewed as being distinct from "normal politics," which is a means for achieving individual self-interest. By contrast, movements often have been viewed as little more than a vent for emotions, cathartic for the participants but ineffective in achieving political goals. The consensus position sees social movements as a means of alleviating personal frustration rather than as an effective way of utilizing existing resources to achieve political change. The conflict perspective, however, emphasizes social movements as a rational, potentially effective, and historically significant means of bringing about change. Effective change is possible only after the oppressed group has achieved true consciousness, that is, an understanding of the political and economic causes of its oppression. From the conflict perspective, it is not the presence of social movements that requires explanation, but rather their absence.

The term *social movement* was first used by German scholar Lorenz von Stein in 1842 and referred specifically to proletarian communist and socialist movements (Heberle 1951, p. 4).

Von Stein believed that the goal of social movements was to bring about basic changes in the distribution of property and in labor relationships. Fundamental social change was also a key characteristic of social movements for Marx. To effect change, he believed, subordinates must create a revolutionary social movement. Social movement theory starts with Marx's notion that a *Klasse an sich* (class in itself) is in a state of false consciousness and begins to act consciously and rationally only when it mobilizes into a *Klasse für sich* (class for itself) (see chapter 7).

The Social-Psychological Approach

The consensus view that collective behavior and social movements are irrational has its origins in the sociology of social psychologist Gustav Le Bon, a French aristocrat who viewed with disfavor the French Revolution and the overthrow of the old order. Writing at a time when organized crowds were becoming an increasingly important phenomenon, Le Bon argued that when "individuals are gathered together in a crowd for purposes of action, observation proves that, from the mere fact of their being assembled, there result certain new psychological characteristics" (Le Bon 1896, p. 3). For Le Bon, "bonds of loyalty to the old order had been broken" (Coser 1971, p. 362), and this breakdown in social control made collective behavior more likely. In crowd situations, the conscious personality of the individual member almost disappears, and a collective mind emerges. Dominated by a single impulse and acting almost identically, people get caught up in the frenzy of the crowd and become less rational. The two ideas of importance postulated by Le Bon are the breakdown of social order and the psychology of the mob. Ironically, Le Bon is usually remembered for the second idea, which is discredited, and not for the first, which is crucial to an understanding of social movements.

French social psychologist Gabriel Tarde also made early contributions to our understanding of social movements. Writing in 1898, Tarde distinguished between crowds and publics, observing that **crowds** can grow only as large as the voice can carry and the eye can see. At a higher level of technology, **publics** come into existence; they were made possible by the development of printing and, later, by radio and television. Printing, according to Tarde, enables "contagion without contact" to occur. Thus, of the major divisions that persist in the treatment of collective behavior, von Stein contributed the idea of social movements, Le Bon gave us crowds, and Tarde gave us publics.

American sociologist Robert Park (1921) pulled these and other ideas into a distinctive treatment of social movements that has largely persisted to this day. He introduced the notions of social order and social change into the study of social movements and foreshadowed the contemporary idea that social order is most easily seen when it is most seriously challenged, a point Park made at the macrosociological level.

For Park, social movements have their origin in crowds. Collective behavior goes through five stages: a milling stage, produced by vague discontent and distress; a stage of violent, confused, disorderly, but enthusiastic popular movements; the development of a leadership structure, organization, and formal doctrines and dogmas; acceptance and institutionalization of the organization and the doctrine; and finally the death of the movement.

Park's notion of stages, as well as his pulling together of the notions of leadership structure, organization, doctrine, and institutionalization, was an important contribution to the study of social movements. Park includes mass migration, crusades, and revolutions within the category of social movements. He also considers public opinion, arguing that "political manipulation of the movements and tendencies of popular opinion has now reached a point of perfection where it can and will be studied systematically" (Park and Burgess 1921, p. 443). From 1921 through the early 1940s, Park's work remained the key work on social movements, although a number of other works appeared during this period.[1]

The Stages of Social Movements

Dawson & Gettys (handwritten)

The idea of stages presented in Park's work persists in the work of C. A. Dawson and W. E. Gettys, who outlined five stages in the life cycle of a social movement: unrest, excitement, formalization, institutionalization, and dissolution (Dawson and Gettys 1934, pp. 708–9). Resemblance to the stages conceived by Park in 1921 is readily apparent.

Dawson and Gettys's first stage is **unrest,** characterized by boredom, restlessness, a sense of injustice, and disruption of life. Frustration results from confrontation with situations that cannot be explained by traditional ideology. In the second stage, **excitement**, the unrest "becomes focused on certain conditions, and when certain 'causes' of misery are identified . . . proposals for action fill the air." The third stage, **formalization**, is achieved when the "chain of officers is worked out, fund raising is systematized, and the ideology of the movement is clarified." For Dawson and Gettys, the formalization process "converts an excited mass into a disciplined membership." In the fourth stage, **institutionalization**, definite patterns have developed, traditions have been established, and vested interests have been identified. "Efficient bureaucrats replace zealous agitators as leaders, and members feel themselves

supporters of a worthy organization rather than campaigners in a sacrificial crusade." The fifth and final stage is **dissolution** (see Horton and Hunt 1968, pp. 499–500; Dawson and Gettys 1934, pp. 708–9).

Historian Crane Brinton (1965) limits his work to revolutionary social movements. He uses the analogy of disease to chart the course of revolutions:

> The outlines of our fever chart work out readily enough. In the society during the generation or so before the outbreak of the revolution, in the old regime, there will be found signs of the coming disturbance. . . . Then comes a time when the full symptoms disclose themselves, and when we can say the fever of revolution has begun. This works up . . . to a crisis frequently accompanied by delirium, the rule of the most violent revolutionists, the Reign of Terror. After the crisis comes a period of convalescence, usually marked by a relapse or two. Finally the fever is over, and the patient is himself again, perhaps in some respects actually strengthened by the experience, immunized at least for a while from a similar attack, but certainly not wholly made over into a new man. . . . Societies which undergo the full cycle of revolution are perhaps in some respects the stronger for it; but they by no means emerge entirely remade. (Brinton 1965, pp. 16–17)

Applying this theory to four modern, Western revolutions—the English Revolution (1649), the American Revolution (1776), the French Revolution (1789), and the Russian Revolution (1917)—Brinton argues that these momentous cataclysms were by no means historically unique. On the contrary, the English, French, and Russian revolutions "have courses in general surprisingly similar. All have a social or class rather than a territorial or nationalist basis" (Brinton 1965, p. 24). The English and French revolutions were carried out by the commercial middle class, while the Russian Revolution was carried out by the proletariat or the industrial working class. All three revolutions "are begun in hope and moderation, all reach a crisis in a

---

1. C. P. Edwards published *The Natural History of Revolution* in 1927. According to Heberle, Jerome Davis's *Contemporary Social Movements* (1930) was "the first textbook on modern social movements to be published in America. While useful, the book does not provide 'a comprehensive, methodical, comparative sociological analysis of social movements'" (Heberle 1951, pp. 2–3). Carl H. Dawson and W. E. Gettys published an analysis of social movements in their textbook *An Introduction to Sociology* in 1934. Crane Brinton's work, *The Anatomy of Revolution*, appeared in 1938. In 1939, Herbert Blumer's article "Social Movements" appeared in Park's *An Outline of the Principles of Sociology*. Hadley Cantril's *Psychology of Social Movements* appeared in 1941. 1946 saw the appearance of *Social-Economic Movements* by Harry W. Laidler.

reign of terror, and all end in something like dictatorship"—that of Oliver Cromwell in England, Napoleon Bonaparte in France, and Lenin and Stalin in the Soviet Union (Brinton 1965, p. 24). The American Revolution differed from the others studied in that it was primarily a territorial and nationalist revolution and only in a limited sense a social one. That is, the goal of the American Revolution (at least in its later stages) was to achieve independence from foreign domination, not to redistribute wealth and transform society. The American Revolution, therefore, "does not show the victory of the extremists over the moderates" (Brinton 1965, p. 24). (For a case study of the Reign of Terror that followed the French Revolution, see Box 9.1.)

Brinton concludes that eight stages characterize true or classic revolutions. The first stage, like that of Park and of Dawson and Gettys, is the accumulation of unrest. The second stage comes when the intelligentsia or the educated class becomes alienated and defects from the ruling class. Stage three occurs when economic incentives for revolt emerge along with social beliefs (an ideology) that serve to justify the revolt. Stage four develops when hesitation or weakness on the part of the rulers is accompanied by revolutionary outbreak. This stage occurs when the interests of the state and the elite no longer coincide and the mechanisms of social control break down (see also Skocpol 1979). Stage four ends with the success of the movement. In stage five, moderate revolutionaries rule. In stage six, radical revolutionaries begin to take power, and stage seven is reached with the eruption of a reign of terror. In stage eight, moderates regain power. They consolidate the achievements of the revolution, restore some aspects of the prerevolutionary society, and produce some return to normality.

Social Movements as Groups

In 1951, Rudolf Heberle published *Social Movements: An Introduction to Political Sociology*. The key to the study of social movements for Heberle is group or class consciousness, shared general goals, and integrating ideologies. Social movements require a "sense of group identity and solidarity." Important distinctions of method are made between (a) the study of the thought or philosophy of a movement (for example, socialism) with the intent of showing its logical consistency or inconsistency, or its empirical validity or lack of it; (b) the study of thought in terms of its function within the collectivity (as ideology rather than philosophy); and (c) the study of the social-psychological processes by which ideas are accepted by the masses as their "constitutive values." This last approach addresses the issue of who joins movements and looks for the reasons why they join.

Building on the seminal perception of Marx and von Stein that ideas are linked to social structure, Heberle examines social movements from a number of interrelated perspectives. First, he examines ideologies, the spiritual and intellectual foundations of group cohesion. He then examines the social-psychological factors of interests, sentiments, and resentments that serve as the basis on which ideologies are accepted and which are tied to the social foundations of society, especially to the distribution of goods and services. He also examines the internal structure of social movements, including the distribution of power, influence, and authority within them, and the relation of the social movement to political parties. Next he explores the movement's strategy and tactics, which may be influenced by such factors as the movement's size and the society's structure (the distribution of power). Finally, he explores the function of the movement within the larger society.

Heberle states that "the chances of an idea's becoming part of the creed of a mass movement depend not so much upon its intrinsic values as upon its appeal to the interests, sentiments, and resentments of certain social strata and other groups," including primary groups, ethnic groups, and social classes. "The particular significance of an appeal to a certain social class or classes . . . has its explanation in the fact that major social and political changes will always affect the distribution of societal income and wealth and thereby induce changes in the relative power position of the classes to one another. . . . Ideologies are linked with the social situation of certain classes" (Heberle 1951, p. 14; see also chapter 6).

Heberle's aims are to "provide the theoretical goals for the study of concrete social movements" (Heberle 1951, p. 17) and to provide a general theory of social movements and political parties. He treats social movements "as a special kind of social group" (Heberle 1951, p. 9), distinguishing social movements from other politically oriented social groups, notably pressure groups and parties. Pressure groups have limited political goals, such as the passing or blocking of a particular piece of legislation, and often use public opinion to put pressure on political parties. Social movement goals are more general and less limited than the goals of pressure groups; for example, social movement goals might be bringing about equal rights for women or an end to the threat of nuclear war.

Distinguishing between social movements and political parties is harder. Both have comprehensive aims and political programs, both may seek to create basic change, and both involve organized groups. They differ, however, in that political parties can occur only within the body politic, only within the state, while social movements "need not be restricted to a particular state or to a national society" (Heberle 1951, p. 11). Parties exist within the institutionalized political system, whereas movements are an extrainstitutionalized means of participation by nonelites (see chapter 11).

The essential characteristics of social movements, then, are commotion, stirring, and unrest related to "collective attempts to reach a visualized goal" (Heberle 1951, p. 6). Movements are intended either to "change the patterns of human relations and social institutions" or to resist such changes. Short-lived, relatively spontaneous mass actions such as wildcat strikes and riots are not social movements but may occur within the framework of

social movements as the first symptoms of social unrest. Heberle views social movements as special kinds of groups, which he terms *social collectivities*, rather than social processes, but he asserts that both social collectivities and social processes are part of social change.

Social Movements and Social Change

In 1957, sociologist Herbert Blumer defined social movements as a process outside the realm of culturally established or defined behavior. Like Le Bon, Blumer treats social movements as a special category of collective behavior. The collective-behavior aspect of social movements has three dimensions. The first is a sense of transcending power that comes from identification with a large group or participation in large group activities. Thus, on the basis of either identification or conscious participation, one is influenced by a sense of the collectivity that supports, reinforces, influences, inhibits, or otherwise controls the individual. The second dimension of collective behavior is its modes of communication, which differ from those in smaller groups. Psychological crowds communicate through uncontrolled circular reactions, social movements through chainlike transmissions, mass media through one-way communication, and purveyors of public opinion through simplified two-way communication with no dialogue or interplay. The third dimension of collective behavior is its mobilization of large masses of people. The functions of leadership, coordination, and control are fulfilled differently in large groups than in smaller groups.

Having thus established how collective behavior differs from small group behavior in the dimensions of transcending identification, modes of communication, and leadership, Blumer turns to the notion of groups that are regulated by established rules, definitions, or norms. He says that collective behavior lies outside this area of cultural prescription:

> Instead, it is concerned with large group activity that comes into being and develops

along lines that are not laid out by pre-established social definitions. Such activity and
the organization of people which it presup-
poses are formed or forged to meet undefined or unstructured situations. This is true
in such typical cases of collective behavior as
crowd behavior, the formation of public
opinion, the shift in popular interest in
music, literature, and entertainment, the
operation of fashion, the generation of social
unrest, and the rise of a social movement.
The characteristic behavior of each such
instance is not an expression of a pre-established prescription but is produced out of a
forging process of interaction. (Blumer 1957,
p. 130)

⤝The term *social movement* refers either to collective efforts to transform some area of established social relations or to "a large unguided
change in social relations involving, however
unwittingly, large numbers of participants"
(Blumer 1957, p. 145). Social movements,
according to Blumer,

> are one of the chief ways through which
> modern societies are remade. . . . In the face
> of such pervasive conditions as increasing
> social contacts, extending communications,
> technological innovation, mobility, institu-
> tional encroachment, and the breaking down
> of traditional cultural forms, people in mod-
> ern societies are forced to seek new ways of
> living and to develop new kinds of social
> relations. . . . [These factors give rise to] col-
> lective enterprises which seek deliberately to
> achieve specific goals. But in addition to such
> organized and consciously directed move-
> ments there is another kind that is fostered
> even more by the dynamic character of mod-
> ern society. I refer to the relatively undi-
> rected and essentially unorganized change of
> people in a common direction—as in the
> case of an extension of a democratic philoso-
> phy or the growth of interest in science.
> Such diffuse movements, without a direct
> leadership or an organized membership, are
> especially likely to arise and to flourish in a
> world marked by dislocation and . . . new
> currents of communication. *They are probably*

the most important type of social movement.
(Blumer 1957, pp. 145–6; italics added)

Blumer argues that most previous work either
dealt with the psychology of participants or
concentrated on the ideology or history of
"grandiose political movements of a revolutionary or quasi-revolutionary character" and
"rarely made any noticeable contribution to
theoretical knowledge of social movements"
(Blumer 1957, p. 146). These earlier efforts
tended to

> ignore what seems to be so essential to social
> movements deliberately seeking change,
> namely, the intricate play of factors which
> must be skillfully employed to forge and
> direct a movement, as well as the fortuitous
> circumstances that facilitate their use. A con-
> sciously directed and organized movement
> cannot be explained merely in terms of the
> psychological disposition or motivation of
> people, or in terms of the diffusion of an ide-
> ology. Explanations of this sort have a decep-
> tive plausibility, but overlook the fact that *a
> movement has to be constructed* and has to
> carve out a career in what is practically
> always an opposed, resistant, or at least
> indifferent world. Thus, conscious move-
> ments have to depend on effective agitation,
> the skillful fomentation and exploitation of
> restlessness and discontent, an effective pro-
> cedure for the recruitment of members and
> followers, the formation of a well-knit and
> powerful organization, the development and
> maintenance of enthusiasm, conviction, and
> morale, the intelligent translation of ideology
> into homely and gripping form, the develop-
> ment of skillful strategy and tactics, and,
> finally, leadership which can size up situa-
> tions effectively, time actions, and act deci-
> sively. These are the ingredients of successful
> movements. To ignore them through preoc-
> cupation with the causes of movements leads
> to inadequate and distorted knowledge. (Blu-
> mer 1957, p. 147)

⚹Blumer thus defines social movements as being
outside culturally established behavior. In social
movements, as in other types of collective

behavior, the individual experiences a transcending power through identification with or participation in large group activities. Social movements, which begin as a response to undefined or unstructured situations, may involve conscious attempts to transform social relations or an unwitting breaking down of old forms and the establishment of new ones. Although initially unstructured, large-scale mobilization requires leadership and organization if it is to emerge as a purposive movement seeking social change. Noting that the irrational components of social movements have been overemphasized, Blumer focuses on the rationality and deliberation that can go into the production of new institutions. Thus, Blumer, perhaps more than anyone else, was responsible for pulling together a variety of disparate contributions and wielding them into a field of study, the study of collective behavior.

Structural Conditions for Collective Behavior ~Smelser~

Neil Smelser's *Theory of Collective Behavior* (1962) is within the tradition of Parsons, Lipset, and other structural-functionalists who believe that the central variable for understanding social processes is culture (see chapter 1). The central variables in Smelser's theory are legitimacy of values, normative guides to action, mobilization of motivation, and skills and information built into the situation.

Smelser defines collective behavior as "mobilization on the basis of a belief which redefines social action" (Smelser 1962, p. 8). These beliefs focus on the existence of extraordinary forces and "involve an assessment of the extraordinary consequences which will follow if the collective attempt to reconstitute social action is successful. The beliefs on which collective behavior is based (we shall call them *generalized beliefs*) are thus akin to magical beliefs" (Smelser 1962, p. 8). Since social movements, for Smelser, are a form of collective behavior

and since collective behavior is defined in terms of beliefs that are magical and behavior that is not institutionalized, social movements are also defined in such terms and are, therefore, irrational.

Smelser distinguishes six stages in the emergence of movements. First, the structural conditions must be conducive to social movements. Second, under conditions of structural conduciveness, there may be a structural strain in the social system, for example, when basic societal beliefs are in conflict. Third, pressed by structural conduciveness and structural strain, people may begin to develop a generalized belief. Fourth, given the growth and spread of a generalized belief, precipitating factors may occur. Fifth, these precipitating factors may be followed by mobilization for action. Finally, in response to mobilization, authorities may exercise social control.

Smelser's work dominated the field from the time of its publication in 1962 through the next decade and remains a very powerful orientation to the study of social movements.

Who Joins Social Movements: The Irrationality Model

Since textbooks are, by definition, compendiums of what is known, in order to see how a field has changed over time it is useful to review not only the key theoretical and empirical works but also the treatment of such works in the standard college textbooks. The treatment of collective behavior and social movements in sociological textbooks has changed over the years. Early textbooks define them as basically irrational action, and, to that extent, the definitions are more ideological than diagnostic (see chapter 1). An early edition of a textbook by sociologists Paul B. Horton and Chester L. Hunt argues that social movements at times act as pressure groups but that most pressure groups are not social movements. The difference, they claim, is that pressure groups simply want norms and values interpreted to their benefit, while social movements attempt to change norms and values (Horton and Hunt 1968, p. 418).

The major thrust of Horton and Hunt's argument is that "frustration and confusion, rather than poverty and misery, spawn social movements" (Horton and Hunt 1968, p. 483). They argue that "in a stable, well-integrated society with very few social tensions or alienated groups there are few social movements. Contented people rarely join social movements. Those who are at peace within themselves and with their society are likely to be fully absorbed in their own activities" (Horton and Hunt 1968, p. 485).

This argument contains several logical errors. To begin with, Horton and Hunt confuse psychological and sociological variables. In their argument that frustrated and confused individuals produce social movements the independent variable is psychological. But Horton and Hunt go on to argue that well-integrated societies contain few alienated groups or social tensions. The implication is that alienation and social tension are caused by lack of societal integration and that in well-integrated societies there are contented people and no social movements. If this is true, then the frustration and social tensions must come from societies that lack integration. Thus, the major variable leading to social movements is lack of integration (a sociological variable) rather than frustration (a psychological variable). In fact, it follows that social tensions and frustration are produced by lack of integration.

Horton and Hunt argue further that "in a changing, continuously disorganized society, the fully contented person is a rarity. More people in such a society believe they perceive social injustice and become dissatisfied or alienated. It is the dissatisfied who build social movements. The frustrated and misplaced, the restless and rootless, those who putter in boredom, those who seethe with hostility, and those who are oppressed by the futility of their present lives. These are the material of which most social

movements are built" (Horton and Hunt 1968, p. 485). Note again the shift in their logic. It is disorganized society that produces discontented people. One would think that a rational and discontented person would attempt to do something about the situation. Yet, for Horton and Hunt, frustration (a personality variable), not social disorganization (a sociological variable), produces social movements.

In spite of this emphasis on psychological variables, Horton and Hunt associate irrational states of mind with a variety of social conditions, including high rates of geographic mobility, marginality, social isolation, upward or downward social mobility, and lack of family ties (Horton and Hunt 1968, pp. 485–88). But while social factors are mentioned, they are clearly considered less important than psychological factors. Horton and Hunt's interpretation resembles that of Heberle (1951), who speaks of the joiners of social movements in the following terms: "The neurotic, maladjusted, unbalanced or psychotic seem attracted not so much by the ideas [of a movement] as by the sense of oneness, of belonging, which appeases their feelings of insecurity, of helplessness, of isolation" (quoted in Horton and Hunt 1968, p. 488). This was clearly the dominant view of the 1950s and 1960s.

Horton and Hunt distinguish between extremist and nonextremist movements, arguing that nonextremist movements are less irrational, especially when the movements are generated by consensus "among the more influential members of the society." The existence of misfits does not cause social movements,

> but when social unrest is intense and alienation and anomie become normal, then the homeless, the status cliff-hangers, and the misfits become the shock troops of mass movements which can set an entire nation on fire. . . . The ultimate consequences depend upon the actions of responsible leaders of the society. If they perceive social injustices in need of correction and social tensions in need of resolution, assume lead-

ership, and channel this mass protest into constructive social reforms, the main features of the social system may be conserved. But if they seek to block social reforms passionately sought and long overdue . . . they guarantee the eventual destruction of the social system. (Horton and Hunt 1968, p. 489)

The question of whether joiners of social movements are rational or irrational is more subtly treated in a recent edition of another textbook, that of sociologists Leonard Broom and Philip Selznick (1979). Even though the authors quote a 1964 work by historian George Rudé, who notes that the potential for rationality may exist, they dismiss the notion out of hand. Rudé had studied preindustrial crowds and argued that rioters in preindustrial societies had "precise objects and rarely engaged in indiscriminate attacks on either property or persons." Rudé observed that "the crowd was by no means 'irrational.'" Referring to Rudé, Broom and Selznick write:

This analysis interprets a type of riot as a rational form of protest. If the interpretation is accepted, the actions of individual rioters cannot be dismissed as the product of mental disturbance or criminality but must be assessed for underlying grievances. On the other hand, as a form of purposeful activity, riots have serious limitations. Although riots may call attention to grievances, not all participants engage in rioting with such a clear purpose, and they may be distracted by fantasy, false rumors, or anger. Moreover, riots may be self-defeating if they provoke repression or destroy resources the rioters themselves need. In other words, the riotous protest is a desperate form of action, and as such may exact costs from the rioters as well as from their targets. (Broom and Selznick 1979, pp. 241–42)

Note the qualifiers: "type of riot," "if this interpretation is accepted," "although riots may." And note the caution that rioting is ultimately irrational because it may cost more than it gains. Clearly, any concession to the idea that violence might be productive is modified by an underlying disbelief. The willingness to accept evidence rests on the authors' consensus ideology rather than on an assessment of data. The extensive protest movements of the 1960s forced many theorists to reevaluate their dismissal of social movements as irrational, yet in this late 1970s book the violent protest issue is raised and then dismissed.

The general hypothesis of Broom and Selznick is that social movements and collective behavior occur in response to a set of conditions such as floods, new highways, or cuts in Social Security. People in similar objective conditions and subject to the same confluence of events comprise what is known as an **aggregate.** Aggregates are composed of large numbers of people who have no preexisting relations and who lack a common organization (for example, slaves under most conditions, fat people, teenagers). From time to time, aggregates with mutual interests may form temporary groups called masses, crowds, and publics (see Vander Zanden 1979). When their response is especially violent, it is assumed that irrational people are joining the movement, since presumably nonviolent and effective alternatives exist for bringing about social change, making violence unnecessary.

When these unconnected people are drawn together in mutual action, is their behavior rational or irrational? This question cannot be decided abstractly, without data. When collective behavior and social movements have been seen as irrational responses to structural strain, they have been treated differently from such "rational" or institutionalized forms of political action as pressure groups and lobbies. It is claimed on one hand that irrational people, not conditions, create social movements and on the other hand that irrational people are more likely to join social movements under conditions of social strain. Author Chalmers Johnson (1966) solves the problem by arguing that social movements arise from an irrational response to structural strain. Thus, either the goals or the means to achieve them may not be rational.

But Johnson's solution, while logical, is not empirically correct. Experience shows that, although irrational people may join social movements, rational people may also. The goals or the means may not be rational, but then again they may be. One key to the problem rests with understanding who has the power to define the group, its members, or its goals and means either as legitimate and sane or as illegitimate and insane (see below).

⚹In sum, many sociologists see social movements as irrational because they characterize collective action as an attempt to alleviate frustration rather than a means to achieve legitimate goals (see also Gurr 1969). Further, certain acts (such as violence) are always seen as irrational by pluralist theorists because institutionalized, nonviolent alternatives (for example, courts, petition, elections) are believed to be available. Pressure groups, by contrast, are considered rational because they are seen as using productive and acceptable means for achieving goals, that is, means defined as legitimate by the people in power. Increasingly since the 1970s, however, a small but growing group of sociologists have disagreed with this perception on logical, empirical, and sometimes moral grounds. Why have so many sociologists been prone to perceive social movements as the result of personal aberrations of the world's misfits? In Gouldner's (1970) terms, we must look at their domain assumptions and their life experiences in order to answer this question.

Sociologist Douglas McAdam (personal communication) has suggested that in the period before the 1960s analysts needed to confront such antidemocratic movements as McCarthyism, German National Socialism, and the fascism of Mussolini and Franco. Similarly, Le Bon was an aristocrat looking back at what for him was the debacle of the French Revolution. Under these circumstances, the belief of some sociologists in the irrationality of all social movements is explained by their opposition to particular movements. The intellectual task was perceived, subconsciously perhaps, not so much as explaining but as debunk-

ing. But the civil rights and antiwar movements of the 1960s and the rise of the feminist movement, with which many sociologists wholeheartedly agreed, diminished the impact of the irrationality argument as the rational aspects of social movements have become more visible. Yet to avoid falling into the same trap as before, sociologists must be alert to the role that personality (rational or irrational) plays in all social phenomena (see Roy 1984, p. 504).

Critique of the Irrationality Model

The idea that social movements are part of irrational collective behavior is inherent in the work of Le Bon and carried through in the works of Park, Blumer, and Smelser. Recent work indicates, however, that the behavior of those who join movements is not in fact disorganized but follows inherent structures not apparent to people looking in from the outside (Horton and Horton 1979; Anderson-Sherman 1982). Blumer's description of collective behavior (including social movements) as not controlled by established rules or norms is therefore an incomplete definition. If social movements are related to social change, they must produce some things that are new—new norms, new beliefs, or new institutions. This does not mean, however, that the movements themselves are unstructured or unguided by culture. While they may not be governed by the rules of the dominant society, they may be oriented to them; also, movements may have rules of their own. Thus, crowds may be orderly, and social movements may be rational in addressing interests, organized and powerful in procuring resources, and effective in achieving their goals.

⚹ Blumer's analysis can mistakenly lead us to visualize the participants of social movements as irrational misfits. It excludes the culturally relative possibility that some members of the society might in fact see potentials for change not seen by others and act rationally to bring about better future conditions. Blumer comes close to confusing the society with the state and accepting the rules of the dominant group in society as the only rules. While he does not make this error, his conceptualization is conducive to this kind of misinterpretation. Smelser, however, commits the error of viewing social movements as outside the pale of acceptable behavior. As one critic charges,

> Unfortunately, . . . [just] when collective theorists are coming to see the continuities between everyday behavior and routine social processes, Smelser's emphasis is on the discontinuities and differences. When other sociologists are coming to see the rational components in collective behavior, Smelser's emphasis is on the nonrational components; when sociologists emphasize the diversity of beliefs, motives, and perceptions in collective behavior that lead to heterogeneity of crowd behavior and of differential participation in social movements, Smelser emphasizes the homogenizing effects of generalized beliefs. (Oberschall 1973, p. 22)

By starting with the notion of magical beliefs, Smelser continues in the long tradition that implicitly, if not explicitly, assigns social movements and all of collective behavior to the category of irrational action. By contrast, Karl Mannheim's distinction among three types of political thought—ideological (based on the past), diagnostic (based on a realistic assessment of the present and the immediate future), and utopian (based on an unrealistic diagnosis of the present while focusing on a "better" future)—may be more fruitful (see Sherman 1976).

A further problem arises with respect to Smelser's work. Since each variable adds to the probability of social movement behavior, Smelser refers to his theory as value-added, contrasting his value-added approach with the natural history approach. The value-added approach assumes that a series of variables can be isolated and stated in such a way that the variables reflect the dynamics of reality. Thus, when events in the real world correspond to the order of the variables, certain other events,

and only these events, will occur. Smelser, a positivist who takes a "scientific" approach, argues for the need to base generalizations on a large number of cases. In attempting to include a large number of cases, however, he broadens his categories to such a degree that he is in danger of lumping together under the rubric of collective behavior unrelated phenomena, including fads, fashions, and crazes as well as social movements.

The natural history approach, by contrast, centers on a limited number of case histories. Skocpol, for example, argues that a successful social revolution that rapidly transforms the political, economic, and social basis of a society is a relatively distinct phenomenon best studied in its own right without being included in a broader category of collective behavior. She adds that "ironically, theoretical approaches that set out to avoid the pitfalls of a too-historical approach to revolutions can end up providing little more than pointers toward various factors that case analysts might want to take into account, with no valid way to favor certain explanations over others" (Skocpol 1979, pp. 33–34).

As long as social movements and violence are considered to be outside the normal political process and adherents of social movements are perceived as irrational misfits, movements cannot be placed along a continuum of normal political behavior from voting to rebellion and revolution. We argue that what integrates these behaviors is that they are all in fact forms of political participation.

In order to create a typology that includes social movements as well as political parties, voting as well as civil disobedience, it is necessary to get rid of the idea of irrationality. Once irrationality is discarded, the concept of political participation can be used as the key distinguishing variable. Participating groups may be divided into **contenders,** those jockeying for a more advantageous position within the system, and **challengers,** those outside the system trying to get in (see Tilly 1978). The goal of both groups may be a redistribution of wealth. For example, contenders may attempt to influence the polity to dispense money in their direction rather than providing it for another group, while challengers such as the poor may desire a more progressive tax rate. In addition to redistribution of wealth, the goal of some groups might be to restructure society. Only the notion of political participation unifies these diverse categories and distinguishes them from other forms of collective behavior, such as religious sects, which may or may not have political goals.

Contemporary Work on Social Movements

The Resource Mobilization Model

The study of social movements began to change in the 1960s and has changed even more in the 1970s. Sociologists Ralph Turner and Lewis Killian, for example, while acknowledging their debt to Blumer, note that in the revised edition of their work on social movements they have "greatly increased the attention to conflict and violence as aspects of collective behavior and as normal features of social life" (Turner and Killian 1972, p. ix). Similarly, sociologist Jeffery M. Paige argues that "men risk their lives only with the greatest reluctance; when, in Peru, Angola, or Vietnam, they do so, it is usually because their opponents have left them with no other choice" (Paige 1975, p. ix). Sociologist William Gamson argues that his data undermine the idea that "violence is the product of frustration, desperation, and weakness. It is an act of last resort by those who see no other means of achieving their goals" (Gamson 1975, p. 81). Sociologist Barrington Moore argues that "revolutionary violence may contribute as much as peaceful reform to the establishment of a relatively free society" (Moore 1966, p. 20).

⚹ Resource mobilization theorists claim that social movements do not result from frustration alone since frustration is relatively constant throughout human societies, and deep frustration and discontent can exist without leading to social movements. Instead, social movements arise when groups have the resources and organizations necessary to mobilize effectively. Mobilization of resources depends not only on the mass base but on the presence of effective elite leadership. If elite sponsors are available, it is possible for resources to flow into the organization. Inherent in this model is the notion that social movements involve the self-interested behavior of the members. Seen in this light, little difference exists between social movements and interest groups (see Turner and Killian 1972).

Sociologists Mayer Zald and John McCarthy (1979), using the resource mobilization model, state that the first stages of group action are random and disorganized. Well-defined action awaits the emergence of leaders, whose function is to provide a definition of the situation and to develop an appropriate ideology. The ideology directs action toward specific targets and defines legitimate forms of organization. The members provide the money and manpower to carry out defined tasks. The size and intensity of a movement reflect the existence of grievances that the political leadership must deal with. If grievances are settled, the movement either disappears or becomes institutionalized.

⚹ Gamson attacks the assumptions of the pluralist theorists that many diverse groups compete in an open political system and that this competition meets the needs of the population by producing "regular and orderly change with the consent of the governed" (Gamson 1975, p. 5). From the perspective of the pluralists, collective behavior and social movements are abnormalities or pathologies, unfortunate occasional events that result when democracy fails to produce orderly change. Pluralists believe that challenging groups can be successful only if they accept the pluralist structure and use institutionally approved means to attain their goals. The chief flaw in the pluralist argument, according to Gamson, is that outsiders cannot effectively utilize the pressure group system because of the overriding power and influence of elites.

The resource mobilization model differs from the pluralist model in that it allows for a rational element in collective behavior. Rebellion may be "politics by other means," and the "absence of rebellion is in need of explanation as much as its presence" (Gamson 1975, p. 139). Gamson resolves the issue of rationality or irrationality empirically by asking whether challenging groups in American society have been successful or unsuccessful. Sampling fifty-three movements from a universe of forty-five hundred challenging groups between 1800 and 1945, he finds a positive correlation between violent tactics and successful outcomes. Gamson defines successful outcomes as achieving two goals: acceptance by the larger society and new advantages for the aggrieved group. Acceptance by society of a social movement is a condition that may move it within the pluralist model—that is, instead of being a challenger outside the system, the social movement becomes a contender within it. Gamson concludes that noninstitutionalized and even violent tactics are often effective and that the most violent movements may in fact be the most successful. Examples of successful movements that used violence include the American Federation of Labor and the International Longshoreman's Association.

The Political Process Model

Another recent theory is the political process model. For sociologist Charles Tilly (1978), *collective action* is a broad term that covers phenomena ranging from strikes to revolutions and is the joint product of pressures for mobilization from below and the degree of opportunity or repression from above. Thus, Tilly returns to Le Bon's twin focus on the causes of movements and the degree of social control.

Collective action can be seen either as the result of choices made by individuals or as the result of external forces over which individuals have little control. Tilly, who believes that both

exteriority and voluntarism have a role in collective behavior, attempts to synthesize these two positions where possible.[2] He explains collective action in terms of both the people who take part in the movement and the context or situation in which the group acts. Action from below is labeled the **mobilization model;** action from above, the **polity model.** The interaction of the mobilization and polity models determines collective action.

Tilly conceptualizes modern polities as consisting of the government, member groups that contend with each other for resources, and challengers who are more or less excluded from contention. Challengers take collective action when their interests are aroused, when they have an organization through which action can take place, and when they can mobilize sufficient assets or resources. The collective action of a challenging group is also influenced by the amount of opportunity or threat it faces. For example, do external groups (in particular, powerful elites) tolerate, facilitate, or repress collective action?

Toleration involves acts or attitudes on the part of elites that neither raise nor lower the cost of collective action. **Facilitation** involves any action that lowers the cost of such action. **Repression**, the opposite of facilitation, is defined as any action that raises the cost of collective action. Clearly, the relative power or potential effectiveness of a challenging group depends, in part, on the degree of facilitation or repression exhibited by the polity. Facilitation and repression, in turn, depend on the polity's relative power, resources, organization, and motivation or interests. Among the policy alternatives of polities is the choice between raising the cost of collective action by repression or lowering the cost by facilitation. For example, the federal government, through the use of police force, raised the cost of col-

---

2. Skocpol (1979), on the other hand, rejects the notion that purposive action plays a significant role in the generation of one type of collective behavior, successful social revolutions. Her theoretical emphasis is on external constraints, as we will see in chapter 13.

lective action in the early days of the labor movement in the United States. In contrast, the government increasingly facilitated the civil rights movement from the early 1950s through the 1960s by means of favorable legislation and the distribution of government funds, gradually raising the cost beginning in the 1970s.

Interests are hard to define. At a minimum, they represent a potential gain or loss for the individual or group. A major problem in the study of interests is having to choose between accepting the group's definition of its interests and assuming that the group is not the best articulator of its interests. In other words, the analyst must ask whether an individual's or a group's statement of its interests should be accepted or whether some other indicator or criterion should be used. The Marxist solution is to use the group's objective conditions, that is, its position in the economic system, as an indicator of its interests (see chapters 3 and 7).

Tilly's synthesis infers long-term interest from the group's social position but also takes account of the group's utterances and actions to infer its short-term interest. In order for collective action to occur, an interest must be held in common by people who share a salient characteristic as part of their identity. This interest-based identity is the basis on which interpersonal bonds are established. The people must also acquire the resources necessary for action. Thus, interests (the potential gain or loss to the individual or group), organization (based on shared characteristics with which people identify and around which they develop interpersonal bonds), and the acquisition of resources (including the mobilization of the group from passivity to action) are the bases for collective action. As noted, these are necessary but not sufficient conditions for collective action. The environment in which the individuals with salient characteristics exist must also be considered.

Tilly argues that collective action comes at a cost but also brings benefits in the form of collective goods, such as equal rights legislation. Contenders (members) and challengers (out-

siders), therefore, weigh the expected cost-benefit ratio and decide on the potential gains to themselves. Some individuals and groups are more willing to take risks than others.

Tilly argues that the amount of risk that a group takes depends on whether its members are "zealots," "misers," "run-of-the-mill types," or "opportunists." **Zealots** are defined as those "who, compared to other groups, set an extremely high value on some collective good in terms of the resources required to achieve that good—willing to expend life and limb, for instance, in order to acquire self-government." **Misers** are those who "value the resources they already hold so highly that hardly any available collective good can draw them into expending their mobilized resources on collective action—we should expect misers to act together defensively when they act at all." **Run-of-the-mill** members are those "who aim for a limited set of collective goods, making the minimum expenditure of resources necessary for the acquisition of these goods, and remaining inactive when the current combination of mobilization and opportunity makes a net loss on the exchange likely." **Opportunists** are those who "strive to maximize their net return—the difference in value between resources expended and collective goods obtained—regardless of which collective goods they acquire" (Tilly 1978, p. 88).

Nonparticipation presents a serious challenge to the logic of social movements. Economist Mancur Olson (1965) argues that collective action, although rational for groups, is not rational for individuals because they can share the benefits of a successful movement—for example, civil rights for minority groups—without the investment of their own time, energy, and resources. The movement's achievements, like public television, are collective goods, available regardless of individual contribution. Participation in social movements may thus be irrational because one can get the benefits without incurring the costs. However, considerable nonmaterial benefits can result from movement participation, including the feeling that one has contributed toward the achievement of collective goods or the avoidance of collective ungoods.

In addition to the factors emphasized by the resource mobilization and political process models, the international political and economic context plays a major role in the success or failure of social movements. We turn now to an examination of the political economy of the world system.

The Political Economy of the World System (PEWS) Model

Neither the resource mobilization model nor the political process model expressly builds in macrolevel international variables. Sociologists Immanuel Wallerstein, Theda Skocpol, Jeffrey Paige, Eric Wolf, and others consider world political and economic factors more explicitly. While these theories will be treated more fully in the next chapter, the conceptual framework is introduced here.

Wallerstein (1974) divides the nations of the world into those in control of the wealth or capital and those from whom capital is accumulated. The crucial factor for Wallerstein is not discrete nation-states but the political-economic relations at work in the political economy of the world system (PEWS). Social movements in Wallerstein's model are seen as the reactions of nations and groups at the **periphery,** from whom surplus capital is accumulated by the **core** nations.

Earlier models of international relations dealt with the nations of Europe and Africa in terms of relations between colonizing and colonized nation-states. The PEWS model, on the other hand, sees the center as containing core processes, such as international banking functions and multinational corporations, as well as core states, that is, key states that act within the core. The core is broader than any specific group of states, functions, or institutions.

In the PEWS model, accumulating nations may be included within the core. The key core powers today include the United States and Japan. As the history of Africa and other parts of the world shows, the development of nation-states over the last 150 years has been a history of core states imposing statehood on tribal areas. Statehood facilitates the expropriation of resources from the people at the grass-roots level through the creation of an administrative apparatus, a military force, and an infrastructure including ports, transportation, and communication. All these structures are necessary to control the peripheral area and connect it to the world economy. Semiperipheral states function to control peripheral states within particular regions. Since the governments of peripheral and semiperipheral societies function in the interest of the political world economy, it makes little sense to conceptualize them as independent nation-states. Rather, they are in many respects epiphenomena, that is, secondary phenomena accompanying the political economy of the world system and caused by it.

There is a movement today from tribal societies to nation-states as well as from colonies and trust territories to independent states. At the same time, many states contain regions that militate for autonomy, if not independence (the Basque country and Catalonia in Spain, for example). These processes may best be understood by combining the political-economy-of-the-world-system perspective with the political process model. Many apparently local phenomena, such as urban riots, guerrilla warfare, and certain types of terrorism, as well as the civil rights and women's liberation movements in the United States, may be analyzed as social movements influenced by world political and economic factors. A more thorough treatment of these topics occurs in chapter 13.

Summary

Social movements are a major link between the social structure and the political sphere, an avenue through which nonelites can participate in the decisions that affect society's fate.

Contemporary research challenges the still prevalent assumption that social movements are irrational responses to frustration. Since we believe that the notion of social movements as fueled by irrational and frustrated misfits is dangerous, a good deal of time and space has been devoted to showing the origins, pervasiveness, and limitations of this idea.

Some sociologists argue that political events are best analyzed by studying a society's basic values, while others argue that social-structural and economic variables play a much more critical role. The key unit of analysis for some is the nation-state, for others the political world economy. Some think that political sociology can be a fairly precise science producing propositions that help make relatively universal statements; others believe that situations are relatively unique and that comparative historical analysis helps us interpret and understand

but not predict or produce timeless and universal propositions. All these approaches have been applied to the study of social movements.

Attempting to answer the questions above in abstract terms is futile. Over a hundred years of trying to produce a conceptual definition of social movements based on some *differentia specifica* (differentiating criteria) have failed to produce a uniform, accepted, and useful typology, although they have helped clarify our understanding. As we see in the next chapter, historical and comparative analysis of specific events and classes of events may be more productive in understanding social change. The political economy of the world systems model, in conjunction with the political process and resource mobilization models, will be used to increase our understanding of the processes of political change and societal transformation in the modern world.

CHAPTER THIRTEEN

The Social and Economic Bases of Political Developments

Preview

Violence and Determinism

Peasant Revolutions
Comparative Historical Analysis of Agrarian Revolutions
North Atlantic Capitalism and Twentieth-Century Peasant Revolutions

Democratic Modernization: England

The So-Called "Mau Mau" Revolution
The Kikuyu
The First Kikuyu Response: Working Within the Pluralist System
The "Mau Mau" Revolt

The Origins of the U.S. Civil Rights Movement

Summary and Epilogue

Preview

The theme of this chapter is social and political change. Since the fifteenth century, world events have become increasingly intertwined. Events such as the Vietnam War, the American civil rights movement, and the nationalist and socialist revolutionary movements of Asia, Africa, and Central and South America are best understood in the context of comparative and historical analysis. This analysis takes into account the dialectical relations between the core and the periphery of world economic and political transactions.

From the perspective of the world political economy (see Wallerstein 1974; see also chapter 12), the world system, which is more of an economic than a political entity, is larger than any political unit. Its essential feature is the extent to which the constant accumulation of capital is its driving force. The key terms of analysis—core, periphery, and semiperiphery—take on a variety of meanings depending on the context (for example, core states, core processes, core products, or core zones), but at the most basic level the core refers to capital accumulation, the periphery to those from whom surplus capital is accumulated, and the semiperiphery to those in an intermediary condition.

Though a number of historical examples will be used, the focus of this chapter is not on history but on contemporary trends. One trend is modernization.[1] Others include the origin and spread of capitalism and democracy. The potential for social change is explored through examination of the contemporary political and economic base of the world's peoples.

---

1. Wallerstein (1984) argues that the concept of modernization is a euphemism for the outmoded concept of evolutionary progress and does not account for qualitative change occurring in the world today.

The global economic base is indicated by data from the World Bank. Of the 125 nations listed in the 1985 World Bank yearbook, 35 were low-income countries. These 35 countries had a combined population of 2.3 billion, with an average per capita gross national product (GNP) of $260 per year. Agriculture accounted for 37 percent of the distribution of gross domestic product in these low-income countries. The 58 middle-income countries had a combined population of 1.2 billion with an annual per capita GNP of $1,310. The proportion of gross domestic product generated by agriculture averaged 15 percent. In the 19 industrialized countries, agriculture accounted for 3 percent of the gross domestic product, and the average GNP per capita was $11,060. There were 729 million people living in the industrialized countries. In addition, 5 capital-surplus oil exporters and 8 East-European nonmarket (socialist) economies were represented.

All of these countries, including the United States, contain different tribal societies and ethnic groups, some of which are horticultural or hunting and gathering peoples. Some countries are more or less involved in the capitalist system, while others are still basically peasant societies. The transformation of these societies into new economic and political forms generates political conflict both among the societies and within them.

Although the potential for social and political change can be explored by examining case histories, before analyzing this material, it is useful to consider a number of crucial issues. When, if ever, is violence rational in the accomplishment of national liberation or the suppression of dissent? Are political situations sometimes so structurally determined that no room for purposive individual action exists (see Gouldner 1980, p. 17)? Skocpol (1979) argues, for example, that given the historical circumstances the French, Russian, and Chinese revolutions were inevitable. Others argue that events are not predetermined and that purposive action can make a difference (see chapter 12). Thus, whether people have true or false consciousness is important, for without an adequate understanding of the world as it is, as it might be, and as it can be, rational, purposive action is not possible.

Violence and Determinism

Violence may at times be useful, rational, and unavoidable. Manifest violence, such as contemporary terrorism, may be the result of more gradual and latent violence, such as expropriation of land from the peasants. If peasants had not been driven off the land by the Enclosure Laws, England might not have been able to modernize (see below). If the Kikuyu tribesmen had not been driven off the land over a period of almost one hundred years, the so-called "Mau Mau" Revolution of 1952–1960 might not have occurred in Kenya (see below). Thus, what appears to be sudden violence may in fact be the result of more gradual forces. Without violence, change might not take place, and change can improve conditions.

The fact that violence is sometimes the policy of choice, however, does not tell us when violence is required or when it can be avoided. An informed diagnosis of conflict situations and an awareness of a variety of conflict-resolution techniques can maximize the potential for peaceful change. Sociologists Reinhard Bendix (1978) and Barrington Moore (1966) argue that social events are not necessarily structurally determined and that human insight, will, and purposive action can make a difference (Gouldner 1980). Author John Burton (1979) argues that scholarship and third-party intervention can play an important role in the process of international conflict management. New social inventions that provide alternatives to revolution, rebellion, terrorism, and war are required.

As sociologist Harold Pepinsky (1982) points out, both superordinates and subordinates are parties to rule violation, and the process of blame attribution is partly a social construction of reality. The development of new methods of dispute resolution represents an important and growing political movement of the last decade. Consistent with the social construction of reality perspective, we argue that the frame of reference brought to the situation by the participants must be examined in order to understand and deal with social reality. This puts us on the side of those who believe that purposive action is possible.

Oddly enough, the so-called *real politik* model of modern diplomacy also allows for both individual action and determinism. This model gives more latitude for purposive action to superordinates than to subordinates, but because of the emphasis on the freedom of action, powerful states often fail to take structural considerations into account. We will see an example of this shortly when we consider the case of Kenya.

The model of power diplomacy developed by political scientist Hans Morganthau and others holds that international political decisions are made by the most powerful nations on the basis of their own interest and their assessment of the consequences of alternative actions by other nations. This model is taught to aspiring diplomats at some of America's most prestigious schools (for example, the Fletcher School of Law and Diplomacy). That Henry Kissinger, President Nixon's secretary of state, failed to understand the conditions under which power diplomacy is appropriate and potentially effective and the conditions under which it is not is illustrated by his attempt to use power politics rather than third-party methods of conflict management in the Vietnam War. Kissinger believed that with the power and resources of the United States behind him he could negotiate a peace treaty with the North Vietnamese and later be able to coerce the South Vietnamese into acquiescing to the terms of the agreement. As history shows, the South Vietnamese did not prove so tractable and the negotiations failed.

One approach that favors determinism is positivism, which argues that science is the only source of valid knowledge and that valid knowledge must include general laws. Pioneering sociologists such as Herbert Spencer and William Graham Sumner argued that, although it is possible to understand the natural laws of society, it is rarely possible to change them. Today, however, we realize that few, if any, universal laws exist. One reason for this is that human social conditions vary with respect to historical context. Since history does not often repeat itself, it is important to develop a concept of world time.

Some of the best work on social change has been done by those who use the comparative and historical method rather than the positivist method (see Moore 1966; Wolf 1969; Skocpol 1979; and Paige 1975). For example, Barrington Moore, using case studies and the concept of world time, argues that it was easier for democracy to develop prior to the twentieth century than it is today (Moore 1966, pp. 424–25). Changes in social conditions in the twentieth century make either fascism or communism more likely routes than democracy in the development of an industrial society.

Below, we examine several case studies that utilize the historical and comparative approach to social change.

Peasant Revolutions

Comparative Historical Analysis of Agrarian Revolutions   *Skocpol*

Theda Skocpol (1979) analyzes successful social revolutions from below that occur in agrarian societies. Successful social revolution involves the rapid transformation of a society's political system as well as the transformation of the class structure within the society. Skocpol excludes from her main consideration revolutions from above, political revolutions that do not involve

a class transformation, unsuccessful revolutionary attempts, and transformations by more gradual, nonrevolutionary means.

Skocpol argues that there have been relatively few successful social revolutions. Her historical and comparative analysis focuses on France in the eighteenth century and Russia and China in the twentieth century. The pre-revolutionary regimes in these countries were controlled by the Bourbon monarchy in France, the Romanov czars in Russia, and the Manchu dynasty in China, respectively.

Under the old regime, if members of the landed upper class are not powerful enough to prevent local rebellion, they can benefit from a cooperative relation with the state. The state, in turn, uses its repressive force to maintain local control in return for upper-class compliance and support. Members of the landed upper class also enjoy opportunities to amass private fortunes through state service. Since the function of the state is not only to maintain internal control but also to deal with the external world in terms of economic and military competition, it requires resources gained through taxation and military conscription. Thus, the state and the landed upper class have both common and conflicting interests.

An additional factor in the old regime is the potential power of the peasants. All three of these societies contained a class of peasants who enjoyed well-established rights in small plots of land and strong local communities. When the social welfare of these peasants was disturbed because of a change in their relation with the landholders, their interests changed from preserving the status quo to increasing their control over that land necessary for survival.

The power of all three major groups was limited. The power of the peasants was limited by the smallness of their holdings, that of the landed upper class by their inability to control the peasants, and that of the state by the interest of the upper class in using state positions to build private fortunes. The holding of office by members of the upper class represented an obstacle to control of the state by the monarchy.

In other words, the protobureaucratic state within agrarian societies lacked the power of the modern state.

Yet in terms of world time more advanced modern states already existed in the world arena in which Bourbon France, Manchu China, and Romanov Russia had to compete. The state required additional economic and military resources in order to compete in this international arena. One way to increase resources, rapid economic transformation (modernization), was blocked by small holdings, local markets, antiquated commercial customs, seigneurial (landlord) rights, and the early stage of industrialization that these countries were in. Other routes to increasing the state's resources were to tax the peasants and the upper class and to recruit soldiers.

In all three societies, the old political regimes came under increasing international economic constraints and military pressure. France suffered a number of military defeats in the eighteenth century, as did Russia in the Crimean War (1850s), the Russian-Japanese War (1904–1905), and World War I (1914–1918). China also suffered from wartime defeats. As a result of these external pressures, the state had a need for both increased taxation and increased mobilization of military recruits. Given the limits of squeezing resources from the peasantry, the state put pressure on the holdings of the landed upper class and at the same time ceased to cooperate in protecting that class's accumulation of surplus wealth from the peasants, taking more of it for itself.

Under these circumstances, a severe conflict of interest arose between the landed upper class and the state that weakened their combined power to control the peasants. In an atmosphere of decreased repression, the revolutionary leadership was able to mobilize discontented urban workers and peasants and foment a revolution.

The revolutionary leaders came, in part, from educated elites marginal to the prerevolutionary power and wealth apparatus who recognized the importance of political ideology.

Ideologies have universalistic properties that unite people from diverse backgrounds, provide a basis for mobilizing the masses, justify the use of violent means in the achievement of an ultimate end, and facilitate the development of organizations that support the ideology (see chapter 6). The ideology of the French Revolution may be labelled republicanism or classical liberalism, that of the Russian Revolution, Marxism, and that of the Chinese Revolution, Maoism.

In the period following the revolutionary crisis, the new political leaders worked not so much to establish the government in the name of the interests of the revolutionary class but rather to establish and maintain state power itself. The new politicians were state-building leaders who, aware that changes in world political and economic reality required changes in government, proceeded to collectivize and modernize the economy as well as the administrative apparatus. In the forty years that followed the Russian Revolution, for example, the U.S.S.R. made economic changes that had taken England two hundred years to accomplish. Thus, the results of these three revolutions included a more powerful, centrally organized state structure, a new ideology, and the replacement of the old landed upper class and the peasantry by more centralized means of agricultural production.

North Atlantic Capitalism and Twentieth-Century Peasant Revolutions   Wolf

Eric R. Wolf (1969) is another historical and comparative social scientist who sees the world market as a critical variable in social change. Wolf studies six peasant revolutions of the twentieth century, in Mexico, Russia, China, Algeria, Vietnam, and Cuba. In the preface to his book *Peasant Wars of the Twentieth Century*, Wolf indicates the reasons he undertook this study:

> Spatially insulated from other continents and their tribulations by virtue of her geographic

position and by her extraordinary prosperity, America finds herself ill prepared in the twentieth century to understand the upheavals which are now shaking the poor nations of the world. Yet ignorance courts disaster. Viet Nam has become a graveyard because Americans did not know enough or care enough about a little-known part of Southeast Asia. The roads to the Mekong delta, to Tay Ninh, to Khe San are strewn with the wreckage of false premises, perceptions, and evaluations. Therefore it is important to America that she bend all her available knowledge—and her considerable power of passion and compassion—to the task of comprehending the world in which she has become a stranger. . . . There will be other "Viet Nams" in the future, unless America reverses her present course. If we must know more in order to live in a changed world, if we must know more so we can act with clear reason rather than with prejudice, with humanity rather than with inhumanity, with wisdom rather than with folly, all of us must undertake the task of understanding in order to learn and of learning in order to understand. This is no longer an undertaking only for the academic specialist, if indeed it has ever been; it is an obligation of citizenship. (Wolf 1969, pp. ix–x)

Wolf argues that to understand one revolution is not to understand all revolutions. Each situation must be studied in its own uniqueness. Sequences of causation and events are "not universal, and therefore cannot form the basis of a universal dogma. The relations between army and party, between proletariat, peasantry, and middle-class intellectuals are variably conjugated in different situations and not exhausted in simple formulas" (Wolf 1969, p. 99). Yet it is possible to identify some of the critical variables and to look for overall patterns. Wolf makes it clear that revolution and revolt can occur with or without the external effects of the world market. Self-sufficient societies are not immune from internal exploitation and surplus accumulation. From the time of permanent settlement, an exchange of surplus exists between rulers and producers that creates

equilibrium. The surplus provides insurance against hard times and protection against enemies. When the members of the lower class believe that the degree of appropriation is creating unnecessary hardship and that they are being exploited for the benefit of the upper class, they may rebel or revolt if they possess sufficient resources and organization.

Wolf concentrates on twentieth-century revolutions in the context of North Atlantic capitalism, in which the cultural belief in **possessive individualism**—the belief that land, labor, and wealth are all commodities to be bought and sold for profit rather than use—has become predominant. Land can be made into a commodity in various ways: by force, by colonization of new land, or by encouraging the **yeoman** or the middle peasant to develop commercial agriculture. In some peasant societies, the impact of North Atlantic capitalism has transformed wealth, labor, and capital into commodities. In the process, the peasants have become alienated from their tools, the work process, their surplus, and themselves. These factors have played a role in revolutions in Mexico, China, Russia, Algeria, Vietnam, and Cuba—the six revolutions that Wolf examines.

Wolf argues that, before capitalism, peasants often had a modicum of security based on social relations and a communal sharing of resources. Capitalism destroyed this social matrix as well as the social insurance that went with it. At the same time that peasants lost access to communal lands, the countertrend of turning crops grown for local use into cash crops intended for larger markets came into existence. Food surpluses in one area became available for others. Health care improved and mortality rates fell. Yet land was often not available for the growing number of peasants, and population increased faster than resources.

The pressures of increased population and the unavailability of land led members of the affected classes either to seek refuge in old traditional forms or create a new social order. The advance of capitalism produced a "crisis in the exercise of power" (Wolf 1969, p. 282). Tribal chiefs, mandarins, and landed nobility were replaced by entrepreneurs, credit merchants, and professionals. Autonomous land-owning farmers (peasants) were replaced by industrial workers. The power of the old elite was eclipsed by that of the new.

This readjustment process takes time. In the early stages, "the power holders of the older order coexist with the power holders of the new." Further, "the old is not yet overcome and remains to challenge the new; the new is not yet victorious" (Wolf 1969, p. 283). Wolf argues that "such a situation of weak contenders, unable to neutralize each other's power, seems to invite the rise or perpetuation of an autocratic central executive, attempting to stand 'above' the contending parties and interest groups, and to consolidate the state by playing off one group against the other" (Wolf 1969, p. 284). Thus France attempted to exercise autocratic rule in Vietnam and Algeria, as did Nationalist leader Chiang Kai-Shek in China and the czars in Russia. Such dictatorship is possible because of the relative weakness of the social classes and political forces within the society, which "ultimately becomes evident in the dictatorship's impotent struggle against challengers from within, unless it can find allies strong enough to sustain it against the challenge" (Wolf 1969, p. 282). Further, "where the social dislocations produced by the market go unchecked . . . the crisis of power also deranges the networks which link the peasant population to the larger society, the all-important structure of mediation intervening between center and hinterland. For example, where the peasants' welfare is no longer the responsibility of the landlord then the function of the police gains in importance. Increased commercialization and capitalization of rent produce dislocations and tensions which often weaken the agents of the process themselves" (Wolf 1969, p. 285).

As noted, in precapitalist society the peasants are linked to the broader society by a series of social and economic relationships. Feudal societies are characterized by ceremonial obligations between lords and serfs. When the old

nobility is replaced by a new professional and commercial elite (a circulation of elites, in Pareto's terms), at least two possibilities may occur: an alliance between the old and new elites or disruption of traditional social relations.

In Germany and Japan, the new elite made alliance with the old, and traditional social obligations between upper and lower classes were maintained. Thus, social dislocation was minimized, but a conservative, nationalist dictatorship prevailed. In parts of China, however, social dislocations were more severe. Traditionally, arguments over the amount of rent to be paid the landlord by the tenant were mediated by an exchange in which the landlord granted a "discount on the rent in return for the tenant's reliable performance in paying rent" (Wolf 1969, p. 285). In much of Southeast China, as interdependence with North Atlantic capitalism grew, the direct relations between landlord and peasants were taken over by agents who collected rent and interest and who hired and paid labor on an impersonal basis. These agents, who became the economic mediators between landlord and peasant, also disrupted the old system of social relations and obligations, replacing it with a system of monetized relations of economic exchange (this is the role played by Indians in contemporary South Africa and other "middleman minorities" elsewhere). Wolf argues that the obedience of these agents to market demands is such that they "maximize returns, regardless of the immediate consequences of their actions" (Wolf 1969, p. 286). In all six societies, such agents rendered the process of commodity formation bureaucratic and impersonal.

> [Agents] remove themselves physically from these consequences; at the same time they lose their ability to respond to social cues from the affected population. Instead, they couple economic callousness with a particular kind of structurally induced stupidity, the kind of stupidity which ascribes to the people themselves responsibility for the evils to which they are subject. Defensive stereotypes take the place of analytical intelligence,

in one of those classical cases of blindness with which the gods strike those whom they wish to destroy.

At the very same time, the political mediators who man the relays of power connecting state and village also face increased uncertainty. The traditional power holders . . . have had their power curtailed, unless they enter into collusion with economic agents to their mutual advantage and to the disadvantage of the state. In either case, however, they can no longer shield the local populations against encroachment from outside, a role which in the past often rebounded to their own interests. The new power holders, on the other hand, find their exercise of power already shorn of effectiveness by the axiom that economic transformation takes precedence over social order. If they are aware of social dislocations caused by the spread of the market, they may be able to raise their voice in protest, but they cannot—at the cost of losing their position— stop them of their own accord. They thus lack control over the decisive processes which affect society; this would involve the mobilization of dissatisfied populations against a state of which they are primary beneficiaries. (Wolf 1969, pp. 286–87)

The new power holders tend to be educated individuals who "answer to a much larger social field and communication network than the traditional power holder, and yet experience every day the very real limitations of their power" (Wolf 1969, p. 288). Political movements may provide a home for these marginal intellectuals, who may find such a constituency among industrial workers or dissatisfied peasants. All of Wolf's cases exhibited a "fusion between the 'rootless' intellectuals and their rural supporters" (Wolf 1969, p. 289).

The poor peasants' and the landless laborers' position of weakness prevents them from joining the rebellion. For these classes, the strength to join the rebellion must come from some external power. In Mexico, for example, external power was provided by the presence of the Constitutionalist army in Yucatan. In Russia, after the collapse of the army in World War I, the peasant soldiers returned home trained and armed, ready to join the revolution.

While the poor peasants are limited in their ability to rebel unless they can join with an external force, the rich peasants are unlikely to rebel because they like things the way they are. Thus, the segment of the peasantry most likely to rebel, according to Wolf, is the middle peasants and the "poor but 'free' peasants" (Wolf 1969, p. 292). The middle peasants are most likely to be concerned with tradition and most vulnerable to the pressures of economic change. While they stay on the farm, their children become urban workers. Given these circumstances, Wolf argues that it is "the very attempt of the middle and free peasant to remain traditional that makes him revolutionary" (Wolf 1969, p. 292). One factor that may increase the middle peasants' power to rebel is simply distance from the political and military center of the society.

But neither a rebellion nor a series of rebellions or acts of resistance adds up to a revolution. Wolf argues that

> no cultural system—no complex of economy, society, polity and ideology—is ever static; all of its component parts are in constant change. Yet as long as these changes remain within tolerable limits, the over-all system persists. If they begin to exceed these limits, however, or if other components are suddenly introduced from outside, the system is thrown out of kilter. The parts of the system are rendered inconsistent with each other; the system grows incoherent. Men in such a situation are caught painfully between various old solutions to problems which have suddenly shifted shape and meaning, and new solutions to problems they often cannot comprehend. (Wolf 1969, pp. 295–96)

Under such circumstances, a peasant uprising can, "without conscious intent, bring the entire society to the state of collapse" (Wolf 1969, p. 296).

An additional group that requires consideration is the military. In Mexico and Algeria, "the peasant rebellions of the hinterland set fire to the pre-existing structure; but it fell to the army and its leadership to forge the organizational balance wheel which would enable the post-revolutionary society to continue on its course." On the other hand, "in Russia, China, and Viet Nam . . . the roles of army and party were reversed. In these . . . cases, it was the political parties of middle-class revolutionaries who engineered the seizure of power and created the social and military instruments which conquered the state, and ensured transition to a new social order" (Wolf 1969, p. 297).

In sum, in examining these six revolutions, Wolf looks for common factors that lead to peasant revolution and finds that the middle peasant plays a major role by reacting to world market forces in a way that contributes to social transformation.

Sociologist Jeffery Paige (1975) has attempted the difficult job of going beyond historical and comparative analysis to the creation of systematic theory. Paige argues that the effects of world political and economic forces in the nineteenth and early twentieth centuries created great change in Latin America, Asia, and Africa. The main role of these areas in the international marketplace, with the exception of a few countries that rely heavily on exporting petroleum or minerals, has been as suppliers of agricultural products. These countries are economically dependent on their major crops, with about 90 percent of their exports going to developed markets. They are dual-economy countries, divided into export and nonexport sectors. Outside the cities, the nonexport agricultural areas tend to be composed of poor subsistence agriculturalists.

Paige analyzes 135 export sectors in seventy countries from 1948 through 1970 and also examines three case studies—Angola, Peru, and Vietnam. The key variable in Paige's work is the relation between the upper class (noncultivators) and the people who directly farm the land (cultivators), and he argues for the need to understand the dialectical relationship between these classes. The upper class can be either a landed aristocracy or a commercial or industrial elite. A landed upper class increases its wealth through enlarging holdings rather than improving efficiency, creating a land concentration based on the expropriation of land from the peasants.

Where land is the income base for the upper class, economic power and productivity are low and maintaining a servile labor force becomes necessary. Because of inefficiency, the resources tend to be zero-sum, that is, not readily expandable to accommodate a rising standard of living for all, and political control is required to ensure the servility of the labor force. Thus, the rights of cultivators are minimal, and the focus of conflict is likely to be on both politics and property.

For both cultivators and noncultivators, wealth can be based either on land or on capital. The distribution and use of these variables produce four types of agricultural organization: the hacienda or manor economy, plantations, small holdings, and sharecropping or migratory wage labor systems.

In **haciendas** or **manor economies,** both cultivators and noncultivators receive their source of income from the land. The most likely form of agrarian social movement in manor economies is revolt. **Plantations** involve invested capital on the part of noncultivators and wage labor on the part of cultivators. In plantation systems, the most likely form of social movement is labor reform. In a **small-holding system,** the capital necessary for cultivation is provided by such noncultivators as bankers and grain operators, while cultivators obtain their income from the sale of products grown on the land. The most likely form of agrarian social movement in small-holding systems is commodity reform, an attempt by the cultivators to control the profits from the crop or commodity they produce. Finally, where land is the source of income for the noncultivator but not for the cultivator, a system of **migratory wage labor** or **sharecropping** exists. This last combination of land and capital has the greatest revolutionary potential.

Prior to the emergence of the industrial

plantation and the commercial small holding as major forms of agriculture, much of the Third World's agricultural production involved an agricultural upper class that acquired its wealth not from capital but from land. In these haciendas or manor economies, large estates tend to dominate the community. The lord of the manor controls the peasants and maintains the privileges of the manor by repression and disenfranchisement. Occasionally, the peasants may try to seize the land, but for the most part such efforts fail because the peasants are conservative, unorganized, and lacking in political solidarity.

Agrarian revolt becomes possible when the power of the landed upper class is weakened, which may happen when a previously colonial country achieves independence and the upper class no longer has the support of the colonial military. Revolts may also occur when the relative power of the peasants increases through external support derived from left-wing labor unions, religious organizations, or socialist or reformist political parties. Ironically, communist parties are not likely to form an alliance with the peasants, since peasants believe in private property and distrust an ideology that calls for its abolition. In addition, communist parties are more likely to focus on the urban proletariat rather than the peasantry as the agents of historical change. Unless these external groups gain control of the central government, however, successful peasant revolt is unlikely. The impulse of the peasants is for a short-term land rush. They lack the class solidarity and political organization necessary for a more sustained, systematic societal transformation. Revolt is the most likely form of social movement in commercial haciendas. One result of a successful revolt may be the transformation of the subsistence peasant into a commercial farmer (see Paige 1975, pp. 40–44).

The greatest potential for revolution exists when the upper class depends on land for its income and the cultivators are paid at least partly in wages. In sharecropping, the cultivator lives on the estate, growing some of the crop for his or her own subsistence and some for the landowner as rent. In the migratory wage labor system, the cultivator does not live on the estate but instead travels between his or her village home and the fields of the landowner and is paid wages.

As in the case of the commercial hacienda, where the upper class depends on land for its wealth a zero-sum political and economic situation tends to exist since land is finite. The upper class, therefore, is not capable of making (and is often not willing to make) political and economic concessions. Social order is maintained not through the lower classes' acceptance of upper-class domination as legitimate but by laws favorable to upper-class interests. As long as the balance of power favors the upper class, the lower class complies.

The lower class may initially adopt the democratic, pluralist ideology of the upper class, as in the case of Kenya from the 1920s to the 1940s (see below), and recognize the need for revolution only when it becomes clear that the democracy of the colonial power does not include them. When increased repression on the part of the colonial power coincides with the growing strength of the peasant movement and a weakening of the position of the upper class, revolution is possible.

Sharecropping and migratory wage labor systems tend to generate different forms of revolution. In sharecropping systems, the ideology is more likely to be communist or socialist, while migratory wage labor systems are more likely to produce nationalist revolutionary movements. In both cases, compromise is unlikely, and guerrilla warfare leads to seizure of the state followed by land redistribution.

The revolutionary potential may also vary by crop. Revolution is more likely, for example, where the crop is rice than where it is cotton. Rice is a water-based rather than a land-based crop often grown under sharecropping conditions where the cultivator does not own the land but depends for his or her income on working cooperatively with others to ensure an effective irrigation system. With little landed security and a tradition of cooperation, the rice grower has a tendency to develop a radical ideology. Under such conditions, the potential political power of the peasants is strong, and revolutionary activity is likely. Cotton, on the other hand, is a land-based crop grown on centralized plantations. Cotton growers work under bureaucratic supervision on the plantation, a condition that promotes political conservatism, while rice growers are organized as a community. The communal ties create strong solidarity among rice growers. Thus, in export-based agricultural systems where the noncultivators are landed and the cultivators are paid in wages, a cotton economy tends to have less revolutionary potential than a rice economy.

Market pressures for a greater supply are translated into a demand for greater productivity. Since small holdings and plantations tend to be the most efficient forms of organization for production, pressure grows for transformation of less productive forms of agricultural production into either small holdings or plantations.

Large-scale commercial agriculture on plantations is possible where the crop requires year-round labor and where substantial savings in transportation costs can be achieved by primary processing that reduces the commodity in bulk. Plantations are owned by noncultivators and cultivated by wage laborers. Under such systems, workers are paid a wage, and profits are generally good due to a nonzero-sum economic structure. Increases in wages can be achieved without a decrease in profit because of increased productivity, greater efficiency, larger markets, higher prices, or inflation. Under these conditions, the nature of conflict between owner and worker is likely to be over wage increases, and since the pie can be expanded the conflict in most cases does not spread beyond the demand for increased wages. Thus, agrarian revolt or revolution is not a likely outcome of a plantation system.

Agricultural change in Third World countries has been in the direction of plantations or small holdings. Since most crops cannot be harvested year round, cannot be reduced in bulk for transport, and are not efficiently processed at the source of production, the small holding rather than the plantation tends to be the most efficient organization of agricultural production.

Most of the world's crops are most economically and efficiently produced under the small farm system that is well known in the United States. Under this system, the upper class surrenders direct control of cultivation, the land is owned by those who work it, and their income is derived from the commercial sale of commodities to middlemen. It is not surprising that most conflict between the owners of small holdings and the middlemen is over the control of profits from the sale of the crop (commodity) under production. Upper-class noncultivators process, transport, export, manufacture, and sell the finished commodity, making a profit as middlemen and moneylenders.

Small farmers tend to be politically conservative and structurally isolated. Since they are divided by economic competition and differences in wealth and status, they lack class solidarity and tend not to be politically organized.

Small holders operate in nonzero-sum situations. Yet in shrinking markets or where expansion through technological innovation is difficult, these farmers are likely to demand a larger share of the profits. Their target is the middlemen, and the competition is for control of the commodity market. They are unlikely to want a redistribution of property. Unless moved toward revolution by an unyielding stance on the part of the upper class, they usually have modest goals and use moderate tactics to achieve them. The most likely outcome is that they get a "greater share of profits through an inflated currency" (Paige 1975, p. 49); in other words, farm prices go up but so does the price of goods the farmer must buy.

The importance of the combination of capital and wages is that conflict is likely to take place over economic issues. Where a nonzero-sum economic structure exists, peaceful, mutually satisfactory settlements are possible. Where the upper class has no economic reserves and no capacity to generate a surplus, on the other hand, it must rely on force to maintain the status quo.

The possibility for revolutionary change comes after the peasant is transformed into a wage laborer. The elimination of subsistence farming allows for the breakup of large estates into more efficient small holdings. Whether a cultivator's major source of income is land or wages makes a difference. If the income source is land, cultivators tend to avoid risk, compete among themselves for rewards, and become structurally isolated and dependent on non-cultivators. Their avoidance of risk leads to a conservative ideology. While competitiveness leads to individual action, isolation and dependence lead to weak solidary structures,[2] with the net result that cultivators whose income source is land tend to be politically weak. Cultivators paid in wages, on the other hand, accept risk, tend to cooperate, and are both independent and interdependent. Acceptance of risk makes them receptive to radical ideology, cooperation leads toward collective action, and interdependence and independence lead toward strong solidarity. The result is that the political power of wage-earning cultivators is strong and the chances for revolution high.

This section introduced the historical context for contemporary revolutionary movements. We have seen that the dislocations of the early stages of modernization may lead to revolution and in some cases to totalitarianism. In all societies examined the peasant class played a crucial role in the economic and political transformation. In the next section, we examine the case of England, the first nation to undergo modernization and one of the few to emerge from the process as a democracy.

---

2. By weak solidary structures we mean cases where individuals perceive only weakly, if at all, their common interests and where cooperation toward collective ends is minimal.

Democratic Modernization: England

Author Barrington Moore, Jr., (1966) argues that there are three basic routes to modernization. The first is capitalism coupled with parliamentary democracy (England, France, the United States), the second combines capitalism and fascism (Germany and Japan), and the third is communism (China and the Soviet Union). Each of these types of modernization occurs within a particular sociohistorical time frame. The key factors that allow for democratic, capitalist modernization are the tradition of immunity of the average citizen from the arbitrary power of the ruler, the right to resist unjust authority, and the idea of the contract "as a mutual agreement freely undertaken by free persons" (Moore 1966, p. 417). An additional structural variable that allows for democratic modernization is the elimination of the peasants as a social class.

Moore asks, "Why did the process of industrialization in England culminate in the establishment of a relatively free society?" (Moore 1966, p. 3). The key actors in the drama of modernization in England were the state (monarchy), the aristocrats (nobles), the bourgeoisie (merchants, artisans, tradespeople), the yeomanry (early capitalist farmers), and the peasants. Feudal England was based on a moral economy (Tilly 1978, p. 6); land and tenural relations bound lord and serf together. Thus, land had a military and social in addition to economic significance. However, the rule of the Tudor kings (1485–1603) and their need for money, which derived from the cost of preparing to face the Armada (the famed Spanish fleet) and the need to consolidate royal power, helped make the command of money more important than the command of men or of land. This change "marks the transition from the medieval conception of land as the basis of political functions and obligations to the modern view of it as an income-yielding investment. Landholding tends, in short, to become commercialized" (Tawney 1912, pp. 188–89). Another factor in England's modernization was the emergence of the wool trade with the continent as an important economic activity. "Royal peace and wool had to combine in a specific way to set up one of the significant forces propelling England toward both capitalism and a revolution that would make capitalism eventually democratic. . . . Men ceased to see the agrarian problem as a question of finding the best method of supporting people on the land and began to perceive it as the best way of investing capital in the land. They began to treat land more and more as something that could be bought and sold . . . in a word, like modern capitalist private property" (Moore 1966, pp. 7–8). "Possessive individualism" began to replace the notion of a "moral economy" (Tilly 1978, p. 6).

The changed attitude led to a boom in the land market that began around 1580 and lasted about fifty years. One consequence of this land boom was the enclosure movement, that is, fencing off for the landlord's use land traditionally used by peasants for pasture or cultivation. "Propelled by the prospect of profits to be made either in selling wool or by leasing their lands to those who did and thereby increasing their rents, the lords of the manors found a variety of legal and semilegal methods to deprive the peasants of their rights of cultivation in the open fields and also their rights to use the common for pasture of their cattle, the collection of wood for fuel, and the like" (Moore 1966, p. 9). (Below, we will see that the British used similar tactics during the twentieth century in Kenya.)

Additional enclosures were perpetrated by the yeoman class, which ranged from the lesser gentry to the more prosperous peasants. These "ambitious, aggressive, small capitalists . . . were the chief force behind peasant enclosures. . . . Those who promoted the wave of agrarian capitalism, the chief victors in the struggle against the old order, came from the yeomanry and . . . from the landed upper classes. The main victims of progress were as

usual the ordinary peasants" (Moore 1966, p. 11).

Persistence of old habits helps explain why the peasants clung to preindustrial attitudes. The medieval system of agriculture involved peasant holdings in the form of a series of narrow strips randomly scattered amid those of other peasants in unfenced or open fields. Since cattle grazed on these fields after harvesting, the harvest had to come in at about the same time for all concerned, and the operations of the agricultural cycle had to be more or less coordinated. In addition, the peasants could graze their cattle on the common land. There was some leeway for individual variation within these arrangements, but mainly there was a strong need for cooperative organization that could easily settle disputes.

The enclosures, or fencing off of the commons, drove peasants off the land and turned both ploughed strips and commons into pastures for the aristocracy's cattle. "Large numbers of the peasants, cast adrift, were becoming a menace to good order, to the point where intermittent revolts occurred" (Moore 1966, p. 13).

The crown sporadically attempted to assist the peasants, but even more important, was *perceived* as siding with the peasants. Therefore, "royal policy tended to wield commercially minded elements in town and countryside, united by many other bonds as well, into a coherent opposition to the crown." In the meantime, the growth of commerce had created a market for agricultural products that "set in motion a process leading toward commercial and capitalist agriculture in the countryside." The gentry were most successful in adapting to these changes, becoming "the main representatives of a decisive historical trend modifying the structure of English rural society." Under the impact of commerce and some industry, English society was breaking apart from the top down in a way that allowed pockets of radical discontent, produced by the same forces, to burst temporarily into the limelight.

Matters came to a head in the Civil War (1642–1649), which climaxed with the execution of King Charles I in 1649. The demands of the rebel leaders were clear and straightforward: "They opposed interference with the landlord's property rights" (Moore 1966, pp. 14–17).

Prior to the Civil War, one of the royal institutions that provided some protection for the peasants against enclosure was the court of the Star Chamber. The Star Chamber, named for the Chambre d'Étoile at Westminster Palace, was a royal court where anyone, including the poor, could have a petition heard. This court was subject neither to influence by the powerful nor to bribery by the rich, and its decisions had the power of royal authority behind them. The Star Chamber protected the peasants from being driven off the land through enclosures; when it was abolished by parliament in 1641, the peasants lost this protection.

> Through breaking the power of the king, the Civil War swept away the main barrier to the enclosing landlord and simultaneously prepared England for rule by a "committee of landlords," a reasonably accurate if unflattering designation of Parliament in the eighteenth century. . . . The outcome of the struggle was an enormous if still incomplete victory for an alliance between parliamentary democracy and capitalism. . . .
>
> Both the capitalist principle and that of parliamentary democracy are directly antithetical to the ones they superseded and in large measure overcame during the Civil War: divinely supported authority in politics, and production for use rather than for individual profit in economics. Without the triumph of these principles in the seventeenth century it is hard to imagine how English society could have been modernized peacefully—to the extent that it actually was peaceful—during the eighteenth and nineteenth centuries. (Moore 1966, pp. 19–20)

Thus, the aristocracy survived, but money rather than birth became the basis of the new aristocratic order.

Moore argues that although "revolutionary violence may contribute as much as peaceful reform to the establishment of a relatively free society," violence need not take the form of revolution. "A great deal may occur through the framework of legality. . . . Such were the enclosures that followed the Civil War and continued through the early Victorian era" (Moore 1966, p. 20). Enclosures were now enforced through acts of a parliament dominated by wealthy, commercially minded landlords.

The landlords did not work the land, although they maintained ownership of it and leased it to tenant farmers, middle-level capitalists who had the responsibility for raising the working capital necessary to plant crops and hire labor. Landlords collected enough income from the tenant farmers to support themselves and pay taxes on the land. Thus, the upper class was transformed into a capitalist class that maintained aristocratic control, the middle class (tenant farmers) was transformed into a capitalist class with limited power, and the peasants were transformed into wage earners.

This transformation was made possible by advanced agricultural techniques, including greater use of fertilizers, new crops, and crop rotation, which necessitated the consolidation of small holdings, enclosures, and the replacement of leases for life with leases for a term of a few years. Rising food prices and labor shortages encouraged landlords to enlarge holdings and rationalize cultivation by increasing the size of estates and by increasingly operating on commercial principles. As the size of holdings increased, land ownership became concentrated in fewer hands. These factors ultimately "destroyed the medieval peasant community" (Moore 1966, p. 25).

What happened to the people displaced by this process? The enclosures of common fields, the loss of commons, and the requirements of a money economy resulted in a steady rise in destitution. By 1832, nearly one-half of the families in some villages were in regular receipt of poor relief, and many more families received intermittent relief. "In the previous century these families had been self-supporting small farmers or not too badly off cottagers, able to obtain the necessaries of life in an open-field economy." The surplus peasant "was caught in the end between alternatives that meant degradation and suffering, compared with the traditional life of the village community. That the violence and coercion which produced these results took place over a long space of time, that it took place mainly within a framework of law and order and helped ultimately to establish democracy on a firmer footing, must not blind us to the fact that it was massive violence exercised by the upper classes against the lower" (Moore 1966, pp. 28–29).

Thus, "the violence of the seventeenth and eighteenth centuries . . . prepared the way for peaceful transition in the nineteenth. . . . Perhaps the most important legacy of a violent past was the strengthening of Parliament at the expense of the king." Parliament emerged "mainly as an instrument of a commercially minded, landed upper class." The other main consequence of the Civil War "was the destruction of the peasantry [which] meant that modernization could proceed in England without the huge reservoir of conservative and reactionary forces" that contributed to fascist dictatorships in Germany and Japan. Also, the possibility of peasant revolutions in the Russian and Chinese manner was eliminated (Moore 1966, p. 30).

The importance of world time and events external to particular societies is demonstrated by the effect of the French Revolution on developments in England. The English upper classes, fearing an attack on their privileges equivalent to that experienced by the French aristocracy, closed ranks. The period of reform or toleration for lower-class demands ended and was replaced by a period of repression. However, with the defeat of the French in the Battle of Waterloo (1815), the British upper classes felt more secure and England moved again into a period of social and political reform.

The landed classes reached the peak of their powers before the end of the nineteenth century and subsequently concentrated on protecting their position and privileges. But by now English industrial capitalism was able to develop both internally and throughout the world economy. Although the landed gentry and the nobility retained considerable political power, the Reform Bill of 1832, which gave industrialists the right to vote, and the Corn Bill of 1846, which repealed tariffs on imported grains, clearly showed the landed classes the limits of their power and extended democracy to the middle and lower classes. This process was to continue throughout the nineteenth century.

Thus, Moore believes violence from below cannot be examined without looking at the dialectical relations between the upper classes, the government, and world market conditions. Clearly, modernization in England would have followed a different route without the passage of the enclosure laws and the destruction of the peasant class. The price of democracy was the elimination of this class through violent means.

The So-Called "Mau Mau" Revolution

The same attitude that led the British toward the enclosure movement and the destruction of the peasantry in England was evident in the colonialization of the Third World. A case in point is the relations of the British with the Kikuyu tribe in Kenya.

Prior to 1850, Europeans and the Kikuyu had little contact. In terms of the world political economy model, the Kikuyu were in an area external to the system and had not yet been peripheralized. By the 1850s, however, sporadic contact began to occur, and with the opening of the Suez Canal in 1869 the race among European countries for control of East Africa heated up. Control of the headwaters of the Nile, located in what is now called Uganda, came to have great geopolitical significance. In order to control Uganda, a viable railroad link to a seaport was required. The path from

Uganda to the nearest seaport, Mombasa, led through Kikuyuland.

The British brought to East Africa a policy of making the colonies pay their own way. In some cases, minerals or export crops provided the basis for such payment, but the Kikuyu had no minerals or crops of commercial value. The British interest in Kikuyuland was in the rail route needed to protect their control of the Nile. This required that the tribes in the area be subdued and the administrative apparatus necessary for operating the rail line be in place. Since the Kikuyu could pay neither the costs of building the railroad nor the costs of the British colonial administration, it was decided to open the land for settlement by the whites.

Into the land of the Kikuyu came the English settlers. Like colonists everywhere, they brought with them attitudes that defined the natives' land as uninhabited, the native people as barbarians, and the native religion as heathen. On the basis of these attitudes, developed during the earliest voyages of discovery and continuing to this day, they took over the land, which they defined not only as free but as underutilized, and by so doing transformed a landed agricultural people into alienated wage laborers and serfs.

A series of policies and laws effected this transformation. The government and the settlers worked purposively to drive the natives off their land and create a class of urban wage laborers through taxation, low wages, land appropriation, restrictions on cash crops, laws, and force. Hut (property) and poll taxes, coupled with the restriction on cash crops, forced a number of family members to leave the land and take wage-laborer jobs, freeing the land for white or European settlement.

The Kikuyu

Kikuyu culture and social organization are integrated, and some elements of Kikuyu culture might have made accommodation with the British possible. These same elements of the social and cultural organization of Kikuyu life later provided the resources and the organizational basis for the development of revolutionary organization and leadership.

The basic social unit among the Kikuyu is the family, which widens out by a "natural process of growth and division" (Kenyatta 1962, p. 297). The symbol of the kinship bond is the family land. Land is not only a symbol, however; it is also the key to the autonomous subsistence economy of this basically vegetarian people. The whole social organization derives from the relation of social units to the land.

Preparation for complex social life takes place through practical education. Kikuyu children learn by experience and from an early age are given work within their ability. Technical aspects of socialization are acquired within the age-group, while other aspects of the culture are learned within the family. European education, by contrast, separates the individual from the family and creates a relation of the individual to the state. Yet cultural similarities between the European and Kikuyu educational systems also exist. Children in both educational traditions, for example, learn equality, cooperation, and democratic competition (see Kenyatta 1962).

As age-groups rise within the Kikuyu social hierarchy, their progress is marked by a series of initiation rites and ceremonies. One of the most important is the circumcision ceremony, which moves members of the age-grade to marriageable status. Since the family is the basis of social organization, marriage and courtship are of special importance. While marriage takes place on the basis of free choice within the tribe, it is also important for creating family linkages.

Marriage is a further step toward adulthood. The Kenyan independence leader Jomo Kenyatta notes that not until he has a family does a man have a "chance to show his capacity for wise administration and for dealing intelligently and justly with people." If he has demonstrated these qualities, then by the time he has children entering adolescence he may be chosen from his age-group as one "mature enough to take part in . . . tribal government" (Kenyatta 1962, p. 303). Such an individual, who is expected to act in the interests of the community as he has for his family, is likely to be selected "by the elders as one who will play an important part in public affairs later on, but not until he has passed successive age-grades and acquired the experience which will qualify him to take full responsibility in tribal matters. By that time he is probably the leader of almost a miniature tribe of his own relatives, as well as his age-grade, and his family life will give evidence of his ability in government" (Kenyatta 1962, p. 303).

The same social factors that give marriage special importance also encourage large families. Men have as many wives as they can support, since the more wives a man has the more children he will father. Both male and female children are useful in production. Also, females are the connecting link between generations, while males are important in war. The taking of a second wife is often initiated by the first wife, who sees subsequent wives not as threats but as companions and coworkers. Husbands, as well as each wife, have their own hut. The times when the husband visits each of his wives are strictly regulated by custom, thus minimizing jealousy. Since typically there are more females than males between the ages of fifteen and twenty, when most Kikuyu marry, polygamy has the interesting side effect of ensuring that all women marry. As a result, there is no word in the Kikuyu language for either *spinster* or *prostitute*.

Kikuyu social organization provided the organizational base for the "Mau Mau" independence movement. Oaths and initiation rites became the basis for the solidarity of this movement. Seen through British eyes, various aspects of Kikuyu life, viewed separately, did not make sense. Oath taking, circumcision practices, and polygamy confirmed to the British that the Kikuyu were indeed savages. The misperception on the part of the British of the social nature of oaths and the practice of circumcision was part of the causal process that led to the "Mau Mau" independence movement and blinded the British to alternative

scenarios, such as a peaceful settlement of their disputes with the Kikuyu.

The British saw themselves as bringing civilization to the native. Listen to the voice of a colonial administrator:

> The reaction of a native race to control by a civilized government varies according to the nature, and to the form of government, but in every case a conflict of some kind is inevitable, before the lower race fully accepts the dictum of the ruling power. It may come quickly or it may be postponed, and it is often better if it comes quickly. (Mungeam 1966, p. 277)

The view of the British military in East Africa was similar to that of the civilian administration. The military's goal was to subdue the natives as quickly as possible with the fewest English casualties. As one soldier states: "In my view, any means to achieve those ends are justified. In the long run, inflicting heavy casualties on an enemy will shorten the duration of the conflict, it will teach a lesson and will result in a more enduring peace than less violent means" (Mungeam 1966, p. 277).

The Africans had their own perception of reality, as indicated by the following story, told by a young Kikuyu man about a conversation he had with his grandfather as a boy:

> "Do you see those big blue gum trees on a line at the edge of the forest?" he asked me, pointing to some Eucalyptus trees. "Yes, grandfather." "Those trees were planted by your great uncle, my elder son, on his third year after his circumcision. They mark the boundary between the Native Reserve and the Forest Reserve which is under Government control. All the land west of those trees was alienated by Government in 1910. By that time we had a lot of millet growing where you see those blue gum trees growing inside the forest. Today we are forbidden to collect firewood from that forest which was ours; we are not allowed to cut even strings for binding together wood when building a hut. Do you see that small hut under the tree?" "Yes, grandfather." "That is the Forest

Guard's hut. It is built on my step-brother's land, Gateru. The boundary went through his land leaving him with only a small portion. Today if the Forest Guards catch a person with any forest property, he would be accused and fined or imprisoned. We buy or work for firewood and all building materials from our former lands which the European has not planted or taken care of.

"My grandson, there is nothing as bad on this earth as a lack of power." (Barnett and Njama 1966, p. 86)

The grandson would grow up to become a general in the independence movement.

The First Kikuyu Response: Working Within the Pluralist System

Political process theory tells us to look for social organization in judging the resources of a social movement (Tilly 1978; McAdam 1982). Kikuyu tribal organization provided one basis for the "Mau Mau" social movement, and the British provided the interest by transforming an independent people into wage laborers. The result was the rise of political consciousness among the Kikuyu and the development, beginning in the 1920s, of a variety of contender Kikuyu political organizations, such as the Kikuyu Association, the Young Kikuyu Association, and the East African Association. For the most part, these political organizations adopted the British democratic-pluralist ideology. They brought grievances to various British commissions and sought redress through democratic means. In each case, the findings went against them.

Along with political consciousness, strong dissent also started early. In 1922, Harry Thuku, head of the Young Kikuyu Association, verbally attacked the government for "stealing Kikuyu land" (Barnett and Njama 1966, p. 36). As Tilly (1978) notes, the extent to which the polity is tolerant or repressive in reaction to protest plays an important role in the development of social movements. Thus, the decision to arrest Thuku and hold him for "deportation on charges of being 'dangerous to peace and good order'" (Barnett and Njama 1966, p. 37) was a decision that had important consequences. With adequate analysis, this decision might have been avoided.

The arrest of Thuku was followed by a general strike. Thousands of Africans assembled outside the jail and demanded his release. "The police, frightened and tense, perhaps, by this unexpected show of African strength, responded to a shot fired by one of their members by opening fire on the crowd. When the shooting had stopped, twenty-one Africans lay dead on the street and a much larger number were injured" (Barnett and Njama 1966, p. 37). Still there was pressure for the use of pluralistic processes. Demands of indigenous organizations included (1) title to deeds of African-held land, as well as

> (2) the return of alienated land, or just compensation, (3) removal of restrictions on the planting by Africans of commercial crops . . . (4) the training and employment of Africans as agricultural instructors, (5) compulsory primary education for African children, sufficient secondary and high schools, and opportunities for higher education . . . (6) abolition of the *kipande* system,[3] exemption of women from Hut and Poll Taxes, and removal of other measures which restricted freedom of movement or compelled Africans to leave their *shambas* (gardens) to work for Europeans, and (7) elected representation in the Legislative Council, as well as in other governing bodies, and a promise of ultimate African predominance. (Barnett and Njama 1966, pp. 37–38)

Many of these demands could have been met without the British feeling that the land had been turned over to the rebels. Instead, the British responded with still more repression.

Even after the Kikuyu Central Association (KCA) was declared illegal in 1940, the Kikuyu still attempted to use pluralist techniques to resolve their grievances. The Kenya African

---

3. All African males sixteen years of age or older had to carry an identification and employment card. Failure to comply meant arrest and imprisonment.

Union was formed in 1944, and as late as 1946 its aims were still democratic reform. British repression, however, continued. A small number of intellectuals who were members of many associations provided a cross-linkage between organizations. With continued repression, this cross-linkage would in time contribute to the formation of a single independence movement. By the 1950s, any hopes for democratic reform were gone. It was clear to the Kikuyu nationalists that constitutional means were ineffective, and the stage was set for a movement for national independence that utilized violent as well as nonviolent means.

The "Mau Mau" Revolt

Part of the recruitment process inducting Kikuyu into the "Mau Mau," the Kikuyu independence movement, included a "terrible" oath that had its roots in Kikuyu culture.[4] The taking of the oath involved the following rituals: using animal fat and blood, stepping over the small intestine of a goat, dedicating one's life and risking the possibility of one's death to an unrelenting fight for freedom, and calling down a curse upon the taker of the oath if any of the covenants was broken. Even a taker of the oath has described it as horrible because of its militancy, its ritual, and the potential cost of disobedience.

> The Kikuyu are . . . a very puritanical people regarding sexual deviancy or exhibitionism. Even minor public displays of emotion toward the opposite sex are likely to be frowned upon and few Kikuyu are willing to discuss the intimacies of their sexual life with more than one or two very close friends. Traditionally, sexual taboos were calculatedly "broken" only within the framework of certain puberty rites and important oaths. Thus, a person accused of killing through witchcraft had to submit, if he maintained his

innocence, to a public oath in which he swore, while inserting his penis in the vagina of a sheep, that he did not commit the crime in question and calling on the wrath of Ngai [a God] to destroy him if he were lying. Again, if a man were accused of having impregnated a girl and he denied it, he would have to publicly swear, while biting a piece of sweet potato or the tip of a bunch of bananas which had been inserted in the girl's vagina by an old woman, that if he'd ever had intercourse with the girl, the oath should kill him. Modern versions of both these oaths were common features of the Warriors' Oath. (Barnett and Njama 1966, p. 126)

The oaths and the rituals that accompanied them involved violating Kikuyu norms, and this resulted in awe and fear. They became very effective in binding the oath taker to the movement.

The process of labeling the movement and creating laws to outlaw the pluralist associations took on a life of its own. The oath was made illegal by the British government, and on May 31, 1950, nineteen Africans were arrested for administering it. In August of the same year, the "Mau Mau" society was officially proscribed. The government, of course, did not see the oath within the context of Kikuyu culture. The press ignored the Kikuyu as a people and, by concentrating on disembodied cultural traits and the manufactured entity of "Mau Mau," gave the movement a fierce, inhuman, and barbaric image in the Western mind. In focusing on isolated acts of violence by the Kikuyu, the press ignored years of fruitless peaceful protest as well as the violence perpetrated upon the Kikuyu.

Many historians mark the declaration of a State of Emergency on October 20, 1952, and the subsequent migration of many Kikuyu warriors into the forests to avoid arrest as the point at which dissent transformed a pluralist challenge into a nationalist revolution (Barnett and Njama 1966, p. 69). Starting in the early 1950s, random acts of violence occurred, probably initiated by local leaders and possibly

---

4. It should be noted that the term *Mau Mau* was created by the government press and has no literal meaning in Kikuyu or Swahili.

related in part to the initiation oaths taken by movement members. The following article from the *New York Times* of September 29, 1952, presents a typical treatment of a "Mau Mau" raid:

New Raids in Kenya
Dread Mau Mau Native Group Kills 2 African Chiefs

Nairobi, Kenya, Sept. 28 (AP)—The police announced today the murderous native Mau Mau society had struck again, killing two African chieftains and slaughtering 350 cattle and sheep owned by white settlers in the foothills of Mount Kenya.

The latest blow of the anti-white society—sworn to drive the British out of Africa—took place while the colonial legislature was considering emergency laws to crack down on the terrorists.

The raided district is about 1000 miles from Nairobi. The Mau Mau struck after a night meeting, slaughtering the livestock with spears, swords, and knives. They cut telegraph lines to hamper police action, but authorities said about 1000 suspected members had already been rounded up.

Meanwhile, increasing numbers of people were in jail or awaiting trial for suspected membership in the "Mau Mau" organization.

After eight years of civil war (1952–1960), the British government succeeded in defeating the "Mau Mau." Yet the British also gave up the struggle to keep Kenya as a colony, and in 1963 Kenya was granted independence. Jomo Kenyatta, the legendary and feared "Mau Mau" leader, became prime minister (Brinton et al. 1967).

The analysis of the "Mau Mau" revolution illustrates the effects of the political world economy on events within a particular nation-state, the political process model, and the role of perceptions in political behavior (see chapter 12). The colonial state of Kenya was created as a result of world political-economic dynamics, namely, Britain's need to control the Nile River and the Suez Canal. Political-process factors such as interests, repression/facilitation, organization, and resources played a vital role in the development of both such pluralist Kikuyu associations as the KCA and the nationalist liberation movement. Finally, Kenyan independence was achieved partly as a result of misperceptions—the British perception that the Kikuyu were less than fully human and the initial Kikuyu perception that the British pluralist system included them. These misperceptions, combined with the political process and the world political economy, led to an escalating cycle of violence and repression and finally to independence.

More recently, a different constellation of political-economic factors and misperceptions have produced an analogous conflict in South Africa. Rapid economic growth and an increasing demand for labor after World War II created a politically conscious black working class, a development that motivated the white-controlled government to impose a policy of apartheid (racial segregation and discrimination). In the 1950s and 1960s, the government denied the demands of the moderate African National Congress (ANC) for an end to apartheid, jailing or murdering the ANC's leaders. Today, the government must confront the demands of a new, more militant black leadership for a radical restructuring of the political system. While the ANC's tactics were peaceful (its jailed leader, Nelson Mandela, was an admirer of Gandhi), today's black protests are increasingly violent, bringing about more repression by the government. The struggle is affected by the world political economy—the decisions of multinational corporations, subject to public-opinion pressures in their own countries, to continue their operations in South Africa or to disinvest, thereby withdrawing their economic support. Thus, the cycle of violence and repression continues.

In the traditional academic literature on social movements, the nation-state has functioned as the unit of analysis. That is, social movements are conceived of as national phenomena, arising in a particular country as a result of factors endemic to that society at that moment in time. In this sense, social movement analysis has tended to be ahistorical and national in focus.

We propose a broader focus for movement analysis—linking the generation of a particular insurgent challenge to international historical processes. In the next section, we see how the combined political process and political world economy models can be used to analyze the origins of a movement closer to home—the civil rights movement in the United States.

The Origins of the U.S. Civil Rights Movement

The American civil rights movement originated out of the collapse of the southern cotton economy during the period of America's ascendance from the semiperiphery to the core of the world political economy following World War I. Prior to World War I, the United States consumed most of the goods it produced. Slavery had ensured the South of an abundant supply of cheap labor. Following the Civil War, Reconstruction jeopardized this supply. The Compromise of 1876, produced by an alliance of northern industrialists and southern planters and lasting until 1920, eliminated blacks from a role in national politics. During this period, national politics was dominated by northern industrial interests affiliated with the Republican Party.

Debt bondage, cotton tenancy, and castelike restrictions (for example, Jim Crow laws) bound blacks to the land nearly as effectively as slavery. From 1876 through 1920, cotton remained—despite some lean years—an important cash crop. Mutual interest bound British investors, southern planters, northern mill owners, and cotton brokers.

World War I interrupted the flow of European immigrants to the northern industrial states, and at the same time wartime production pushed the demand for labor to record levels. Northern industry attempted to fill the resulting labor shortage by recruiting southern blacks. The result was a record out-migration of blacks both to northern states and to south-

ern cities. The South reacted by passing laws against recruiting blacks for out-of-state jobs. Thus, the alliance of North and South that had produced the Compromise of 1876 began to break down. After the war, passage of restrictive immigration laws reduced the influx of foreign labor even further and increased the demand for black labor, and after 1920 the South decreased its efforts to prevent black migration northward. The reason for the South's change of policy was the decline of "King Cotton."

Until 1881, the United States imported twice as much as it exported, creating a foreign debt paid for in large part by the export of cotton. Since America supplied much of the world's cotton, it was hazardous for other nations to invest in cotton production outside the United States. The development of new cotton regions would have required proper climate and soil, considerable capital investment, and processing and transport capabilities. In short, potential investors needed evidence that the risk of capital investment would result in long-term profits. These conditions did not exist outside the United States as long as American cotton was readily available.

A series of events reducing the risk for foreign cotton investment began with the end of World War I. By the turn of the twentieth century, industry replaced western migration and agriculture as the key to the American economy, and foreign trade began to increase. World War I saw the transformation of the United States from a debtor nation to the world's foremost creditor nation. As the industrial capacity of the United States increased, high tariffs were placed on imported goods to protect the budding American manufacturing from foreign competition. It became difficult for foreign debtor nations to trade their goods for the U.S. dollars necessary to pay off their debts. With creditor status, the United States' need to export cotton in order to pay foreign debt obligations disappeared. High tariff policies destroyed "the purchasing power of the South's foreign customers" (Molyneaux 1936, p. 43).

With high debts owed to the United States

and no dollars being produced from exports due to high tariffs, it became impossible for the American export trade to survive. A collapse soon followed as prices tumbled, American investors began to reduce their loans, and exports declined significantly (Fite and Reese 1973, p. 502). At the same time, internal processes were at work that undermined the viability of southern cotton farming. The boll weevil infestations of 1920 and 1922 destroyed 16 million bales of American cotton. Whether the United States could regain the ability to produce cotton was questionable; even if it could, the world might no longer be able to buy American cotton. The first cracks in the systemic factors that had prevented capital investment in non-American cotton were now visible.

Following the loss of crops due to the boll weevil infestations, the South staged a comeback. In 1924 and 1925, 29,735,000 bales of cotton were produced, a substantial increase over prior years and a sign that the United States was still capable of meeting world demands. The overproduction, however, had the side effect of substantially reducing the price of cotton. By 1927, the South was able to cut production and restore the supply/demand equilibrium. The South had demonstrated that it could produce enough cotton for home and world consumption as well as control production and prices.

Meanwhile, however, foreign production increased, and bankers in New York and Britain began investing in cotton production in foreign fields. The U.S. share of the world market in cotton dropped from 60 percent in 1929 to 40 percent in 1935. Thus, as a result of high tariffs and cheap money, and as a consequence of the transformation of the United States from a debtor to a creditor nation following World War I, the South lost its role as producer of a needed balance-of-payment commodity. The Depression reduced cotton's dominant role in the South's economy, and New Deal policies further diminished cotton's economic impor-

tance by reducing cotton acreage in an effort to stimulate demand. Competition from synthetic fibers as well as from foreign production further reduced the demand for American cotton.

The collapse of the southern cotton economy, which was tied to world economic processes, in turn stimulated an expansion of political opportunity and institutional development within the southern black community. From 1910 through 1960, the South lost nearly 5 million blacks through out-migration. This movement resulted both from the push of a declining cotton economy and from the pull of northern jobs. Migrants were drawn disproportionately from states with the lowest black voter registration. Eighty-seven percent of the total number of black migrants from the South in the period from 1910 to 1960 settled in seven key northern industrial states. The disproportionate migration of blacks to these states greatly enhanced the electoral significance of the black vote. Thus, black migration was not so much a general exodus from the South as a selective move from those areas where the political participation of blacks had been severely limited to areas with key electoral influence. It "was a move, almost literally, from no voting to voting" (Brooks 1974, p. 17).

The organizational resources available to the southern black population increased simultaneously with the expansion in political opportunity. The demographic transition from south to north resulted in a dramatic reorganization of black life. The number of black farm operators declined from 915,000 in 1920 to only 267,000 in 1959. Many displaced agricultural workers moved out of the South, while others moved to urban regions within the South. The collapse of the cotton economy undermined the oppressive system of social controls. A system of "political domination based on terror and disenfranchisement was no longer essential to the southern ruling class in order to insure their labor needs" (Piven and Cloward 1979, p. 191). For example, the number of lynchings of blacks by whites decreased from 57 per year in the period from 1910 to 1919 to 3 per year in the period from 1940 to 1949.

The years between 1930 and 1954 were a time of development for black urban communities. The concentration of blacks in southern cities replaced the isolation of tenant farms and allowed for greater ease of communication. These factors, along with increased education, better jobs, and higher incomes, encouraged the development of political, religious, and economic institutions within the black community and led to the organizational structure from which black insurgency developed in the 1950s and 1960s. This organizational structure was dominated by a growing black middle class and the development of black churches, black colleges, and local chapters of the NAACP (National Association for the Advancement of Colored People, an early civil rights organization) throughout the South.

Clearly, the organizational strength of the black community in the South around the middle of the twentieth century was a function of the dramatic demographic transformation set in motion by the collapse of the cotton economy. The declining viability of domestic cotton production facilitated the emergence of the civil rights movement by shaping the organizational capacity as well as the political opportunity for successful insurgency.

Summary and Epilogue

Recent scholarship has taken us a long way from the pluralist model of democracy and the frustration-aggression theory of social movements discussed in chapter 12.

The inevitability of violence in social change is a disputed issue in political sociology. In accounting for revolution, Tilly, Wolf, Skocpol, Paige, and Moore focus on the role of violence and of purposive human action in the relations among different segments of the social structure. Skocpol's model is deterministic, holding

that revolutions occur whenever certain conditions exist, namely, when the interests of the old upper class and the government cease to coincide. Wolf agrees with Skocpol that successful social revolutions manifest, and perhaps require, a split between the old upper class and the emerging upper class. Where the peasant has some organizational and other resources, peasant revolution becomes possible.

Tilly argues that revolutions as well as other forms of social movements are products of the interaction between groups with various interests, resources, organizations, and power. Among other factors, the potential for purposive action from below is influenced by the degree of facilitation or repression from above. Similarly, Moore argues that the balance of power between the upper class and the government influences the likelihood of democratic, communist, or fascist transformation. He claims that the ability of preindustrial nations to move toward democracy and competitiveness in the world economy depends on their ability to deal with the peasant class. If that class cannot be transformed, it must be eliminated in order for democratic modernization to proceed. Moore believes that it is harder for this to occur in the twentieth century than it was in previous centuries. Thus, we see today a trend toward communism and fascism.

While Moore indicates that modernization is impeded where a large peasant population exists, Paige notes that impediments to modernization are also produced by large landholders, who stand in the way of land redistribution and social and political reform. These realities need to be considered in debates over levels of economic development, human rights, and the fate of democracy.

Tilly's and Moore's models allow room for purposive action, which implies that roles are played in world affairs both by ideas and by people's ability to act successfully on the basis of those ideas. The ideas are often ideological or utopian. In this book, we have attempted to provide tools that can take us beyond ideology and utopia toward a diagnostic view of the world as it is and as it could be. These tools include the predominantly micro-level analysis introduced by Tilly and the predominantly macro-level analysis of Wallerstein, which together allow us to see the world political and economic context within which nations act, as well as the internal processes that occur within particular societies. Clearly, there is a connection between these levels.

An adequate model of social movements needs to incorporate many different variables, including both a psychological analysis of revolutionaries at the micro-sociological level and a sociological and economic analysis of revolution at the macro-sociological level. It is necessary to know the psychological traits that make some people more willing than others to engage in collective behavior, and also to understand when radical action is likely to occur because of conditions that make such action a rational form of adaptive behavior. While it is difficult to synthesize a model of revolutionary behavior that incorporates all of these factors, we have attempted such a synthesis by using the PEWS and the political process models to interpret events such as the Kenyan independence movement and the U.S. civil rights movement. These case studies illustrate the effects of both world political and economic pressures and internal political processes on domestic social movements.

Most of the world's people are still involved in subsistence or export agriculture. Clearly, as long as world market forces tend toward the accumulation of resources through the expropriation of land, labor, and resources from peasant societies, the potential for violent confrontation will remain. No day goes by without newspaper reports of civil war, guerrilla warfare, political terrorism from below, state terrorism from above, regional wars, and separatist movements. In the next twenty years, more than a hundred new nations are likely to come into existence, and the process by which this occurs will not always be peaceful.

In this book we have tried to incorporate a number of innovative approaches. First, we have maintained that political behavior can be understood best as arising out of people's location in the social structure and out of past and present ideological beliefs and political thought. Second, we have noted that both generalizing science and comparative case studies add to understanding. Third, we have shown that the social construction of reality plays a role in political life. This idea contrasts with the position that politics and resources constitute a zero-sum game, that we must look at the world from the perspective of one particular vantage point, and that the outcome is best determined by the use of coercion and manipulation by those with the greatest power and resources. Such a view precludes the possibility that a situation may be only socially constructed as zero-sum and that a process of social deconstruction and reconstruction can in fact lead to defining the situation as non-zero-sum. As sociologists W. I. Thomas and Dorothy Swaine Thomas (1928) pointed out, if a situation is defined as real, it is real in its consequences. To achieve the social reconstruction of reality, neutral third-party collaborative problem solving may be more appropriate than power negotiations between principals. We offer that possibility as a way of shedding the outworn skin of our past and moving peacefully and productively toward the future.

Bibliography

Abercrombie, Nicholas; Hill, Stephen; and Turner, Bryan S. 1980. *The Dominant Ideology Thesis*. Boston: Allen & Unwin.

Acker, Joan R. 1980. Women and Stratification: A Review of Recent Literature. *Contemporary Sociology* 9:25–35.

Adams, Robert McC., 1966. *The Evolution of Urban Society*. Chicago: Aldine.

Adorno, Theodore; Frenkel-Brunswick, E.; Levinson, D.; and Sanford, R. 1950. *The Authoritarian Personality*. New York: Harper & Row.

Alba, Richard D., and Moore, Gwen. 1982. Ethnicity in the American Elite. *American Sociological Review* 47:373–83.

Almond, Gabriel, and Verba, Sidney. 1965. *The Civic Culture*. Boston: Little, Brown.

Anderson, Charles H. 1974. *The Political Economy of Social Class*. Englewood Cliffs, N.J.: Prentice-Hall.

Anderson-Sherman, Arnold. 1982. The Social Construction of "Terrorism." In *Rethinking Criminology*, edited by Harold E. Pepinsky, pp. 85–103. Beverly Hills, Calif.: Sage.

Apetheker, Herbert. 1968. Power in America. In *C. Wright Mills and The Power Elite*, edited by G. Domhoff and Hoyt Ballard, pp. 133–64. Boston: Beacon Press.

Apter, David E., ed. 1964. *Ideology and Discontent*. New York: Free Press.

Arblaster, Anthony. 1984. *The Rise and Decline of Western Liberalism*. London: Basil Blackwell.

Aristotle. 1923. *The Politics of Aristotle*. Translated by Benjamin Jowett. Oxford: Clarendon Press.

Aron, Raymond. 1968. *Main Currents in Sociological Thought*. Vols. I, II. Garden City, N.Y.: Doubleday.

Aron, Raymond. 1970. *Main Currents in Sociological Thought*. Vol. I. Garden City, N.Y.: Doubleday Anchor Books.

Auletta, Ken, 1982. *The Underclass*. New York: Random House.

Bachrach, Peter. 1967. *The Theory of Democratic Elitism: A Critique*. Boston: Little, Brown.

Balbus, Isaac D. 1971. The Concept of Interest in Pluralist and Marxian Analysis. *Politics and Society* 1:151–77.

Baltzell, E. Digby. 1958. *Philadelphia Gentlemen: The Making of a National Upper Class*. New York: Free Press.

Balz, Dan. 1984. White Men Reassert Their Force in Electorate. *Washington Post*, 26 December, p. A12.

Balz, Dan. 1985. Vote Turnout Increased in November. *Washington Post*, 8 January.

Barnes, Samuel H.; Kaase, Max; and Allerbeck, Klause R. 1979. *Political Action: Mass Participation in Five Western Democracies*. Beverly Hills, Calif.: Sage.

Barnett, Donald L., and Njama, Karari. 1966. *Mau Mau from Within: Autobiography and Analysis of Kenya's Peasant Revolt*. New York: Monthly Review Press.

Baron, James N., and Bielby, William T. 1980. Bringing the Firms Back In: Stratification, Segmentation, and the Organization of Work. *American Sociological Review* 45:437–65.

Baron, James N., and Bielby, William T. 1984. The Organization of Work in a Segmented Economy. *American Sociological Review* 49:454–74.

Barringer, Felicity. 1983. Industry's Influence Chronicled: Liberal Group Lists Access to Regulators. *Washington Post*, 12 October.

Beck, E. M.; Horan, Patrick; and Tolbert, Charles M. II. 1978. Stratification in a Dual Economy. *American Sociological Review* 43:704–20.

Becker, Howard, and Barnes, Harry E. 1952. *Social Thought from Lore to Science.* Vol. 2. Washington, D.C.: Dover Publications, Harren Press.

Beeghley, Leonard. 1978. *Social Stratification in America.* Santa Monica, Calif.: Goodyear Publishing.

Bell, Daniel. 1961. *The End of Ideology.* New York: Collier Books.

Bendix, Reinhard. 1978. *Kings or People: Power and the Mandate to Rule.* Berkeley: University of California Press.

Berelson, Bernard R.; Lazarsfeld, Paul F.; and McPhee, William V. 1965. *Voting.* Chicago: University of Chicago Press. First published in 1954.

Berger, Peter L., and Luckmann, Thomas. 1967. *The Social Construction of Reality.* Garden City, N.Y.: Doubleday.

Berger, Suzanne, ed. 1981. *Organizing Interests in Western Europe: Pluralism, Corporatism, and the Transformation of Politics.* New York: Cambridge University Press.

Bernstein, Basil. 1971. Class, Codes, and Control. *Theoretical Studies Toward a Sociology of Language.* Vol 1. London: Routledge & Kegan Paul.

Bierstedt, Robert. 1974. *Power and Progress: Essays on Sociological Theory.* New York: McGraw-Hill.

Birnbaum, Pierre. 1982. *The Heights of Power: An Essay on the Power Elite in France.* Translated by Arthur Goldhammer. Chicago: University of Chicago Press.

Blank, Robert H. 1980. *Political Parties: An Introduction.* Englewood Cliffs, N.J.: Prentice-Hall.

Blau, Peter M., and Duncan, Otis Dudley. 1967. *The American Occupational Structure.* New York: John Wiley.

Blauner, Robert. 1964. *Alienation and Freedom.* Chicago: University of Chicago Press.

Block, Fred. 1977. The Ruling Class Does Not Rule: Notes on the Marxist Theory of the State. *Socialist Revolution* 33:6–29.

Bluhm, William T. 1974. *Ideologies and Attitudes: Modern Political Culture.* Englewood Cliffs, N.J.: Prentice-Hall.

Blumberg, Paul. 1980. *Inequality in an Age of Decline.* New York: Oxford University Press.

Blumenthal, Sidney. 1985. The Conservative Elite. *Washington Post,* 22–25 September.

Blumer, Herbert. 1939. Social Movements. In *An Outline of the Principles of Sociology,* edited by Robert E. Park. New York: Barnes & Noble.

Blumer, Herbert. 1957. Collective Behavior. In *Review of Sociology: Analysis of a Decade,* edited by J. B. Gittler, pp. 127–58. New York: John Wiley.

Bollen, Kenneth A., and Jackman, Robert W. 1985. Political Democracy and the Size Distribution of Income. *American Sociological Review* 50:438–58.

Boorstin, Daniel. 1953. *The Genius of American Politics.* Chicago: University of Chicago Press.

Bottomore, T. B. 1964. *Elites and Society.* London: Penguin Books.

Bottomore, Tom. 1979. *Political Sociology.* New York: Harper & Row.

Boulding, Kenneth. 1981a. *Ecodynamics: A New Theory of Societal Evolution.* Rev. ed. Beverly Hills, Calif.: Sage.

Boulding, Kenneth. 1981b. *Evolutionary Economics.* Beverly Hills, Calif.: Sage.

Bowles, John. 1961. *Western Political Thought: An Historical Introduction from the Origins to Rousseau.* London: University Paperbacks, Methuen.

Breiger, Ronald L. 1981. The Social Class Structure of Occupational Mobility. *American Journal of Sociology* 87:578–611.

Brink, W., and Harris, L. 1963. *The Negro Revolution in America.* New York: Simon & Schuster.

Brint, Steven. 1984. "New-Class" and Cumulative Trend Explanations of the Liberal Political Attitudes of Professionals. *American Journal of Sociology* 90:30–72.

Brinton, Crane. 1965 *The Anatomy of Revolution.* Rev. ed. New York: Alfred E. Knopf. First published in 1938.

Brinton, Crane; Christopher, John B.; and Wolff, Robert Lee. 1967. *A History of Civilization.* 3d ed. 2 vols. Englewood Cliffs, N.J.: Prentice-Hall.

Broder, David S. 1980. *Changing of the Guard.* New York: Simon & Schuster.

Broder, David S. 1983. GOP's "Gender Gap" Gets Scrutiny. *Washington Post,* 5 September, p. A14.

Broder, David S. 1984. Zigzagging in Search of Identity. *Washington Post,* 15 July, pp. A1, A15.

Brooks, T. R. 1974. *Walls Come Tumbling Down: A History of the Civil Rights Movement,*

1940–1970. Englewood Cliffs, N.J.: Prentice-Hall.

Broom, Leonard; Jones, F. L.; McDonnel, Patrick; and Williams, Trevor. 1980. *The Inheritance of Inequality.* London and Boston: Routledge & Kegan Paul.

Broom, Leonard, and Selznick, Philip. 1979. *Essentials of Sociology.* New York: Harper & Row.

Brownstein, Ronald. 1985. On Paper, Conservative PACs Were Tigers in 1984—But Look Again. *National Journal,* 29 June.

Bruce-Briggs, B., ed. 1979. *The New Class?* New Brunswick, N.J.: Transaction Books.

Buchwald, Art. 1981. Pin-Picking Pandemonium: Who's Who in Militants and Moderates. *Washington Post,* 17 October.

Burch, Philip H., Jr. 1980. *Elites in American History: The New Deal to the Carter Administration.* New York: Holmes & Meier.

Burke, Edmund. 1790. *Reflections on the Revolution in France.*

Burke, Edmund. 1893. Thoughts on the Cause of the Present Discontents. In *The Works of Edmund Burke.* Bohn's Standard Library ed. London: George Bell and Sons. First published in 1770.

Burton, John. 1979. *Deviance, Terrorism, and War: The Process of Solving Unsolved Social and Political Problems.* New York: St. Martin's.

Burton, John. 1982. *Dear Survivors: Planning After Nuclear Holocaust: War Avoidance.* Boulder, Colo.: Westview Press.

Burton, John. 1984. *Global Conflict: The Domestic Sources of International Crises.* College Park, Md.: University of Maryland, Center for International Development.

Butler, David; Penniman, Howard R.; and Ranney, Austin, eds. 1981. *Democracy at the Polls: A Comparative Study of Competitive National Elections.* Washington, D.C.: American Enterprise Institute.

Campbell, Angus; Converse, Philip E.; Miller, Warren E.; and Stokes, Donald E. 1960. *The American Voter.* New York: John Wiley.

Campbell, Angus; Converse, Philip E.; Miller, Warren E.; and Stokes, Donald E. 1966. *Election and the Political Order.* New York: John Wiley.

Campbell, Mildred. 1960. *The English Yeoman Under Elizabeth and the Early Stuarts.* 2d ed. London: Merlin Press.

Campell, Bernard. 1982. *Humankind Emerging.* Boston: Little, Brown.

Cantril, Hadley. 1941. *A Psychology of Social Movements.* New York: John Wiley.

Caplan, Arthur L., ed. 1978. *The Sociobiology Debate.* New York: Harper & Row.

Carneiro, Robert L. 1970. How Did the State Evolve? *Science* 169:733–38.

Cavanagh, Thomas E., and Sundquist, James L. 1985. The New Two-Party System. In *The New Direction in American Politics,* edited by John E. Chubb and Paul E. Peterson, pp. 33–69. Washington, D.C.: Brookings Institution.

Chafetz, Janet Saltzman. 1984. *Sex and Advantage.* Totowa, N.J.: Rowman & Allanheld.

Chagnon, Napoleon A. 1968. *Yanomamo, The Fierce People.* New York: Holt, Rinehart & Winston.

Chagnon, Napoleon A. 1974. *Studying the Yanomamo.* New York: Holt, Rinehart & Winston.

Chambers, William Nisbet. 1963. *Political Parties in a New Nation: The American Experience, 1776–1809.* New York: Oxford University Press.

Chambers, William Nisbet, and Burnham, Walter Dean, eds. 1967. *The American Party Systems.* New York: Oxford University Press.

Childe, Gordon. 1950. The Urban Revolution. *Town Planning Review* 21.

Chirot, Daniel. 1977. *Social Change in the Twentieth Century.* New York: Harcourt Brace Jovanovich.

Chubb, John E. 1983. *Interest Groups and the Bureaucracy: The Politics of Energy.* Stanford, Calif.: Stanford University Press.

Clark, Gordon L., and Dear, Michael. 1984. *State Apparatus: Structures and Languages of Legitimacy.* Boston: Allen & Unwin.

Clark, Grahme, and Piggot, Stuart. 1965. *Prehistoric Societies.* New York: Alfred A. Knopf.

Clymer, Adam. 1983. Poll Shows Problems of Low Voter Turnout. *New York Times,* 25 September, p. 33.

Cohen, Rosalie; Fraenkel, Gerd; and Brewer, John. 1968. The Language of the Hard-Core Poor: Implications for Culture Conflict. *Sociological Quarterly* 9:19–28.

Coleman, Richard P., and Rainwater, Lee. 1978. *Social Standing in America.* New York: Basic Books.

Collins, Randall. 1975. *Conflict Sociology: Toward an Explanatory Science.* New York: Academic Press.

Comte, Auguste. 1896. *The Positive Philosophy.* Translated and condensed by Harriet

Martineau. 3 vols. New York: Calvin Blanchard. First published in 1855.

Comte, Auguste. 1875–1877. *System of Positive Polity*. Translated by Federic Harrison et al. London: Longmans, Green.

Converse, Philip E. 1964. The Nature of Belief Systems in Mass Publics. In *Ideology and Discontent*, edited by David Apter, pp. 206–61. New York: Free Press.

Converse, Philip E. 1976. *The Dynamics of Party Support: Cohort-Analyzing Party Identification*. Beverly Hills, Calif.: Sage.

Coser, Lewis. 1956. *The Functions of Social Conflict*. Glencoe, Ill.: Free Press.

Coser, Lewis A. 1971. *Masters of Sociological Thought*. New York: Harcourt Brace Jovanovich.

Cullen, John B., and Novick, Shelley M. 1979. The Davies-Moore Theory of Stratification: A Further Examination and Extension. *American Journal of Sociology* 84:1424–37.

Czudnowski, Moshe M., ed. 1982. *Does Who Governs Matter? Elite Circulation in Contemporary Societies*. DeKalb, Ill.: Northern Illinois University Press.

Czudnowski, Moshe M., ed. 1983. *Political Elites and Social Change: Studies of Elite Roles and Attitudes*. DeKalb, Ill.: Northern Illinois University Press.

Dahl, Robert A. 1961. *Who Governs?* New Haven and London: Yale University Press.

Dahl, Robert A. 1970. *A Preface to Democratic Theory*. Chicago: University of Chicago Press. First published in 1956.

Dahl, Robert A. 1982. *Dilemmas of Pluralist Democracy*. New Haven and London: Yale University Press.

Dahrendorf, Ralf. 1959. *Class and Class Conflict in Industrial Society*. Stanford: Stanford University Press.

Dahrendorf, Ralf. 1968. *Essays in the Theory of Society*. Stanford, Calif: Stanford University Press.

Dahrendorf, Ralf. 1979. *Life Chances: Approaches to Social and Political Theory*. Chicago: University of Chicago Press.

Darling-Hammond, Linda. 1985. *Equality and Excellence: The Educational Status of Black Americans*. New York: College Board Publications.

Davis, Jerome. 1930. *Contemporary Social Movements*. New York: Appleton-Century-Crofts.

Davis, Kingsley. 1955. The Origin and Growth of Urbanization in the World. *American Journal of Sociology* 60.

Davis, Kingsley, and Moore, Wilbert E. 1945. Some Principles of Stratification. *American Sociological Review* 10:242–49.

Dawson, Carl H., and Gettys, W. E. 1934. *An Introduction to Sociology*. New York: Ronald Press.

Dawson, Richard E.; Prewitt, Kenneth; and Dawson, Karen. 1977. *Political Socialization*. 2d ed. Boston: Little, Brown.

Della Fave, L. Richard. 1980. The Meek Shall Not Inherit the Earth. *American Sociological Review* 45:955–71.

Denitch, Bogden. 1981. *Democratic Socialism: The Mass Left in Advanced Industrial Societies*. Montclair, N.J.: Allanheld, Osmun.

Deutsch, Martin; Bloom, Richard D.; Brown, Bert R.; Deutsch, Cynthia P.; Goldstein, Leo S.; John, Vera P.; Katz, Phyllis A.; Levinson, Alma; Peisach, Estelle Cherry; and Whitman, Martin. 1967. *The Disadvantaged Child*. New York: Basic Books.

Dewar, Helen. 1984. Party Struggles with Definition of Democrat. *Washington Post*, 13 March, pp. A1, A7.

Dionne, E. J., Jr. 1983. Why Everyone Else Seems to Vote. *New York Times*, 20 March, p. 4E.

DiTomaso, Nancy. 1980. Class Politics and Public Bureaucracy: The U.S. Department of Labor. In *Classes, Class Conflict, and the State*, edited by Maurice Zeitlin, pp. 135–52. Cambridge, Mass.: Winthrop.

Domhoff, G. William. 1967. *Who Rules America?* Englewood Cliffs, N.J.: Prentice-Hall.

Domhoff, G. William. 1974. *The Bohemian Grove and Other Retreats*. New York: Harper Books.

Domhoff, G. William. 1978. *The Powers That Be*. New York: Vintage Books.

Domhoff, G. William, ed. 1980. *Power Structure Research*. Beverly Hills, Calif.: Sage.

Domhoff, G. William. 1983. *Who Rules America Now?* Englewood Cliffs, N.J.: Prentice-Hall.

Domhoff, G. William, and Ballard, Hoyt B., eds. 1968. *C Wright Mills and the Power Elite*. Boston: Beacon Press.

Dowse, Robert E., and Hughes, John A. 1972. *Political Sociology*. London: John Wiley.

Drennen, D. A. 1972. *Karl Marx's Communist Manifesto*. Woodbury, N.Y.: Barron's Education Series.

Drew, Elizabeth. 1983. *Politics and Money*. New York: Macmillan.

Drucker, Philip. 1965. *Cultures of the North Pacific Coast*. San Francisco: Chandler.

Duncan, Greg, and Coe, Richard D. 1984. *Years of Poverty, Years of Plenty*. Ann Arbor:

Institute for Social Research, University of Michigan.

Durkheim, Emile. 1949. *The Division of Labor in Society.* Translated by George Simpson. Glencoe, Ill.: Free Press. First published in 1893.

Durkheim, Emile. 1966. *Suicide.* Glencoe, Ill.: Free Press. First published in 1897.

Duverger, Maurice. 1967. *Political Parties.* Translated by Barbara and Robert North. New York: John Wiley. First published in France in 1951; first English edition published in 1954.

Dye, Thomas. 1976. *Who Is Running America?* Englewood Cliffs, N.J.: Prentice-Hall.

Edsall, Thomas B. 1984a. Candidates Find It Easy to Give Spending Curbs the Runaround. *Washington Post,* 3 June, p. A4.

Edsall, Thomas B. 1984b. GOP Purchasing Technological Edge. *Washington Post,* 18 June, pp. A1, A6.

Edsall, Thomas B. 1984c. *The New Politics of Inequality.* New York: W. W. Norton.

Edwards, C. P. 1927. *The Natural History of Revolution.* Chicago: University of Chicago Press.

Eisenstadt, S. N. 1969. *The Political Systems of Empires.* New York: Free Press.

Eisenstadt, S. N., and Roniger, L. 1984. *Patrons, Clients, and Friends: Interpersonal Relations and the Structure of Trust in Society.* New York: Cambridge University Press.

Eldersveld, Samuel J. 1982. *Political Parties in American Society.* New York: Basic Books.

Engels, Friedrich. 1973. *Karl Marx and Friedrich Engels: Selected Works.* Vol. 7. Moscow: Progress.

Epstein, Cynthia Fuchs, and Coser, Rose Laub, eds. 1980. *Access to Power: Cross-National Studies of Women and Elites.* London: Allen & Unwin.

Etzioni, Amitai. 1985. The World-Class University That Our City Has Become. *Washington Post,* 28 April, pp. C1, C4.

Evans, Peter; Rueschemeyer, Dietrich; and Skocpol, Theda, eds. 1985. *Bringing the State Back In.* New York: Cambridge University Press.

Ewen, Lynda Ann. 1978. *Corporate Power and Urban Crisis in Detroit.* Princeton: Princeton University Press.

Fainsod, Merle. 1963. *How Russia Is Ruled.* Rev. ed. Cambridge, Mass.: Harvard University Press.

Ferguson, Thomas, and Rogers, Joel, eds. 1981. *The Hidden Election: Politics and Economics in the 1980 Presidential Campaign.* New York: Pantheon Books.

Feuer, Lewis S. 1975. *Ideology and the Ideologists.* New York: Harper & Row.

Fidler, John. 1981. *The British Business Elite: Its Attitudes to Class, Status, and Power.* Boston: Routledge & Kegan Paul.

Field, G. Lowell, and Higley, John. 1980. *Elitism.* London: Routledge & Kegan Paul.

Fischer, David. 1965. The Social Basis of Parties in 1800. In *The Early American Party System,* edited by Norman K. Risjord, pp. 94–110. New York: Harper & Row.

Fite, G. C., and Reese, J. E. 1973. *An Economic History of the United States.* Boston: Houghton Mifflin.

Form, William, and Rytina, Joan. 1969. Ideological Beliefs and the Distribution of Power in the United States. *American Sociological Review* 34:19–31.

Freeman, Jo. 1973. The Origins of the Women's Liberation Movement. *American Journal of Sociology* 78:792–811.

Freitag, Peter. 1975. The Cabinet and Big Business: A Study of Interlocks. *Social Problems* 23:137–52.

Fried, Morton H. 1967. *Evolution of Political Society: An Essay in Political Anthropology.* New York: Random House.

Friedrichs, Robert W. 1970. *A Sociology of Sociology.* New York: Free Press.

Galbraith, John Kenneth. 1978. *The Affluent Society.* New York: New American Library. First published in 1958.

Gamson, William. 1975. *The Strategy of Social Protest.* Homewood, Ill.: Dorsey Press.

Gans, Herbert J. 1962. *The Urban Villagers.* New York: Free Press.

Garraty, John A., and Gay, Peter, eds. 1981. *The Columbia History of the World.* New York: Harper & Row.

Gelb, Leslie. 1982. In This Town, The Currency Is Power. *New York Times,* 16 April.

Geyelin, Philip. 1984. The World As It Isn't. *Washington Post,* 15 July, p. 88.

Giddens, Anthony. 1973. *The Class Structure of the Advanced Societies.* New York: Harper & Row.

Gilder, George F. 1981. *Wealth and Poverty.* New York: Basic Books.

Ginsberg, Benjamin, and Shefter, Martin. 1985. Institutionalizing the Reagan Regime. Paper presented at the Meetings of the American Political Science Association, New Orleans.

Girvetz, Harry K. 1963. *The Evolution of Liberalism.* New York: Collier Books.

Goldstone, Jack. 1980. A New Look at Gamson's The Strategy of Social Protest. *American Journal of Sociology* 85:1017–42.

Goldthorpe, John H. 1980. *Social Mobility and Class Structure in Modern Britain*. Oxford: Clarendon Press.

Goodman, Paul. 1967. The First American Party System. In *The American Party Systems*, edited by William Nisbet Chambers and Walter Dean Burnham. New York: Oxford University Press.

Gould, James A., and Truitt, Willis H., eds. 1973. *Political Ideologies*. New York: Macmillan.

Gouldner, Alvin W. 1970. *The Coming Crisis of Western Sociology*. New York: Basic Books.

Gouldner, Alvin W. 1979. *The Future of Intellectuals and the Rise of the New Class*. New York: Seabury Press.

Gouldner, Alvin W. 1980. *The Two Marxisms: Contradictions and Anomalies in the Development of Theory*. New York: Seabury Press.

Greenstone, David J., ed. 1982. *Public Values and Private Power in American Politics*. Chicago: University of Chicago Press.

Gurr, Ted Robert. 1969. *Why Men Rebel*. Princeton, N.J.: Princeton University Press.

Haber, Robert A. 1968. The End of Ideology as Ideology. In *Reader in Political Sociology*, edited by Frank V. Lindenfeld. New York: Funk & Wagnalls.

Hacker, Andrew, ed. 1972. *The Federalist Papers*. New York: Simon & Schuster.

Hadley, Arthur T. 1978. The Rich, Happy, Educated Nonvoter. *Washington Post*, 12 November.

Hamilton, Richard F. 1972. *Class and Politics in the United States*. New York: John Wiley.

Hamilton, Richard F. 1982. *Who Voted for Hitler?* Princeton: Princeton University Press.

Harrington, Michael. 1972. *Socialism*. New York: Bantam Books.

Harrington, Michael, 1984. *The New American Poverty*. New York: Penguin Books.

Hartsock, Nancy C. M. 1983. *Money, Sex, and Power: Toward a Feminist Historical Materialism*. New York: Longman.

Hartz, Louis. 1955. *The Liberal Tradition in America*. New York: Harcourt Brace Jovanovich.

Hearnshaw, F.J.C. 1933. *Conservatism in England*. London: Macmillan.

Heberle, Rudolf. 1951. *Social Movements: An Introduction to Political Sociology*. New York: Appleton-Century-Crofts.

Held, David; Anderson, James; Gieber, Bram; Hall, Stuart; Harris, Laurence; Lewis, Paul; Parker, Noel; and Turok, Ben. 1983. *States and Societies*. New York: New York University Press.

Henderson, Nell. 1986. Computers Are Reshaping U.S. Elections. *Washington Post*, 20 January.

Herman, Edward S. 1981. *Corporate Control, Corporate Power*. New York: Cambridge University Press.

Hess, Robert D., and Chipman, Virginia C. 1965. Early Experience and the Socialization of Cognitive Modes in Children. *Child Development* 36:869–86.

Himmelweit, Hilde E.; Humphries, Patrick; and Katz, Michael. 1981. *How Voters Decide: A Longitudinal Study of Political Attitudes and Voting Extended over Fifteen Years*. London: Academic Press.

Hobhouse, Leonard T. 1964. *Liberalism*. New York: Oxford University Press. First published in 1911.

Hochschild, Jennifer. 1981. *What's Fair? American Beliefs About Distributive Justice*. Cambridge, Mass.: Harvard University Press.

Hodge, Robert W.; Siegel, Paul M., and Rosse, Peter H. 1964. Occupational Prestige in the United States, 1925–63. *American Journal of Sociology* 70:286–302.

Hoffman, Martin L., and Saltzstein, Herbert D. 1967. Parent Discipline and the Child's Moral Development. *Journal of Personality and Social Psychology* 5:45–57.

Hofstadter, Richard. 1969. *The Idea of a Party System*. Berkeley: University of California Press.

Horowitz, Irving Louis. 1972. *Foundations of Political Sociology*. New York: Harper & Row.

Horton, James Oliver, and Horton, Lois E. 1979. *Black Bostonians: Family Life in the Antebellum North*. New York: Holmes and Meier.

Horton, Paul B., and Hunt, Chester L. 1968. *Sociology*. New York: McGraw-Hill.

Huber, Joan, and Form, William H. 1973. *Income and Ideology*. New York: Free Press.

Hunter, David E., and Whitten, Phillip M. 1979. *Anthropology: Contemporary Perspectives*. 2d ed. Boston: Little, Brown.

Hunter, Floyd. 1980. *Community Power Succession: Atlanta's Policy-Makers Revisited*. Chapel Hill: University of North Carolina Press.

Huntington, Samuel B. 1981. *American Politics:*

The Promise of Disharmony. Cambridge, Mass.: Harvard University Press.

Hyman, Herbert H. 1969. *Political Socialization: A Study in the Psychology of Political Behavior*. Glencoe, Ill.: Free Press.

Hyman, R., and Fryer, R. H. 1977. Trade Unions: Sociology and Political Economy. In *Trade Unions Under Capitalism*, edited by Tom Clarke and Laurie Clements, pp. 152–74. Glasgow: Fontana.

Jaher, Frederic Cople. 1982. *The Urban Establishment: Upper Strata in Boston, New York, Charleston, Chicago, and Los Angeles*. Urbana: University of Illinois Press.

Janowitz, Morris. 1978. *The Last Half-Century: Societal Change and Politics in America*. Chicago: University of Chicago Press.

Jencks, Christopher. 1979. *Who Gets Ahead?* New York: Basic Books.

Jenkins, J. Craig. 1981. On the Neofunctionalist Theory of Inequality. *American Journal of Sociology* 87:177–79.

Jennings, M. Kent, and Niemi, Richard G. 1981. *Generations and Politics: A Panel Study of Young Adults and Their Parents*. Princeton, N.J.: Princeton University Press.

Johnson, Chalmers. 1966. *Revolutionary Change*. Boston: Little, Brown.

Kann, Mark E. 1982. *The American Left: Failures and Fortunes*. New York: Praeger Books.

Kater, Michael H. 1983. *The Nazi Party: A Social Profile of Its Members and Leaders, 1919–1945*. Cambridge, Mass.: Harvard University Press.

Kautsky, Karl. 1903. *The Social Revolution*. Chicago: Charles H. Kerr.

Kenyatta, Jomo. 1962. *Facing Mount Kenya*. New York: Vintage Books.

Kerbo, Harold R., and Fave, L. Richard Della. 1979. The Empirical Side of the Power Elite Debate: An Assessment and Critique of Recent Research. *Sociological Quarterly* 20:5–22.

Kerckhoff, Alan C.; Campbell, R. T; and Trott, J. M. 1982. Dimensions of Educational and Occupational Attainment in Great Britain. *American Sociological Review* 47:347–64.

Kessler, Ronald C. 1982. A Disaggregation of the Relationships Between Socioeconomic Status and Psychological Distress. *American Sociological Review* 47:752–64.

Kettler, David; Meja, Volker; and Stehr, Nico. 1984. Karl Mannheim and Conservatism: The Ancestry of Historical Thinking. *American Sociological Review* 49:71–85.

Key, V. O., Jr. 1958. *Politics, Parties, and Pressure Groups*. New York: Crowell.

Keynes, John Maynard. 1936. *The General Theory of Employment, Interest, and Money*. New York: Harcourt Brace Jovanovich.

Knoke, David. 1976. *Change and Continuity in American Politics*. Baltimore: Johns Hopkins University Press.

Knoke, David. 1983. Organization Sponsorship and Influence Reputation of Social Influence Associations. *Social Forces* 61:1065–87.

Knoke, David, and Wood, James R. 1981. *Organized for Action: Commitment in Voluntary Association*. New Brunswick, N.J.: Rutgers University Press.

Kohn, Melvin, 1969. *Class and Conformity: A Study in Values*. Homewodd, Ill.: Dorsey Press.

Kohn, Melvin, and Schooler, Carmi. 1982. Job Conditions and Personality: A Longitudinal Assessment of Their Reciprocal Effects. *American Journal of Sociology* 87:1257–86.

Komarovsky, Mirra. 1962. *Blue-Collar Marriage*. New York: Random House.

Kornhauser, William. 1959. *The Politics of Mass Society*. New York: Free Press.

Korpi, Walter. 1983. *The Democratic Class Struggle*. Boston: Routledge & Kegan Paul.

Kottak, Conrad Phillip. 1979. *Cultural Anthropology*. 2d ed. New York: Random House.

Krause, Charles A. 1978. *Guyana Massacre: The Eyewitness Account*. With exclusive material by Laurence M. Stern, Richard Harwood, and the staff of the *Washington Post*. New York: Berkley.

Krause, Elliot A. 1982. *The Division of Labor*. Westport, Conn.: Greenwood Press.

Kriesberg, Louis. 1970. *Mothers in Poverty: A Study of Fatherless Families*. Chicago: Aldine.

Ladd, Everett Carll. 1981. The Brittle Mandate: Electoral Dealignment and the 1980 Presidential Election. *Political Science Quarterly* 96:1.

Ladd, Everett Carll, Jr. 1977. *Where Have All the Voters Gone?* New York: W. W. Norton.

Laidler, Harry W. 1946. *Social-Economic Movements*. New York: Thomas Y. Crowell.

Lane, Robert E. 1962. *Political Ideology*. New York: Free Press.

LaPalombara, Joseph, and Weiner, Myron, eds. 1966. *Political Parties and Political Development*. Princeton, N.J.: Princeton University Press.

Laumann, Edward O., and Knoke, David. 1986. *National Policy Domains: An Organizational Perspective on Energy and Health.* Madison: University of Wisconsin Press.

Laumann, Edward O.; Knoke, David; and Kim, Yong-Hak. 1985. An Organizational Approach to State Policy Formation: A Comparative Study of Energy and Health Domains. *American Sociological Review* 50:1–19.

Lazarsfeld, Paul F.; Berelson, Bernard; and Gaudet, Hazel. 1968. *The People's Choice.* New York: Columbia University Press. First published in 1944.

Le Bon. Gustave 1896. *The Crowd.* London: T. Fisher Urwin.

LeMasters, E. E. 1975. Blue Collar Aristocrats: Life Styles at a Working-Class Tavern. Madison: University of Wisconsin Press.

Lenski, Gerhard. 1966. *Power and Privilege: A Theory of Social Stratification.* New York: McGraw-Hill.

Lenski, Gerhard, and Lenski, Jen. 1974. *Human Societies: An Introduction to Macrosociology.* 2d ed. New York: McGraw-Hill.

Lewis, Oscar. 1959. *Five Families.* New York: Basic Books.

Liebman, Arthur. 1979. *Jews and the Left.* New York: John Wiley.

Liebman, Robert C., and Wuthnow, Robert, eds. 1983. *The New Christian Right.* New York: Aldine.

Lindemann, Albert S. 1983. *A History of European Socialism.* New Haven: Yale University Press.

Lipset, Seymour Martin. 1959. Political Sociology. In *Sociology Today,* edited by Robert K. Merton, Leonard Broom, and Leonard S. Cottrel, Jr., pp. 81–115. New York: Harper & Row.

Lipset, Seymour Martin. 1963. *The First New Nation.* Garden City, N.Y.: Doubleday.

Lipset, Seymour Martin, ed. 1978. *Emerging Coalitions in American Politics.* San Francisco: Institute for Contemporary Studies.

Lipset, Seymour Martin. 1981. *Political Man: The Social Bases of Politics.* Garden City, N.Y.: Doubleday Anchor Books. First published in 1960.

Lipset, Seymour Martin. 1984. Jews Are Still Liberal and Proud of It. *Washington Post,* 30 December, pp. C1, C2.

Lipset, Seymour M., and Schneider, William. 1983. *The Confidence Gap: Business, Labor, and Government in the Public Mind.* New York: Free Press.

Lipset, Seymour Martin; Trow, Martin; and Coleman, James. 1956. *Union Democracy.* New York: Free Press.

Lukes, Steven. 1979. *Power: A Radical View.* London: Macmillan.

Mann, Judy. 1982. Ratings. *Washington Post,* 22 October.

Mannheim, Karl. 1936. *Ideology and Utopia.* New York: Harcourt Brace Jovanovich.

Mannheim, Karl. 1940. *Man and Society in an Age of Reconstruction.* New York: Harcourt Brace Jovanovich.

Mannheim, Karl. 1953. Conservative Thought. In *Essays on Sociology and Social Psychology,* edited by Paul Kecskemeti, pp. 74–164. New York: Oxford University Press. Originally published in 1927.

Mannheim, Karl. 1971. *From Karl Mannheim.* Edited by Kurt H. Wolff. New York: Oxford University Press.

Mannheim, Karl. 1985. *Conservatism.* Text and translation edited and introduced by David Kettler, Volker Meja, and Nico Stehr; translated by Elizabeth R. King. London: Routledge & Kegan Paul. First published in 1927.

Marcuse, Herbert. 1964. *One-Dimensional Man.* Boston: Beacon Press.

Marger, Martin N. 1981. *Elites and Masses: An Introduction to Political Sociology.* New York: Van Nostrand Reinhold.

Margolis, Diane Rothbard. 1979. *The Managers.* New York: William Morrow.

Marsden, Peter. 1985. Latent Structural Models for Relationally Defined Social Classes. *American Journal of Sociology* 90:1002–21.

Marshall, Lorna. 1965. The Kung Bushmen of the Kalahari Desert. In *People of Africa,* edited by J. L. Gibbs, pp. 241–78. New York: Holt, Rinehart & Winston.

Martin, Judith. 1979. Transporting Foibles Across Class Lines. *Washington Post.* 23 February.

Martineau, Harriet. 1896. *The Positive Philosophy of Auguste Comte.* London: George Bell & Sons.

Marx, Karl. 1852. *The Eighteenth Brumaire of Louis Bonaparte.* Translated by Daniel de Leon, 1898. New York: International Publishing Co.

Marx, Karl. 1956. *Selected Writings in Sociology and Social Philosophy.* Translated by T. B.

Bottomore; edited by T. B. Bottomore and Maximilien Rubel. New York: McGraw-Hill.

McAdam, Douglas. 1982. *Political Process and the Development of Black Insurgency, 1930–1970.* Chicago: University of Chicago Press.

McCarthy, John D., and Zald, Mayer N. 1973. *The Trend of Social Movements in America: Professionalization and Resource Mobilization.* Morristown, N.J.: General Learning Press.

McConnell, Grant. 1966. *Private Power and American Democracy.* New York: Knopf.

Merton, Robert K. 1968. *Social Theory and Social Structure.* New York: Free Press.

Michels, Robert. 1962. *Political Parties.* Translated by Eden and Cedar Paul. New York: Free Press. First published in 1911.

Milbrath, Lester W. 1965. *Political Participation: How and Why People Get Involved in Politics.* Chicago: Rand McNally.

Miliband, Ralph. 1969. *The State in Capitalist Society.* New York: Basic Books.

Miliband, Ralph. 1982. *Capitalist Democracy in Britain.* New York: Oxford University Press.

Mill, John Stuart. 1956. *On Liberty.* Indianapolis: Bobbs-Merrill. First published in 1859.

Miller, Arthur H. 1981. What Mandate? What Realignment? *Washington Post,* 18 June.

Miller, Walter B. 1958. Lower Class Culture as a Generating Milieu of Gang Delinquency. *Journal of Social Issues.* 14:5–19.

Miller, Warren E.; Miller, Arthur H.; and Schneider, Edward J. 1980. *American National Election Studies Data Sourcebook, 1952–1978.* Cambridge, Mass.: Harvard University Press.

Mills, C. Wright. 1956. *The Power Elite.* New York: Oxford University Press.

Mills, C. Wright. 1959. *The Sociological Imagination.* New York: Oxford University Press.

Mintz, Beth. 1975. The President's Cabinet, 1897–1972:A Contribution to the Power Structure Debate. *The Insurgent Sociologist* 5:131–48.

Mizruchi, Mark S. 1982. *The American Corporate Network, 1904–1974.* Beverly Hills, Calif.: Sage.

Molyneaux, P. 1936. *The Cotton South and American Trade Policy.* World Affairs Book No. 17. New York: National Peace Conference.

Montesquieu. 1962. *The Spirit of the Laws.* Rev. ed. 2 vols. Translated by Thomas Nugent. New York: Hafner. First published in 1748.

Moore, Barrington, Jr. 1966. *Social Origins of Dictatorship and Democracy: Lord and Peasant in the Making of the Modern World.* Boston: Beacon Press.

Moore, Gwen. 1979. The Structure of a National Elite Network. *American Sociological Review* 44:673–92.

Mosca, Gaetano. 1939. *The Ruling Class.* Edited and revised with an introduction by Arthur Livingston. Translated by Hannah D. Kahn. New York: McGraw-Hill. First published in 1896 and revised in 1923 under the title *Elementi di scienza politica.*

Mosse, George L. 1964. *The Crisis of German Ideology: Intellectual Origins of the Third Reich.* New York: Grosset & Dunlap.

Moynihan, Elizabeth B. 1981. Mail Call on Capitol Hill. *New York Times Magazine,* 15 November.

Mueller, Claus. 1973. *The Politics of Communications.* New York: Oxford University Press. Reprinted as *The Politics of Communications: A Study in the Political Sociology of Language, Socialization, and Legitimation,* New York: Oxford University Press, 1975.

Mungeam, G. H. 1966. *British Rule in Kenya 1895–1912: The Establishment of Administration in the East African Protectorate.* Oxford: Clarendon Press.

Murray, Charles. 1984. *Losing Ground: American Social Policy, 1950–1980.* New York: Basic Books.

Mussen, Paul H., and Wyszynski, Anne B. 1952. Personality and Political Participation. *Human Relations* 5:65–82.

Nash, George H. 1976. *The Conservative Intellectual Movement in America Since 1945.* New York: Basic Books.

New York Times. 1980. Over the Years, "None of the Above" Got More Votes. 21 September.

Nie, Norman; Verba, Sidney; and Petrocik, John R. 1979. *The Changing American Voter.* Enlarged ed. Cambridge, Mass., and London: Harvard University Press.

Nisbet, Robert A. 1966. *The Sociological Tradition.* New York: Basic Books.

Nisbet, Robert A. 1980. *History of the Idea of Progress.* New York: Basic Books.

Nordlinger, Eric A. 1981. *On the Autonomy of the Democratic State.* Cambridge, Mass.: Harvard University Press.

Novak, Michael, ed. 1980. *Democracy and Mediating Structures: A Theological Inquiry.* Washington, D.C.: American Enterprise Institute.

Nyden, Philip W. 1985. Democratizing Organizations: A Case Study of a Union Reform Movement. *American Journal of Sociology* 90:1179–1204.

Oberschall, Anthony. 1973. *Social Conflict and Social Movements*. Englewood Cliffs, N.J.: Prentice-Hall.

O'Connor, Len. 1975. *Clout: Mayor Daley and His City*. Chicago: Henry Regnery.

Offe, Claus. 1972. Political Authority and Class Structure. *International Journal of Sociology* 2:1.

Oglesby, Carl, ed. 1969. *The New Left Reader*. New York: Grove Press.

Oliver, Pamela. 1984. If You Don't Do It, Nobody Else Will: Active and Token Contributors to Local Collective Action. *American Sociological Review* 49:601–11.

Olson, Mancur. 1965. *The Logic of Collective Action*: Cambridge, Mass.: Harvard University Press.

Orum, Anthony M. 1978. *Introduction to Political Sociology: The Social Anatomy of the Body Politic*. Englewood Cliffs, N.J.: Prentice-Hall.

Oshansky, Mollie. 1969. How Poverty Is Measured. *Social Security Bulletin* 32:37–41.

Ostrander, Susan A. 1984. *Women of the Upper Class*. Philadelphia: Temple University Press.

Padover, Saul K., ed. 1939. *Thomas Jefferson on Democracy*. New York: Appleton-Century-Crofts.

Paige, Jeffery M. 1975. *Agrarian Revolution: Social Movements and Export Agriculture in the Underdeveloped World*. New York: Free Press.

Palen, J. John. 1975. *The Urban World*. New York: McGraw-Hill.

Parenti, Michael. 1977. *Democracy for the Few*. 2d ed. New York: St. Martin's.

Parenti, Michael. 1978. *Power and the Powerless*. New York: St. Martin's.

Pareto, Vilfredo. 1935. *The Mind and Society*. 4 vols. Translated by Andrew Bongiorno and Arthur Livingston. Edited by Arthur Livingston. New York: Harcourt Brace Jovanovich.

Pareto, Vilfredo. 1966. *Sociological Writings*. Selected and introduced by S. E. Finer. Translated by Derick Mirfin. New York: Praeger. (See especially the introduction by Finer.)

Park, Robert E., ed. 1939. *An Outline of the Principles of Sociology*. New York: Barnes & Noble.

Park, Robert E., and Burgess, Ernest W. 1921. *Introduction to the Science of Sociology*. Chicago: University of Chicago Press.

Parkin, Frank. 1971. *Class Inequality and Political Order*. New York: Praeger.

Parsons, Talcott. 1951. *The Social System*. New York: Free Press.

Parsons, Talcott. 1964. *Social Structure and Personality*. Glencoe, Ill.: Free Press.

Parsons, Talcott, ed. 1965. *Theories of Society*. Glencoe, Ill.: Free Press.

Parsons, Talcott. 1969. *Politics and Social Structure*. New York: Free Press.

Pepinsky, Harold E. 1982. *Rethinking Criminology*. Beverly Hills, Calif.: Sage.

Pessen, Edward. 1984. *The Log Cabin Myth*. New Haven: Yale University Press.

Pfeiffer, John E. 1969. *The Emergence of Man*. New York: Harper & Row.

Pfeiffer, John E. 1977. *The Emergence of Society: A Prehistory of the Establishment*. New York: McGraw-Hill.

Piven, Frances Fox, and Cloward, Richard A. 1971. *Regulating the Poor: The Functions of Public Welfare*. New York: Random House.

Piven, Frances F., and Cloward, Richard A. 1979. *Poor People's Movements*. New York: Vintage Books.

Plato. 1955. *The Republic*. Translated by Benjamin Jowett. New York: Random House.

Polsby, Nelson. 1983. *The Consequences of Party Reform*. New York: Oxford University Press.

Polsby, Nelson. 1984. *Political Innovation in America*. New Haven: Yale University Press.

Poulantzas, Nicos. 1968. *Political Power and Social Classes*. London: NLB and Sheed and Ward.

Powell, G. Bingham, Jr. 1980. Voting Turnout in 30 Democracies: Partisan, Legal, and Socio-Economic Influences. In *Electoral Participation*, edited by Richard Rose. Beverly Hills, Calif.: Sage.

Prewitt, Kenneth, and Stone, Alan. 1973. *The Ruling Elites*. New York: Harper & Row.

Price, David. 1984. *Bringing Back the Parties*. Washington, D.C.: Congressional Quarterly Inc.

Rainwater, Lee. 1966. Crucible of Identity: The Black Lower Class Family. *Daedalus* 95:172–216.

Rakove, Milton L. 1975. *Don't Make No Waves, Don't Back No Losers*. Bloomington: University of Indiana Press.

Ranney, Austin, ed. 1981. *The American Elections of 1980*. Washington, D.C.: American Enterprise Institute.

Raspberry, William. 1985. The Cure Is in Black America. *Washington Post,* 1 July.

Rawls, John. 1971. *Theory of Justice.* Cambridge: Belknap Press.

Reeves, Richard. 1984. How Ideas Shape Presidential Politics. *New York Times Magazine,* 15 July.

Reid, T. R. 1980. The Largest Political Party in America. *Washington Post,* 3 November.

Rich, Spencer. 1984a. The Skeptics Are Wrong— Anti-Poverty Programs Do Work. *Washington Post,* 6 May, pp. F1, F4.

Rich, Spencer. 1984b. Children Are the Largest Group of Impoverished Americans. *Washington Post,* 21 December.

Rich, Spencer. 1985a. Welfare Cuts Cause Severe Income Loss. *Washington Post,* 11 July.

Rich, Spencer. 1985b. Poverty Rate Dips Sharply. *Washington Post,* 28 August.

Riesman, David; Denney, Ruel; and Glazer, Nathan. 1953. *The Lonely Crowd.* New York: Doubleday Anchor Books.

Ringle, Ken. 1982. The List Peddlers. *Washington Post,* 17 October, pp. D1, D3.

Roberts, Steven V. 1983. The G.O.P.: A Party in Search of Itself. *New York Times Magazine,* 6 March, p. 31ff.

Robinson, Robert V. 1984. Reproducing Class Relations in Industrial Society. *American Sociological Review* 49:182–96.

Robinson, Robert V., and Kelley, Jonathan. 1979. Class as Conceived by Marx and Dahrendorf: Effects on Income Inequality and Politics in the United States and Great Britain. *American Sociological Review* 44:38–58.

Ronen, Dov. 1979. *The Quest for Self-Determination.* New Haven: Yale University Press.

Rose, Arnold. 1967. *The Power Structure.* New York: Oxford University Press.

Rosenberg, Morris. 1954. Some Determinations of Political Apathy. *Public Opinion Quarterly* 18:34–66.

Rothenberg, Randall. 1984. *The Neoliberals.* New York: Simon & Schuster.

Rothman, Robert A. 1978. *Inequality and Stratification in the United States.* Englewood Cliffs, N.J.: Prentice-Hall.

Roy, William G. 1984. Class Conflict and Social Change in Historical Perspective. In *Annual Review of Sociology,* edited by Ralph H. Turner. Palo Alto, Calif.: Annual Reviews.

Royko, Mike. 1971. *Boss: Richard J. Daley of Chicago.* New York: New American Library.

Rubin, Lillian Breslow. 1976. *Worlds of Pain.* New York: Basic Books.

Ruesh, Jungen. 1958. The Tangential Response. In *Psychopathology of Communications,* edited by Paul H. Huch and Joseph Zubin. New York: Grune & Stratton.

Rush, Michael, and Althoff, Philip. 1972. *An Introduction to Political Sociology.* Indianapolis: Bobbs-Merrill.

Sabato, Larry J. 1981. *The Rise of Political Consultants.* New York: Basic Books.

Sabato, Larry J. 1985. *PAC Power.* New York: W. W. Norton.

Sabine, George H., and Thorson, Thomas L. 1973. *A History of Political Theory.* 4th ed. Hinsdale, Ill.: Dryden Press.

Sahlins, Marshall. 1958. *Social Stratification in Polynesia.* Seattle: University of Washington Press.

Sahlins, Marshall. 1968. *Tribesman.* Englewood Cliffs, N.J.: Prentice-Hall.

Sahlins, Marshall. 1972. *Stone Age Economics.* Chicago: Aldine.

Sahlins, Marshall, and Service, Elman, eds. 1960. *Evolution and Culture.* Ann Arbor: University of Michigan Press.

Sanday, Peggy Reeves. 1981. *Female Power and Male Dominance: On the Origins of Sexual Inequality.* New York: Cambridge University Press.

Scaff, Lawrence A. 1981. Max Weber and Robert Michels. *American Journal of Sociology* 86:1269–86.

Schneider, Eugene V. 1968. The Sociology of C. Wright Mills. In *C. Wright Mills and the Power Elite,* edited by G. Domhoff and Hoyt Ballard, pp. 12–21. Boston: Beacon Press.

Schumpeter, Joseph. 1950. *Capitalism, Socialism, and Democracy.* New York: Harper & Row.

Scimecca, Joseph. 1981. *Society and Freedom.* New York: St. Martin's.

Segal, David R. 1974. *Society and Politics: Uniformity and Diversity in Modern Democracy.* Glenview, Ill.: Scott, Foresman.

Seidman, Steven. 1983. *Liberalism and the Origins of European Social Thought.* Berkeley: University of California Press.

Seliger, Martin. 1976. *Ideology and Politics.* London: George Allen & Unwin.

Sennet, Richard, and Cobb, Jonathan. 1972. *The Hidden Injuries of Class.* New York: Random House.

Sewell, W. H., and Shah, V. P. 1967. Socio-Economic Status, Intelligence, and the Attainment of Higher Education. *Sociology of Education* 40:123.

Sherman, Arnold K. 1976. *The Sociological Theory of Karl Mannheim: The Structure of Knowledge, Education, and Freedom.* Unpublished Ph.D. dissertation. Albany, N.Y.: State University of New York at Albany.

Sherman, Arnold K., and Femminella, Francis X. 1984. Ethnic Ego-Identity and the Dilemma of Universalism. *Humanity and Society* 8:304–18.

Sherman, Arnold K., and Scimecca, Joseph A. 1984. Karl Mannheim, Religious Values and The Lost Art of Social Diagnosis. *International Review of History and Political Science* 21:39–41.

Shils, Edward. 1960. The Intellectual in Political Development of New States. *World Politics* 12:329–68.

Shils, Edward. 1968. The Concept and Function of Ideology. In *International Encyclopedia of Social Science*, pp. 66–67. New York: Macmillan.

Shils, Edward. 1981. *Tradition.* Chicago: University of Chicago Press.

Shupe, Anson D., Jr. 1979. Social Participation and Voting Turnout: The Case of Japan. *Comparative Political Studies* 12:229–56.

Shupe, Anson, and Stacey, William A. 1982. *Born Again Politics and the Moral Majority: What the Surveys Really Show.* Lewiston, N.Y.: Edwin Mellen.

Sigel, Roberta. 1985. The Gender Gap—Generation Gap or Marriage Gap? Paper presented at the Meetings of the American Political Science Association, New Orleans.

Silk, Leonard, and Silk, Mark. 1980. *The American Establishment.* New York: Basic Books.

Simmel, Georg. 1956. *Conflict and the Web of Group Affiliations.* Translated by Kurt H. Wolff. New York: Free Press. First published in 1908.

Singer, Charles. 1959. *A Short History of Scientific Ideas to 1900.* New York: Oxford University Press.

Sjoberg, Gideon. 1965. *Preindustrial City: Past and Present.* Glencoe, Ill.: Free Press.

Skocpol, Theda. 1979. *States and Social Revolutions.* Cambridge: Cambridge University Press.

Smelser, Neil J. 1962. *Theory of Collective Behavior.* New York: Free Press.

Sorel, George. 1950. *Reflections on Violence.* Glencoe, Ill.: Free Press. First published in 1908.

Steiner, N. K. 1965. *Local Government in Japan.* Stanford, Calif.: Stanford University Press.

Steinfels, Peter. 1979. *The Neoconservatives.* New York: Simon & Schuster.

Stephens, John D. 1980. *The Transition from Capitalism to Socialism.* Atlantic Highlands, N.J.: Humanities Press.

Stockton, Ronald R., and Wayman, Frank Whelon. 1983. *A Time of Turmoil: Values and Voting in the 1970s.* East Lansing: Michigan State University Press.

Stolte, John F. 1983. The Legitimation of Structural Inequality. *American Sociological Review* 48:331–42.

Sundquist, James L. 1983. *Dynamics of the Party System.* Rev. ed. Washington, D.C.: Brookings Institution.

Sussman, Barry. 1982. Both Parties Lost the Elections: They Were Rejected by the Two-Thirds Who Didn't Vote. *Washington Post,* 28 November.

Swanson, Guy E. 1960. *Birth of the Gods: The Origin of Primitive Beliefs.* Ann Arbor: University of Michigan Press.

Sweezy, Paul M. 1968. Power Elite or Ruling Class? In *C. Wright Mills and the Power Elite,* edited by G. Domhoff and Hoyt Ballard, pp. 115–32. Boston: Beacon Press.

Szymanski, Albert. 1978. *The Capitalist State and the Politics of Class.* Cambridge: Worthrop.

Szymanski, Albert. 1983. *Class Structure: A Critical Perspective.* New York: Praeger Books.

Talmon, J. L. 1952. *The Origins of Totalitarian Democracy.* London: Mercury Books.

Tarde, Gabriel. 1969. *On Communication and Social Influence.* Chicago: Phoenix Books. First published in 1898.

Tawney, R. H. 1912. *The Agrarian Problem in the Sixteenth Century.* London: Longmans, Green.

Taylor, Charles Lewis, and Jodice, David. 1983. *World Handbook of Political and Social Indicators.* 3d ed. New Haven and London: Yale University Press.

Templeton, F. 1966. Alienation and Political Participation. *Public Opinion Quarterly* 39:249–61.

Therborn, Goran. 1978. *What Does the Ruling Class Do When It Rules?* New York: Schocken Books.

Thomas, Elizabeth Marshall. 1959. *The Harmless People.* New York: Vintage Books.

Thomas, William I., and Thomas, Dorothy Swain. 1928. *The Child in America.* New York: Alfred A. Knopf.

Thorpe, Francis Newton. 1909. *The Federal and State Constitutions, Colonial Charters, and Other Organic Laws of the States, Territories, and Colonies Now or Heretofore Forming the United States of America.* Vol. 5. Washington, D.C.: United States Government Printing Office.

Thurow, Lester C. 1980. *The Zero-Sum Society.* New York: Basic Books.

Tilly, Charles. 1978. *From Mobilization to Revolution.* Reading, Mass.: Addison-Wesley.

Time Magazine. 1977. The American Underclass. 19 August.

Tocqueville, Alexis de. 1951. *Democracy in America.* Edited by Phillips Bradley. New York: Alfred A. Knopf.

Tocqueville, Alexis de. 1955. *The Old Regime and the French Revolution.* Translated by Stuart Gilbert. Garden City, N.Y.: Doubleday Anchor Books. First published in 1856.

Tocqueville, Alexis de. 1966. *Democracy in America.* Edited by J. P. Mayer and Max Lerner. Translated by George Lawrence. New York: Harper & Row. Part I first published in 1835, Part II in 1840.

Touraine, Alain. 1983. *Solidarity.* Translated by David Denby. New York: Cambridge University Press.

Trilling, Lionel. 1954. *The Liberal Imagination.* Garden City, N.Y.: Doubleday.

Tsiantar, Dody. 1984. Study Finds Jewish Vote Less Firm for Democrats. *Washington Post,* 14 November.

Tumin, Melvin M. 1953. Some Principles of Stratification: A Critical Analysis. *American Sociological Review* 18:287–394.

Turner, Jonathan H. 1984. *Social Stratification: A Theoretical Analysis.* New York: Columbia University Press.

Turner, Ralph H., and Killian, Lewis M. 1972. *Collective Behavior.* Rev. ed. Englewood Cliffs, N.J.: Prentice-Hall. First published in 1957.

United States Bureau of the Census. 1975. *Historical Statistics of the United States: Colonial Times to 1970.* Part 2. Bicentennial Edition.

United States Bureau of the Census. 1986. *Statistical Abstracts of the United States.* Washington, D.C.: United States Government Printing Office.

Useem, Michael. 1983a. Business and Politics in the United States and the United Kingdom. *Theory and Society* 12:281–308.

Useem, Michael. 1983b. *The Inner Circle: Large Corporations and the Rise of Business Political Activity in the U.S. and U.K.* New York: Oxford University Press.

Vander Zanden, James W. 1979. *Sociology.* New York: John Wiley.

Vanfossen, Beth Ensminger. 1979. *The Structure of Social Inequality.* Boston and Toronto: Little, Brown.

Veblen, Thornstein. 1899. *The Theory of the Leisure Class.* New York: Macmillan.

Verba, Sidney, and Nie, Norman H. 1972. *Participation in America: Political Democracy and Social Equality.* New York: Harper & Row.

Viereck, Peter. 1964. The Philosophical "New Conservatism." In *The Radical Right,* edited by Daniel Bell, pp. 188–99. Garden City, N.Y.: Doubleday.

Vivelo, Frank Robert. 1978. *Cultural Anthropology Handbook: A Basic Introduction.* New York: McGraw-Hill.

Walker, Jack. 1966. A Critique of the Elitist Theory of Democracy. *American Political Science Review* 60:185–95.

Wallace, Michael, and Kallenberg, Arne L. 1982. Industrial Transformation and the Decline of Craft: The Decomposition of Skill in the Printing Industry, 1931–1978. *American Sociological Review* 47:307–25.

Wallerstein, Immanuel. 1974. *The Modern-World System: Capitalist Agriculture and the Origins of the European World-Economy in the Sixteenth Century.* New York: Academic Press.

Wallerstein, Immanuel. 1979. *The Capitalist World Economy: Essays.* New York: Cambridge University Press.

Wallerstein, Immanuel. 1984. In *Sociological Theory 1984.* Edited by Randall Collins. San Francisco: Jossey-Bass.

Walsh, Edward. 1981a. Cuyahoga Crunch: Decline of Industrial Belt Hurts Democrats. *Washington Post,* 18 August.

Walsh, Edward. 1981b. Fast-Growing Florida: Influx of People Puts Politics in Flux. *Washington Post,* 19 August.

Warner, W. Lloyd; Meeker, Marchia; and Eells, Kenneth, eds. 1949. *Social Class in America.* Chicago: Science Research Associates.

Washington, George. 1940. Farewell Address. In *The Writings of George Washington,* edited by John C. Fitzpatrick. Washington, D.C.

United States Government Printing Office. First published in 1796.

Waxman, Chaim I., ed. 1968. *The End of Ideology Debate*. New York: Funk & Wagnalls.

Weber, Max. 1947. *The Theory of Social and Economic Organization*. Translated by Alexander Henderson and Talcott Parsons. Glencoe, Ill.: Free Press.

Weber, Max. 1951. *The Religion of China: Confucianism and Taoism*. Translated and edited by Hans H. Gerth. Glencoe, Ill. Free Press. First published in 1916.

Weber, Max. 1952. *Ancient Judaism*. Translated and edited by Hans H. Gerth and Don Martindale. Glencoe, Ill.: Free Press. First published in 1917–1919.

Weber, Max. 1958a. *From Max Weber*. Edited by Hans H. Gerth and C. Wright Mills. New York: Oxford University Press.

Weber, Max. 1958b. *The Protestant Ethic and the Spirit of Capitalism*. Translated by Talcott Parsons. New York: Charles Scribner's. First published in 1904–1905.

Weber, Max. 1978. *Economy and Society*. 2 Vols. Edited by Guenther Roth and Claus Wittich. Berkeley: University of California Press.

Weisman, Steven R. 1980. What Is a Conservative? *New York Times Magazine*, 31 August.

Weissberg, Robert. 1974. *Political Learning, Political Choice, and Democratic Citizenship*. Englewood Cliffs, N.J.: Prentice-Hall.

Where We Stand: A Political Statement of the Democratic Socialists of America. 1982. Washington, D.C.: Democratic Socialists of America.

Whitt, J. Allen. 1979. Toward a Class-Dialectical Model of Power: An Empirical Assessment of Three Competing Models of Political Power. *American Sociological Review* 44:81–100.

Whitt, J. Allen. 1982. *Urban Elites and Mass Transportation: The Dialectics of Power*. Princeton, N.J.: Princeton University Press.

Whyte, William H., Jr. 1956. *The Organization Man*. New York: Simon & Schuster.

Williams, Thomas Rhys. 1983. *Socialization*. 2d ed. Englewood Cliffs, N.J.: Prentice-Hall.

Wilson, Edmund. 1953. *To the Finland Station*. Garden City, N.Y.: Doubleday.

Wolf, Eric R. 1969. *Peasant Wars of the Twentieth Century*. New York: Harper & Row.

Wolfe, Alan. 1981. *America's Impasse: The Rise and Fall of the Politics of Growth*. New York: Pantheon Books.

Wolfinger, Raymond E., and Rosenstone, Steven J. 1980. *Who Votes?* New Haven and London: Yale University Press.

Wolin, Sheldon F. 1976. The New Conservatives. *New York Review of Books*, 5 February.

World Bank, The. 1985. *World Development Report*. Washington, D.C.: The World Bank.

Wright, Erik Olin. 1978. Race, Class, and Income Inequality. *American Journal of Sociology* 83:1368–97.

Wright, Erik Olin. 1979. *Class Structure and Income Determination*. New York: Academic Press.

Wright, Erik Olin. 1985. *Classes*. London: Verso.

Wright, Erik Olin; Costello, Cynthia; Hachen, David; and Sprague, Joey. 1982. The American Class Structure. *American Sociological Review* 47:709–26.

Wrong, Dennis H. 1961. The Oversocialized Conception of Man in Modern Sociology. *American Sociological Review* 26:183–93.

Wrong, Dennis H. 1980. *Power: Its Forms, Bases, and Uses*. New York: Harper & Row.

Yago, Glenn. 1980. Corporate Power and Urban Transportation: A Comparison of Public Transit's Decline in the United States and Germany. In *Classes, Class Conflict, and the State*, edited by Maurice Zeitlin, pp. 296–323. Cambridge, Mass.: Winthrop.

Yago, Glenn. 1984. *The Decline of Transit: Urban Transportation in German and United States Cities, 1900–1970*. New York: Cambridge University Press.

Yankelovich, Daniel. 1979. Who Gets Ahead in America. *Psychology Today* 13:28–43.

Zald, Mayer, and McCarthy, John D., eds. 1979. *The Dynamics of Social Movements*. Cambridge, Mass.: Winthrop.

Zeitlin, Maurice, ed. 1980. *Classes, Class Conflict, and the State*. Cambridge, Mass.: Winthrop.

Index